RETHINKING HELL

Rethinking Hell

Readings in Evangelical Conditionalism

Edited by
CHRISTOPHER M. DATE,
GREGORY G. STUMP,
and JOSHUA W. ANDERSON

CASCADE *Books* • Eugene, Oregon

RETHINKING HELL
Readings in Evangelical Conditionalism

Copyright © 2014 Wipf and Stock Publishers. All rights reserved. Except for brief quotations in critical publications or reviews, no part of this book may be reproduced in any manner without prior written permission from the publisher. Write: Permissions, Wipf and Stock Publishers, 199 W. 8th Ave., Suite 3, Eugene, OR 97401.

Cascade Books
An Imprint of Wipf and Stock Publishers
199 W. 8th Ave., Suite 3
Eugene, OR 97401

www.wipfandstock.com

ISBN 13: 978-1-62564-598-2

Cataloging-in-Publication data:

Rethinking hell : readings in evangelical conditionalism / edited by Christopher M. Date, Gregory G. Stump, and Joshua W. Anderson, with a foreword by John G. Stackhouse.

xxx + 338 p. ; 23 cm. Includes bibliographical references and index.

ISBN 13: 978-1-62564-598-2

1. Hell—Biblical teaching. 2. Future punishment—biblical teaching. 3. Immortality—biblical teaching. I. Date, Christopher M. II. Stump, Gregory G. III. Anderson, Joshua W. IV. Stackhouse, John Gordon. V. Title.

BS680.H43 D172 2014

Manufactured in the U.S.A.

The image "Hell Triangle: Three Views of Final Punishment" was provided by © Ronnie Demler & RethinkingHell.com.

To the "widows" of Rethinking Hell,
our wives whose support for us is, unlike immortality, unconditional:
Starr Date, Michele Stump, Natalie Anderson,
Anchalee Grice, and Ruth Peoples.

Contents

Foreword by John G. Stackhouse Jr.   ix

Preface by Gregory G. Stump   xv

Acknowledgments   xix

Permissions   xx

Abbreviations   xxiii

Editor's Introduction by Christopher M. Date   xxvii

PART ONE: Rethinking Hell

1. Igniting an Evangelical Conversation—*Peter S. Grice*   3

2. Introduction to Evangelical Conditionalism
   —*Glenn A. Peoples*   10

PART TWO: Influential Defenses of Conditionalism

3. The Final End of the Wicked—*Edward W. Fudge*   29

4. The Nature of Final Destiny—*Stephen H. Travis*   44

5. Judgment and Hell—*John R. W. Stott*   48

6. The Destruction of the Finally Impenitent
   —*Clark H. Pinnock*   56

7. The Case for Conditional Immortality
   —*John W. Wenham*   74

PART THREE: Biblical Support for Conditionalism

8. The Doom of the Lost—*Basil F. C. Atkinson*   99

9. New Testament Teaching on Hell—*E. Earle Ellis*   116

10. Does Revelation 14:11 Teach Eternal Torment?
    —*Ralph G. Bowles*   138

Contents

11 The General Trend of Bible Teaching
    —*Harold E. Guillebaud*   155

12 Claims about "Hell" and Wrath
    —*Anthony C. Thiselton*   174

PART FOUR: Philosophical Support for Conditionalism

13 Is the Soul Immortal?—*Philip E. Hughes*   185

14 Divine Justice—*Henry Constable*   198

15 Divine and Human Punishment in the New Testament
    —*Christopher D. Marshall*   207

16 A Kinder, Gentler Damnation?—*Nigel G. Wright*   228

17 The Future of the Totally Corrupt
    —*Richard G. Swinburne*   234

PART FIVE: Historical Considerations

18 The Development of Gehenna between the Old and
    New Testaments—*Kim G. Papaioannou*   245

19 Conditionalism in the Early Church
    —*LeRoy E. Froom*   260

PART SIX: Conditionalism and Evangelicalism

20 Hell and Evangelical Unity—*Evangelical Alliance*   281

21 Diverse Christian Beliefs about Life beyond Death
    —*Roger E. Olson*   289

22 Equally Orthodox Christians—*Ben Witherington III*   292

Appendix A: Recommended Reading   305

Bibliography   307

Ancient Document Index   319

Foreword

"Ron Hobbs should go to hell."

That was my fervent theological conclusion as a small boy growing up in northern Ontario.

As a precocious five-year-old literally fresh off the Cunard Line boat from England and starting grade 1 in northern Ontario, I had a difficult time connecting with my new Canadian schoolmates. Small, and with an impossibly thick West Country accent, I was an attractive target and immediately made sport of by the available bullies. (I am not kidding about "immediately": I was attacked on the schoolyard leaving for home on my first day.) Chief among the tiny thugs who loomed large over my life, however, was Ron Hobbs—two years older and much, much bigger.

Ron, in the inscrutable providence of the *deus absconditus*, lived in the house directly behind mine. I had to cross through his family's yard to walk the mile to the elementary school we both attended. Ron quickly sized up the situation and concluded he could have a great deal of fun lying in wait for the little English boy at various points along the route. Perhaps he could jump me immediately upon my setting foot in his backyard. Perhaps he could hide along one of the paths in the woods we used as a shortcut between our suburban bungalows and the school. Perhaps instead he could guess that I would take the long way around, via the road. In as close to an actual cat-and-mouse game that two boys could play, however grimly, I was pursued by this nasty creature for two years.

Yes, two solid years. My parents possessed many good qualities, but responsiveness to the worries of their first-born son, when his younger sisters were more obviously vulnerable and demanding, was not among them. So it was two full years before the elder of my two younger sisters, having watched me get pinned down on the asphalt yet again and get my face punched by Ron Hobbs yet again, told my mother tearfully that

Foreword

she was afraid for me. Roused now to action, my parents spoke to the Hobbses and, decent people that they surely were, the bullying stopped.

Before it did, however, and from time to time thereafter, I devoutly wished Ron Hobbs in hell. He had made every morning's walk to school and every afternoon's walk home an exercise in terror. I spent hours at night and during class frantically considering which route today might help me elude him. I comforted myself on particularly bad days with the teaching I received from my evangelical Sunday School teachers about hell: Ron Hobbs would surely go there, and he couldn't get there fast enough for me.

How long, however, should Ron be kept there? Being a child of lively imagination, as I went to sleep one night—and I couldn't have been older than eight at the time—I tried to imagine what it would be like to exist in total darkness and in terrible pain *with no hope of it ever ending*. It took a little while to compose the experience in my mind, but then suddenly it was real. And it was horrible. And I have never forgotten it. Indeed, I can summon up at will now the icy grip on my throat of abject despair. *"Forever" is a long time.*

I hated Ron. Let's not resort to euphemism. I wanted him punished. Even as a boy, though, I thought, *Not forever*. How could "forever" make sense? Ron made two years of my life pretty bad, so my intuition was, and is, that *someone* needed to make that right. And if a long stretch of significant suffering is the way to make such things right—as the Bible, and many of the world's religions, assert—then Ron should suffer accordingly.

But forever? That seemed both illogical and unworthy of the God I had known, especially in the face of Jesus. God was frighteningly just, to be sure. There was no sugar-coating in my Sunday School! But he was *just*, not vindictive; scarily fair, yes, but not mean. So the teaching I received of the damned being sustained by God to endure unending torment seemed incongruous to me. And when I was a teenager reading science fiction and thriller novels by the boxload, the figure of the brilliant torturer who found clever medical devices to keep his victim alive and conscious for yet another round of torment struck me as devilish, not divine.

To this day, I have wondered why Christians prefer—as many seem to do—believing in eternal conscious torment (ECT). Now, I understand hatred. I understand vengefulness. And these natural reactions to evil rose in my heart into a whole new register when I discovered as a man that someone I loved had been abused as a girl, and frequently, by her

Foreword

parents. It was all I could do to resist hatching my own real-world plot of death preceded by exquisite suffering for these wretches. But even then, even in my darkest musings, I never approached wishing them eternal conscious torment. It just didn't make any sense. At some point, a sinner has suffered commensurately with the evil he or she has done, and that is that. No?

Not, it is sometimes said in reply, if you're dealing with the glory of God. For God's glory is infinite, and God's goodness is infinite, and God's love is infinite, and so any sin against all those infinities must entail infinite suffering.

I have studied just enough mathematics, however, and quite a bit more theology to be suspicious of "infinities." Infinity often messes up math equations, and I have found it certainly messes up a variety of theological discussions as well. Well-meaning Christians often use "infinite" when they should say "great" or even "perfect," such as when they refer to God's patience. Thank God that God's patience is *not* infinite! If it were, justice and peace would be infinitely deferred. No, we need to beware of using "infinite," and even more of *equating* "infinities" as if we are speaking of the same things just by putting "infinite" in front of each element.

Yes, God's goodness has no limits. He is, as the philosophical theologians sometimes put it more carefully, *maximally* good. God's power is also maximal, as is God's wisdom, and love, and so on. God is as good and as great as good and great can be. But to sin against this superb and supreme being does not thereby bring down upon your head the entire weight of God's glory. Any sin, however small, separates one from God, yes. Only the righteous can ascend God's holy hill, yes. Nothing impure can enter the kingdom of heaven, yes and amen. But this appropriate binary language (in/out; good/bad) is not sufficient to deal with all that must be dealt with in the question of the just deserts of human evil.

Ron Hobbs treated me much, much worse than did every other child in that school. My intuition is that he therefore deserved much, much worse punishment than did they. Isn't yours the same? So of course, it seems to me, there must be degrees of punishment exactly proportioned by "the Judge of all the earth" to the degrees of transgression.

"But God is infinitely good," one hears in response, "and so there are no degrees of sin. Once you've sinned against God, you deserve to suffer forever." Really? Pick your favorite horrible villain, from history or from fiction: No one deserves to suffer any less than does he or she? Isn't there something wrong with any theological "equation" that ends up with "Caligula/de Sade/Hitler/Stalin = your friend or relative who decided, for whatever reason, not to accept God's salvation"? At least, don't we *hope* that there is?

That is the question I want to pose in this foreword. In the book that follows, there are chapters upon chapters of high-quality argument: exegesis of Scriptures, logical deductions, inferences to best explanations, metaphors and thought experiments, and more. I've never seen such a book, in fact, that piled up such a rich array of reasons to hold to a particular theological idea. But these resources won't do the reader any good who doesn't have any desire to change his or her mind, who *prefers* to think of ECT as the right way to think about judgment and hell.

So I ask you to consider this basic question: Wouldn't it be *great* to be able to believe that God did not keep the damned on a spit, rotating forever in the flames of eternal hellfire? Wouldn't it be a *relief* not to think of the saints getting on with the joyful business of the Age to Come without expending considerable energy trying not to think about their loved ones writhing in everlasting agony? Wouldn't it be *reassuring* not to have to try to bend one's mind and, worse, one's heart into a shape that could somehow give glory to God for afflicting people forever, that could somehow call majestic what seems obviously monstrous?

Don't get me wrong. And don't get these authors wrong. Ron Hobbs should go to hell. If he didn't repent of his sins and receive the stupendous gift of salvation in the sufferings of Jesus Christ on his behalf, then he is every bit the vicious little predator he seemed to be way back then, and hell is precisely what he deserves. He ought to pay for every moment of misery he inflicted on me, to the last drop.

Even more important, of course, is the offense of sin against God. God is offended and offended against by sin, and sin must be dealt with thoroughly on God's behalf as well as on any of ours. But some Christians seem to think they must be zealous on God's behalf and require the worst punishment they can imagine. We must be careful, to paraphrase Bonhoeffer, not to be more judgmental than God.

I don't want to believe in a God who keeps Ron Hobbs in the fire any longer than his sins warrant—do you? And how much suffering does it take to make up for two years of bullying? Or, in the case of my beloved friend, ten years of abuse? A lot, yes. A horrible lot. But not an eternity of it. There is only so much evil one can work in a human lifetime. Infinity

Foreword

just seems immediately, and wildly, out of proportion to a finite amount of sin, however large and virulent.

Now, maybe, of course, the traditional view of ECT is right. If it is, if ECT is truly what the Bible teaches, then I'll do my very best to believe it and teach it. I won't like it, but that doesn't matter: I love God and I trust him above my own reason and experience and moral intuition. Despite whatever might be the theological sophistication I have acquired over the years, if the Bible says it, I'll believe it, and that settles it.

But if I don't *have* to understand the Bible that way, . . . if I don't *have* to believe in eternal conscious torment, . . . if someone or, even better, a group of reputable someones can make a powerful case for a view of God's justice that seems proportionate to human evil . . . and not stretching out infinitely, then why wouldn't I rejoice to be granted this alternative?

Ten years or so after Ron Hobbs stopped besetting me, I had moved to another part of town, had hit puberty pretty hard, and had worked out enough to play football for my high school team. One night, inside our local hockey arena, I was walking along during an intermission munching a snack, and I nearly bumped into a much smaller fellow about my age who seemed strangely familiar. I stopped. He hadn't noticed me, as he was smoking a cigarette and staring out onto the ice as the Zamboni cleaned it for the next period of play. But I stared. It was Ron Hobbs. Menace of my childhood, now within striking range—and I was four inches and thirty pounds bigger than he was.

And I felt, looking at that small teenager forlornly looking off into space, that *God* should deal with him, not me. God would know what to do with him. God would save him, if he would be saved, and punish him rightly if he wouldn't. And what I still thought, as I thought when I was small, was that Ron Hobbs didn't deserve an eternity of hopeless pain. God was perfectly wrathful, but not insatiably bloodthirsty. And I have certainly been glad in the subsequent decades to find an interpretation of Holy Scripture that does not require me to believe in a God and Father of our Lord Jesus Christ that was actually fiercer about Ron Hobbs than I was.

This book will give you the grounds to believe in an entirely good, entirely righteous God who knows the difference between small sins and large ones, between awful little sinners and awfully big ones, between pathetic foolishness and satanic malevolence—and who judges each aright. Why wouldn't you want to rejoice in such a theology?

John G. Stackhouse Jr.

Preface

It was a number of years ago that the idea for this book first came to me. I believe it was when my nine-year-old daughter walked into my office, looked over several of my bookshelves with a quizzical expression, and finally asked, "Daddy, why do you have so many books about hell?" It struck me as a good question, similar to one that many friends and colleagues have asked me over the twenty years I have been studying the topic of hell, particularly focusing on the doctrine of conditional immortality: "Why are you so interested in hell?"

It is a reasonable question, since the evidence for my somewhat obsessive interest in the topic is obvious to those around me. I have collected over a hundred books on hell, along with countless articles, blog posts, and other media. In seminary, I regularly focused on the doctrine of hell in projects and papers, and later as a pastor, I led presentations on various views of hell in the church, arranged a debate on hell at an evangelical university, and have raised the topic of final judgment in too many conversations to remember. After helping to forge an international project dedicated to the idea of "rethinking hell," I have now had the privilege of working with some colleagues to select significant excerpts from conditionalist writings to reprint as a book on hell, as well as organizing an international conference on conditionalism. During these years, I have often faced alienation and marginalization from peers who have vehemently disagreed with me, along with the ongoing potential of losing my job over the view of hell that I held. So it truly is a question that should be answered.

The truth is, however, that I am not really that interested in the topic of hell itself. (And to be quite honest, I was never very drawn to the study of any eschatological subject: debates over the timing of Christ's return, views on the nature of the tribulation and millennium, and musing on the intermediate state have always felt very tiresome and speculative to

xv

Preface

me.) Hell is a rather morbid topic, to my mind, and it seems almost in bad taste to spend too much time dwelling upon it, though it is certainly important to understand the doctrine as it relates to God's character and human destiny, and to be able to communicate the reality of judgment, justice, and punishment as part of Christian belief.

My abiding interest in hell, and the reason why I've poured so much of my thought, resources, and conviction into this topic, has to do with the fact that there are so many Christians who claim quite confidently that hell will consist of eternal conscious torment, yet I personally (and surprisingly) have found the biblical, theological, and philosophical evidence for this perspective to be weak and insubstantial. In contrast, I discovered that the case for conditional immortality and the final destruction of the unsaved was comprehensive and compelling: this view seemed to be derived from the clear and consistent language of Scripture, it had an internal coherence that made sense of the overarching narrative of redemptive history, and it resolved philosophical and intuitive difficulties that have plagued generations of Christians and non-Christians alike for centuries.

And yet despite my own experience of the inferiority of the traditional view and the seemingly clear evidence and scriptural basis of the conditionalist view, there were so many other thoughtful and intelligent believers who have claimed the exact opposite—in fact, eternal conscious torment has been the position of the majority of Christians throughout church history. And this is what has made me, and so many others, obsess over the issue. How can it be that the evidence in favor of conditionalism appears so clear to those of us who have been convinced and yet is received with such skepticism by our fellow Christians? This experience is baffling, having an almost Kafkaesque quality to it, and it is honestly what has driven my own obsessive interest in the topic. I just don't understand how I can simultaneously feel so right and so wrong.

For instance, in an article in the alumni publication of the evangelical Christian university where I had worked for a number of years, an "expert" on the topic of hell had this to say about the view I hold:

> There have been individuals within the broad evangelical community who have subscribed to this view of annihilationism, which basically is the idea that the unbeliever will be tormented for a particular amount of time in hell but will eventually be terminated or annihilated. It's the

Preface

idea that fire destroys and brings things to an end—to ashes. It's the idea of conscious, but not eternal torment. I'm not quite sure if there's any biblical basis for this. From what I've seen and what I've read, the problem seems to be more existential, more emotional than scriptural and textual. Annihiliationism is held by some theologians in the church—Clark Pinnock, Edward Fudge—but to be honest, textually speaking I'm not quite sure how they can affirm this.

I remember reading the words "I'm not quite sure if there's any biblical basis for this" and feeling a depth of incredulity and perplexity that confounded me to my core. Of course I understand that Christians have different interpretations of Scripture, but this author's dismissive attitude and ignorance of the careful biblical study of the highest level of evangelical scholars exemplifies the frustrating reality of presumptuous conjectures and careless conclusions that conditionalists face within evangelical circles. Having been told there are no legitimate grounds for holding our view, we have returned to the biblical texts and the theological and philosophical arguments to reexamine if we have indeed misread the texts or misunderstood the evidence for our view somehow. Surely our evangelical brothers and sisters have deeply reflected on the basis for their beliefs and are not simply asserting their view out of blind adherence to the traditional doctrine of eternal conscious torment that has been handed down to them, right? So we research and read some more, looking for the place where we must have gone wrong in our study of the topic. And yet we arrive, in the end, at the same conclusion favoring conditionalism. But when we share these results, once again, traditionalists are adamant that there are no credible reasons for holding our view.

At times, the experience of being dismissed by others as emotional, eccentric, or even heretical, combined with others' unwillingness to actually review the evidence for conditionalism has been both confusing and deeply troubling, particularly given the fact that evangelicals claim to base their beliefs on their study of Scripture and not merely on the authority of any tradition. So my passionate interest in hell has primarily been an exercise in challenging myself and others to test our commitment to the authority of God's revelation in the Bible over unexamined tradition, which would be the same with any other accepted doctrine that did not appear to stand up to exegetical investigation.

Preface

G. K. Chesterton famously said, "The Christian ideal has not been tried and found wanting; it has been found difficult and left untried." Something similar could be said about the doctrine of conditional immortality in terms of most Christians' willingness to explore the topic. Our hope with this book is that it will provide readers with a collection of solid evangelical voices in support of conditionalism in order to make their study of our view as accessible and focused as possible. (It will also save them the hassle of having to track down the many books from which these chapters are taken, most of which are out of print, hard to find, or expensive to obtain.) If our readers still reject this view, it will not be because they have not considered the best arguments for our perspective (although they would benefit tremendously from also reading Edward Fudge's definitive exploration of the topic in his book *The Fire that Consumes*). Hopefully, at the very least, my own friends who get this book can have a more accurate understanding of why I and other conditionalists have such an intense interest in the topic of hell. And perhaps someday my daughter will take up this volume too, and discover just why all those books, in a manner of speaking, have a place on every Christian's shelves.

Greg Stump

Acknowledgments

The editors would like to thank those who have helped to make this book possible through their support, generosity, and encouragement in various ways, including those involved in the Rethinking Hell project (Joseph Dear, Ronnie Demler, Aaron Fudge, Dan Holmes, Nick Quient, Daniel Sinclair, John "JT" Tancock, William Tanksley Jr., and Jeff Whittum), many of whom assisted in our research and helped to review our manuscript; those who helped us trace down permissions for various works, including Richard Eldridge, I. Howard Marshall, Elijah Smith, and Paul Wolfe; those who provided us with archival materials, including Berry Driver, Allison Kirchner, John Roller, David Wenham, and Simon Wenham; those who assisted us with the cost of obtaining permissions, including Debbie Bostian, Katherine Lo, Pat and Kathy Ogle, Shellie Soares, Don and Eileen Stump, Mark and Joanne Stump, and John "JT" Tancock.

We would like to especially thank all those authors or publishers who granted us permission to use various excerpts at no or minimal cost, including Everett Berry, Ralph Bowles, Tom DeVries, the editors of the *Evangelical Quarterly*, LeRoy Froom (grandson of L. E. Froom), Christopher Marshall, Mike Parsons, Jon Pott, E. Randolph Richards and the board of the International Reference Library for Biblical Research, Stephen Travis, Ben Witherington, and Nigel Wright.

Special thanks to Edward Fudge, John Stackhouse, Glenn Peoples, Peter Grice (for bringing us all together) and particularly to our editor at Wipf & Stock, Robin Parry, who painlessly guided us through the process of proposal, submission, and publication.

Permissions

Bowles, Ralph G. "Does Revelation 14:11 Teach Eternal Torment?" *Evangelical Quarterly* 73.1 (2001) 21–36. © Paternoster Periodicals, Nottingham, England. Reprinted by permission from the editors of *Evangelical Quarterly*.

Edwards, David L., and John R. W. Stott. *Evangelical Essentials: A Liberal-Evangelical Dialogue.* © 1988 Hodder and Stoughton, London. Pages 312–20, reprinted by permission of Hodder and Stoughton Limited; all rights reserved.

Ellis, E. Earle. "New Testament Teaching on Hell." In *Eschatology in Bible & Theology.* © 1999 International Reference Library for Biblical Research (IRLBR), Fort Worth, TX. Reprinted by permission from IRLBR; all rights reserved.

Evangelical Alliance Commission on Unity and Truth among Evangelicals (ACUTE). *The Nature of Hell: A Report by the Evangelical Alliance Commission on Unity and Truth Among Evangelicals ACUTE.* © 2000 Evangelical Alliance, London. Portions of chapters 9 and 10 reprinted by permission from the Evangelical Alliance; all rights reserved.

Froom, LeRoy E. *The Conditionalist Faith of Our Fathers.* © 1959 LeRoy E. Froom. Portions of chapters 44–46, 51–52, 54, and 63 reprinted by permission from the Froom estate; all rights reserved.

Fudge, Edward W. "The Final End of the Wicked." In *Journal of the Evangelical Theological Society* 27.3 (1984) 325–34. © Edward Fudge. Reprinted by permission of the author; all rights reserved.

Permissions

Hughes, Philip E. *The True Image*. © 1989 Wm. B. Eerdmans Publishing Company, Grand Rapids. Chapter 37 reprinted by permission of the publisher; all rights reserved.

Marshall, Christopher D. *Beyond Retribution*. © 2001 Wm. B. Eerdmans Publishing Company, Grand Rapids. Portions of chapter 4 reprinted by permission of the publisher; all rights reserved.

Olson, Roger E. *The Mosaic of Christian Belief*. © 2002 Roger E. Olson. Portions of chapter 14 reprinted by permission of InterVarsity Press, Downers Grove, IL; all rights reserved.

Papaioannou, Kim G. *The Geography of Hell in the Teaching of Jesus*. © 2013 Wipf and Stock, Eugene, OR. Portions of Part I and of "Synopsis and Synthesis" reprinted by permission of the publisher.

Pinnock, Clark H. "The Destruction of the Finally Impenitent." *Criswell Theological Review* 4.2 (1990) 243–59. © Criswell College, Dallas, TX. Reprinted by permission of the publisher; all rights reserved.

Swinburne, Richard G. *Responsibility and Atonement*. © 1989 Oxford University Press, Oxford. Pages 179–84, reprinted by permission of the publisher; all rights reserved.

Thiselton, Anthony C. *Life After Death*. © 2011 Wm. B. Eerdmans Publishing Company, Grand Rapids. Portions of chapter 9 reprinted by permission of the publisher; all rights reserved.

Travis, Stephen H. *Christ Will Come Again: Hope for the Second Coming of Jesus*. © 2004 Clements, Toronto, Ontario. Portions of chapter 6 reprinted by permission from the publisher; all rights reserved.

Wenham, John W. "The Case for Conditional Immortality." In *Universalism and the Doctrine of Hell*, edited by Nigel M. de S. Cameron. © 1992 Baker Academic, a division of Baker Publishing Group, Grand Rapids. Reprinted by permission of the publisher; all rights reserved.

Witherington, Ben III. *The Bible and Culture* blog. © Ben Witherington III. Portions of "Hell? No??" (http://www.patheos.com/blogs/bibleandculture/2011/03/16/hell-no/), "Matthew 10:28—Why Annihilationism is not Universalism" (http://www.patheos.com/blogs/bibleandculture/2011/03/

Permissions

18/mt-10–28-why-anihilationism-is-not-universalism/), and "And Now—The Case for Permanent Residence in Hell" (http://www.patheos.com/blogs/bibleandculture/2011/03/19/and-now-the-case-for-permanent-residence-in-hell/) reprinted by permission of the author; all rights reserved.

Wright, Nigel G. *The Radical Evangelical: Seeking a Place to Stand.* © 1996 Nigel Wright. Portions of chapter 7 reprinted by permission of the author; all rights reserved.

Abbreviations

Reference Works

ANF   *Ante-Nicene Fathers.* Edited by Philip Schaff et al. 10 vols. Peabody, MA: Hendrickson, 1996.

APOT   *Apocrypha and Pseudepigrapha of the Old Testament.* Edited by R. H. Charles. London: Oxford University Press, 1913.

DCB   *Dictionary of Christian Biography, Literature, Sects and Doctrines; during the First Eight Centuries.* Edited by William Smith and Henry Wace. 4 vols. London: 1877–87.

NPNF   *Nicene and Post-Nicene Fathers.* First series 14 vols; second series 14 vols. Edited by Philip Schaff et al. Reprint. Peabody, MA: Hendrickson, 1996.

OTP   *Old Testament Pseudepigrapha.* Edited by James Charlesworth. 2 vols. 1983. Reprint. Peabody, MA: Hendrickson, 2010.

TDNT   *Theological Dictionary of the New Testament.* Edited by Gergard Kittle and Gerhard Friedrich. Translated by Geoffrey Brimiley. 10th ed. 10 vols. Grand Rapids: Eerdmans, 1977.

Periodicals

CTR   *Criswell Theological Review*
EuroJTh   *European Journal of Theology*
ExpTim   *Expository Times*

Abbreviations

JBL	*Journal of Biblical Literature*
JETS	*Journal of the Evangelical Theological Society*
JTS	*Journal of Theological Studies*
NTS	*New Testament Studies*
WTJ	*Westminster Theological Journal*

Scriptures and Other Ancient Sources

ESV	*English Standard Version*

Scriptures

Hebrew Bible/Old Testament

Gen
Exod
Lev
Num
Deut
Josh
Judg
Ruth
1–2 Sam
1–2 Kgs
1–2 Chr
Ezra
Neh
Esth
Job
Ps (*pl.* Pss)
Prov
Eccl (or Qoh)
Song
Isa
Jer
Lam

Ezek
Dan
Hos
Joel
Amos
Obad
Jonah
Mic
Nah
Hab
Zeph
Hag
Zech
Mal

New Testament

Matt
Mark
Luke
John
Acts
Rom
1–2 Cor
Gal
Eph
Phil
Col
1–2 Thess
1–2 Tim
Titus
Phlm
Heb
Jas
1–2 Pet
1-2-3 John

Jude
Rev

Apocrypha/deuterocanonical books

1–2 Esd
Jdt

Old Testament Pseudepigrapha

As. Mos.	*Assumption of Moses*
4 Macc.	*4 Maccabees*
Pss. Sol.	*Psalms of Solomon*

Early Church Fathers

Barn.	*Epistle of Barnabas*
1 Clem.	*First Clement*
2 Clem.	*Second Clement*
Diogn.	*Letter of Diognetus*
Ign. Eph.	Ignatius' *Letter to the Ephesians*
Ign. Magn.	Ignatius' *Letter to the Magnesians*
Ath. Res.	Athanasius' *On the Resurrection of the Dead*
Orig. Prin.	Origen's *First Principles*
De Inc.	Athanasius' *On the Incarnation of the Word*

Editor's Introduction

It has been my experience that Christians are frequently shocked to discover that many notable and respected evangelical scholars are conditionalists and have rejected the traditional view of hell as eternal conscious torment. Contributing to this phenomenon is the fact that few such scholars in the twentieth and twenty-first centuries have written book-length defenses of conditionalism. Edward Fudge is one of a handful of exceptions; most have instead articulated or defended conditionalism in smaller portions of books written about other topics, or covering a variety of topics, many of which are difficult to obtain. It is therefore not always easy to direct curious traditionalists (not to mention hostile ones) to these authors' published support for conditionalism.

Rethinking Hell: Readings in Evangelical Conditionalism is meant to serve as a resource to help solve that problem by compiling some of what these various conditionalist scholars have written into one convenient publication, saving inquisitive traditionalists and universalists, and the conditionalists who love them, hundreds of dollars—and precious real estate on the bookshelf. However, the works featured in this volume were written and published across decades and centuries, in multiple countries, differ in style, and overlap at times in content. For these reasons and others, creating a wide-ranging collection but with the feel of a single book required some effort.

In no case has an author's originally intended meaning been changed or muzzled, even where one or more of the editors disagrees with it, or otherwise does not endorse it. A number of minor, mostly stylistic changes have been required, however, in order to unify the original works collected in this volume. For example, works have been edited to conform to American spelling and standards of punctuation. "Saviour," for example, has become "Savior," quotes are enclosed in quotation marks (double-quotes) rather than in apostrophes (single-quotes), and commas

Editor's Introduction

and periods precede closing quotation marks. Likely to go unnoticed by all but the most meticulous comparisons of these reproductions to their originals are replacements of "for ever" with "forever," "per cent" with "percent," and so on.

Abbreviated citations of biblical and other ancient texts have been made to conform to a unified standard. Endnotes have been converted to footnotes. Works originally cited in long-form footnote citation are instead cited in short-form, with their expanded details included in a comprehensive bibliography at the end of the book. The style of all headings have been modified to conform to a unified style. Divine pronouns (he, him, his, etc.) originally capitalized have been made lower-case.

In most cases, original citations of different editions of the same book have been updated to cite a single shared edition, the one exception being Edward Fudge's *The Fire That Consumes*. Where an author cites or quotes *The Fire That Consumes*, the edition cited is indicated by the year in which the cited edition was published (1982 or 2011). Most citations of early church fathers have been modified to quote and cite Roberts and Donaldson's *The Ante-Nicene Fathers* or Schaff and Wace's *The Nicene and Post-Nicene Fathers*, to make it easier for readers to look up the cited text.

Part One consists of two introductory chapters of original content from members of the Rethinking Hell team. Part Two reproduces the works of those authors consistently identified, even by traditionalists, as being most responsible for reigniting the modern debate over conditionalism. In an effort to avoid duplication of themes and ideas as much as possible in the remaining authors, original works or excerpts thereof have been chosen that complement one another, and have been organized into groups with others that focus on similar topics: Scripture in Part Three, philosophy in Part Four, history in Part Five, and evangelicalism in Part Six. The book is thus laid out in such a way as to be read from beginning to end, while at the same time enabling readers to more easily locate works in categories in which they're specifically interested.

Each editor was responsible for one or more parts of the book, which entailed writing short introductions to their sections and biographical sketches introducing their chapters' authors, as well as proofreading reproduced works by comparing them to their originals. Greg was responsible for Part Two, and wrote the preface as the book was his original idea. Joshua was responsible for Parts Four and Six, and I oversaw Parts One, Three, and Five. I also compiled the bibliography, converted the original

Editor's Introduction

works into manuscript form through a combination of optical character recognition and manual transcription, and prepared the final manuscript for submission to our publisher.

We hope and pray with confidence that *Rethinking Hell: Readings in Evangelical Conditionalism* will personally edify you, the reader. If you are already convinced of conditionalism, you will find encouragement in the caliber of scholarship supporting your view, and may find yourself better prepared to articulate and defend it. If, on the other hand, you currently believe in the traditional view of hell, or that eventually everyone will be saved, even if you remain convinced of it after reading this book, you'll better understand why so many of us have felt forced to reject it in favor of conditionalism. Hopefully, like the authors in Part Six, you'll begin to see us as your brothers and sisters in Christ, if you don't already.

Or, quite possibly, you'll find yourself rethinking hell, too.

Chris Date

PART ONE

Rethinking Hell

1

Igniting an Evangelical Conversation

PETER S. GRICE

Peter Grice is a founder of the Rethinking Hell project, a global network of evangelical scholars, teachers, and laypeople who are exploring the doctrine of conditional immortality. He also serves as president of Think Christianity, which promotes Christian thought in contemporary life, and director of the TELOS Program®, a unique Christian worldview and apologetics training program. Peter writes and teaches on topics such as science, culture, and worldviews, and contributed a chapter on reason and Christian faith to the book True Reason: Confronting the Irrationality of the New Atheism. *He lives in Brisbane, Australia with his wife Anchalee and son Lewis.*

MUCH LIKE HELL ITSELF, conditionalism usually takes you by surprise. At least, that's how it was for a number of evangelical Christians who stumbled into a clearing at the turn of the twenty-first century, and began to encounter this paradigm together.

Like most card-carrying evangelicals, we had blissfully assumed that when it comes to widely held Christian beliefs, all of the theological dust had settled. In our tradition, a relatively obscure doctrine like conditional immortality isn't supposed to resurface and challenge the dominant view. We are open to this kind of thing in principle, of course, as good students of the Protestant Reformation. But we are ready, with unwritten laws about how biblical such challenges could possibly be, and from which inauspicious sources they must surely emanate.

Those were my cynical expectations too, so I was not prepared for conditionalism to commend itself with such biblical force, in an unmistakably evangelical voice. Neither did I anticipate that the response from critics would prove to be lackluster, at least thus far. Hardly any of us did, in fact. Nor did we expect a steady stream of others emerging from the woods, pondering with us the same issues, and noticing those discrepancies in the terrain.

Only some of the new conditionalists were left scratching their heads, however, since among our company were those who had arrived on the scene a little sooner, including, as would become clear, some of the world's leading Bible scholars and teachers. Even they weren't there first, given the long history of conditionalism—which of course has something to do with the present volume.

In terms of the Christian milieu, the renowned evangelical leader and critic of conditionalism, J. I. Packer, had just been succeeded at Regent College by a notable proponent of our view, John G. Stackhouse Jr. For conditionalists, this symbolized a shift we'd been noticing for some time. Packer's longstanding influence could be compared to that of another architect of contemporary evangelicalism, the late John Stott, who instead embraced conditionalism (a position he'd held tentatively for some fifty years) and pleaded for more open dialogue. Late last century, and not without irony, Packer had urged caution on this issue to the National Association of Evangelicals in the United States, who came close to ruling that conditionalism—and by implication Stott himself—was incompatible with evangelicalism. Perhaps due to the remarkably narrow margin, the real significance of this is often overlooked: conditionalism was deemed to be acceptable. This would be the case in the United Kingdom as well, when with less fanfare the Evangelical Alliance would formally review the doctrine, and explicitly conclude that it is indeed a legitimate alternative view on hell.

Meanwhile, a landmark written defense of conditionalism had been quietly straddling the two centuries, simultaneously fueling the controversy and helping to resolve it. Edward Fudge's *The Fire That Consumes*, an enduring work which many credit with the resurgence of this view in our time, was to receive an endorsement and new foreword in 2011 by another leading conditionalist scholar, Richard Bauckham of Cambridge.

In the same year, the popular American pastor Rob Bell published a book on hell that drew the ire of many evangelicals, and in some circles his name became a byword for one who departs from the fold. It seemed as though Bell had crossed a line, not so much for critiquing the traditional view, but for appearing to advocate universalism in its stead. What really concerned many was that a doctrine that was long ago condemned by the church could return so swiftly on the wings of popular Christian culture, exploiting new forms of media for their ease of communication and rapid distribution. If the printing press could catalyze the Protestant Reformation, it stands to reason that the advent of the internet in our time may yet lead to more doctrinal revision. Without any guarantees that this be done on biblical grounds, evangelicals in particular have become unsettled. Universalism was indeed on the rise, appearing in other books and publications, and harnessing new media forms with the theatrical release of the documentary *Hellbound?* Conditionalism had its own foray into cinema as well, in the form of *Hell and Mr. Fudge*, a feature-length biographical film about the social ramifications of Edward Fudge's theological plight in the 1980s.

Those kinds of tensions and concerns need to be managed well, and this may require the established position to be more open to scrutiny. Numerous credible voices are saying that traditionalism is not as biblically defensible as has long been assumed. Some have even suggested that the doctrine of hell is the unfinished business of the Reformation. If this is the case, or at least plausibly so, then it makes sense that both universalism and conditionalism should be reappearing now, when many younger evangelicals are eagerly searching the internet to see if these things are so.

What role would those of us in the "Rethinking Hell" project play in all of this? As proponents of conditional immortality the most obvious task is to commend our perspective to new audiences. This is a privilege that we have embraced, being fully convinced that conditionalism gives the most defensible reading of the relevant biblical texts, and faithfully represents the revealed character of God. Given its worthy credentials, there is still a concerning lack of awareness of this view, to the point where it is regularly conflated with universalism. This situation hasn't been helped by the general difficulty involved with accessing some of the most important recent literature on this subject. The present work is an important step toward a remedy, building upon the foundation laid by Edward Fudge and anticipating continued academic exploration of the topic, in an effort to produce a robustly evangelical theology of conditional immortality. For this cause, and in pursuit of healthy engagement with this topic among our evangelical brothers and sisters, we will continue to press forward as a movement, providing materials via our website in a variety of media formats (http://www.rethinkinghell.com), hosting academic conferences, debates, and other kinds of conversations.

However, we are not just satisfied with commending our own view. We are also advocates for evangelical unity, and well-positioned to notice when this is being challenged. We long for a healthier, more irenic conversation about hell, free from some of the lingering antagonisms that unnecessarily drag us down. More than ever before, the non-Christian world is watching, and we have a responsibility to deal with controversy in light of the high calling to Christian charity.

To this end, we are helping to frame the conversation around mutual understanding. There are three main views on hell, and if we never deal with the topic as a trichotomy, it may be difficult to know which one is correct. One of our offerings, the "hell triangle" diagram, serves as a reminder of this, and a useful platform for discussion. A brief rundown of the three views may assist the reader in navigating some of the discussions in this book.

The traditional and most familiar view of everlasting conscious torment is indicated in the bottom left corner of the triangle. At the apex, universalism draws sinners figuratively upward from hell, believing them to be restored to God after a temporary period of refinement. Then in the bottom right corner, conditionalism renders unsaved sinners permanently destroyed, including any finite period of conscious suffering. With this basic arrangement, one is able to reflect upon similarities and differences between the views. The biblical metaphor of fire is also useful for distinguishing the three positions, understood variously as fire which torments, or refines, or completely consumes.

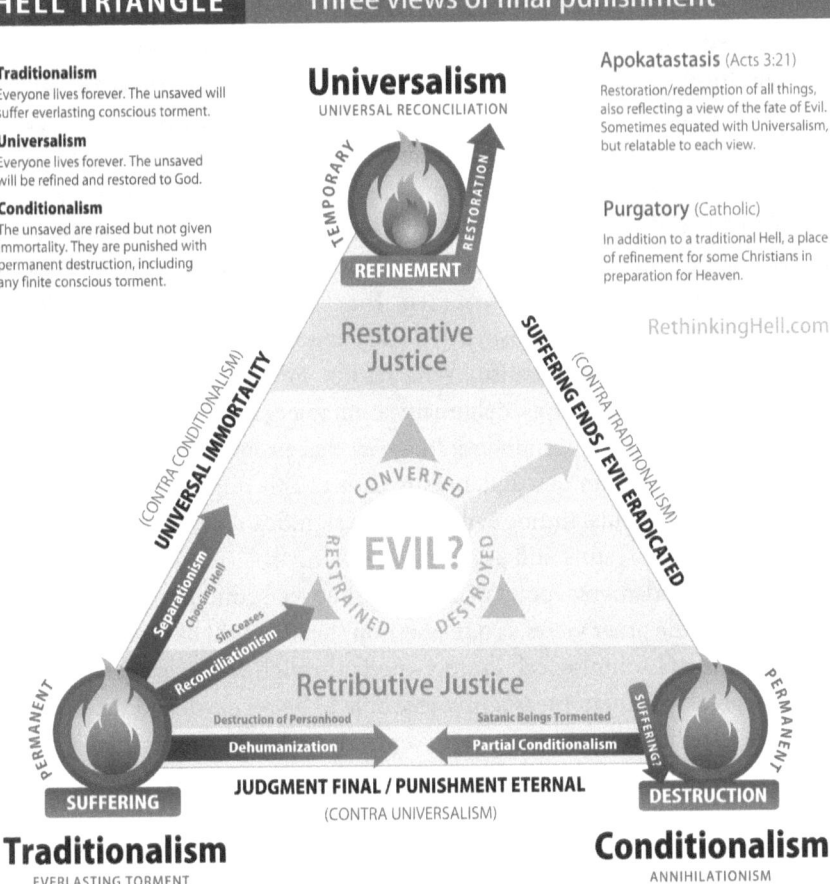

The triangle's center and edges deal with an important biblical consideration, the eventual reconciliation of "all things," which prompts the question of what happens to evil beings should they persist in evil. Universalists contend that the reconciliation includes the conversion of all evil beings into good. Conditionalists also contend for a universal scope, but one that is established after recalcitrant evil has been destroyed. Traditionalists maintain that containment is enough, so that evil is eradicated from a redeemed realm of the cosmos, albeit not from the entire created order.

Some traditionalists are not content with that solution, however, noting that if evil beings continue to curse God in hell, for example, this is not a satisfying picture. Reconciliationists, as they are known, hold that evil thoughts and deeds do cease in hell, and its inhabitants remain subdued. This is one of the three not-so-traditional variations, seen as trajectories on the diagram, and perhaps partial concessions to other main views. The second tendency out of traditionalism is that of separationism, which departs significantly from reconciliationism in saying that evil beings are only in hell because they continue to choose to be there, instead of with God. Some have seen this as problematic because it leaves open the possibility that they might change their minds in hell, so that salvation could occur even then. The third contemporary modification to historic traditionalism avoids this upward beckoning, by creeping instead toward conditionalism. Whereas our view describes the cessation of unsaved human beings, dehumanization refers to the cessation only of human identity or personhood, in a way that progressively degenerates into something akin to a dull, beastly nature. This might seem to resolve the problem of outstanding evil, but at the significant cost of bequeathing an ex-human creature still under punishment.

The fundamental point of departure between conditional immortality and all the other views, is our assertion that the right biblical frame for eschatology is ontological. From Genesis through to Revelation, we see that ongoing human life is a privilege able to be revoked, and that it was revoked, when humankind was prevented from living forever (Gen 3:22). We are not innately immortal, but this gift of eternal life will be given to those who are rescued from death by our Savior (2 Tim 1:10). The Old Testament language of a definitive destruction of the wicked, often by fire, cannot be dismissed lightly as merely "temporal," for it follows language constructions of finality, and the fire itself is called "eternal." Only the righteous, it turns out, can dwell figuratively within the eternal burning of God's holy fire (Isa 33:14–15), which to all God's enemies is an agent of destruction. Only the saved "can no longer die," Jesus taught, being "considered worthy of taking part in the age to come" (Luke 20:35–36). The fact that the unsaved will be resurrected to face a final judgment (an important evangelical affirmation in this context) in no way demands that they will live eternally. Though to imagine an eternity of torment is a fearful thing, we should instead fear that God might "destroy both soul and body in hell" (Matt 10:28).

Understood ontologically, the Bible's various terms referring to either living forever or being forever destroyed, help to show how the biblical frame never actually bifurcates into a heaven and hell seen as separate living quarters but instead emphasizes the present world being redeemed along a climactic timeline, so that the heavenly kingdom is something that manifests here in transformative power. Given impending judgment, the burning biblical question is always about who will be brought *back* to life, or preserved alive, in order to inherit the glorious promises of the age to come. Conversely, it's about who would pass away along with the present evil age, once the kingdom of God is fully installed in all its conquering glory.

As you journey through these readings in conditionalist thought, you will encounter much more detail about this view, seen from various perspectives. Whatever your convictions, please don't drop out of this important conversation. You can join us, and many other evangelical brothers and sisters, via the website at www.rethinkinghell.com. There you will find articles, interviews, debates, reference information, news of events, and more. Importantly, we trust you will find there the spirit of evangelical unity and conviction. If you are not yet convinced, but are willing just to engage in dialogue, you have already stumbled into the same clearing as us, for subjecting one's views to biblical scrutiny is the essence of rethinking hell.

2

Introduction to Evangelical Conditionalism

GLENN A. PEOPLES

Glenn Peoples runs the popular New Zealand blog Right Reason and podcast Say Hello to My Little Friend. There and elsewhere he writes and speaks on theology and biblical studies, moral and social philosophy, and philosophy of religion. He completed undergraduate studies in Theology at the Bible College of New Zealand (now Laidlaw College), followed by an MTh and a PhD in Philosophy at the University of Otago. Peoples is the author of the article, "Fallacies in the Annihilationism Debate," JETS 50.2 (2007) 349–55.

CONDITIONAL IMMORTALITY IS A term that just forty years ago most evangelical Christians had never heard.[1] Today it is a familiar guest at theological discussions about human nature and destiny. It is the view that human beings are mortal, that we depend entirely on the grace of God for our existence, that eternal life is made possible only through the resurrection of Jesus of Nazareth, and that immortality—endless life—is the gift of God that he will bestow upon those who are saved through

---

1. I include those who do not spend time in the literature on historical theology, otherwise this observation about what "most" evangelicals are familiar with would not be true.

Christ, at the resurrection of the dead. It can be contrasted with a familiar story told widely in churches, a story that it has become convenient to call "traditionalism" because of its broad acceptance and respectable pedigree: that the souls of human beings live on when the mortal body gives up the ghost, to return to the body (or a new one) at the resurrection of the dead in order to be assigned its eternal home—joy in heaven or torment in hell forever.

In recent decades evangelical conditionalism was thrust into the limelight among popular evangelical books with the 1982 publication of Edward Fudge's *The Fire That Consumes*.[2] The responses to Fudge's work have ranged from delight to outrage, along with everything in between. Thirty years later the shape of evangelical discussions about eternal life and judgment has been permanently changed. One of the reasons for that change, evangelical conditionalists maintain, is that many traditionalists, never having been exposed to the case for "the other side," were simply not prepared for how mundane, simply stated, and biblically grounded that case really was, and found themselves not only taken off guard but, like Fudge, won over.

Here the case for evangelical conditionalism is summed up under four of its principle arguments: firstly the question of immortality, secondly the biblical vision of eternity, thirdly the theological explanation of the atoning death of Christ as a substitution, and finally the biblical description of the fate of the lost as destruction.

Immortality

In much of the historical literature on conditional immortality, there has been a sustained focus on the doctrine of the immortality of the soul, especially when the doctrine began to attract renewed attention from the time of the Reformation. By that time things had reached the point where the Fifth Lateran Council (1513) declared, "We do condemn and reprobate all who assert that the intelligent soul is mortal." And asserting it Christians were. For many of them (e.g., William Tyndale, Jon Frith, Martin Luther, George Wishart, Archbishop John Tillotson, Henry Layton, and many others) the central issue was the state of the dead prior to the resurrection, where rejecting the soul's immortality was synonymous with embracing the doctrine of "soul sleep," the view that death is a state

---

2. The book is now in its third edition.

of total unconsciousness, rather than survival in heaven, hell, or purgatory. For others, however (e.g., William Whiston, John Locke, Bishop William Warburton, and numerous since then), denying the immortality of the soul went hand in hand with recognizing that everlasting life in any shape or form was a gift of God, and the result of separation from God is the denial of that gift and final death. Eternal life in the sense of life without end is not a natural human possession. We are bereft of it because of sin, and God promises to give it to those who are united to Christ. Immortality is therefore not universal or inherent but *conditional*. God alone has immortality in himself and he will give eternal life "to them who by patient continuance in well doing seek for glory and honor and immortality."[3] While "those who belong to Christ" at the resurrection of the dead will "put on immortality," immortality is never promised to those who reject God.[4] This is the significance of that familiar biblical promise of eternal life, and the warning that the wages of sin is death. This, surely, is the point of the Garden of Eden narrative in Genesis 2–3. This is the way in which God's people will have victory over "the final enemy," which is death.[5] Eternal life is made possible and received only through Christ. However, once the widespread doctrine of the immortality of the soul is added to a biblical theology, this picture is distorted. Now the issue is not the biblical one of *obtaining* eternal life. Everyone has eternal life! The issue now must be one of where or how that eternal life will be spent: in the bliss of heaven or the horror of hell?

Some contemporary spokespeople for the traditional view of hell distance themselves from the issue of the soul's immortality, insisting that it is not a driving force in their outlook. Robert Peterson, for example, reassured readers that

> I do not accept traditionalism because I believe in the immortality of the soul. Rather, I believe in the immortality of human beings (united in body and soul after the resurrection of the dead) because the Bible teaches that there will be "eternal punishment" for the lost and "eternal life" for the saved (Matt 25:46).[6]

The truth is, however, that like many traditionalists Dr. Peterson believes in the immortality of the soul, body or not, for he maintains that

3. Rom 2:7. See also 1 Tim 6:16.
4. 1 Cor 15:23, 53.
5. 1 Cor 15:26.
6. Fudge and Peterson, *Two Views*, 89.

the soul lives on when the body dies, entering what is frequently called the "intermediate state." That the soul will be reunited with a body at the resurrection is not, in the traditional Reformed view, what grants a person immortality, but rather a person's soul is immortal already. This is clearly taught in Peterson's own doctrinal standard (that held by Covenant Theological Seminary), the Westminster Confession of Faith:

> After God had made all other creatures, He created man, male and female, with reasonable and immortal souls . . . (Chapter 4)

> The bodies of men, after death, return to dust, and see corruption: but their souls, which neither die nor sleep, having an immortal subsistence, immediately return to God who gave them: the souls of the righteous, being then made perfect of holiness, are received into the highest heavens, where they behold the face of God, in light and glory, waiting for the full redemption of their bodies. And the souls of the wicked are cast into hell, where they remain in torments and utter darkness, reserved to the judgment of the great day. (Chapter 23)

Historically, many of the proponents of the doctrine of the eternal torments of the lost—in fact those who were responsible for cementing the place of that view within Christian theology—did indeed argue from the immortality of every human soul to the doctrine of eternal torment in hell. Clement of Alexandria made the argument in approximately AD 195: "All souls are immortal, even those of the wicked, for whom it were better that they were not deathless. For, punished with the endless vengeance of quenchless fire, and not dying, it is impossible for them to have a period put to their misery."[7] But it was Augustine of Hippo, more than any other theologian of the first half millennium of Christian history, who galvanized the doctrine of the immortality of all human souls, as well as the role that this belief was to play in the doctrine of hell. How can the lost live forever in hell when immortality is the gift of God to his people? One answer was that of Marcus Minucius Felix in the third century: "That clever fire burns the limbs and restores them, wears them away and yet sustains them, just as fiery thunderbolts strike bodies but do not consume them."[8] The fire had strange properties so that it did not devour its fuel like normal fire. Augustine's solution was the same as that

---

7. A Post-Nicene Fragment from "The Book on the Soul."

8. Felix, Marcus Minucius, *Octavius*, chapter 35. Cited in Jürgens, *Early Fathers*, 1:110.

of Clement. The fire cannot destroy that which is immortal. Augustine argued that his opponents, those who say anything that can suffer in fire is not really immortal, are overlooking one crucial thing: "there is something which is greater than the body," namely the soul. This is his key response: "For the spirit, whose presence animates and rules the body, can both suffer pain and cannot die. Here then is something which, though it can feel pain, is immortal." Since the spirit of the living is immortal but can still suffer pain when the body suffers without being harmed, so too the soul in eternity can suffer forever but not die.[9] Thus began a mainstay for proponents of what became the traditional view of hell. William Shedd used the argument explicitly when arguing that the suffering of the age to come must be endless: "Scripture speaks of but two aeons, which cover and include the whole existence of man, and his whole duration. If, therefore, he is an immortal being, one of these must be endless."[10] Today, while retaining the fruit of this argument, proponents of the traditional view of hell increasingly distance themselves from it.

There were, however, other voices among the church fathers who did not share the stance of Clement of Alexandria and Augustine.[11] Among writers like Ignatius of Antioch, the author of the *Epistle of Barnabas*, Irenaeus of Lyons, Arnobius of Cicca, and even Athanasius the Great, modern conditionalists find a view much more like their own than like that of many Christians. In the view of these fathers—representing the earliest post-apostolic perspective, Christ came so that he could save people from the impending consequences of sin, and thereby "breathe immortality into His church" so that those within would not "perish,"[12] saying that if God did not save us and chose instead "to reward us according to our works, we should cease to be."[13] They taught that instead of living forever, the one who rejects God's kingdom in favor of other things "shall be destroyed with his works."[14] They taught Christians that we are like God's other creations in the sense that they "endure as long as God wills that they should have an existence and continuance," and that "it is

9. *City of God* 21.3.2; NPNF 1.2:453.

10. Shedd, *Theology*, 687.

11. Athenagorus, earlier than these two, overtly taught the immortality of the soul (and appears to be the earliest Christian writer to do so). However he did not make an argument for the doctrine of eternal torment on this basis.

12. *Ign. Eph.* 17; ANF 1:56.

13. *Ign. Magn.* 10; ANF 1:63.

14. *Barn.* 21; ANF 1:149.

the Father of all who imparts continuance for ever and ever on those who are saved." The one who rejects the gift of life, however, "deprives himself of continuance for ever and ever," and he "shall justly not receive from Him length of days for ever and ever."[15] This is a punishment which is eternal, but not because the lost themselves will live forever. Instead the punishment is eternal insofar as what the lost will miss out on is eternal. "That punishment falls upon them because they are destitute of all that is good. Now, good things are eternal and without end with God, and therefore the loss of these is also eternal and never-ending."[16] Among these fathers we read that a being "cannot be immortal which does suffer pain," and that those who are finally lost, regardless of whether their souls survive the death of their bodies in this world, will finally die "man's real death, this which leaves nothing behind," and "being annihilated, pass away vainly in everlasting destruction."[17]

Evangelical conditionalists share this outlook, finding in it a major theme of biblical theology. The biblical salvation history begins with the tree of life. Human sin results in a loss of access to the tree, sealing the fate of mortal humans: "For dust you are, and to dust you shall return" (Gen 3:19). God engages in a soliloquy about what to do next.

> "Behold, the man has become like one of us in knowing good and evil. Now, lest he reach out his hand and take also of the tree of life and eat, and live forever—" therefore the LORD God sent him out from the garden of Eden to work the ground from which he was taken. (Gen 3:22–24)

The divine pronouncement is cut short. God's reticence is seen in that he will not even express the possibility of the immortality of those who are in rebellion against him. Humanity is driven from Eden with little hope in sight. Death, rather than hell, has become part of the human story, and, to borrow the phraseology of Athanasius, humanity is being undone and "the handiwork of God was in process of dissolution."[18] The first man was created when the dust of the earth and the breath of God were brought together (Gen 2:7), and just as surely as the man did not exist prior to creation, he does not exist when the spirit returns to God who gave it and the dust returns to the earth (Eccl 12:7).

15. *Against Heresies*, 2.34.3; ANF 1:412.
16. Ibid., 5.27.2; ANF 1:556.
17. *Against the Heathen* 2.14; ANF 6:439–40.
18. *De Inc.* 6.1; NPNF 2.4:39.

But immortality is not entirely out of sight, out of mind. In Scripture it is a promise that emerges from the mist, obscure at first. Proverbs 12:28 promises that "In the way of righteousness there is life; along that path is immortality" (literally *no dying*). More clearly still in Dan 12:2 the hope of resurrection to eternal life appears, where "many of those who sleep in the dust of the earth shall awake, some to everlasting life, and some to shame and everlasting contempt."[19] The biblical doctrine of immortality emerges most fully in the New Testament, where Jesus not only affirms the doctrine of the resurrection of the dead, but claimed to *be* "the resurrection and the life," and promised that all who believe in him will have eternal life, and to that end will be raised up on "the last day" (John 6:40).

What conditionalists point out, however, is that eternal life in all of its verbal expressions—and in particular when it is described in terms of "immortality"—is exclusively promised as a gift to those who are saved through Christ. Ongoing life is portrayed as lost in Adam, and recovered in Christ—but only *through* Christ. St. Paul described the grace of God as follows:

> This grace was given us in Christ Jesus before the beginning of time, but it has now been revealed through the appearing of our Savior, Christ Jesus, who has destroyed death and has brought life and immortality to light through the gospel. (2 Tim 1:9b–10)

Similarly, although the resurrection of the lost is mentioned a number of times in the New Testament, the contrast between their resurrection and that of the people of God is precisely the fact that while they take part in the "resurrection of judgment," it is only the people of God who will take part in the "resurrection of life" (John 5:29). In his great chapter on the resurrection (1 Cor 15), all of Paul's talk of the mortal putting on immortality falls within the context of describing the resurrection of "those who belong to Christ" (v. 23). He similarly speaks to the Romans of immortality as something sought out by those who do good: "to those who by patience in well-doing seek for glory and honor and immortality, he will give eternal life" (Rom 2:7). Although immortality is seldom mentioned by name in the New Testament, whenever it is, it is either a

---

19. Evangelical conditionalists are careful to point out that although this passage in Daniel is often quoted as though it described the eternal sufferings of the damned in hell, in reality it does no such thing, saying only that they will forever be held in "contempt." The same is true of many individuals who are no longer alive; Hitler, Stalin, Vlad the Impaler, and so on. These are all still held in contempt in spite of their no longer being alive to appreciate the fact.

reference to God's immortality or a reference to immortality as a gift to those who will receive it through Christ.

None of this suggests to evangelical conditionalists that those who receive eternal life will be inherently immortal in a way that implies that God would be literally incapable of ending their lives. But whether inherent or not—that distinction is not made explicit in Scripture—immortality, living forever, "continuance" forever (to use the language of Irenaeus), is something that is the gift of God.[20] This outlook contrasts strongly with the view of many theologians. Article 37 of the Belgic confession makes this explicit: "The evil ones will be convicted by the witness of their own consciences, and shall be made immortal—but only to be tormented in the everlasting fire prepared for the devil and his angels." Similarly, when responding to evangelical conditionalist Edward Fudge who observes the biblical teaching that immortality is a gift to God's people only, Robert Peterson frankly admits that the Bible only ever explicitly attributes immortality to God and the saved. And yet, he claims that since the Bible teaches eternal torment, it must be the case that "Fudge errs when he rejects the immortality of the lost."[21] This is an issue where conditionalists set aside such claims and confessions in favor of what we see as the clearly expressed teaching of the biblical writers that immortality in any shape or form is something that is conditional. God gives it to some and not others, and as a direct consequence, those who in the end find themselves on the outside cannot and will not live forever.

---

20. This distinction is sometimes abused in responses to conditionalists. Christopher Morgan, for example, claims that, contrary to the conditionalists, "Satan, the beast and the false prophet are punished forever," by which he means tormented forever. He goes on, "Do they somehow have inherent immortality? Of course not. God will keep them in existence endlessly in order to punish them. Similarly, the wicked will be punished consciously forever in hell, not because they exist as immortal souls but because God will sustain them" (Morgan, "Annihilationism," 205). The innuendo is that conditionalists use an argument that depends on the claim that God is *capable* of destroying the lost in hell since they are not inherently immortal. But in the first place, as seen above, the argument from the immortality of the soul to the doctrine of eternal torment was clearly made by Augustine, a fact that many today might prefer to forget. Secondly, the conditionalists' point is not simply that God is able to destroy the lost (as though we accuse proponents of the traditional view of denying this), but rather than immortality *per se*, regardless of whether it is had inherently or simply in virtue of being sustained forever, is claimed in Scripture to be a gift to God's people that is not a universal expectation.

21. Fudge and Peterson, *Two Views*, 103.

A World Without Evil

A second biblical consideration that drives the conditionalist position is the vision of eternity spelled out by the biblical writers. "Spelled out" may be too strong a term, because the details of what eternity will be like are not spelled out, but in broad strokes Scripture does address the question. Its answer, conditionalists observe, includes the claim that all sin and all remnants of evil will be no more. There are a couple of ways to think about this. One way is to ask the Barthian line: *How much more!* How much more it would be beautiful, good, harmonious, or elegant that there is no eternal duality of good and evil. How much simpler and more pleasing it would be if evil was no more and everything that existed was good! As do many conditionalists, I agree with all of this, but that is not the argument to which evangelical conditionalists would appeal. The point is not to make a judgment about what we think would be better, but instead to appeal to biblical material describing the way things will be, whether one thinks it better or not.

The biblical writers anticipate a time when everything that exists will be united under Christ. St. Paul told the Ephesians that our own redemption is part of a wider plan, regarding which God has "made known to us the mystery of his will according to his good pleasure, which he purposed in Christ, to be put into effect when the times will have reached their fulfilment—to bring all things in heaven and on earth together under one head, even Christ."[22] Using an accountant's terminology, Paul says that all the totals will be summed up, the accounts settled, and all ownership will be in Christ's name. As Lincoln observes, this is "a restoration of harmony with Christ," and even more, "Christ is the one in whom God chooses to sum up the universe, in whom he restores the harmony of the cosmos."[23]

There is a similar idea—also from St. Paul—in his first letter to Corinth.

> Then the end will come, when he hands over the kingdom to God the Father after he has destroyed all dominion, authority, and power. For he must reign until he has put all his enemies under his feet. The last enemy to be destroyed is death. For he "has put everything under his feet." . . . When he has done this,

---

22. Eph 1:9–10.
23. Lincoln, *Ephesians*, 34.

then the Son himself will be made subject to him who put everything under him, so that God may be all in all.[24]

This strong thread of Paul's thought finds anticipation among the Old Testament prophets, whose hope in the redemptive work of God in history led them to look, not for heaven rather than hell, but for a world transformed entirely, where nations say, "come and let us go up to the mountain of the LORD," where they will learn and keep his ways, and where "the earth shall be full of the knowledge of the LORD as the waters cover the sea."[25]

Such a vision invites the question: What room is left for evil? It is not tucked away on the other side of creation, where sin persists, albeit contained in misery, or simply dormant yet unredeemed.[26] Creation itself will be brought into a state of sinless perfection to the praise of God's glory, and the dualistic portrait of eternity with heaven on one side and hell on the other finds no home in Scripture, as it did in the theology of Aquinas: "In order that the happiness of the saints may be more delightful to them and that they may render more copious thanks to God for it, they are allowed to see perfectly the sufferings of the damned."[27]

Isaac Watts was more succinct:

---

24. 1 Cor 15:24–28.

25. Isa 2:3; 11:9.

26. At this juncture there is a division of opinion among those who affirm the picture of hell as eternal torment. On the one hand are those who claim that in reality there will *never* be a world without sin, for in fact the perpetual sinful state and continual sinning of those in hell may be what justifies their eternal torment (e.g., Carson, *Gagging*, 533–34). On the other hand there are those who, apparently in harmony with St. Augustine, say that those who find themselves in hell will no longer have any ability to sin. Paul Helm adds his voice to this minority report: "Although hell is a place of sinners, there is no reason to think that it is a heaven for sinners. . . . So hell is a place of pain, but not of defiance or resistance" (Helm, *Last Things*, 114). For a focused defense of the view that there is no sin in hell, see Saville, "Hell without Sin." What the conditionalist observes here is, firstly, that by far the dominant view among traditionalists (as Helm and Saville agree) has been that sinning will not stop in hell, and secondly, that even this modified view where sinning ceases must accept that it allows *sinfulness* to continue forever (for the alternative would involve everyone being sanctified), and suffering and sorrow existing forever (an evil in the classical conception of goodness, for if there is suffering, regret, and sorrow, things are clearly less than ideal) which reduces, rather than resolves, the problem of sin in a world where Christ is "all in all."

27. *Summa Theologica*, Volume 5, Third Part, Supplement, Question 94, "Of the Relations of the Saints Towards the Damned," Article 1.

> What bliss will fill the ransomed souls
> When they in glory dwell
> To see the sinner as he rolls
> In quenchless flames of hell.[28]

In Scripture, however, there is no eternal dualism of horror and bliss, good and evil. There is no eternal plan A and plan B, there is only the question of whether we will remain a part of everything that is summed up in Christ or whether we are part of the world that is passing away with its sinful desires.[29]

Substitutionary Atonement

The person of Christ is an illustration of many of the central tenets of the Christian faith. In Christ the character of God is made known to us. In Christ the pattern of Christian sanctification is portrayed. In Christ the resurrection of the dead is both made possible and demonstrated. And, evangelical conditionalists maintain, in Christ the consequences of sin are revealed as Jesus intervened in history and took them upon himself. Jesus died for sinners.

It is true that there are several models of the atonement that deserve to be called mainstream, penal substitution—the view that Jesus was punished instead of those for whom he died—being only one of them. All such views, however, take substitution as an integral part of them. In ransom theories of the atonement (including the *Christus Victor* view currently enjoying a resurgence), Christ pays his life as a ransom for ours, leaving death and hell with no claim on those saved through Christ. In the satisfaction theory of the Western Catholic tradition, Jesus' sacrifice was accepted by the Father instead of the need for punishment.

---

28. Cited in Bloesch, *Last Things*, 223. If we are looking for examples that emphasize not so much the delight of the righteous as they spectate on the excruciating suffering of the lost, but simply on the eternal existence of evil and suffering, here too Watts obliges only too willingly:

> There is a dreadful hell,
> And everlasting pains:
> There sinners must with devils dwell
> In darkness, fire, and chains.

("There is Beyond the Sky" in Watts, *Divine Songs*, 20.)

29. 1 John 2:17.

The common theme in all of this, regardless of the rationale for the atonement (although perhaps especially for the penal substitutionary model), is that Christ, the sinless son of God, is part of an exchange: his life for the lives of others.

The New Testament is replete with the language of Jesus dying for sin, for sinners, and for us. Whatever else this might mean, it at least means that in Christ's passion and ultimately his death we see what comes of sin. In order to put himself in the place of sinners, "the just for the unjust" as St. Peter says, humiliation, suffering, sorrow, and even alienation from God were not enough.[30] As Edward Fudge succinctly put it, "Jesus died the sinner's death."[31] In taking human nature to himself and laying down his life, Jesus in his sacrificial death gives us a picture of what would have come to us all were it not for God's saving intervention. Especially if one is favorably disposed towards a penal substitutionary view of the atonement, but even if one is not, the death of Christ shows us what we are saved from, as Christ tasted death for us all.[32] In identifying with sinners and standing in their place, Jesus bore what they would have borne. Abandonment by God, yes. Suffering, yes. But crucially, death.

Destruction

Lastly and perhaps most clearly, evangelical conditionalists observe that Scripture uses a range of language and images to refer to the fate of humanity without salvation through Christ: punishment, darkness, fire, death, destruction, being blotted out, and so on. Without any doubt, however, the overwhelming preponderance of the clearest such language speaks of the final death and destruction of the enemies of God.

Jesus told his disciples that rather than fearing men who can kill the body, they should "be afraid of the One who can destroy both soul and body in hell."[33] There is no doubt as to what it means for men to kill the

---

30. 1 Pet 3:18, "For Christ also suffered once for sins, the righteous for the unrighteous, that he might bring us to God."

31. Fudge, *Fire that Consume* (2011), 179.

32. Heb 2:9, "But we see him who for a little while was made lower than the angels, namely Jesus, crowned with glory and honor because of the suffering of death, so that by the grace of God he might taste death for everyone."

33. In order to compare the usage of *apollumi* (destroy) in relevantly similar contexts, we may observe that in the Synoptic Gospels whenever this verb is used in the active voice to describe what one person or agent does to another, the intended

body. Here God's power to kill the whole person in Gehenna (unhelpfully translated "hell") is affirmed by Jesus. But this is no isolated proof text. The fact is stressed often and emphatically in Scripture, and a small sample is enough to make the point. In Matt 7:13–14 the Lord warns that we should seek the narrow path that leads to life, and that the way to destruction, by contrast, is wide, and followed by many. In Matt 13:40–42, Jesus interpreted his own parable of the weeds to warn that just as weeds are destroyed in a furnace, so evildoers will be rooted out and destroyed at the end of the age.

The truth is that we are all familiar with evangelistic texts like Rom 3:23, but less often do we pause to think about the simple words they use—"the wages of sin is death, but the gift of God is eternal life." Conditionalists offer the modest exhortation that we allow such texts to speak, and not subconsciously revise them so that by the time they have passed through our doctrinal filter, they say something else. Second Thessalonians 1:9 speaks of a future time, "when the Lord Jesus shall be revealed from heaven with his mighty angels, in flaming fire taking vengeance on them that know not God, and that obey not the gospel of our Lord Jesus Christ: who shall be punished with everlasting destruction from the presence of the Lord, and from the glory of his power." As a final example, 2 Pet 2:6 tells us of God that "by turning the cities of Sodom and Gomorrah to ashes he condemned them to extinction, making them an example of what is going to happen to the ungodly." We would be hard pressed to state the conditionalist view of final punishment any clearer than this. As is said in law, *res ipsa loquitur*—the thing speaks for itself!

This evidence is not cherry-picked. This is the normal way that biblical writers spoke of the coming judgment of God, and eternal torment is not part of the picture. After surveying the overwhelming tendency of the New Testament language highlighted here, Clark Pinnock makes what must be considered a very fair observation:

---

meaning is always literal killing. This pattern is universal, but seven clear examples are: Matt 2:13 (Herod's intention to kill the baby Jesus), Matt 12:14 (the Pharisees conspired on how to kill Jesus), Matt 21:41 (the vineyard owner kills the wicked tenants), Matt 27:20 (the elders and chief priests urge the people to have Barabbas released and Jesus killed), Mark 3:6 (the Pharisees plot to kill Jesus), Mark 9:22 (an unclean spirit often throws a boy into water or into a fire, trying to kill him), and Luke 6:9 (Jesus asks if it is lawful on the Sabbath to save life or kill). Similarly in Matt 10:28 when Jesus warns of God's ability to destroy both soul and body in Gehenna, the verb is active, in the Synoptics, and being used to describe the actions of one person against another.

> Our Lord spoke plainly of God's judgment as the annihilation of the wicked when he warned about God's ability to destroy body and soul in hell (Matt 10:28) . . .
>
> The Apostle Paul creates the same impression when he wrote of the everlasting destruction that would come upon unrepentant sinners (2 Thess 1:9). He warned that the wicked would reap corruption (Gal. 6:8) and stated that God would destroy the wicked (1 Cor 3:17; Phil 1:28). . . . Concerning the wicked, the apostle stated plainly and concisely: "their destiny is destruction" (Phil 3:19). . . .
>
> It is no different in any other New Testament book. Peter spoke of the "destruction of ungodly men" (2 Pet 3:7) and of false teachers who denied the Lord, thus bringing upon themselves "swift destruction" (2:1, 3).[34]

In light of these observations it becomes all the more egregious that so many proponents of the traditional view of hell take their view to represent anything like a "literal" interpretation of what Scripture says on the subject. Of the scant few passages that might appear to give credence to a traditional view, the contexts in which they appear are not the places one would normally expect to find important, direct teaching on the nature of the world to come—and certainly not "literal" teaching, as that term is typically used.[35] As evangelical conditionalists see it, the burden of proof demanded of the conditionalist view seems unfairly heavy, for even if conditionalists show that Scripture teaches repeatedly that the lost will die, will be destroyed, will be cut off, will be consumed and the like, our claims are dismissed as "twisting" or taking things out of context, and in the name of a more compelling case we are offered a paltry list of vague references, parables of questionable interpretation, and figurative imagery. Let Bible translator R. F. Weymouth speak for us:

> My mind fails to conceive a grosser misinterpretation of language than when the five or six strongest words which the Greek tongue possesses, signifying "destroy," or "destruction," are explained to mean maintaining an everlasting but wretched existence. *To translate black as white is nothing to this.*[36]

---

34. Pinnock, "Conditional View," 146.

35. Indeed the only passages of Scripture that have even the *appearance* of prolonged suffering after death for the lost are firstly the tale of Lazarus and the Rich Man in Luke 16:19–31, and secondly some highly symbolic episodes in John's visionary experience in the book of Revelation (chapters 14, 19, and 20).

36. Quoted from a letter to Edward White, in Constable, *Future Punishment*, 55.

Summary Remarks

Together, these four considerations constitute not only a serious case but a clearly *evangelical* case for conditional immortality. That there are still those who label the view "heresy" is extraordinary in light of the evidence. It is possible, of course, to argue for conditionalism—or for any other biblical or orthodox doctrine—in a manner that could not be called evangelical. To appeal to extra-biblical revelation or to require commitment to points of view that clearly fall out of the bounds of historical orthodoxy (for example, denying the bodily resurrection or the resurrection of the lost) would place an argument or the resulting conclusion outside of what could reasonably be called evangelical. In calling this case (and the resulting point of view) evangelical, we are saying that it is one that commends itself to an orthodox Christian point of view that takes the centrality of the gospel and the authority of Scripture seriously. Anyone who is familiar with the literature can be forgiven for having lost count of the times that conditionalists are said to be motivated by pity or some other kindly emotion, or that they would rather suppress the hard biblical truths than face up to them. This is clearly not what is driving these and other arguments. In addition to being undeniably evangelical, the arguments are *thematic* in nature, rather than resting on isolated proof texts. These are themes that are developed throughout Scripture as salvation history unfolds. Thirdly, the case is *perspicuous*. It rests on clear premises that are fairly easily demonstrated or falsified. It is true that at times technical details can be amplified to strengthen the case, and it is also true that many passages of Scripture are complex and require much time and effort to properly explain (a fact that many conditionalists have come to suspect is lost on proponents of the traditional view who confidently and fairly hastily point to proof texts in an apocalyptic vision in John's Revelation). Lastly, the case is *cumulative*, in that none of the arguments depend on the other, but each stands or falls independently. Even if a critic was less convinced of the soundness of one of the arguments, the others would need to be taken seriously in their own right. These four features of the case commend it to an evangelical audience.

The doctrine of conditional immortality, quite contrary to the dire claims of many of its detractors and to the expectations of many as they approach it for the first time, is a point of view that deserves to be taken seriously by anyone with a commitment to the concept of doing theology in a way that is not only systematic, but biblical.

PART TWO

Influential Defenses of Conditionalism

WHILE THE DOCTRINE OF conditional immortality had many evangelical advocates in America and the United Kingdom during the nineteenth century, their influence had waned in the twentieth century. By that point, conditionalism had become relatively unknown to the average evangelical Christian, and was considered by their leaders to be controversial at best, and heretical at worst. John Wenham notes, regarding his presentation of the conditionalist view to an evangelical readership in his 1974 book *The Goodness of God*, that the "acceptance of the manuscript [by Inter-Varsity Press] was a great step forward," being that the two most significant works promoting conditionalism in the early twentieth century—Basil Atkinson's *Life and Immortality* and Harold Guillebaud's *The Righteous Judge*—had both been unable to find a publisher.[1]

However, as the twentieth century came to a close, conditional immortality slowly began to appear more frequently in evangelical books and articles. Most importantly was the publication of Edward Fudge's thoroughly researched and comprehensive defense of conditionalism in the 1982 volume, *The Fire That Consumes*. Soon thereafter, other respected evangelical scholars began to publish their views as well: Stephen Travis publicly allied himself with conditionalism in his 1982 book *I Believe in the Second Coming of Jesus* and Philip Edgecumbe Hughes argued for conditionalism in his 1989 work, *The True Image*. In 1992, British evangelist and apologist Michael Green briefly outlined a conditionalist perspective in his book *Evangelism through the Local Church*.

However, it was with the 1988 publication of *Evangelical Essentials: A Liberal-Evangelical Dialogue*, in which John Stott tentatively defended this view, that conditionalism took the main stage in the evangelical discussion about hell. In a *Christianity Today* cover article, Robert Peterson described the impact of Stott's ideas concerning the issue of final judgment: "It was six pages near the end of the book that exploded like a bombshell within evangelicalism." In these six pages, Stott outlined the

---

1. Wenham, *Facing Hell*, 231.

view of conditional immortality in response to his co-author's questions about the meaning of hell and who might be condemned to go there. As a result of Stott's advocacy of conditionalism, Peterson noted that "traditionalists, who make up most of evangelicalism, were shocked," some even going "so far as to question Stott's salvation. Evangelicals have been debating the subject ever since, both sides producing books and articles defending their views and contesting the opposition."[2]

In the following years, significant Christian theologians, philosophers, and biblical scholars continued to come forward as holding to various forms of conditionalism, including Clark Pinnock, I. Howard Marshall, Richard Swinburne, Dale Moody, E. Earle Ellis, R. T. France, John Stackhouse, Anthony Thiselton, and Richard Bauckham. However, without the influential defenses of conditionalism on the part of earlier evangelical thinkers who dared to challenge the traditional view of hell based on their study of Scripture, this important perspective on final judgment may have remained unknown and unavailable to most evangelicals who wished to thoroughly consider what the Bible has to say on the topic of hell.

2. Peterson, "Undying Worm," 30.

3

The Final End of the Wicked

EDWARD W. FUDGE

Edward Fudge earned both Bachelor's and Master's degrees in Biblical Languages at Abilene Christian University before serving as a minister in the Churches of Christ. He later published The Fire That Consumes, *which is currently in its third edition and remains the definitive defense of conditional immortality. After leaving professional ministry, Fudge earned a Doctor of Jurisprudence from the University of Houston College of Law, and practiced law for many years while continuing his work as an independent theologian, speaker, and author. He is also the author of* The Divine Rescue, Hebrews: Ancient Encouragement for Believers Today, *and the co-author of* Two Views of Hell: A Biblical & Theological Dialogue *(with Robert Peterson). In 2012, an independent feature film,* Hell & Mr. Fudge, *was released, which told the story of Fudge's life, particularly focusing on his study of the doctrine of hell that led to his becoming convinced of the position of conditional immortality. Fudge's written work and teaching ministry on the topic of conditional immortality continue to remain the most highly regarded explanation and defense of this position in evangelical theology.*

His article, "The Final End of the Wicked," was published in 1984 in The Journal of the Evangelical Theological Society *in an effort to continue promoting widespread evangelical reconsideration of the traditional doctrine of eternal conscious torment. In this article, Fudge condensed much of his research from*

The Fire That Consumes into a tightly-argued disputation against traditionalist assumptions and in favor of a conditionalist understanding of the fate of the unsaved.

TODAY, AS A GROWING host of evangelical (and other) scholars bear witness, the evidence for the wicked's final total destruction (rather than the traditional view of unending conscious torture, which sprang from pagan Platonic theories of immortal, indestructible souls) is finally getting some of the attention it demands. Because nearly all of us have completely skirted the relevant material on this subject far too long, I would like to present a concise summary of the case against traditionalism's conscious unending torment and at the same time the case for the total, ultimate, everlasting extinction of the wicked. The "second death" involves an eternal graveyard around which we can no longer merrily whistle.

Jesus once said of some people: "They will go away to eternal punishment, but the righteous to eternal life." Whoever honors him as God's Son and our Savior must receive his teachings as from God. Jesus' words will never pass away (Matt 24:35); they will judge us on the last day (John 12:48).

The question at stake is not, therefore, whether the wicked will suffer "eternal punishment." It is rather of what that punishment consists. Is it, as many Christian preachers since the third century have assumed, unending conscious torture of body and/or soul? Or is it, to use the words of Paul, "everlasting destruction"—in the most ordinary sense of those words (2 Thess 1:9)? Like most readers of *JETS* I had always assumed the former, until a year-long research project forced me to change my mind. Here I will simply summarize some of the pertinent evidence that study uncovered, which I present for the reader's consideration.

The Traditional Position

The traditional position of conscious unending torment is easy to summarize and is perhaps best stated in recent years by Harry Buis.[1] The traditional doctrine rests on three arguments: (1) that the OT is, generally speaking, silent on the subject; (2) that the doctrine of conscious unending torment developed during the intertestamental years and came, by

1. Buis, *Eternal Punishment*.

Jesus' time, to be "the commonly accepted Jewish view" (it is said therefore that we ought to read Jesus and the NT writers with a presumption that they and their original hearers all held to the doctrine of unending conscious torment); (3) that the NT language on the subject requires us to conclude that God will make the wicked immortal for the purpose of torturing them alive forever without end.

If these three points were true, the traditionalist would have a solid case indeed. The multitude of evidence available today (and presented in detail, both biblical and historical, in *The Fire That Consumes*) does not allow us that easy assumption. All three traditional premises prove rather to be false. The traditional doctrine turns out, upon historical investigation, to be a pollution from paganism via the apologists and their followers and not at all the clear teaching of Scripture. The following is a summary of that evidence.

The Old Testament Speaks

Is the OT silent concerning the wicked's final fate? Indeed it is not. It overwhelmingly affirms their total destruction. It never affirms or even hints at anything resembling conscious unending torment. The OT uses about fifty different Hebrew verbs to describe this fate, and about seventy figures of speech. Without exception they portray destruction, extinction, or extermination. Not one of the verbs or word-pictures remotely suggests the traditional doctrine.

The wicked will become like a vessel broken to pieces (Ps 2:9), ashes trodden underfoot (Mal 4:3), smoke that vanishes (Ps 37:20), chaff carried away by the wind (Ps 1:4), a slug that melts (Ps 58:8), straw that is burned (Isa 1:31), thorns and stubble in the fire (Isa 33:12), wax that melts (Ps 68:2) or a dream that vanishes (Ps 73:20). The traditionalist view has to deny that the wicked will ever become like any of those things and affirm that they will indeed be what none of those pictures portrays: an everlasting spectacle of indestructible material in an unending fire.

The Psalms repeatedly say that the wicked will go down to death, their memory will perish, and they will be as though they had never been. The righteous on the other hand will be rescued by God from death and then will enjoy him forever (Pss 9; 21:4–10; 36:9–12; 49:8–20; 52:5–9; 59; 73; 92). Proverbs likewise warns that the wicked will pass away, be overthrown, be cut off, be no more, their lamp put out (Prov 2:21–22; 10:25; 12:7; 24:15–20). We certainly do not see that happen in this life.

The historical books show us actual examples of God's judgments against sin. When the first world became too wicked to continue, God wiped every living creature outside the ark from the face of the earth (Gen 6:7; 7:4). This is a model, Scripture says, for the fiery judgment awaiting the lost at the eschaton (2 Pet 2:5; 3:3–7; Matt 24:38–39). When Sodom became too sinful to endure, God rained down fire and brimstone (burning sulfur) from heaven, obliterating the entire wicked population and even the vegetation, in a moment so terrible the rest of the Bible memorializes it as an example and prototype of divine judgments within history and also at the end of the world (Gen 19:24–29; Deut 29:23; Isa 1:9; 13:19–22; Jer 49:18; 50:40; Lam 4:6; Amos 4:11; Zeph 2:9; Luke 17:28–33; 2 Pet 2:6; Jude 7, 23).

The prophets also speak of God's wrath against sinners. Details of actual judgments against cities and nations become later symbols for the ultimate divine visitation. These prophetic scenes provide much of the later vocabulary of judgment: fire and storm, tempest and darkness, wrath and corpses and worms (Zeph 1:14–18; Isa 66:16–24; Ezek 39:9–22; Dan 12:2). Some of these scenes describe the final judgment of the lost at the end of the world. There we meet utter contempt, worms and fire, taking their last toll. Nothing remains in these pictures of the wicked but ashes: the righteous tread over them with their feet (Mal 4:3) or survey their abhorrent corruption in progress (Dan 12:2; Isa 66:24). The wicked become, in short, as though they had never been (Obad 16).

No, the OT is not silent concerning the end of the wicked. It appears silent to the traditionalist only because it says nothing he expected to find. It is silent, however, about unending conscious torture. But it speaks volumes concerning that penalty first threatened in the Garden of Eden: Those who sin will "surely die" (Gen 3:3; Ezek 18:4).

Between the Testaments

The traditionalist is correct that his doctrine developed during the time between the Testaments, but modern research totally destroys his presupposition that unending conscious torment was "the" Jewish view held by the earliest readers and writers of the NT Scriptures. We cannot be harsh in blaming earlier interpreters for erring at this point, for it was not until our century that English readers had access to much of the pertinent literature involved.[2] It is inexcusable, however, for modern writers to repeat that earlier error in light of the material now handily available. In the following paragraphs I simply summarize the diversity of Jewish views that literature reveals on this subject.[3]

The apocryphal books of 1 Esdras, 3 Maccabees, 1 Baruch, Epistle of Jeremiah, Prayer of Manasseh, and the additions to Daniel and Esther are silent on this subject. The books of Tobit, Sirach, Baruch, 1 and 2 Maccabees and the Wisdom of Solomon agree thoroughly with the OT as they anticipate the total destruction of the wicked.

The first appearance of conscious unending torment in anything resembling biblical literature comes in the apocryphal book of Judith (16:17). There the Jewish heroine warns: "Woe to the nations that rise up against my race. The Lord Almighty will take vengeance on them in the day of judgment, to put fire and worms in their flesh. And they shall weep and feel their pain forever."

The words "fire" and "worms" here come from Isa 66:24, but Judith completely changes Isaiah's picture. The prophet has unburied corpses; Judith has consciously tortured people. Isaiah's fire and worms destroy; Judith's simply torment. In Isaiah the fire and worms are external agents consuming their dead victims; in Judith they are internal agonies perpetually torturing from within. In Isaiah (and all the OT) the victims are destroyed; in Judith they "feel their pain forever." This is clearly the traditionalist picture of hell. But it never appears in the OT even once. And this is the first time it appears in even the Apocrypha.

The testimony of the Pseudepigrapha (a growing list of Jewish and sometimes Christian-edited works, c. 200 BC–AD 100) is even more mixed. Some of these works say the wicked will totally pass away (*Sibylline Oracles*, fragments of a Zadokite work, *Psalms of Solomon*, *4 Esdras*). This is also the consistent witness of the Qumran literature throughout, so far as yet translated.

Other Jewish texts of the period are ambiguous on this point (*Assumption of Moses*, *Testaments of the Twelve Patriarchs*, *Life of Adam and Eve*). Others are inconsistent (*Jubilees*, *1 Enoch*, *2 Baruch*). And some anticipate the conscious unending pain of the traditionalist view (*2 Enoch*, *4 Maccabees*), though some modern scholars do not even concede that much.

2. See especially *APOT*.
3. Cf. further Fudge, *Fire That Consumes* (1982), 119–54.

At the Time of Jesus

The intertestamental literature offers us a rich variety of Jewish expectation regarding the end of sinners. There is clearly no such thing as "the" Jewish view on this topic. Everlasting conscious torment has its advocates, though statistically the evidence is far heavier on the side of ultimate extinction. This destruction is sometimes seen as accomplished by fire, and sometimes it is preceded by a period of conscious anguish and suffering before it is consummated in eternal extinction.

Because of this unquestionable range of Jewish opinion, we cannot continue to presume a single attitude among first-century Jews on this subject. We cannot go on reading Jesus' words, or those of the NT writers, with presuppositions based on a supposed "uniform Jewish view." We must categorically deny the common notion (which traditionalist authors constantly repeat) that Jesus' hearers all held to conscious unending torment and would have heard his cryptic sayings with that sole presupposition. We must do what traditionalist authors have never yet done—study the NT language at face value, determining its meaning according to the ordinary accepted methods and disciplines of proper biblical exegesis.

The NT Language on the Subject

Does the teaching of Jesus and the NT writers require us to expect the conscious unending torment of the wicked? Not unless we ignore the entire OT background to the NT vocabulary involved, then proceed to give to the NT language later definitions imported from pagan Platonic philosophy during the centuries following.

This was one of the most exasperating parts of my year of research. Over and over again I was amazed to see how traditionalist writers took NT words and phrases out of their setting—as if they had no OT background at all—and then forced on them a meaning found nowhere in Scripture. This habit of eisegesis began in the late second century and has generally continued unchallenged until today. A few examples will have to suffice.

Unquenchable Fire

Traditionalists assume that "unquenchable fire" means "unending conscious torment." They do not acknowledge that this expression comes from the OT, where it has the frequent and regular sense of "destruction that cannot be resisted." "Quench" means to "extinguish" or "put out" a fire. The psalmist, for instance, says he will quench his enemies' fire (Ps 118:12), and Heb 11:34 mentions heroes of faith who were able to "quench the violence of fire." But God's fire of punishment cannot be quenched or put out, and so he warns cities and nations in many places (Isa 1:31; 34:10–11; Jer 4:4; 7:20; 17:27; 21:12; Ezek 20:47–48; Amos 5:5–6).

Jesus warns the same in Mark 9:43, 48 when he speaks of the horrible place of punishment where "the fire is not quenched." And what does fire do to its victims if it is not extinguished? It burns them up—exactly as John the Baptist announced concerning sinners' doom in his word about Jesus' eschatological wrath: "He will clear his threshing floor . . . burning up the chaff with unquenchable fire" (Matt 3:12).

Undying Worms

What of "the worm that does not die" (Mark 9:48)? For centuries, traditionalist interpreters have ignored the biblical background of this phrase and have made it mean everything from a tormenting conscience to an everlasting parasite. The Bible itself, however, provides ample definition. Our Lord's expression comes directly from Isa 66:24, which may be the most ignored biblical passage on final punishment, even though its language might be used most often.

The language of Isaiah 66 is figurative, prophetic symbolism. God executes judgment "with fire and with his sword" (v. 16). When the visitation is ended, "many will be those slain by the Lord" (v. 16b). The wicked "will meet their end together" (v. 17). The righteous, on the other hand, "endure" (v. 22). "All mankind" comes to worship God—the wicked are no more (v. 23). This is the setting of the crucial v. 24: "And they will go out and look upon the dead bodies of those who rebelled against me; their worm will not die, nor will their fire be quenched, and they will be loathsome to all mankind." Note that the righteous "go out and look" at the dead bodies of the wicked. This symbolic picture of the future may well reflect an actual incident Isaiah witnessed, when God defeated the army of Assyria in answer to Hezekiah's prayer (2 Kgs 18:17—19:36; Isa 36–37). That night, Isaiah himself reports, "the angel of the Lord went out and put to death a hundred and eighty-five thousand men in the Assyrian camp. When the people got up the next morning—there were all the dead bodies!" (Isa 37:36).

Now Isaiah says the same scene will be reproduced on a vaster scale at the end of time. In the historical event of the prophet's day (37:36) and in the prophetic picture of the future (66:24), the righteous view with satisfaction "dead bodies" or "corpses" of the wicked. These are dead bodies (Hebrew *pĕgārîm*), not living people or imperishable zombies. The righteous view their destruction, not their misery. The prototype to this viewing of enemies who have perished came at the Red Sea (Exod 14:30), and similar scenes are pictured throughout the OT (Pss 58:10; 91:8; Ezek 39:9–22; Mal 4:1–3). Both the maggots (Greek *skōkēx*) and the fire speak of total extinction. Both terms make this picture repulsive or loathsome—they describe disgust, not pity. The picture is one of shame, not pain (the same Hebrew word for "loathsome" in Isa 66:24 appears also in Dan 12:2, where the NJV has "contempt").

Traditionalists have ignored Isaiah's picture, then interpreted Jesus as though his language had no biblical precedent. Free from the Scriptural definitions, the "fire" and "worms" have (as with Judith in the Apocrypha) become something never found in the Bible. The scriptural picture of total destruction has been replaced in traditional explanation with the pagan notion of unending conscious torture.

Gnashing of Teeth

The phrase "grinding of teeth" appears many times in the OT (see Job 16:9; Pss 35:16; 37:12; Lam 2:16), and it always pictures someone so angry at another that he grinds his teeth in rage, like a mad animal straining at the leash. We see the same usage in the NT, where Stephen's enemies "gnashed their teeth at him" (Acts 7:54).

Traditionalist interpretation has ignored the biblical usage of this phrase and has homiletized instead on souls grinding their teeth eternally in excruciating pain. In the Bible, however, the teeth grind in rage, not particularly in pain—though there may well be time for that along the way. Psalm 112:10 is instructive concerning the wicked's end in this regard. The verses just before it describe the final glory of God's people.

Verse 10 then says: "The wicked man will see and be vexed, he will gnash his teeth and waste away; the longings of the wicked will come to nothing." Gnash his teeth as he may, the wicked man's rage does him no good in the end. Even as he grinds his teeth, he comes to nothing (the KJV has "melt away"). Traditionalists make "gnashing of teeth" into conscious unending torment. The Bible pictures it as horrible rage—rage that is frustrated by the wicked's own inexorable destruction.

Smoke that Ascends

The "smoke" that "rises for ever and ever" (Rev 14:11) also deserves defining by prior biblical usage. This picture comes from the destruction of Sodom. The Lord "rained down burning sulfur on Sodom and Gomorrah" (Gen 19:24) until not even vegetation survived. The next morning Abraham looked down on the site "and he saw dense smoke rising from the land, like smoke from a furnace" (19:28).

It is much the same as our image of the mushroom-shaped cloud after an atomic blast. The visible smoke is a certification of accomplished destruction. There are no more cries in Sodom when Abraham views the ascending smoke. All is quiet. The sinners are all destroyed. The rising smoke testifies to their complete extinction.

The same figure reappears in Isa 34:10 of Edom's destruction. God comes against the land with "burning sulfur" and "blazing pitch" (v. 9). The fire "will not be quenched night and day" (v. 10)—it is irresistible and therefore destroys completely (see the same figure in Rev 14:11). Isaiah says "its smoke will rise forever," telling us that Edom's destruction is not only certain (not quenched) and complete (smoke rising) but also irreversible. The desolation will be unending. The verses following describe a land empty of people, the haunt of desert creatures. Conscious pain has ended there, but "its smoke will rise forever"—the extinction is perpetual.

We find the same symbol in Revelation 18–19 concerning the destruction of "Babylon." The city is "fallen" (Rev 18:2), "consumed by fire" (18:8), and those observing "see the smoke" (18:9). Like Sodom of old, "Babylon" is utterly destroyed. The rising smoke testifies to that destruction. Like Edom of old, her destruction will never be reversed or undone, for "the smoke from her goes up for ever and ever" (19:3).

PART TWO—INFLUENTIAL DEFENSES OF CONDITIONALISM

No Rest Day or Night

Revelation 14:1–5 presents John with a glorious vision of the Lamb and 144,000 of his people, the earth's redeemed firstfruits. Three angels announce judgment in increasingly stronger language. The third angel cries with a loud voice: "If anyone worships the beast and his image and receives his mark on the forehead or on the hand, he, too, will . . . be tormented with burning sulfur in the presence of the holy angels and of the Lamb. . . . There is no rest day or night for those who worship the beast and his image" (14:9–11). We have already seen the biblical meaning of fire and brimstone (burning sulfur) as a cipher for total destruction at Sodom and Gomorrah and thereafter (Gen 19:23, 28; Deut 29:23; Job 18:15–17; Isa 30:27–33; 34:9–11; Ezek 38:22ff.). Here the destruction occurs without respite or relief for its victims until it is finished. They have "no rest day or night" until it is over. The victims can anticipate no respite by day or by night. Their suffering is not exclusively a "daytime" activity, nor is it exclusively a "nighttime" activity. There is no intermission in the suffering while it continues. But the other three figures in this scene all suggest that it will finally cease, when the destruction is completed and nothing is left. Then only rising smoke will testify to the everlasting penalty that has been exacted.

The Cup of God's Wrath

This symbol, in the scene at Rev 14:9–11, is a common figure for God's punishment in both OT and NT (see Job 21:20; Pss 60:3; 75:8; Isa 51:17, 22; Jer 25:27–28; Obad 16; Matt 26:39). Since God prepares the drink, he also determines its potency. For some, it might represent a stroke that sends them reeling but from which they recover (Ps 60:3; Isa 51:22). For others, it may mean total and irreversible extinction. The prophets use language like this: "They will drink and drink and be as if they had never been" (Obad 16); they "drink, get drunk and vomit, and fall to rise no more" (Jer 25:27). The figures combine in this passage for the strongest possible picture of punishment. The destruction is total (flaming sulfur), without respite until accomplished (no rest day or night), accomplished (smoke rising) with no hope of recovery (smoke rising forever). Not all commentators understand this passage to refer to the final end of sinners, of course, and we will not argue that point either way. Whatever the case, the symbols are clear in the light of previous biblical usage. None of them refers to unending conscious torment in regular usage, and there is no reason to think any refers to it here. They all, on the other hand, have regular prophetic significance in many passages of Scripture, and the meanings of them all converge on this description of a complete, irreversible destruction and extinction forever accomplished.

The Lake of Fire

The lake of fire is the Bible's last description of final punishment, and it is mentioned four times (Rev 19:20; 20:10, 15; 21:8). It is the fiery lake of burning sulfur, the lake of fire and brimstone. The exact expression "lake of fire (and brimstone/burning sulfur)" does not appear anywhere else in Scripture. Most seem agreed, however, that it stands for the same ultimate destiny that we commonly call "hell," which in turn stands for the word "Gehenna," taking its name from the literal "Valley of Hinnom" (Hebrew *gê' hinnōm*) outside Jerusalem. It is not always noted that "Gehenna" is used for the destiny of the wicked by name only in the Gospels in the NT, since it would be unfamiliar to Gentile or non-Palestinian readers who had not visited or heard of the actual site and its significance throughout history.

The nearest OT parallel to the lake of fire comes in Daniel's dream of four beasts (Dan 7:9–12). There the Ancient of Days (whose appearance is partially attributed to Jesus in Revelation 1) takes his seat on a throne aflame with fire (v. 9). A "river of fire" comes out from his presence (v. 10). The terrible fourth beast is "slain and its body destroyed and thrown into the blazing fire" (v. 11). This is in specific contrast to the other beasts; who are stripped of authority but are allowed to live for a period of time (v. 12).

Unless this vision sheds light on the lake of fire in Revelation, no OT light is to be had. If the passage in Daniel is in the background here, that light reveals a fiery destruction that is expressly not a stripping of authority with the survival of life.

The four occurrences of the lake of fire in Revelation are also instructive. The beast and the false prophet are first to go there. Some interpreters see these as representative of actual persons yet to come. Others regard them as symbolic of persecuting civil government and false religion. In the latter case, the lake of fire clearly stands for their total, utter, absolute annihilation. In the former case, the question is still to be decided on some other basis.

Revelation 20:7–10 builds on the imagery of Ezekiel 38–39, as Satan's hordes surround the camp of God's people but, as in Elijah's day (2 Kgs 1), are destroyed by fire from heaven. Satan, however, is "thrown into the lake of burning sulfur, where the beast and false prophet had been thrown. They will be tormented day and night for ever and ever." Again, if the beast and false prophet are personifications of civil and religious powers opposing Christ, a literal interpretation of conscious unending pain would be impossible. If one's prophetic schema sees these as actual persons yet to come, we only note that the text says nothing about human beings "tormented day and night forever and ever." This is the single most problematic text in the whole Bible for the extinction of all evil, even though it does not specify human beings. In view of the overwhelming mass of material otherwise found throughout Scripture, however, one ought to remember the general hermeneutical rule that calls for interpreting the uncommon in light of the common and the obscure in light of the more clearly revealed.

As the vision continues, however, "death and Hades" are "thrown into the lake of fire" (v. 14). More than 700 years before, Isaiah had foretold a time when God would "destroy the shroud that enfolds all peoples, the sheet that covers all nations," when he "will swallow up death forever" (Isa 25:7–8). Paul had written: "The last enemy to be destroyed is death" (1 Cor 15:26) and had spoken of the time when the saying will come true that "death has been swallowed up in victory" (v. 54). This is the consummation of God's victory over his final foe. Death and Hades are certainly abstractions, not persons, and the lake of fire here means their annihilation. Death will be no more—forever.

Only now do we find sinners included in this dreadful fate. "If anyone's name was not found written in the book of life, he was thrown into the lake of fire" (v. 15). The "book of life" is a symbol based on the ancient city's register of living citizens. Whoever is not listed among the living is instead "in the lake of fire." John makes the identification clear: "The lake of fire is the second death" (v. 14).

The next chapter repeats the fact with elaboration. Overcomers will inherit the new heavens and new earth, but all classes of sinners "will be in the fiery lake of burning sulfur," which again, John adds, "is the second death" (21:8). There is no good reason for not taking John's explanation exactly as it stands, or for importing foreign Platonic definitions of "death" as "separation" into the discussion here. The natural sense is to be preferred, and here it could hardly be made plainer than it is. The final options are "life" or "death." Everything else we have found throughout Scripture accords with this as well.

Paul's Favorite Phrases

Besides all the language we have surveyed so far, Paul's most common phrases on the subject all picture the total extinction of sinners at the end. The wicked, he warns, will die (Rom 6:21, 23), perish (2:12), be destroyed (Gal 6:8; 1 Cor 3:17; 2 Thess 1:9; Phil 1:28; 3:19; see also Jude 10). Nor will they ever come back, for this destruction is to be "everlasting" (2 Thess 1:9).

If we ignore the Bible's own usage of its language, we can make these terms mean whatever we please. But if we let the Bible interpret itself, we have far less choice. For all of Scripture's language on this subject leads us time and time again to the same conclusion: the wicked will finally perish completely and forever in hell. None of the Bible's language suggests unending conscious torment for human beings.

But Is This Punishment "Eternal"?

But can such irreversible extinction properly be called "eternal punishment," such as Jesus speaks of in Matt 25:46? The question is legitimate and the answer is easy to find. Of the seventy occurrences of the adjective "eternal" in the NT, six times the word qualifies nouns signifying acts or processes rather than persons or things. The six "eternal" acts or events are salvation (Heb 5:9), judgment (6:2), redemption (9:12), sin (Mark 3:29), punishment (Matt 25:46), and destruction (2 Thess 1:9).

In four of the six, "eternal" refers to the results or outcome of the action and not the action itself. "Eternal judgment" does not mean that the judging will last forever, but that its outcome will. "Eternal redemption" does not mean that the process goes on without end—for the redemptive work was done once and for all—but that its issue will have no end forever. "Eternal salvation" is the result; we do not look for an eternal act of "saving." And the "eternal" sin is called that because its guilt will never be forgiven, not because the sinning continues throughout eternity.

Given this regular usage of "eternal" to describe the results of an action or process, we suggest that it is perfectly proper to understand the two disputed usages in this same ordinary way. The "everlasting destruction" (2 Thess 1:9) of the wicked does not mean that Christ will be forever in the process of destroying them but that their destruction, once accomplished, will be forever. The wicked will never reappear. Paul's phrase "eternal destruction" is in fact a clearer picture of Jesus' generic term "eternal punishment" in Matt 25:46. This destruction is not accidental, nor is it self-inflicted. It is the penal outcome of God's judgment. It is punishment, in this instance capital punishment. And, unlike even the capital punishment man may inflict, it is irreversible capital punishment. It is, truly, "everlasting" or "eternal" punishment, "everlasting destruction," the second death from which there is no resurrection or return forever. It is the very fate we have met time and time again throughout the Bible. The wicked's destruction will be just as long-lasting as the life of the saved. We give the dualism full weight, in keeping with the regular usage of the word "eternal" with nouns of action and in light of Jesus' clear statement in Matt 25:46 placing "eternal life" and "eternal punishment" side by side. Never, ever after, in all eternity, will the wicked be.

Conclusion

I would like to conclude with the final paragraphs of *The Fire That Consumes*, which aptly bring this summary to a close as they do also the detailed discussion contained in the book:

> Eternal conscious torment is either true or it is not. God's Word gives the only authoritative answer. We wish to humbly receive whatever it says—on this or any subject—then faithfully proclaim it as befits God's stewards. . . . We were reared on the traditionalist view—we accepted it because it was said to rest on the Bible. A more careful study has shown that we were mistaken in that assumption. Both the OT and NT instead clearly teach a resurrection of the wicked for divine judgment, the fearful anticipation of a consuming fire, irrevocable expulsion from God's presence into a place where there will be weeping and grinding of teeth, such conscious suffering as the divine justice individually requires—and finally, the total, everlasting extinction of the wicked with no hope of resurrection, restoration, or recovery. Now we stand on that, on the authority of the Word of God.

We have changed once and do not mind changing again, but we were evidently wrong once through lack of careful study and do not wish to repeat the same mistake. Mere assertions and denunciations will not refute the evidence presented . . . nor will a mere recital of ecclesiastical tradition.

This case rests finally on Scripture. Only Scripture can prove it wrong.[4]

---

4. 1st edition, 1982.

4

The Nature of Final Destiny

STEPHEN H. TRAVIS

Stephen Travis received his PhD from the University of Cambridge and was the Vice-Principal and a lecturer in New Testament at St. John's College in Nottingham, England until his retirement in 2005. He is the author of numerous publications, including Christ and the Judgement of God, Christian Hope and the Future of Man, Exploring the New Testament Vol. 2 *(with I. Howard Marshall and Ian Paul), and many dictionary articles on the topics of eschatology and judgment.*

His book, Christ Will Come Again: Hope for the Second Coming of Jesus, *was originally published in 1982 as* I Believe in the Second Coming of Jesus. *This volume was part of a series of "I Believe In . . ." books edited by Michael Green that were intended to explore various controversial areas of Christian faith, particularly those doctrines that had been subjected to criticism and skepticism in the popular imagination. His main purpose was to enable the Christian to respond to the incredulity of a post-Christian culture towards "the last things" and to explain that hope that lies within them. However, when considering the issue of final human destinies, the issue of hell and its nature were unavoidable. In a chapter entitled "The Dark Side of Hope," Travis outlined a biblical view of judgment and the fate of the unsaved that ultimately landed on the side of conditional immortality.*

IF IT IS TRUE that some people are excluded from God's final kingdom, what form does their destiny take?[1] The traditional view, which we have already noted in Augustine, is the doctrine of eternal punishment—an unending conscious experience of torment and anguish. In the last hundred years considerable ground has been gained by an alternative view, known as "conditional immortality" or "annihilationism." This is the view that after death, or after the judgment, those who have rejected Christ cease to exist. In my view the New Testament does not express itself clearly for one or other of these options. But the following observations are important.

First, we have already seen that Jesus had much more to say about how to avoid exclusion from God's presence than about what form such exclusion might take. His restraint on this matter is very striking when it is set against the full and lurid descriptions in some of the Jewish apocalyptic books (such as *1 Enoch*) which were in circulation in Jesus's time. Even when he used a specific term such as "Gehenna" (e.g., Matt 10:28; Mark 9:43, 45, 47) he gave no descriptive content to it. Gehenna (the Valley of Hinnom) was in fact the valley to the south-west and south of Jerusalem which had become a byword for all that is abhorrent to God ever since it had been a place of child sacrifice in Jeremiah's day (see Jer 7:31f.). There is, incidentally, as far as I know, no evidence earlier than the twelfth century AD for the popular view that the Valley of Hinnom was Jerusalem's rubbish dump in biblical times.

Jesus's language about the destiny of unbelievers is allusive rather than descriptive. Even the parable of the rich man and Lazarus, which might seem to offer a fuller description of conditions in the next world, cannot be used for this purpose. For Jesus is here making use of a popular Jewish tale, and so we would be rash to press the details of the story (Luke 16:19–31). And other New Testament terms, such as Paul's use of "death," "destruction," "corruption," take us no further towards an actual description of hell. Only in the apocalyptic picture-language of Revelation, and one or two places such as Jude 6 and 13, do we find any fuller description. And it is picture-language.

There is good reason for all this restraint. Jesus and his apostles were concerned that people should decide for God and against hell, not out of desire for the comforts of heaven nor out of fear of the discomforts of hell. They wanted people to choose on the only proper grounds—desire

---

1. Travis has said more in *Christian Hope*, 133–36.

for God himself and for the doing of his will. This is why Jesus spent time telling people how to avoid condemnation rather than describing what the existence of the condemned would be like.

There is a second important point. As we have seen, the New Testament understands salvation and condemnation in terms of relationship or lack of relationship towards God. Now, once this idea of relationship is seen to be fundamental, questions about the details of the afterlife become ultimately irrelevant. If we know that heaven means to be with Christ, we do not need to know much else about it. And if hell means being without Christ, that is an enormous tragedy, and the New Testament writers see little point in asking whether the lost continue to be conscious or are annihilated. It is, perhaps, because we have been more concerned about happiness and misery than about godliness and sin that we have kept asking such questions.

Nevertheless, we must say something about the debate between "eternal punishment" and "conditional immortality." If pressed, I must myself opt for the latter. The case for eternal punishment rests primarily on belief in the immortality of the soul, the requirement of divine justice that the sins of this life should be appropriately punished in the next, and the apparently explicit teaching of biblical passages such as Matt 25:34, 41, 46; Mark 9:42f.; 2 Thess 1:9; Rev 14:11; 19:3; 20:10.

Supporters of "conditional immortality," on the other hand, argue as follows. First, immortality of the soul is a non-biblical doctrine derived from Greek philosophy. In biblical teaching man is "conditionally immortal"—that is, he has the possibility of becoming immortal if he receives resurrection or immortality as a gift from God. This would imply that God grants resurrection to those who love him, but those who resist him go out of existence.

Secondly, biblical images such as "fire" and "destruction" suggest annihilation rather than continuing conscious existence.

Thirdly, New Testament references to "eternal punishment" (Matt 25:46; cf. 2 Thess 1:9; Heb 6:2) do not automatically mean what they have traditionally been assumed to mean. "Eternal" may signify the permanence of the result of judgment rather than the continuation of the act of punishment itself. So "eternal punishment" means an act of judgment where results cannot be reversed, rather than an experience of being punished forever.

Fourthly, we must recognize that such New Testament language is picture-language. The fact that Jesus can speak of hell in terms of both "darkness" and "fire" surely makes it clear that such language must not be taken too literally. This of course does not remove our responsibility to take it very seriously, but it indicates that we should be very cautious about pressing such language into, service in defense of eternal punishment.

Fifthly, eternal torment serves no useful purpose, and therefore exhibits a vindictiveness incompatible with the love of God in Christ.

Finally, eternal punishment requires that we believe in heaven and hell existing forever "alongside" each other. It seems impossible to reconcile this with the conviction that God will be "all in all" (1 Cor 15:28). As we saw earlier, in Jesus's teaching the emphasis is not on hell as a place into which the unrepentant are thrown, but rather on the kingdom of God as a realm from which the unrepentant are excluded. So we are back again to the concept of relationship or non-relationship to God. That is what matters.

5

Judgment and Hell

JOHN R. W. STOTT

John Stott (1921–2011) was one of the most significant evangelical leaders in the latter half of the twentieth century, ranked by Time *magazine in 2005 as being among the hundred most influential people in the world. Although more well-known in the UK, where he had a stature equivalent to Billy Graham's in the US, Stott was an important figure in global evangelicalism through his work on the composition of the Lausanne Covenant, a critical manifesto written in 1974 promoting renewed evangelical effort towards evangelism and social responsibility. After an education at the University of Cambridge, Stott served for much of his life as a priest in the Anglican church; however, he had an international ministry through the more than fifty books he wrote, including* Basic Christianity, Why I Am a Christian, The Cross of Christ, *and numerous widely used New Testament commentaries, as well as through his leadership in many evangelical organizations.*

Stott was approached in the 1980s by David Edwards, a fellow Anglican priest on the liberal end of the theological spectrum, to act as a representative evangelical in responding to questions that Edwards had of the conservative Christian movement. The book that resulted from their interactions, Evangelical Essentials: A Liberal-Evangelical Dialogue, *covered topics such as Scripture, the atonement, miracles, and evangelism. Near the end of the book, Edwards brought up the question of whether Stott really believed that all non-*

Christians were lost and would be doomed to hell for eternity. Edwards also picked up on Stott's "consistent preference for 'perish' to refer to the end of those who reject God," before raising an implied challenge for Stott to come clean on his view on hell: "So far as I know, he has never made it clear whether or not this means that he holds the belief that the wicked are ultimately annihilated— the doctrine known as 'conditional immortality.'"[1] With Stott's written reply to Edwards' questions about the fate of the unsaved, he opened up a global and ongoing debate among evangelicals as to the nature and duration of divine judgment.

IT IS WITH GREAT reluctance and with a heavy heart that I now approach this subject. You [David Edwards] quote the Grand Rapids report that describes the unevangelized millions as human beings who, "though created by God like God and for God . . . are now living without God." This is a phrase which I have myself often used, because it seems to me to sum up the poignant tragedy of human lostness. And when it is extended to the possibility that some who live without God now may also spend eternity without him, the thought becomes almost unbearable.

I want to repudiate with all the vehemence of which I am capable the glibness, what almost appears to be the glee, the *Schadenfreude*, with which some evangelicals speak about hell. It is a horrible sickness of mind or spirit. Instead, since on the day of judgment, when some will be condemned, there is going to be "weeping and gnashing of teeth" (Matt 8:12; 22:13; 24:51; 25:30; Luke 13:28), should we not already begin to weep at the very prospect? I thank God for Jeremiah. Israelite patriot though he was, he was charged with the heartbreaking mission of prophesying the destruction of his nation. Its ruin would only be temporary; it would not be eternal. Nevertheless, he could not restrain his tears. "Oh that my head were a spring of water and my eyes a fountain of tears! I would weep day and night for the slain of my people" (Jer 9:1; cf. 13:17; 14:17).

It is within this prophetic tradition of tragedy, of sorrow over people's rejection of God's word, and over the resultant inevitability of judgment, that Jesus wept over the impenitent city of Jerusalem. He cried out: "If you, even you, had only known on this day what would bring you peace . . . !" (Luke 19:41–42; cf. Matt 23:37–38). In this too Paul had the mind of Christ. He wrote of the "great sorrow and unceasing anguish" he felt in his heart for his own race, the people of Israel. His "heart's desire and

---

1. Edwards and Stott, *Essentials*, 292.

prayer to God" was for their salvation. He was willing even, like Moses before him, to be himself "cursed and cut off from Christ" if only thereby his people might be saved (Rom 9:1–4; 10:1; cf. Exod. 32:32). He had the same deep feelings for the Gentiles. For three whole years in Ephesus, as he reminded the church elders of that city, "I never stopped warning each of you night and day with tears" (Acts 20:31; cf. 20:19; Phil 3:18).

I long that we could in some small way stand in the tearful tradition of Jeremiah, Jesus, and Paul. I want to see more tears among us. I think we need to repent of our nonchalance, our hard-heartedness.

What Is Hell?

You raise two main questions in relation to hell. The first concerns what is meant by it, and the second who may be condemned to go there. We both agree that the imagery Jesus and his apostles used (the lake of fire, the outer darkness, the second death) is not meant to be interpreted literally. In any case it could not be, since fire and darkness exclude each other. You comment positively on the Lausanne Covenant's expression "eternal separation from God"; it is a conscious echo both of Jesus' words "depart from me" (Matt 7:23; 25:41) and of Paul's "shut out from the presence of the Lord" (2 Thess 1:9). We surely have to say that this banishment from God will be real, terrible (so that "it would be better for him if he had not been born," Mark 14:21), and eternal. The New Testament contains no hint of the possibility of a later reprieve or amnesty. The biblical phraseology includes, in contrast to "eternal life" and "eternal salvation," "eternal judgment" (Heb 6:2 and possibly Mark 3:29), "everlasting contempt" (Dan 12:2), "eternal punishment" (Matt 25:46), "everlasting destruction" (2 Thess 1:9), and "eternal fire" (Matt 18:8; 25:41). And the imagery supporting this phraseology includes the pictures of the door being shut (Matt 25:10–12) and the great chasm being fixed (Luke 16:26).

You press me, however, to go beyond this. You rightly say that I have never declared publicly whether I think hell, in addition to being real, terrible, and eternal, will involve the experience of everlasting suffering. I am sorry that you use in reference to God the emotive expression "the Eternal Torturer," because it implies a sadistic infliction of pain, and all Christian people would emphatically reject that. But will the final destiny of the impenitent be eternal conscious torment, "forever and ever," or will it be a total annihilation of their being? The former has to be described as traditional orthodoxy, for most of the church fathers, the medieval theologians, and the Reformers held it. And probably most evangelical leaders hold it today. Do I hold it, however? Well, emotionally, I find the concept intolerable and do not understand how people can live with it without either cauterizing their feelings or cracking under the strain. But our emotions are a fluctuating, unreliable guide to truth and must not be exalted to the place of supreme authority in determining it. As a committed evangelical, my question must be—and is—not what does my heart tell me, but what does God's Word say? And in order to answer this question, we need to survey the biblical material afresh and to open our minds (not just our hearts) to the possibility that Scripture points in the direction of annihilation, and that "eternal conscious torment" is a tradition that has to yield to the supreme authority of Scripture. There are four arguments; they relate to language, imagery, justice, and universalism.

First, *language*. The vocabulary of "destruction" is often used in relation to the final state of perdition. The commonest Greek words are the verb *apollumi* (to destroy) and the noun *apòleia* (destruction). When the verb is active and transitive, "destroy" means "kill," as when Herod wanted to murder the baby Jesus and the Jewish leaders later plotted to have him executed (Matt 2:13; 12:14; 27:4). Then Jesus himself told us not to be afraid of those who kill the body and cannot kill the soul. "Rather," he continued, "be afraid of the One [God] who can destroy both soul and body in hell" (Matt 10:28; cf. Jas 4:12). If to kill is to deprive the body of life, hell would seem to be the deprivation of both physical and spiritual life, that is, an extinction of being. When the verb is in the middle, and intransitive, it means to be destroyed and so to "perish," whether physically of hunger or snakebite (Luke 15:17; 1 Cor 10:9) or eternally in hell (e.g., John 3:16; 10:28; 17:12; Rom 2:12; 1 Cor 15:18; 2 Pet 3:9). If believers are *hoi sōzomenoi* (those who are being saved), unbelievers are *hoi apollumenoi* (those who are perishing). The phrase occurs in 1 Cor 1:18, 2 Cor 2:15; 4:3, and in 2 Thess 2:10. Jesus is also recorded in the Sermon on the Mount as contrasting the "narrow . . . road that leads to life" with the "broad . . . road that leads to destruction" (Matt 7:13; cf. also Rom 9:22; Phil 1:28; 3:19; Heb 10:39; 2 Pet 3:7; Rev 17:8, 11; the word used in 1 Thess 5:3 and 2 Thess 1:9 is *olethros*, which also means "ruin" or "destruction"). It would seem strange, therefore, if people who are said to suffer destruction are in fact not destroyed; and, as you put it, it is "difficult to imagine a perpetually inconclusive process of perishing." It cannot, I think, be replied that it is impossible to destroy human beings because they are immortal, for the immortality—and therefore indestructibility—of the soul is a Greek not a biblical concept. According to Scripture only God possesses immortality in himself (1 Tim 1:17; 6:16); he reveals and gives it to us through the gospel (2 Tim 1:10). And by the way, "annihilation" is not quite the same as "conditional immortality." According to the latter, nobody survives death except those to whom God gives life (they are therefore immortal by grace, not by nature), whereas according to the former, everybody survives death and will even be resurrected, but the impenitent will finally be destroyed.[2]

The second argument concerns the *imagery* used in Scripture to characterize hell, and in particular that of fire. Jesus spoke of "the fire of hell" (Matt 5:22; 18:9) and of "eternal fire" (Matt 18:8; 25:41), and in the Revelation we read about "the lake of fire" (20:14–15). It is doubtless because we have all had experience of the acute pain of being burned, that fire is associated in our minds with "conscious torment." But the main function of fire is not to cause pain, but to secure destruction, as all the world's incinerators bear witness. Hence the biblical expression "a consuming fire" and John the Baptist's picture of the Judge "burning up the chaff with unquenchable fire" (Matt 3:12; cf. Luke 3:17). The fire itself is termed "eternal" and "unquenchable," but it would be very odd if what is thrown into it proves indestructible. Our expectation would be the opposite: it would be consumed forever, not tormented forever. Hence it is the smoke (evidence that the fire has done its work) that "rises forever and ever" (Rev 14:11; cf. 19:3).

Four objections are raised to this understanding of "the lake of fire."

(1) There is the vivid picture of hell as a place where "their worm does not die, and the fire is not quenched" (Mark 9:48). It is a quotation from the last verse of Isaiah (66:24), where the dead bodies of God's enemies are consigned to the city's rubbish dump to be eaten by maggots and burned. It is not necessary to apply this as Judith did, however, namely that God would take vengeance on the hostile nations, "to put fire and worms in their flesh" so that "they shall weep and feel their pain forever" (Jdt

---

2. Stott's way of articulating the distinction between annihilationism and conditional immortality is confusing to some, and is not universally agreed upon by evangelicals who use those terms to describe their own views or those of others. Those who call themselves conditionalists are varied in their views of the intermediate state and the consciousness of human beings in death; so, too, are those who call themselves annihilationists.

16:17). Jesus' use of Isa 66:24 does not mention everlasting pain. What he says is that the worm will not die and the fire will not be quenched. Nor will they—until presumably their work of destruction is done.

(2) At the end of the so-called parable of the sheep and goats, Jesus contrasted "eternal life" with "eternal punishment" (Matt 25:46). Does that not indicate that in hell people endure eternal conscious punishment? No, that is to read into the text what is not necessarily there. What Jesus said is that both the life and the punishment would be eternal, but he did not in that passage define the nature of either. Because he elsewhere spoke of eternal life as a conscious enjoyment of God (John 17:3), it does not follow that eternal punishment must be a conscious experience of pain at the hand of God. On the contrary, although declaring both to be eternal, Jesus is *contrasting* the two destinies: the more unlike they are, the better.

(3) But did not Dives cry out because he was "in agony in this fire" (Luke 16:23–24, 28)? Yes, he did. But we must be cautious in interpreting a parable (if it was that) that speaks of "Abraham's bosom" as well as hell fire. Moreover, these two states were experienced immediately after Dives and Lazarus died (vv. 22–23). The natural interpretation would be that Jesus was referring to the so-called "intermediate (or interim) state" between death and resurrection. I myself believe that this will be the time (if indeed we shall be aware of the passage of time) when the lost will come to the unimaginably painful realization of their fate. This is not incompatible, however, with their final annihilation. Similarly, the "torment" of Rev 14:10, because it will be experienced "in the presence of the holy angels and of the Lamb," seems to refer to the moment of judgment, not to the eternal state. It is not the torment itself but its "smoke" (symbol of the completed burning) which will be "forever and ever."

(4) But does the book of Revelation not say that in the lake of fire "they will be tormented day and night forever and ever"? Yes, that sentence occurs, but only once (20:10), where it refers not only to the devil, but to "the beast and the false prophet," just as the noun for "torment" had been used of "the harlot Babylon" (Rev 18:7, 10, 15), though without the addition of the words "forever and ever." The beast, the false prophet, and the harlot, however, are not individual people but symbols of the world in its varied hostility to God. In the nature of the case they cannot

experience pain. Nor can "Death and Hades," which follow them into the lake of fire (20:13). In the vivid imagery of his vision John evidently saw the dragon, the monsters, the harlot, death, and hades being thrown into the lake of fire. But the most natural way to understand the reality behind the imagery is that ultimately all enmity and resistance to God will be destroyed. So both the language of destruction and the imagery of fire seem to point to annihilation.

The third argument in favor of the concept of annihilation concerns the biblical vision of *justice*. Fundamental to it is the belief that God will judge people "according to what they [have] done" (e.g., Rev 20:12), which implies that the penalty inflicted will be commensurate with the evil done. This principle had been applied in the Jewish law courts, in which penalties were limited to an exact retribution, "life for life, eye for eye, tooth for tooth, hand for hand, foot for foot" (e.g., Exod 21:23–25). Would there not, then, be a serious disproportion between sins consciously committed in time and torment consciously experienced throughout eternity? I do not minimize the gravity of sin as rebellion against God our Creator, and shall return to it shortly, but I question whether "eternal conscious torment" is compatible with the biblical revelation of divine justice, unless perhaps (as has been argued) the impenitence of the lost also continues throughout eternity.

The fourth and last argument relates to those texts which have been used as the basis for *universalism*. I am not a universalist, and you tell me that you are not either. So there is no need for me to say more than that the hope of final salvation for everybody is a false hope, since it contradicts the recorded warnings of Jesus that the judgment will involve a separation into two opposite but equally eternal destinies. My point here, however, is that the eternal existence of the impenitent in hell would be hard to reconcile with the promises of God's final victory over evil, or with the apparently universalistic texts which speak of Christ drawing all men to himself (John 12:32), and of God uniting all things under Christ's headship (Eph 1:10), reconciling all things to himself through Christ (Col 1:20), and bringing every knee to bow to Christ and every tongue to confess his lordship (Phil 2:10–11), so that in the end God will be "all in all" or "everything to everybody" (1 Cor 15:28).

These texts do not lead me to universalism, because of the many others that speak of the terrible and eternal reality of hell. But they do lead me to ask how God can in any meaningful sense be called "everything to everybody" while an unspecified number of people still continue in rebellion against him and under his judgment. It would be easier to hold together the awful reality of hell and the universal reign of God if hell means destruction and the impenitent are no more.

I am hesitant to have written these things, partly because I have a great respect for longstanding tradition that claims to be a true interpretation of Scripture, and do not lightly set it aside, and partly because the unity of the worldwide evangelical constituency has always meant much to me. But the issue is too important to suppress, and I am grateful to you for challenging me to declare my present mind. I do not dogmatize about the position to which I have come. I hold it tentatively. But I do plead for frank dialogue among evangelicals on the basis of Scripture. I also believe that the ultimate annihilation of the wicked should at least be accepted as a legitimate, biblically founded alternative to their eternal conscious torment.

6

The Destruction of the Finally Impenitent

CLARK H. PINNOCK

Clark Pinnock (1937–2010) was a highly regarded, though often controversial, evangelical theologian in North America. He studied for his PhD under F. F. Bruce at Manchester University and went on to teach at a number of evangelical seminaries, including Trinity Evangelical Divinity School, Regent College, and McMaster Divinity School. Early in his career, he was considered a defender of conservative evangelical views with the 1967 release of his book, A Defense of Biblical Infallibility. *However, as his views on Scripture shifted and he became known for his advocacy of open theism and an inclusivist view of salvation, Pinnock became an icon of progressive evangelicalism and a target of conservative theologians. His books include* A Wideness in God's Mercy, Flame of Love: A Theology of the Holy Spirit, Most Moved Mover, *and* The Scripture Principle. *Pinnock also wrote the chapter on conditionalism in the book,* Four Views on Hell, *as well as a chapter on annihilationism in* The Oxford Handbook of Eschatology.

In 1990, Pinnock wrote an article entitled, "The Destruction of the Finally Impenitent," published in the Criswell Theological Review, *in which he expressed deep emotional outrage at the traditional view of endless torment and argued for the annihilation of the unsaved. This article represented a significant salvo in the larger theological battle over conditional immortality in the US that had resulted from the earlier work of Wenham, Fudge, Travis, and Stott.*

ALL CHRISTIAN DOCTRINES UNDERGO a certain amount of development over time. Issues such as Christology and soteriology are taken up at various periods in church history and receive a peculiar stamp from intellectual and social conditions obtaining at the time. A variety of factors in society and philosophical thought impact upon the way in which issues are viewed and interpreted. All doctrinal formulations reflect to some extent historical and cultural conditions and have an incarnate or historical quality about them. Not to recognize this is (I think) to be willingly blind to reality.[1]

Eschatology is not an exception to this principle. Indeed it exemplifies it. It illustrates the reality of doctrinal change and development very well, having gone through a number of important changes in time. Consider briefly the following changes in eschatology: the way thinking moved from the expectation in the New Testament and the early church of the nearness of the Second Coming of Christ to the willingness of later orthodox theologians to delay their expectation until the far distant future; from a millennial or chiliast belief in Christ's reign upon the earth, which one finds in the early fathers, to a belief that sees his rule taking place in the world above and beyond history; from placing the final judgment at the end of history to an expectation of it occurring at the moment of death; from an emphasis on the gloriously resurrected body to an emphasis on the naturally immortal soul. Eschatology is one of those doctrines in which interpreters should be careful not to place uncritical confidence in what tradition has said, since it has undergone several large sea changes and does not speak with a single voice.[2]

The aspect of eschatology that we are studying here is the doctrine of divine judgment and hell.[3] As in so many matters, for better or worse, it was Augustine who gave the church its standard way of thinking about hell, a way that would become dominant for the next millennium and a half. Specifically he taught us to view hell as a condition of endless torment

---

1. This is made plain by Hopper, *Modern Theology*, 2:4–31, in chap. 1, which is entitled "The Recognition of Historical and Cultural Relativity."

2. See Travis, *Christian Hope*; Küng, *Eternal Life?*; and Hick, *Death*.

3. For an orientation see Toon, *Heaven and Hell*; Morey, *Afterlife*; and Fudge, *Fire That Consumes*.

of conscious persons in body and soul. In a major section of *The City of God* (book 21), he argues at length against all objections to this grim idea and defends his view vigorously that God plans to torture the wicked both mentally and physically forever. To get a feeling for his orientation, one should consider his argument in answer to one objection: how could a resurrected person burn physically and suffer psychologically forever without being materially consumed or ever losing consciousness? How could they suffer the same kind of burns one would sustain on earth from contact with raging flames and not be consumed by them? To explain this marvel Augustine explains that God has the power to do such things that transcend ordinary nature. He will employ his power to perform miracles to keep them alive and conscious in the fire.

Unfortunately Augustine is not alone in thinking this way but rather speaks for orthodoxy. The Protestant J. Edwards is every bit as rigorous in his doctrine of hell, as is well known. His sermon "Sinners in the Hands of an Angry God" is (in)famous for the picture of God dangling sinners over the flames like a loathsome spider. J. Gerstner, an Edwards scholar, summarizes Edwards' view in this way:

> Hell is a spiritual and material furnace of fire where its victims are exquisitely tortured in their minds and in their bodies eternally, according to their various capacities, by God, the devils, and damned humans including themselves, in their memories and consciences as well as in their raging, unsatisfied lusts, from which place of death God's saving grace, mercy, and pity are gone forever, never for a moment to return.[4]

Not only is it God's pleasure to torture the wicked everlastingly, but it will be the happiness of the saints to see and know this is being faithfully done. It would not be unfair to picture the traditional doctrine in this way: just as one can imagine certain people watching a cat trapped in a microwave oven squirming in agony and taking delight in it, so the saints in heaven will, according to Edwards, experience the torments of the damned with pleasure and satisfaction.

In my paper I do not intend to consider what one might call "revisionist" versions of the traditional doctrine, which in effect take the hell out of hell: for example, views that remove physical suffering from it, or make it into a timeless state, or put it down to the sinner's free choice to live separately from God rather than its being God's will to torment them.

---

4. Gerstner, *Edwards*, 53.

Augustine and Edwards too would certainly have rejected these softening concessions. I want to address the traditional view of the matter as it has actually been held, namely, the everlasting, conscious torment of the finally impenitent in body and soul. I want to do that first because such is the traditional view of hell and second because that view, like my own, takes the Bible's actual imagery of burning fire seriously.

Augustine hardly pauses over the well-known objections that plague the modern mind on the subject. We wonder how this doctrine can possibly be reconciled with the revelation of God in the face of Jesus Christ, a problem made so much worse by the fact that according to Augustine the people God tortures are also the nonelect to whom he has sovereignly/arbitrarily declined to extend his grace or assist in any way to be saved from hell. Thus Augustine cannot even resort to the explanation one hears often today: if hell is what the wicked have asked for, what can God do about it?[5] Edwards, on the other hand, is aware of the problems. Unfortunately, as Gerstner acknowledges, he just ducks the questions and does not really answer them. Edwards seems to grasp the questions we moderns want to ask but does not in the end face them. Gerstner surmises in response to this strange situation that Edwards must have been blinded by the very fire he defended so vigorously.[6] I find this explanation bizarre. More likely, he just could not bring himself to wrap his tongue around the words which his system demanded be said.

For there really is little doubt what Edwards would have said to the objections since he says similar things elsewhere. Our problem, he would say, is that we think God as more loving and merciful than he actually is and want to judge God by our puny moral standards. Torturing the wicked eternally presents no problem to God, as Edwards understands him. I think there must have been times in his life when he just could not bring himself to say the horrible things he believed about hell. At least we have his disciple Gerstner to pronounce the words for him.[7]

How should I begin? Shall I treat the subject in the calm way one would when dealing with another issue? Would it be right to pretend to

5. Silvester, *Arguing*, chap. 7.
6. Gerstner, *Edwards*, 87–90.
7. Many traditionalists other than Gerstner have no difficulty saying what they really think about hell. Listen to A. W. Pink: "Startling as it may sound, it is nevertheless a fact, that the Scriptures speak much more frequently of God's anger and wrath, than they do of his love and compassion." For a booklet along these lines, see Pink, *Eternal Punishment*.

be calm when I am not? To begin calmly would not really communicate a full account of my response. I do not feel calm about the traditional doctrine of hell, and so I will not pretend. Indeed, how can anyone with the milk of human kindness in him remain calm contemplating such an idea as this? Now I realize that in admitting this I am playing into the hands of the critics, when I admit how disturbed the doctrine makes me. They will be able to say that I have adopted arguments on the basis of sentimentality and a subjective sense of moral outrage. In a recent paper, J. I. Packer has said that he dislikes the idea critics of everlasting conscious punishment seem to have of their moral superiority, when it is not spiritual sensitivity, he says, but secular sentimentalism that motivates them (referring in the context to none other than his esteemed evangelical and Anglican colleague J. Stott).[8] Nonetheless, I will take the risk of beginning at the point of my outrage and hope people will hear me and not put it down to sentimentality. To such a charge I would reply: if it is sentimentality that drives me, what drives my opponent? Is it hardheartedness and the desire for eternal retribution? Such recriminations will get us nowhere fast.

Let me say at the outset that I consider the concept of hell as endless torment in body and mind an outrageous doctrine, a theological and moral enormity, a bad doctrine of the tradition that needs to be changed. How can Christians possibly project a deity of such cruelty and vindictiveness whose ways include inflicting everlasting torture upon his creatures, however sinful they may have been? Surely a God who would do such a thing is more nearly like Satan than like God, at least by any ordinary moral standards, and by the gospel itself. How can we possibly preach that God has so arranged things that a number of his creatures (perhaps a large number predestined to that fate) will undergo (in a state of complete consciousness) physical and mental agony through unending time? Is this not a most disturbing concept that needs some second thoughts? Surely the God and Father of our Lord Jesus Christ is no fiend; torturing people without end is not what our God does. Does the one who told us to love our enemies intend to wreak vengeance on his own enemies for all eternity? As H. Küng appropriately asks, "What would we think of a human being who satisfied his thirst for revenge so implacably and insatiably?"[9]

8. Packer, "Evangelicals."
9. Küng, *Eternal Life*, 136.

In a recent book ably defending the traditional view of hell, R. Morey complains that in every generation people keep questioning the belief in everlasting, conscious torment even though the basis of it, as far as he can tell, has been laid out in books like his time and again. Well, I would offer him an explanation for this. Is it a surprise, given the cruelty the doctrine attributes to God's action, that Christians would repeatedly wonder if this were true? It is no wonder to me why they would gravitate to the kind of view I am defending, that the finally impenitent wicked, rather than suffering torture forever, pass out of existence. Their moral sensibilities demand it of them.

The Question before Us

Having said that, I am ready to discuss the question rationally, if not exactly calmly. The question before us is whether Christian theology should contend that the wicked who are finally impenitent suffer everlasting, conscious punishment in body and soul or whether they are more likely to be destroyed in the destruction of a second death? Will the fire of hell torment condemned souls endlessly, or will it destroy and finally consume them? Does God intend to grant the wicked immortality in order to inflict endless pain upon them, or does he will that the wicked, following the last judgment, should finally perish and die? This is the question before us in this exchange of views.[10] I myself will take the position that the finally impenitent wicked suffer extinction and annihilation.[11]

In defending the annihilation of the wicked, I realize that this is the view of a minority among evangelical theologians and church leaders and that I place myself at risk when I oppose the traditional view of hell as endless agony and torment. After all, it is a well-established tradition, and one does not oppose such a tradition without paying a price in terms of one's reputation. Even worse, I recognize that this puts me in some odd company, a fact regularly used against the position I am defending, for it is usually argued that only heretics or near-heretics deny the doctrine

10. Supporting Morey in defense of everlasting, conscious torment today are such names as Hoekema, *The Bible and the Future*, chap. 19; Buis, *Eternal Punishment*; and Erickson, *Theology*, 1234–40. I believe that the majority of conservative theologians would side with this view and that I stand with the minority.

11. Supporting this view among contemporary evangelical theologians may be mentioned such authors as these: Stott in Edwards and Stott, *Essentials*, 312–20; Fudge, *Fire That Consumes*; Hughes, *Image*, chap. 37; and Travis, *Second Coming*, 196–99.

PART TWO—INFLUENTIAL DEFENSES OF CONDITIONALISM

of everlasting punishment and defend extinction. The idea is that if the Adventists or the liberals hold such a view, the view must be wrong. In this way the position can be discredited by association and not need to be taken seriously or worried about.[12] Of course it is not much of an argument, but it proves effective with ignorant people who are taken in by rhetoric of this kind.

So it is that when such a noted evangelical as J. W. Wenham defends annihilationism, it gets put down to liberal influences in the InterVarsity Press and to poor research on Wenham's part for falling into this error.[13] In my case, after *Christianity Today* published my view of hell as annihilation (March 20, 1987), A. Rogers, then the president of the Southern Baptist Convention, saw it as proof that my theology was no longer sound but was going liberal.[14] Therefore, I suppose that I should feel grateful that Morey at least allows the possibility that one might actually be a Christian even if he believes in annihilation.[15] Unfortunately for me, even that is now in some doubt, according to Morey, since I expressed some thoughts about divine omniscience.[16] What does this tell us about the condition of evangelical theology that such a distorted evaluation of a fellow evangelical's work would be possible?

Nevertheless, the view I am advancing does seem to be gaining ground among evangelicals. The fact that no less of a person than J. R. W. Stott has endorsed it now will certainly encourage this trend to continue. It will tend to create a measure of accreditation by association and counter the dirty-tricks tactics used against it. It will be more difficult now to claim that only heretics and near-heretics hold the position, even though I am sure there will be people who will dismiss Stott too as a sound evangelical teacher for saying this.

This is surely a divisive issue at present among evangelicals, something that became clear at the "Evangelical Affirmations" conference held at Trinity Evangelical Divinity School last spring (as reported by *Christianity Today*, June 16, 1989).[17] Stott himself expresses anxiety on that score, lest he should become a source of division in the community

12. See Morey, *Afterlife*, 199–203.
13. Ibid., 203.
14. Rogers, "Response," 106.
15. Morey, *Afterlife*, 204.
16. Morey, *Battle*, 114–17.
17. See Packer, "Evangelicals."

in which he is a renowned leader. The doctrine of hell enters into the struggle for evangelical identity. At the same time we should remember that whether Stott or Wenham or Hughes or anyone else holds the view of the annihilation of the wicked is irrelevant, since truth is not decided on the basis of who holds what opinion. The knife cuts both ways.

What I would ask my readers to do is to entertain the possibility that the Christian tradition has gone wrong in regard to hell as everlasting, conscious torment. It should not be too much to ask since many of them already hold that Augustine got certain other things wrong in his theology. Many will hold, for example, that he was wrong on the doctrine of the millennium, on the practice of infant baptism, and on Gods sovereign/arbitrary reprobation of the wicked. So why should they not entertain the possibility that he may have erred with regard to the doctrine of hell as everlasting, conscious punishment as well? Since as Protestants we accept the fact that Christian doctrines sometimes need reforming in some ways at some times, why would we refuse at least to consider the possibility that it might need to be reformed in this matter too? It can be viewed as a thought experiment.

The Case for the Annihilation of the Wicked

What I want to do is what I am assured cannot be done, namely, to show that the Bible does not teach Augustine's version of the doctrine of hell. Almost all who defend his view admit that the idea of everlasting torment is a genuinely awful concept, but they go on to defend it anyway on the assumption that it is nevertheless mandatory scriptural truth (much as a strict Calvinist argues in defense of his doctrine of the sovereign reprobation of the nonelect—recall Calvin's reference to "the horrible decree"). They tell us that they do not like the doctrine any more than anyone else but have to espouse it because it is a biblical idea and they have no choice but to uphold it. They make it sound like the infallibility of the Bible were at stake. Let us ask then whether the traditional doctrine of hell is biblically and theologically sound. In my view it is not.

1. The strong impression the Bible creates in this reader with regard to the fate of the finally impenitent wicked is a vivid sense of their final and irreversible destruction. The language and imagery used by Scripture is so powerful in this regard that it is remarkable more theologians have

not picked up on it. The Bible repeatedly uses the language of death, destruction, ruin, and perishing when speaking of the fate of the wicked. It uses the imagery of fire consuming (not torturing) what is thrown into it. The images of fire and destruction together strongly suggest annihilation rather than unending torture. It creates the impression that eternal punishment refers to a divine judgment whose results cannot be reversed rather than to the experience of being tormented forever.

Frankly it is a little annoying to be told again and again by the defenders of everlasting torment that there is no biblical case for the annihilation of the wicked. A. Pink, for instance, calls the position an absurdity, while W. Hendriksen says he is aghast that anyone would argue otherwise than for hell as everlasting torment; and Packer attributes the position to sentimentality, not to any scriptural ground. But is it not really quite the other way around? Does the burden of proof not rest with the traditionalists to explain why the strong impression of the destruction of the wicked that the Bible gives its readers should not just be believed?

A brief overview of the Bible will show what I am driving at. The Old Testament gives us a clear picture of the destruction of the wicked (perhaps because it is more oriented to this world than the next) and supplies the basic imagery of divine judgment for the New Testament as well. Consider Psalm 37 where we read that the wicked fade like grass and wither like the herb (v. 2), that they will be cut off and be no more (vv. 9, 10), that they will perish and vanish like smoke (v. 20), and be altogether destroyed (v. 38). Listen to this oracle from the prophet Malachi: "For behold, the day comes, burning like an oven, when all the arrogant and all evildoers will be stubble; the day that comes shall burn them up, says the LORD of hosts, so that it will leave them neither root nor branch" (4:1). The message is plain—the finally impenitent wicked will perish and be no more.

Turning to the New Testament, Jesus' teaching about the afterlife is sketchy in matters of detail. While he certainly referred to a destiny beyond the grave either of bliss or woe, he did not bother to give us a clear conception of it. He was not a systematic theologian but a preacher more concerned with the importance of a decision here and now than with speculations about the furniture of heaven or the temperature of hell. At the same time Jesus said things that support the impression the Old Testament gives us.

He presented God's judgment as the destruction of the wicked. He said that God could and perhaps would destroy body and soul in hell, if he must (Matt 10:28). Jesus' words are reminiscent of John the Baptist's when he said that the wicked are like dry wood about to be thrown into the fire and like chaff to be burned in the unquenchable fire (Matt 3:10, 12). He warned that the wicked will be cast away into hell like so much rejected garbage into the Gehenna of fire (5:30), an allusion to the valley outside Jerusalem where sacrifices were once offered to Moloch (2 Kgs 16:3; 21:6), and possibly the place where garbage actually smoldered and burned in Jesus' day. Our Lord said that the wicked will be burned up there just like weeds when thrown into the fire (Matthew 13:30, 42, 49, 50). The impression is a very strong one that the impenitent wicked can expect to be destroyed.

The Apostle Paul communicates the same thing, plainly thinking of divine judgment as the destruction of the wicked. He writes of everlasting destruction that will come upon the wicked (2 Thess 1:9). He warns that the wicked will reap corruption (Gal 6:8). He states that God will destroy the wicked (1 Cor 3:17; Phil 1:28). He speaks of their fate as a death they deserve to die (Rom 1:32) and which is the wages of their sins (6:23). About the wicked, he states plainly and concisely: "Their end is destruction" (Phil 3:19).

It is no different in the other New Testament books. Peter speaks of "the fire which has been kept until the day of judgment and the destruction of ungodly men" (2 Pet 3:7). The author to the Hebrews speaks of the wicked who shrink back and are destroyed (Heb 10:39). Peter says that false teachers who deny the Lord who bought them will bring upon themselves "swift destruction" (2 Pet 2:1, 3). They will resemble the cities of Sodom and Gomorrah which were "condemned to extinction" (2:6). They will perish like the ancient world perished when deluged in the great Flood (3:6, 7). Jude also points to Sodom as an analogy to God's judgment, being the city which underwent "a punishment of eternal fire" (Jude 7). Similarly, the Apocalypse of John speaks of the lake of fire consuming the wicked and of the second death (Rev 20:14, 15).

At the very least it should be obvious to any impartial reader that the Bible may legitimately be read to teach the final destruction of the wicked without difficulty. I am not making it up. It is not wishful thinking. It is simply a natural interpretation of Scripture on the subject of divine judgment. I think it is outrageous for traditionalists to say that a biblical basis for the destruction of the wicked is lacking. What is in short supply are texts supporting the traditional view.

2. Some advocates prefer to call their position conditional immortality rather than annihilationism because it sounds more positive to the ear. Underlying the doctrine of annihilation, after all, is a belief in conditional immortality, the understanding that our immortality is not a natural attribute of humankind but God's gift. This is clearly an important issue in our discussion because belief in the natural immortality of the soul so widely held by Christians, although stemming more from Plato than the Bible, really drives the traditional doctrine of hell more than exegesis does. Consider the logic: if souls must live forever because they are naturally immortal, the lake of fire must be their home forever and cannot be their destruction. In the same way, the second death would have to be a process of everlasting dying and not a termination of existence, which is impossible. I am convinced that the Hellenistic belief in the immortality of the soul has done more than anything else (specifically more than the Bible) to give credibility to the doctrine of the everlasting conscious punishment of the wicked. This belief, not Holy Scripture, is what gives this doctrine the credibility it does not deserve.

Belief in the immortality of the soul has long attached itself to Christian theology. J. Maritain, for example, states: "The human soul cannot die. Once it exists, it cannot disappear; it will necessarily exist forever and endure without end."[18] To this we must say, with all due respect, that the Bible teaches no such thing. The soul is not an immortal substance that has to be placed somewhere if it rejects God. The Bible states that God alone has immortality (1 Tim 6:16) and that everlasting life is something God gives to humanity by grace (1 Cor 15:51–55). Eternal life is not something we possess by any natural right according to Scripture. Immortality is not inherent in human beings. We are dependent on God for what happens to us after death. Rather than speaking of immortal souls, the Bible refers to resurrected bodies, to persons being reconstituted through the power of God (Phil 3:20). In a word, Jesus Christ "abolished death and brought life and immortality to light through the gospel" (2 Tim 1:10).[19]

---

18. Maritain, *Reason*, 60.

19. Cullmann, *Immortality of the Soul?*; Harris, *Raised*, 187–205; and Wisbrock, *Death*.

The Greek doctrine of immortality has affected theology unduly on this point. It is one of several examples where there has been an undue Hellenization of Christian doctrine. The idea of souls being naturally immortal is not a biblical one, and the effect of believing it stretches the experience of death and destruction in Gehenna into endless torment. If souls are immortal, then either all souls will be saved (which is unscriptural universalism) or else hell must be everlasting torment. There is no other possibility since annihilation is ruled out from the start. This is how the traditional view of hell got constructed: add a belief in divine judgment after death (scriptural) to a belief in the immortality of the soul (unscriptural), and you have Augustine's terrible doctrine.

Nevertheless, I do not call my position conditional immortality. It is a necessary, but not a sufficient condition of my view. Conditional immortality has to be true for a negative reason—to make the destruction of the wicked conceivable, but it does not positively establish annihilation simply because it would still be possible that God might give the wicked everlasting life and condemn them to spend it in everlasting torment. Conditional immortality then, while necessary to belief in annihilation, does not prove that annihilation is true. The key issue remains my first argument: the Scriptures suggest the destruction of the wicked.

3. As I intimated earlier, everlasting torment is intolerable from a moral point of view because it makes God into a bloodthirsty monster who maintains an everlasting Auschwitz for victims whom he does not even allow to die. How is one to worship or imitate such a cruel and merciless God? The idea of everlasting torment (especially if it is linked to soteriological predestination) raises the problem of evil to impossible dimensions. A. Flew was quite right (I think) to say that, if Christians want to hold that God created some people to be tortured in hell forever, then the apologetic task in relation to theodicy is just hopeless.[20] Stott seems to agree: "I find the concept intolerable and do not understand how people can live with it without either cauterizing their feelings or cracking under the strain."[21] I even wonder what atrocities have been committed by those who have believed in a God who tortures his enemies?

Naturally, various attempts have been made by the traditionalists to hide the gruesome problem. C. Hodge and B. B. Warfield, for example, make use of postmillennial eschatology to argue that very few persons

20. Flew, *God*, 56–57.
21. Stott and Edwards, *Essentials*, 314.

relatively speaking) will go to hell anyway. Presumably we do not need to worry much if only a negligible number is tormented while a numerical majority is saved. Such a calculus, however, achieves little: first, because few today would accept the postmillennial premise to begin with, and second, because the tens of millions still suffering everlasting torture even under their scenario are tens of millions too many.

Alternatively it is common to try to hide the moral problem by redefining hell. C. S. Lewis tries this when he pictures hell in *The Great Divorce* as almost pleasant, if a little gray, being the kind of place from which one can take day trips on the bus into heaven and return again to meet with the theological society that meets regularly in hell.[22] This resembles Sartre's picture of hell in *No Exit* as consisting of being cooped up with the other people forever. In these terms, hell is nasty and inconvenient, but certainly no lake of fire. Thus by sheer speculation the biblical warnings are emasculated and the moral problem dealt with by fancy footwork devoid of exegesis. The fact is that the biblical warnings spell a terrible destruction awaiting the impenitent wicked, and if hell is everlasting there is no way to make it other than endless torture. I understand why traditionalists want to take the hell out of hell, but it should not be permitted, because it breaks the concentration and prevents people from seeing the need for theological renewal on this point.

4. The need to correct the traditional doctrine of hell also rests upon considerations of the divine justice. What purpose of God would be served by the unending torture of the wicked except sheer vengeance and vindictiveness? Such a fate would spell endless and totally unredemptive suffering, punishment just for its own sake. Even the plagues of Egypt were intended to be redemptive for those who would respond to the warnings. But unending torment would be the kind of utterly pointless and wasted suffering that could never lead to anything good beyond it. Furthermore, it would amount to inflicting infinite suffering upon those who have committed finite sins. It would go far beyond an eye for an eye and a tooth for a tooth. There would be a serious disproportion between sins committed in time and the suffering experienced forever. The fact that sin has been committed against an infinite God does not make the sin infinite. The chief point is that eternal torment serves no purpose and

---

22. In another place, though, Lewis sounds much like an annihilationist himself. Hell speaks more of finality than of duration, he says, and it exists on the outer rim "where being fades away into nonentity" (*Pain*, 114–15).

exhibits a vindictiveness out of keeping with the love of God revealed in the gospel. We should listen to H. Küng:

> Even apart from the image of a truly merciless God that contradicts everything we can assume from what Jesus says of the Father of the lost, can we be surprised at a time when retributive punishments without an opportunity of probation are being increasingly abandoned in education and penal justice that the idea not only of a lifelong, but even eternal punishment of body and soul, seems to many people absolutely monstrous?[23]

5. Finally, from a metaphysical point of view, everlasting torment gives the clear picture of an unending cosmological dualism. Heaven and hell just go on existing alongside each other forever. But how can this be if God is to be "all in all" (1 Cor 15:28) and if God is making "all things new" (Rev 21:5)? It just does not add up right. Stott asks: "How can God in any meaningful sense be called 'everything to everybody' while an unspecified number of people still continue in rebellion against him and under his judgment?"[24] It would make better sense metaphysically (as well as biblically, morally, and justicewise) if hell meant destruction and the wicked were no more. Otherwise the disloyal opposition would eternally exist alongside God in a corner of unredeemed reality in the new creation.

6. Nevertheless, the reader may be asking, have I not forgotten something important? What about the texts that have always been taken to support the doctrine of everlasting conscious torment? In regard to them I would say that their number is very small. The texts that can be taken to teach this doctrine are few in number and capable of being fairly interpreted in harmony with the majority of verses that teach the destruction of the wicked. I deal with these "difficult" texts in the way that biblical inerrantists or high Calvinists deal with the difficult passages they face.

(1) "Their worm does not die and the fire is not quenched" (Mark 9:48). This imagery is taken from Isa 66:24 where the dead bodies of God's enemies are being eaten by maggots and burned up. It is safe to say there is not a hint of everlasting suffering in the verse. The fire and the worm destroy the dead bodies; they do not torment them. The fire will be

---

23. Küng, *Eternal Life*, 136–37.
24. Edwards and Stott, *Essentials*, 319.

quenched only when the job is finished, not before. The tradition simply misreads the verse.[25]

(2) "They will go away into eternal punishment" (Matt 25:46). I admit that the interpretation of everlasting, conscious torment can be read out of this verse if one wishes to do so. Such a meaning is not at all impossible from the wording, especially if one smuggles the term "conscious" into it as is very common.[26] But there are considerations that would bring the meaning more into line with what I judge to be the larger body of evidence. Jesus does not define the nature of eternal life or eternal death in this text. He just says there will be two destinies and leaves it there. One is free to interpret it to mean either everlasting conscious torment or irreversible destruction. The text allows for both possibilities and only teaches explicitly the finality of the judgment itself, not its nature.[27] Therefore, one's interpretation of this verse in respect to our subject here will depend upon other considerations. In the light of what has been said so far, I think it is better and wiser to read the text as teaching annihilation.

(3) But did not the rich man suffer torment in the flames in a famous parable of Jesus? (Luke 16:23ff.). Yes, this is part of the Jewish imagery Jesus uses. But one should keep two things in mind here: first, the mention of Abraham's bosom (v. 22) should alert us to the fact that we are dealing with imagery, not literal description; and second (and more importantly), the story refers to the intermediate state between death and the resurrection and is not really relevant to our subject. This point should not be missed given the fact that the passage is used regularly (and erroneously) in the traditionalist literature to describe hell, not the intermediate state.[28]

(4) But what about those passages in the book of the Revelation of John that speak of Satan, the false prophet, the beast, and certain evildoers being tormented in fire and brimstone (Rev 14:11; 20:10)? Only in the first case (14:11) are human beings at all in view, and it is likely that what

---

25. Unfortunately, Lane reads the text through Jdt 16:17 and therefore gives the meaning as endless torment (*Mark*, 349).

26. Harris reads it this way (*Raised*, 182–84), as does Gundry: "The parallel between eternal punishment and eternal life forestalls any weakening of the former" (*Matthew*, 516).

27. Brown, *New International Dictionary*, 3:99.

28. For background on the Jewish imagery used in this parable of Jesus, see Marshall, *Luke*, 632–39.

is being described is the moment of their judgment, not their everlasting condition, with the smoke going up forever being the testimony to their final destruction. In the other verse (20:10), it is the devil, the beast, and the false prophet who are the only ones present, and they cannot be equated with ordinary human beings, however we should understand their nature. John's point seems to be that everything that has rebelled against God will come to an absolute end. As Caird comments: "John believed that, if at the end there should be any who remained impervious to the grace and love of God, they would be thrown, with Death and Hades, into the lake of fire which is the second death, i.e., extinction and total oblivion."[29] I think it would be fair to say that the biblical basis for the traditional view of hell has been greatly exaggerated.

Positively I am contending that Scripture and theology give solid support to the doctrine of the annihilation of the wicked. The case is impressive if not quite unambiguous, and the traditional view looks less likely in comparison with it. Yet I would not say that either side wins the argument hands down largely because the Bible does not seem concerned to deal with this question as precisely as we want it to. But it is amusing to hear traditionalists claiming that they alone hold to the infallibility of the Bible as illustrated by their holding to everlasting torment of the wicked.[30] Their position is in fact very weakly established biblically.

Hermeneutical Commentary

A number of fascinating issues surface in this debate, some of which we should at least notice before we close. Some important things are revealed about theological method. First, it appears that the strongest argument for holding the Augustinian view of hell is the long tradition. The scriptural support is rather weak and the objections to it very strong. This raises the question why evangelicals cling tightly to certain ancient traditions and not others (like infant baptism)? Perhaps the issue of liberal theology comes into it. After all, all liberals hate the traditional doctrine of hell, and evangelicals know this well. This means that belief in everlasting torment can serve as a handy litmus test for separating liberals from evangelicals (much like the virgin birth has done for decades). This may account for some of the emotion and stubbornness one encounters

---

29. Caird, *Revelation*, 186–87.
30. Buis, *Eternal Punishment*, 127.

around this subject. But if the best reason for holding to everlasting torment is tradition, then we had better reconsider because it is not a good enough reason.

Second, my own essay illustrates the primary reason why people question the tradition so vehemently. They are not first of all impressed by its lack of a good scriptural basis (that comes later). They are appalled by its awful moral implications. But this means of course that along with Scripture they are employing moral reasoning in their theological method even as their opponents are employing tradition in theirs.

Third, we receive some lessons in biblical interpretation too. How is it that the Bible can be read in such different ways as we have noticed? Does this not suggest that we need a more adequate understanding of hermeneutics? Ought we to press a single verse, the meaning of which we are personally certain, if it goes against a lot of other texts and also broader considerations? Should we be staring at texts or considering wider theological issues in this case? Does our interpretation depend upon larger paradigms?

Fourth, reason is certainly playing a role here too. It gets used in assessing the meaning of texts, in constructing doctrines, and in considering issues surrounding the problem of evil, justice, and metaphysics. The discussion illustrates how reason, even operating in a ministerial role, plays a role in deciding doctrinal questions. Fifth, there is clearly a lot of cultural and situational input too. The traditional view was greatly influenced by the Hellenistic belief in the immortality of the soul. Pusey used hell as a whip to keep people morally observant, and Edwards used it to frighten them into faith. People even oppose annihilation on the grounds that it is not frightening enough and lets the wicked get off too easy! A great deal more than exegesis goes into decisions like these.

Concluding Remarks

First, I hope we remember that eschatology is an area in which what we know by way of specific knowledge is quite limited. The Bible is reserved about giving us detailed information about heaven or hell, so we should try not to be too dogmatic or harsh with one another.

Second, I hope that the traditionalists will not make this issue into one that will divide evangelicals from one another as seems quite possible. Whether the wicked perish or suffer endlessly, hell is a very grim prospect, and I and the others are not trying to lessen it.³¹ To be rejected by God, to miss the purpose for which one was created, to pass into oblivion while others enter into bliss—this will mean weeping and the gnashing of teeth. I do not think we have to be at one another's throats over this. I commended *Christianity Today* earlier and the *Criswell Theological Review* now for their willingness to examine the issue of annihilation.

Finally, take heed to what Stott says:

> I am hesitant to have written these things, partly because I have a great respect for longstanding tradition which claims to be a true interpretation of scripture, and do not lightly set it aside, and partly because the unity of the worldwide evangelical constituency has always meant much to me. But the issue is too important to suppress, and I am grateful to you [D. Edwards] for challenging me to declare my present mind. I do not dogmatize about the position to which I have come. I hold it tentatively. But I do plead for frank dialogue among evangelicals on the basis of Scripture. I also believe that the ultimate annihilation of the wicked should at least be accepted as a legitimate, biblically founded alternative to their eternal conscious torment.³²

---

31. Neither is Wenham who hesitates on this very point (Wenham, "Conditional Immortality," 190).

32. Edwards and Stott, *Essentials*, 319–20.

7

The Case for Conditional Immortality

JOHN W. WENHAM

John Wenham (1913–1996) was Vice-Principal at Tyndale Hall (an Anglican seminary in Bristol, England); an Anglican priest; and the Warden of Latimer House (an evangelical think tank connected to the University of Oxford), a position in which he was preceded by J. I. Packer. During his time in this latter role, he had the opportunity to impact many evangelical students at Oxford, even influencing N. T. Wright to pursue academic work. Wenham's textbook, The Elements of New Testament Greek, *is a well-regarded and widely used resource, and his conservative defense of Scripture,* Christ and the Bible, *is considered by many to be one of the best works on the authority and inerrancy of Scripture. Wenham is also the father of two noted biblical scholars: Gordon Wenham (Old Testament) and David Wenham (New Testament).*

In 1991, John Wenham delivered a paper on conditional immortality at the Fourth Edinburgh Conference in Christian Dogmatics, which was collected in the volume, Universalism and the Doctrine of Hell, *published the following year. This paper represented Wenham's challenge to contemporary evangelical theologians, including his old friend and colleague J. I. Packer, to more accurately understand the tenets of conditional immortality and to respond to the arguments on the basis of biblical interpretation.*

THIS PAPER IS DELIBERATELY restricted in scope. The *presupposition* on which it is based is an acceptance of the canonical books of the Old and New Testaments as divinely inspired and harmonious in their teaching when interpreted in the natural and intended sense. There is therefore no discussion of critical questions which see one part of Scripture in conflict with another. By way of *definition*: belief in conditional immortality is the belief that God created Man only potentially immortal. Immortality is a state gained by grace through faith when the believer receives eternal life and becomes a partaker of the divine nature, immortality being inherent in God alone. It is a doctrine totally different from universalism, which I have long believed quite irreconcilable with Scripture. It shares the doctrine of judgment held by the upholders of everlasting torment in almost every particular—except for one tremendous thing: it sees no continuing place in God's world for human beings living on in unending pain, not reconciled to God. The wrath of God will put an end to sin and evil.

An Answer Awaited

I am grateful for the opportunity of expounding this case, for it is seventeen years since I tentatively committed myself to it in print. This was in my book *The Goodness of God*,[1] where I dealt with the subject of "Hell" in one short chapter. I could do little more than outline the main points of the case for unending conscious torment and for conditional immortality (the latter in seven pages) as convincingly as I could and leave the reader to make his choice. I said, however, that I felt under no obligation to defend any doctrine more shocking than conditionalism until the arguments of L. E. Froom, Basil Atkinson, and Harold Guillebaud[2] had been effectively answered.

---

1. Since republished as *The Enigma of Evil*.
2. Froom, *Conditionalist Faith*; Atkinson, *Immortality*; Guillebaud, *Judge*. (Basil Atkinson, an eccentric bachelor academic, was the main adviser of the Cambridge Inter-Collegiate Christian Union during the years when the Inter-Varsity Fellowship was being built up and conservative evangelicals were trying to extricate themselves from liberalism. He was the great pillar of orthodoxy and was not slow to oppose any deviation from evangelical tradition, as I knew to my cost when during the war I questioned current "worldliness" taboos. At no other time has anyone been so rude to me in print!)

PART TWO—INFLUENTIAL DEFENSES OF CONDITIONALISM

I had learned the doctrine from Basil Atkinson in (I suppose) about 1934. Hitherto I had held the doctrine of unending torment, which had been particularly impressed on me by R. A. Torrey.[3] The torments of the lost had occupied a considerable place in my prayers and I felt deflated when I first heard their everlastingness questioned. But I was fairly certain that Basil Atkinson was right.

In spite of his censures he and I remained good friends and in 1940 we had a considerable correspondence in which I put many questions to him. When I left Cambridge in 1938 I had to teach doctrine at St. John's Hall, Highbury. There till 1941 I taught conditionalism with much reserve and restraint. After that I had twelve years out of direct academic work, before joining the staff of Tyndale Hall, Bristol. Here I taught with rather less reserve, particularly after a Tyndale House Study Group in 1954 that was devoted to The Intermediate State and the Final Condition of the Lost. Here some of the best brains in IVF studied the subject for (I think) three days. Though bringing home to me the great difficulty of coming to assured conclusions about the intermediate state, I was more than ever persuaded that the final end of the lost was destruction in the fires of hell.

Matters reached crisis point in 1973, when I presented Inter-Varsity Press with the MS of *The Goodness of God*. IVP had already published my *Christ and the Bible*, which I had let them have on condition that they would publish its sequel, concerning the moral difficulties of the Bible. I thought that hell was too big a subject to treat in this book and decided simply to content myself with presenting the biblical images without comment. IVP sent the MS to a discerning reader who then asked for help on this topic. So I wrote half-a-dozen pages advocating conditional immortality. At this IVP was up in arms and a long correspondence ensued, which ended with a conference with some of their senior people. I was astonished at how little they had thought about the subject. But at least we were agreed that the biblical research we were promoting should be more concerned about fundamental doctrines than archaeological minutiae and they allowed me to try to state both doctrines as fairly as I could. This was a great step forward for neither Atkinson nor Guillebaud had been able to find a publisher. So I have been waiting since 1973 for a reply to the massive work of Froom (2,476 pages), to Atkinson's closely argued 112 pages, to Guillebaud's sixty-seven and (more important) to

3. Torrey, *Bible*, 303–14.

the one additional book that has appeared on the conditionalist side: Edward Fudge's *The Fire That Consumes*.

An Answer Attempted

To my knowledge there have been four serious attempts at reply. In 1986 The Banner of Truth Trust republished the work of the Reformed theologian W. G. T. Shedd, *The Doctrine of Endless Punishment*, first published in 1885, which faithfully reasserts the doctrine of the Westminster Confession, chapter 32 of which says:

> The bodies of men after death return to dust, and see corruption; but their souls, (which neither die nor sleep) having an immortal subsistence, immediately return to God who gave them. The souls of the righteous, being then made perfect in holiness, are received into the highest heavens, where they behold the face of God in light and glory, waiting for the full redemption of their bodies; and the souls of the wicked are cast into hell, where they remain in torments and utter darkness, reserved to the judgment of the great day. Besides these two places for souls separated from their bodies, the Scripture acknowledgeth none.

In 1989 the same Trust published Paul Helm's *The Last Things: Death, Judgment, Heaven and Hell*. In 1990 J. H. Gerstner's *Repent or Perish* was published, which has four chapters directed specifically against Fudge. In the same year J. I. Packer published his Leon Morris Lecture, "The Problem of Eternal Punishment," which he declares to be "a dissuasive . . . particularly from conditionalism."[4]

The extraordinary thing about these replies is that none of them actually addresses the arguments used by the conditionalists. Shedd, it is true, refers to the eighteenth-century Anglican Bishop Warburton, who "denied that the immortality of the soul is taught in the Old Testament." Shedd's reply is that it "is nowhere formally demonstrated, because it is everywhere assumed."[5] He then proceeds to demolish views that, as far as I know, no conditionalist holds. Similarly I did not recognize the conditionalism to which Helm refers—he gives no references. He says annihilationists hold that "when the impenitent die they do not go on

---

4. Packer, "Eternal Punishment," 25.
5. Shedd, *Endless Punishment*, 50–51.

to await the judgment, but they go literally out of existence."[6] He does, however, acknowledge that "Scripture does not teach the immortality of the soul in so many words."[7]

When we come to Gerstner and Packer an important new factor has arisen: J. R. W. Stott and P. E. Hughes, two leading conservative evangelicals, have written sympathetically of conditionalism.[8] In *Essentials*, his dialogue with David Edwards, Stott writes that he holds his belief in the ultimate annihilation of the wicked "tentatively." He also expresses his hesitation in writing this (although he has told me that he has spoken about it for thirty or forty years), "partly because I have great respect for longstanding tradition which claims to be a true interpretation of Scripture, and do not lightly set it aside, and partly because the unity of the worldwide evangelical constituency has always meant much to me."[9] He says he prefers to describe himself as "agnostic," which, he tells me, is how the late F. F. Bruce also described his position. Since in his view Scripture does not come down unequivocally on either side, he pleads "that the ultimate annihilation of the wicked should at least be accepted as a legitimate, biblically founded alternative to their eternal conscious torment."[10] Hughes, who lectured at Westminster Theological Seminary, Philadelphia, and was one of the editors of *Westminster Theological Journal*, has no such hesitations. He says, "It would be hard to imagine a concept more confusing than that of death which means existing endlessly without the power of dying. This, however, is the corner into which Augustine (in company with many others) argued himself."[11] He wrote to me that he had "long been of this judgment and common Christian candor compelled me to state my position." Gerstner pitches into Hughes, Stott, and Fudge for their revolt against hell. It is a wonderful example of circular argument. He assumes that the Bible teaches what he believes about hell and then proceeds to show that they believe otherwise. He just does not seriously address their arguments. Not sharing his beliefs about hell is

---

6. Helm, *Last Things*, 117.

7. Ibid., 118.

8. See Edwards and Stott, *Essentials*, 312–29. Incidentally I find Stott's way of distinguishing annihilationism and conditional immortality on p. 316 somewhat confusing. Hughes, *Image*, chap. 37.

9. Edwards and Stott, *Essentials*, 319.

10. Ibid., 320.

11. Hughes, *Image*, 403.

equated with a rejection of hell itself, which it is absurd to attribute to such as Stott, Hughes, and Fudge.

Packer is in some ways even more disappointing. With all his capacity for reading and digesting material and with his gift of lucid exposition, one hoped to see the conditionalist arguments carefully considered. He had certainly read the slight treatments of Stott and Hughes and was aware of Fudge's work, but he shows no signs of having read Fudge, Froom, or Atkinson and provides no answers to their arguments, but gives instead answers to arguments they do not use.

While not answering the conditionalist arguments with any seriousness, these writers do of course state their own case. They set out certain well-known texts and claim that their meaning is "obvious."[12] Of conditionalist interpretations Packer says: "I will say as emphatically as I can, that none of them is natural. . . . Conditionalists' attempts to evade the natural meaning of some dozens of relevant passages impress me as a prime case of avalanche-dodging."[13]

The Biblical Data

I would claim that the natural meaning of the vast majority of relevant texts is quite otherwise. Of course, what seems natural and obvious to a person with one set of presuppositions may not seem so to someone with a different set. What we must try to do is to think the way the biblical writers thought and clear our minds of ideas from other cultures. This makes the Old Testament very important, but demands of space make it necessary to pass over the Old Testament, though earlier writers and Fudge quite properly pay it considerable attention. But this is not central to the debate and we will simply quote one sentence of Fudge: "The Old Testament utilizes some fifty Hebrew words and seventy-five figures of speech to describe the ultimate end of the wicked—and every one

---

12. E.g., Packer, "Eternal Punishment," 24. I was reminded by a theologian for whose learning and acuteness I have profound respect of another old book, not republished: Goulbum, *Everlasting Punishment*. He takes the same line: "Most certain it is that the objectors do not *found* their views on Holy Scripture . . . probably none of them would maintain that Scripture on the surface favours them." Similarly Hendriksen says: "The passages . . . are so numerous that one actually stands aghast that in spite of all this there are people today who affirm that they accept Scripture and who, nevertheless, reject the idea of never-ending torment" (*Hereafter*, 197).

13. Packer, "Eternal Punishment," 24.

sounds ... like total extinction."[14] He also shows that in the Apocrypha and pseudepigrapha the Old Testament view predominates, although the notion of endless torment is beginning to appear in Jewish literature.

When we come to the New Testament, the words used in their natural connotation are words of destruction rather than words suggesting continuance in torment or misery. When preparing this paper I found in my files thirty pages of foolscap (dating, I think, from the '40s) on which I had attempted to jot down from the RV all passages referring to life after death. This is certainly not a complete list, but I have worked through it again and this interesting statistic results. I found 264 references to the fate of the lost.

Ten (that is 4 percent) call it Gehenna, which conjures up at once the imagery of the rubbish tip in the Valley of Hinnom outside Jerusalem, where the maggots and the fire destroy the garbage.[15] Two of these call it the Gehenna of fire.

There are twenty-six other references (that is 10 percent) to burning up, three of which concern the lake of fire of the Apocalypse.[16] Fire naturally suggests destruction and is much used for the destruction of what is worthless or evil. It is only by a pedantic use of the modern concept of the conservation of mass and energy that it is possible to say that fire destroys nothing. It has a secondary use as a cause of pain, as in the case of Dives.

Fifty-nine (22 percent) speak of destruction, perdition, utter loss, or ruin.[17] Our Lord himself in the Sermon on the Mount uses destruction, which he contrasts with life, as the destination of those who choose the broad road (Matt 7:13). Paul uses it of "the objects of his wrath—prepared for destruction" (Rom 9:22); of "those who oppose you" who "will be destroyed" (Phil 1:28); of the enemies of the cross of Christ whose "destiny is destruction" (Phil 3:19). "The man of lawlessness is ... doomed to destruction" (2 Thess 2:3); harmful desires "plunge men into ruin and

---

14. Fudge, "Challenge," 4. See also Fudge, *Fire That Consumes* (1982), 87–116.

15. Matt 5:22, 29, 30; 10:28; 18:9; 23:33; Mark 9:43, 45, 47; Luke 12:5.

16. Matt 3:7, 12; 7:19; 13:40, 42, 50; 18:8f; 25:41. Mark 9:43, 48f.; Luke 3:7, 17; 1 Cor. 3:13; 2 Thess 1:7; Heb 6:8; 10:27; 12:29; 2 Pet 3:7, 10; Jude 7, 23; Rev 20:14f.; 21:8.

17. Matt 7:13, 27; 10:6, 28, 39; 15:13; 16:25f; 21:41, 44; 22:7; Mark 8:35f; 12:9; Luke 6:49; 9:25; 13:3, 7; 17:29, 33; 19:10, 27; 20:18; John 3:16, 36; 6:39; 12:25; Acts 2:25, 31; 13:41; Rom 2:12; 9:22, 29; 14:15; 1 Cor 1:18; 10:10; 15:18; 2 Cor 2:15; 4:3; Phil 1:28; 3:19. 1 Thess 5:3; 2 Thess 1:9; 2:8, 10; 1 Tim 6:9. Heb 10:39; Jas 4:12; 2 Pet 2:1, 3, 12; 3:7, 9, 16; 1 John 2:17; Jude 5, 10f.

destruction" (1 Tim 6:9). Hebrews 10:39 says "we are not of those who shrink back to destruction, but of those who believe and are saved." Second Peter speaks of "destructive heresies . . . bringing swift destruction . . . their destruction has not been sleeping" (2:1–3); "The present heavens and earth are reserved for fire, being kept for the day of judgment and destruction of ungodly men" (3:7). The old order will disappear and "the elements will be destroyed by fire" (3:10–12). The beast will "go to his destruction" (Rev 17:8, 11). The very common word *apollumi* is frequently used of eternal ruin, destruction, and loss, as in John 3:16 "should not perish," but it is also used of the lost sheep, the lost coin, and the lost son, who though metaphorically dead and whose life was in total ruin was restored (Luke 15).

Twenty cases (8 percent) speak of separation from God,[18] which carries no connotation of endlessness unless one presupposes immortality: "depart from me" (Matt 8:23); "cast him into the outer darkness" (Matt 22:13); he "shall not enter" the kingdom (Mark 10:15); "one will be taken and the other left" (Luke 17:34); "he is cast forth as a branch" (John 15:6); "outside are the dogs, etc." (Rev 22:15). This concept of banishment from God is a terrifying one. It does not mean escaping from God, since God is everywhere in his creation, every particle of which owes its continuing existence to his sustaining. It means, surely, being utterly cut off from the source and sustainer of life. It is another way of describing destruction.

Twenty-five cases (10 percent) refer to death in its finality, sometimes called "the second death."[19] Without resurrection even "those who have fallen asleep in Christ have perished" (1 Cor 15:18). This has been brought out with great force by a number of modern theologians like Oscar Cullmann, Helmut Thielicke, and Murray Harris.[20] They show that the teaching of the New Testament is to be sharply contrasted with the Greek notion of the immortality of the soul, which sees death as the release of the soul from the prison of the body. What the Christian looks forward to is not a bodiless entrance "into the highest heavens" at death,

---

18. Matt 7:21; 8:11; 10:32; 22:13; 25:30, 41, 46. Mark 8:38; 10:15; Luke 12:9; 13:27f; 14:21, 34; 16:26; 17:34; John 15:6; Eph 5:5; 2 Thess 1:9; Rev 22:15.

19. Luke 20:36; John 8:51; 11:26; Rom 1:32; 4:17; 5:12; 6:13; 11:15; 1 Cor 15:22, 54; 2 Cor 2:15; 5:4; 7:10; Eph 2:5; 2 Tim 1:10; Heb 5:7; Jas 5:20; 1 John 3:14; 5:16; Jude 12; Rev 2:7, 10; 20:6, 14; 21:8.

20. Cullmann, *Immortality of the Soul?*; *Immortality and Resurrection*. Thielicke, *Death and Life*; Harris, *Raised*. See also the recent work of the Oxford Dominican, Tugwell, *Human Immortality*.

but a glorious transformation at the *parousia* when he is raised from death. Life is contrasted with death, which is a cessation of life, rather than with a continuance of life in misery.

One hundred and eight cases (41 percent) refer to what I have called unforgiven sin:[21] adverse judgment, in which the penalty is not specified (e.g., "they will receive greater condemnation," Mark 12:40); life forfeited, with the wrath of God resting on the unbeliever (John 3:36); being unsaved, without specifying what the saved are delivered from (Matt 24:13). Other passages show salvation contrasted with lostness (Matt 16:25), perishing (1 Cor 1:18), destruction (Jas 4:12), condemnation (Mark 16:16), judgment (John 3:17), and death (2 Cor 17:10), never with everlasting misery or pain.

Fifteen cases (6 percent) refer to anguish[22]—this this includes tribulation and distress (Rom 2:9), deliverance to tormentors (Matt 18:34), outer darkness (Matt 22: 13), wailing and grinding of teeth (Matt 25:30), the undying worm (Mark 9:48), beaten with many stripes (Luke 12:47), the birth-pains of death (Acts 2:24), and sorer punishment (Heb 10:29).

There is one verse (Rev 14:11)—this represents less than a half percent—which refers to human beings who have no rest, day or night, the smoke of whose torment goes up forever and ever, which we shall come back to in a moment.

It is a terrible catalogue, giving most solemn warning, but in all but one of the 264 references there is not a word about unending torment and very many of them in their natural sense clearly refer to destruction.

Immortality of the Soul

There is thus a great weight of material which *prima facie* suggests destruction as the final end of the lost. The view gains most of its plausibility

---

21. Matt 12:36, 41; 18:18; 23:35f.; Mark 3:29; 12:40; 16:16; Luke 3:9; 11:31, 50; 12:10, 20; 20:35f.; 20:47; 21:19; John 3:17; 5:28; 8:21, 24; 12:48; Acts 2:40; 4:12; 8:22; 10:42; 13:26, 38f., 47; 15:1, 11; 16:17, 30; 24:25; 26:18; Rom 1:16, 18; 2:3, 5, 16; 3:6; 4:7; 5:9; 8:24; 9:27; 10:9f.; 11:26, 32; 14:10; 1 Cor 1:21; 3:13; 9:22; 10:33; 11:32; 15:2, 17; 16:22; 2 Cor 6:2; Eph 5:6; Phil 4:3; Col 3:6, 25; 1 Thess 1:10; 2:16; 4:6; 5:9; 2 Thess 1:8; 2:10; 1 Tim 2:4; 4:10; 2 Tim 1:9, 18; 2:10; 4:1, 14, 16; Tit 2:11, 13; 3:5; Heb 2:10; 5:9; 6:1; 9:27f; 10:27; Jas 1:21; 2:13; 5:12; 1 Pet 1:5, 9; 4:5f., 17; 2 Pet 2:9. 1 John 2:28; 4:17; Jude 15, 21; Rev 3:5; 6:10, 17; 7:10; 11:18; 22:12.

22. Matt 18:34; 22:13; 24:51; Mark 9:48; Luke 12:46; 13:28; 16:23f., 28; Acts 2:24; Rom 2:9; 2 Thess 1:6; Heb 10:29; 2 Pet 2:17; Jude 13.

from a belief that our Lord's teaching about Gehenna has to be wedded to a belief in the immortality of the soul. A fierce fire will destroy any living creature, unless that creature happens to be immortal. If man is made immortal, all our exegesis must change. But is he? From Genesis 3 onwards man looks mortal indeed; we are clearly told that God alone has immortality (1 Tim 6:16); immortality is something that well-doers seek (Rom 2:7); immortality for the believer has been brought to light by the gospel (2 Tim 1:10)—he gains immortality (it would appear) when he gains eternal life and becomes partaker of the divine nature; immortality is finally put on at the last trump (1 Cor 15:53). No, say the traditionalists, God in making man made him immortal, so that he must live on, not only beyond death, but also beyond the second death, forever and ever. The fires of hell will continue to inflict pain on persons they cannot consume.

Now the curious thing is that when asked for biblical proof of the immortality of the soul, the answer usually given is that it is nowhere explicitly taught, but that (as we have already quoted from Shedd) "it is everywhere assumed." Goulburn similarly says that the doctrine of man's immortality "seems to be graven on man's heart almost as indelibly as the doctrine of God's existence."[23] The great Herman Bavinck defends it as a biblical doctrine, but says that it is better demonstrated by reason than by revelation.[24] That life-beyond-death is repeatedly taught in Scripture and is instinctively believed by everyone I readily agree, but of its nature and endurance we know nothing except by revelation. If anything has become pellucidly clear to me over the years it is this: philosophizings about the afterlife are worthless, we must stick to Scripture and Scripture alone. Certainly something as important as the immortality of the soul and the endless pain of the lost cannot be *assumed!*

Passages Relied on for Endlessness of Punishment

What are these "dozens of relevant passages" that we conditionalists attempt to evade by "various exegetical expedients"?[25] They seem in fact to be fourteen in number.

---

23. Goulburn, *Everlasting Punishment*, 68.
24. Quoted in Fudge, *Fire That Consumes* (1982), 53 n. 11.
25. Packer, "Eternal Punishment," 24.

There are seven passages that speak of everlasting punishment (Matt 25:46), everlasting fire (Matt 18:8; 25:41), an eternal sin (Mark 3:29), everlasting destruction (2 Thess 1:9), everlasting judgment (Heb 6:2), and the punishment of everlasting fire (Jude 7). Fudge rightly devotes a chapter early in his book to the meaning of *aionios* and shows (as is well known) that it has two aspects. It has a qualitative sense, indicating "a relationship to the kingdom of God, to the age to come, to the eschatological realities which in Jesus have begun already to manifest themselves in the present age."[26] This aspect is perhaps best translated "eternal." When I analyze my own thoughts, I find that (rightly or wrongly) everlastingness has virtually no place in my concept of eternal life. Everlasting harp-playing or hymn-singing or even contemplation is not attractive. What the heart yearns for is deliverance from sin and the bliss of being with God in heaven, knowing that the inexorable march of death has been abolished forever. *Aionios* also has an aspect of temporal limitlessness which can be rightly translated "everlasting." It is common to argue that since everlasting punishment is set against everlasting life in Matt 25:46, and since the life lasts as long as God, so must the punishment. This was the position of Augustine, of which Hughes writes:

> Augustine insisted ... to say that "life eternal shall be endless, punishment eternal shall come to an end, is the height of absurdity" (*City of God* 21.23).... But, as we have seen, the ultimate contrast is between everlasting *life* and everlasting *death* and this clearly shows that it is not simply synonyms but also antonyms with which we have to reckon. There is no more radical antithesis than that between life and death, for life is the absence of death and death is the absence of life. Confronted with this antithesis, the position of Augustine cannot avoid involvement in the use of contradictory concepts.[27]

To this we might add three further considerations: (1) It would be proper to translate "punishment of the age to come" and "life of the age to come," which would leave open the question of duration. The Matthean

26. Fudge, *Fire That Consumes* (1982), 49. Cf. Carson, *John*, 202: "*zoe aionios* here makes its first appearance in the Fourth Gospel. Properly it means 'life of the age to come,' and therefore resurrection life. But in John's Gospel that life may in some measure be experienced before the end.... The eternal life begun by the new birth is nothing less than the eternal life of the eternal Word."

27. Hughes, *Image*, 403. The rest of his discussion in this chapter is excellent, meriting careful study.

parallel to the *aionios* of Mark 3:29 is indeed "age to come" (Matt 12:32). (2) We have a number of examples of once-for-all acts that have unending consequences: eternal redemption (Heb 9:12), Sodom's punishment of eternal fire (Jude 7). (3) Just as it is wrong to treat God and Satan as equal and opposite, so it is wrong to assume that heaven and hell, eternal life and eternal punishment, are equal and opposite. Both are real, but who is to say that one is as enduring as the other?[28]

There are three passages that speak of unquenchable fire, two in the teaching of the Baptist (Matt 3:12 = Luke 3:17) and one from our Lord who speaks of going away "into Gehenna into the unquenchable fire" (Mark 9:43). The chaff of course is burnt up by the irresistible fire—there is nothing to suggest that the fire goes on burning after it has destroyed the rubbish. The same Markan passage (9:48) gives us the one reference to the undying worm, which (as we have seen) is a quotation from Isa 66:24 that depicts corpses being consumed by maggots, which fits precisely the imagery of the rubbish of Jerusalem.

There is nothing in any of these ten texts that even suggests (let alone requires) an interpretation contrary to the natural interpretation of the great mass of texts telling of death, destruction, perishing, and consumption by fire. Nor has the imagery of outer darkness and grinding of teeth any bearing on the question of endlessness.

This leaves us with one passage in Jude and three passages in the book of Revelation. Jude has spoken of the people saved from Egypt and the destruction of those who did not believe; and of angels kept in eternal chains in the nether gloom awaiting the day of judgment, when they will suffer as Sodom suffered; he then goes on to speak of those who defile the Christian love feasts "for whom the nether gloom of darkness has been reserved forever" (v. 13). These immoral Christians will suffer the same fate as the fallen angels: nether gloom till the day of judgment, then destruction.

In the book of Revelation two passages speak of the smoke of torment rising forever and ever. 14:11 says of those with the mark of the beast, tormented with burning sulfur, "the smoke of their torment goes

28. There is the further question as to whether the life of the age to come should be thought of as in time at all. Post Einsteinians naturally think of space and time as so related that creation would be the creation of space-time, the two being inseparable. This is a philosophical question the Bible does not address, but it does use time-language concerning heaven. However, this may well be because this is the only category in which we can think.

up forever and ever; and they have no rest, day or night, these worshippers of the beast." 19:3 says of the great whore, "the smoke from her goes up forever and ever." Finally, 20:10 speaks of the devil "thrown into the lake of fire and brimstone where the beast and the false prophet were, and they will be tormented day and night forever and ever."

Of these three passages two are concerned with nonhuman or symbolic figures: the devil, the beast, the false prophet, and the great whore, and only one refers to men. But the imagery is the same and they need to be examined together. The mind of John of the Apocalypse is steeped in Holy Scripture and it is to the Old Testament that we must go for enlightenment. After Noah's flood, the second great demonstration of divine judgment is the raining down of burning sulfur on the cities of Sodom and Gomorrah. What is left is total irreversible desolation and dense smoke rising from the land (Gen 19:24–28). This fearful example is recalled by Moses (Deut 29:23), Isaiah (13:19), Jeremiah (50:40), Lamentations (4:6), Amos (4:11), Zephaniah (2:9), Peter (2 Pet 2:6), Jude (7), and Jesus himself (Luke 17:28–32). It seems best to interpret the lake of fire and brimstone, the smoke and the torment of the Apocalypse in the light of this great archetypal example. The concept of second death is one of great finality; the fire consumes utterly, all that is left is smoke, a reminder of God's complete and just triumph over evil.

The third passage (Rev 14:11) is the most difficult passage that the conditionalist has to deal with. I freely confess that I have come to no firm conclusions about the proper interpretation of the book of Revelation. While I would not want to be guilty of undervaluing its symbolism, I am nonetheless chary about basing fundamental doctrine upon its symbolism. Certainly, on the face of it, having no rest day or night with smoke of torment going up forever and ever, sounds like everlasting torment. But, as Stott points out, the torment "experienced 'in the presence of the holy angels and ... the Lamb,' seems to refer to the moment of judgment, not to the eternal state."[29] This is the time of which Jesus gave warning (Luke 12:8) when the unbeliever is denied before the angels of God. Final judgment is an experience of unceasing and inescapable pain, and as at Sodom all that is left is the smoke of their torment going up forever. It is a reminder to all eternity of the marvelous justice and mercy of God. The proof texts of the Westminster Confession add the passage concerning the rich man and Lazarus (Luke 16:19–31), which is indeed

---

29. Edwards and Stott, *Essentials*, 318.

one of great exegetical difficulty.[30] But the scene with Lazarus in hades can hardly represent the final state of the lost seeing hades itself is to be cast into the lake of fire (Rev 20:14), and in any case there is no reference to the everlastingness of that place of torment. So this "avalanche," these "dozens," these fourteen passages whose natural meaning we are attempting to evade reduces to perhaps one, and that is far from insuperable, representing less than a half of one percent of the New Testament passages on the doom of the lost. So both Old and New Testaments taken in their natural sense seem to be almost entirely, if not entirely, on the conditionalist side.

The nub of the whole debate is the question of the natural meaning of the texts, but there are other objections to the conditionalist position which should be briefly looked at.

Other Objections to Conditionalism

1. *Belief in endless torment is said to have been the view of Jesus and the Jews of his day, of the New Testament writers and fathers of the church, of the reformers, and all Bible-believers, and never seriously questioned till the twentieth century.*[31] I myself, resting largely on the authority of Charles

---

30. Useful points are made about this passage in Froom, *Conditionalist Faith*, 1:234–51, Atkinson, *Immortality*, 49f., Fudge, *Fire That Consumes* (1982), 203–8. It is clear that it is not intended as a literal description of the world of the life-to-come. Hades is the sheol of the Old Testament, the immediate destination of all who die, bad and good, normally and rightly translated in NIV as "the grave." Here they sleep the sleep of death awaiting the resurrection. Luke's story is a highly figurative fable-parable, which, if taken literally, does not agree with the Old Testament. From the context its primary aim is seen to be the necessity of living according to the way God has revealed now, there being no room for repentance after death. The motif of roles reversed after death was common in contemporary folk-lore. What is difficult to understand is that Jesus should use such material knowing that it did not correspond to the literal reality. Possibly it is something like modern stories about St. Peter at the pearly gates and how he treats his suppliants. The preacher can use such stories to make his points effectively without danger of his hearers taking him literally.

31. Packer, "Eternal Punishment": "directly from Jesus, and the apostolic teaching" (19); belief in "everlasting conscious distress . . . belonged to the Christian consensus from the first. Fathers, medievals, and moderns up to the time of the Enlightenment were unanimous about it; Protestants, Catholics and Orthodox were divided on many things, but not on this. The consensus existed . . . because Bible-believers of all schools of thought found it inescapable" (22).

Hodge,[32] at one time believed this to be true. But it is quite untrue. It was certainly an almost unchallenged view during the Middle Ages, but it was not so either in first-century Judaism or in the early fathers or at the Reformation and most certainly not in the nineteenth century, which was the heyday of conditionalism among evangelicals.[33] This is all meticulously documented in Froom's great volumes, and Fudge devoted three chapters to the intertestamental period and four to the period from post-apostolic times to the present day—something over a quarter of his book.

2. *Belief in annihilation is said to miss out on the awesome dignity of our having been made to last for eternity.*[34] But how a long period of hopeless, ceaseless pain, "learning" (in Packer's words) "the bitterness of the choice" the unbeliever has made, can be said to enhance the dignity of man, I fail to see. Long-term imprisonment is one of the horrors of our supposedly civilized society and long-term prisoners normally gain a hang-dog look. What would be the effect of such unending "learning"

---

32. Hodge, *Systematic Theology*, 3:870.

33. Packer says "it was never queried with any seriousness (by evangelicals) until the twentieth century" ("Eternal Punishment," 23). B. L. Bateson in a private communication writes: "(that statement) is absolute nonsense. The subject was much discussed by evangelicals in the nineteenth century, not only in Britain, but also in the United States and at least fifty books and pamphlets appeared and many items of correspondence appeared on both sides in Christian magazines. Here are some of the best works: Edward White, Congregationalist, *Life in* Christ, 1878, 3rd ed., 541pp. E. Petavel, D.D., Swiss pastor, *The Problem of Immortality*, 1878, 600pp. Richard Whately, Protestant Archbishop of Dublin, *A View of the Scripture Revelation concerning a Future State*. There were nine editions from 1829 of which the later ones were conditionalist. Canon Henry Constable, *The Duration and Nature of Future Punishment*. Six editions between 1868 and 1886. W. R. Huntingdon, D.D., Rector of All Saints, Worcester, U.S.A., *Conditional Immortality*, 1878, 202pp. J. H. Pettingell, Congregational minister, *The Life Everlasting*, 1882, 761pp. Reginald Courtenay, Bishop in Jamaica, *The Future States*, 1843. H. H. Dobney, Baptist minister, *The Scripture Doctrine of Future Punishment*, 1846. J. M. Denniston, Scottish Presbyterian missionary to Jamaica, *The Perishing Soul*, 2nd ed., 1874. Dr. Cameron Mann, Protestant Episcopal Bishop of N. Dakota, *Five Discourses on Future Punishment*, 1888. Dr. Joseph Parker, Congregational minister of the City Temple, London from 1874 for 28 years proclaimed conditionalism in the 25 volumes of *The People's Bible*." Bateson then goes on to mention R. W. Dale, whose book on the atonement was the most recommended book on the subject in my student days and W. H. A. Hay Aitken, who was a well-known mission preacher and Canon of Norwich Cathedral. More about these men and many others can be found in Froom, *Conditionalist Faith*, vol. 2; see also Fudge, *Fire That Consumes* (1982), 394–402.

34. Packer, "Eternal Punishment," 24.

which yields no reformation? Certainly not awesome dignity. Or is it the believer who has this dignity? Surely he gains his dignity by grace, rather than by creation?

3. *Believing in annihilation the Christian "will miss out on telling the unconverted that their prospects without Christ are as bad as they possibly could be. . . . Conditionalism cannot but impoverish a Christian and limit our usefulness."*[35] It seems to me to be a complete fallacy to think that the worse you paint the picture of hell the more effective your evangelism will be. I felt a growing distaste as I read through Shedd and a worse distaste as I read through Gerstner. This is not the God that I am trying to present to unbelievers. Shedd quotes Jonathan Edwards: "Wrath will be executed in the day of judgment without any merciful circumstances . . . in hell there will be no more exercises of divine patience." Faber likewise says

> O fearful thought! one act of sin
> Within itself contains
> The power of *endless* hate of God
> And *everlasting* pains.[36]

Packer says, "every moment of the unbeliever's . . . bitterness . . . furthers the glory of God."[37] But the God whom I know had compassion on the crowds "because they were harassed and helpless, like sheep without a shepherd" (Matt 9:36). He teaches us to think of him as like a good earthly father who won't give a snake to the son who asks for a fish (Luke 11:11). "He knows how we are formed, he remembers that we are dust" (Ps 103:14). Faber said rightly, there is no place where kindlier judgment is given than in heaven.[38] I think that the ordinary decent person who is groping his way through life, ignorant of God, battered and perplexed by the sinful world around him, is helped best by introducing him or her to the Jesus of the Gospels in his gentleness, truthfulness, and power. As we talk, while not hiding the seriousness of sin, we must see that the love of God gets through. To present God as the one whose "divinely executed retributive process"[39] will bring him into everlasting torment unless he

---

35. Ibid.
36. Edwards, Sermon 12; Faber's Hymn on Predestination; both quoted by Shedd, *Endless Punishment*, 196.
37. Packer, "Eternal Punishment," 24.
38. The hymn: "There is a wideness in God's mercy."
39. Packer, "Eternal Punishment," 24.

believes, is hardly likely to help. To any normal way of thinking (and Jesus has told us when we think about God to think how a human father acts) this depicts God as a terrible sadist, not as a loving Father.

Whether in practice the adoption of conditionalism makes our evangelism less effective, it is impossible to say. Many preachers of endless torment have been greatly used by God, but it is doubtful whether that part of the message affected the conviction. Equally I have no reason to think that the adoption of conditionalism impairs a man's evangelism. Basil Atkinson was always on the look-out to put in a word for Jesus. I was very touched when one day I heard that he, a man whose mind lived in academia and Christian theology, had gone up to a group of lads lounging around in the Cambridge market-place and told them that Jesus loved them. I haven't noticed that John Stott's or Michael Green's conditionalism has made them any less of evangelists. In personal talks I often find myself explaining the self-destructive power of sin and of its ultimate power to destroy absolutely. I explain that that is how God has made the world. Judgment expresses his wrath against the abominable thing he hates.

The Glory of Divine Justice

4. *We are said to miss out on the glory of divine justice, and, in our worship, on praise for God's judgments.*[40] We should have "a passionate gladness" that God's "adorable justice" should be done for the glory of our Creator.[41] I cannot see that this is true. In my book *The Enigma of Evil* I try to grapple with all the moral difficulties of the Bible and many of the difficulties of providence. My main theme is to show how God's judgments reflect the goodness of the God we adore. The one point at which I am so seriously perplexed that I have to devote a whole chapter to it is the subject of hell. My problem is not that God punishes, but that the punishment traditionally ascribed to God seems neither to square with Scripture nor to be just. Many stress that on the cross Jesus suffered the pains we deserve. But, though he suffered physical torture, the utter dereliction of separation from the Father, and death, he did not suffer endless pain. I know that no sinner is competent to judge the heinousness of sin, but I cannot see that endless punishment is either loving or just.

40. Ibid., 21.
41. Ibid.

C. S. Lewis was brought up in Northern Ireland where that extraordinary hell-fire preacher W. P. Nicholson had exerted so great an influence. In one of his early books, *The Pilgrim's Regress*, he tells of his spiritual pilgrimage in allegory. Chapter 1 starts in Puritania, where he dreams of a boy who is frustrated by the prohibitions of his elders. He is told that they are the rules of the Steward, who has been appointed by the Landlord who owns the land. One day his parents take him to see the Steward:

> when John came into the room, there was an old man with a red, round face, who was very kind and full of jokes, so that John quite got over his fears, and they had a good talk about fishing tackle and bicycles. But just when the talk was at its best, the Steward got up and cleared his throat. He then took down a mask from the wall with a long white beard attached to it and suddenly clapped it on his face, so that his appearance was awful. And he said, "Now I am going to talk to you about the Landlord.
>
> "The Landlord owns all the country, and it is *very very* kind of him to allow us to live on it at all—very, very kind." He went on repeating "very kind" in a queer singsong voice so long that John would have laughed, but that now he was beginning to become frightened again. The Steward then took down from a peg a big card with small print all over it, and said, "Here is a list of all the things the Landlord says you must not do. You'd better look at it." So John took the card: but half the rules seemed to forbid things he had never heard of, and the other half forbade things he was doing every day and could not imagine not doing: and the number of rules was so enormous that he felt he could never remember them all.
>
> "I hope," said the Steward, "that you have not already broken any of the rules?" John's heart began to thump, and his eyes bulged more and more, and he was at his wit's end when the Steward took off the mask and looked at John with his real face and said, "Better tell a lie, old chap, better tell a lie. Easiest for all concerned," and popped the mask on his face all in a flash. John gulped and said quickly, "Oh, no, sir." "That is just as well," said the Steward through the mask. "Because, you know, if you did break any of them and the Landlord got to know of it, do you know what he'd do to you?"
>
> "No, sir," said John: and the Steward's eyes seemed to be twinkling dreadfully through the holes of the mask. "He'd take you and shut you up for ever and ever in a black hole full of snakes and scorpions as large as lobsters—for ever and ever.

And besides that; he is such a kind, good man, so very, very kind, that I am sure you would never *want* to displease him." "No, sir," said John. "But, please, sir . . ." "Well," said the Steward. "Please, sir, supposing I did break one, one little one, just by accident, you know. Could nothing stop the snakes and lobsters?" "Ah! . . ." said the Steward; and then he sat down and talked for a long time, but John could not understand a single syllable.

However, it all ended with pointing out that the Landlord was quite extraordinarily kind and good to his tenants, and would certainly torture most of them to death the moment he had the slightest pretext. "And you can't blame him," said the Steward. "For after all it is his land, and it is so very good of him to let us live here at all—people like us, you know." Then the Steward took off the mask and had a nice, sensible chat with John again, and gave him a cake and brought him out to his father and mother. But just as they were going he bent down and whispered in John's ear, "I shouldn't bother about it all too much if I were you." At the same time he slipped the card of the rules into John's hand and told him he could keep it for his own use.[42]

Unending torment speaks to me of sadism, not justice. It is a doctrine I do not know how to preach without negating the loveliness and glory of God. From the days of Tertullian it has frequently been the emphasis of fanatics. It is a doctrine that makes the Inquisition look reasonable. It all seems a flight from reality and common sense.[43]

---

42. Lewis, *Regress*, 29–31. The Roman Catholic Gerard Hughes (*Surprises*, 34), like C. S. Lewis, indulges in a fantasy. God is seen as a relative (Uncle George) who has a fiery torture-chamber in his basement. The child knows that he has got to say that he loves him, when in reality he loathes him. I simply do not know how to avoid this honest and commonsensical impression in preaching everlasting torment.

43. I have a suspicion (though I may well be wrong) that many of the sincere Christians who hold this doctrine don't *quite* believe it themselves. They are tempted to whittle down some of the Bible's teaching. Jesus speaks of the many on the broad road to destruction in contrast to the few on the road to life, but Charles Hodge says, "We have reason to believe . . . that the number of the finally lost in comparison with the whole number of the saved will be very inconsiderable" (Shocking adjective!) (Hodge, *Systematic Theology*, 3:870). Packer, "Eternal Punishment," says that hell is "unimaginably dreadful" (p. 20), "far, far worse than the symbols" (p. 25) and he recommends that we "do not attempt to imagine what it is like." But is it not the preacher's *duty* to exercise his imagination in a disciplined way to bring home to his hearers the dread truth, whatever it is? It seems to me that Fudge is a most unwavering preacher of hell, not tempted to whittle down what the Bible actually says. Its solemn teaching appears to be that our destiny is sealed at death, and this gives great urgency to our preaching. (See Heb 9:27, "It is appointed for men to die once, and after that comes judgment."

Some argue that destruction is no punishment, since many an unbeliever wants to die, so mere death would be a denial of justice. This assumes that the first death is the end and that there is no Day of Judgment and that we are not judged according to our works. This is plainly unscriptural and not the view of any conditionalist that I know. The very wicked who have suffered little in this life will clearly get what they deserve. Perhaps a major part of the punishment will be a realization of the true awfulness of their sin, in its crucifixion of the Son of God and in its effects on others. The horror (particularly of the latter) would be greater for some than for others.

5. *Conditionalists, we are told, "appear to back into" their doctrine "in horrified recoil from the thought of millions in endless distress, rather than move into it because the obvious meaning of Scripture beckons them."*[44] As I have already shown, I was drawn to conditionalism by Scripture rather than by a horrified recoil from the other doctrine. But I do plead guilty to a growing horror at the thought of millions in endless distress, which I find exceedingly difficult to reconcile not only with the goodness of God, but also with the final supremacy of Christ. If there are human beings alive suffering endless punishment, it would seem to mean that they are in endless opposition to God; that is to say, we have a doctrine of endless sinning as well as of suffering. How can this be if Christ is all in all? I plead guilty also to failing to see how God and the saints could be in perfect bliss with human beings hopelessly sinning and suffering.[45] Packer tells us that God's joy will not be marred by the continuance in being of the damned, so that the Christian's joy will not be either.[46]

These speculations don't look to me like the beckonings of Scripture's obvious meaning. I have thought about this subject for more than fifty years and for more than fifty years I have believed the Bible to teach

---

2 Cor 5:10, "We must all appear before the judgment seat of Christ so that each one may receive good or bad, according to what he has done in the body." Rom 2:5–8, "On the day of wrath . . . he will render to every man according to his works: to those who by patience and well doing seek glory and honor and immortality, he will give eternal life; but for those who are factious and do not obey the truth, but obey wickedness, there will be wrath and fury." John 3:36, "He who does not obey the Son shall not see life, but the wrath of God rests upon him." John 8:24, "I told you that you would die in your sins, for you will die in your sins unless you believe that I am he.")

44. Packer, "Eternal Punishment," 24.
45. See also Hughes, *Image*, 406.
46. Packer, "Eternal Punishment," 24.

the ultimate destruction of the lost, but I have hesitated to declare myself in print. I regard with utmost horror the possibility of being wrong. We are all to be judged by our words (Matt 12:37) and teachers with greater strictness (Jas 3:1). *Whichever side you are on, it is a dreadful thing to be on the wrong side in this issue.* Now I feel that the time has come when I must declare my mind honestly. I believe that endless torment is a hideous and unscriptural doctrine that has been a terrible burden on the mind of the church for many centuries and a terrible blot on her presentation of the gospel. I should indeed be happy if, before I die, I could help in sweeping it away. Most of all I should rejoice to see a number of theologians (including some of the very first water) joining Fudge in researching this great topic in all its ramifications.

PART THREE

Biblical Support for Conditionalism

IN HIS FOREWORD TO Robert Peterson's defense of traditionalism, *Hell on Trial*, John MacArthur commends the work for shining "the clear light of Scripture on a truth too often made murky by critics and so-called scholars who find ways to manipulate the text rather than letting the Bible speak plainly for itself."[1] Murray Harris says, "The New Testament contains sufficient warnings of the dire, eternal consequences of rejecting Christ to leave us in no doubt that the early church rejected both universalism and annihilationism."[2] Paul Helm wrote that the arguments for annihilationism are "weak, even interpreted charitably. But they appear immeasurably weaker when the positive teaching of Scripture about life after death is added."[3] In the eyes of J. I. Packer, conditionalists can maintain their view only by dodging a veritable avalanche of biblical data in support of the traditional view of hell.[4] So it is that readers of these authors are given the impression that the Bible is so undeniably clear in its affirmation of eternal conscious punishment in hell that we are left with "no doubt" as to its truthfulness, and conditionalist authors are only "so-called scholars" evading the obvious meaning of a torrent of biblical data, marshalling arguments which, to put it charitably, are "weak"—even immeasurably so.

Others see things differently, and write with seemingly leveler heads. "Exegesis does not move with dogmatic certainty on this difficult and dark question of destiny," writes Dale Moody.[5] "It is a problem that still requires careful consideration," he continues, "free from the hurling of unreasonable epithets, before more certain conclusions can be

---

1. Peterson, *Hell on Trial*, vii.
2. As cited in Dixon, *The Other Side*, 94.
3. Helm, *Last Things*, 119. Helm here refers to forms of annihilationism in which the lost do not rise unto judgment at the resurrection, but his reasoning would apply equally to the evangelical view that the wicked are destroyed *after* rising.
4. Packer, "Eternal Punishment," 12.
5. Moody, *Hope of Glory*, 108.

drawn."[6] Francis Chan humbly admits, "The debate about hell's duration is much more complex than I first assumed. While I lean heavily on the side that says it is everlasting, I am not ready to claim that with complete certainty."[7] "The annihilation of the damned," writes Fred Thompson, "is not expressly ruled out as the eventual reward for their wickedness."[8] Perhaps, then, Scripture does not as clearly rule out conditionalism as its most outspoken critics seem to think.

If the testimony of Scripture is as black and white as those critics contend, why are other well-respected exegetes less certain? Why do still other conservative evangelicals embrace conditionalism, despite what is alleged to be its utter dearth of biblical support? Edward Fudge reports that some of the most outspoken critics of conditionalism blame compromise, sentimentalism, pluralism, and "the exaltation of human reason."[9]

> But what if they all are mistaken, unknowingly distracted from the real answer by centuries of tradition, human assumptions, and denominational creeds? What if the muting of hell is due neither to emotional weakness nor loss of gospel commitment?
>
> What if the biblical foundations thought to support unending conscious torment are less secure than has been widely supposed? . . . I have spoken with evangelical university and seminary professors, and have heard from still others, who have carefully restudied all that the Bible says about the destiny of the wicked and have felt the necessity to reorder their understanding.[10]

The influential defenses of conditionalism in part 2 ought to convince the honest reader that conditionalism is a plausible interpretation of Scripture, one borne from a firm commitment to its authority, reliability, and perspicuity. In the chapters that follow, five evangelical scholars of unquestionable caliber present thorough cases for conditionalism from both Old and New Testaments, buttressed by support from ancient Jewish and Christian writers, carefully examining what are thought by many traditionalists to be the biblical texts which most clearly teach eternal conscious punishment.

6. Ibid., 112.
7. Chan and Sprinkle, *Erasing Hell*, 86.
8. Thompson, *Heaven and Hell*, 361.
9. Fudge, *Fire That Consumes* (2011), 3.
10. Ibid.

8

The Doom of the Lost

BASIL F. C. ATKINSON

Basil Atkinson (1895–1971) earned his PhD from Magdalene College, Cambridge and served as the under-librarian of the University of Cambridge from 1925 to 1960. Throughout his career he published widely in theology and remained an active leader in the Cambridge Inter-Collegiate Christian Union; he also played a decisive role in the formation of Inter-Varsity Fellowship of Evangelical Unions.

Atkinson was well known as an evangelical bulwark at Cambridge—and he was also perhaps the most influential conditionalist of his generation. Both Harold Guillebaud and John Wenham confess to Atkinson's role in their coming to take this view. In Life and Immortality, *his final work, Atkinson lays out his exegetical case against the natural immortality of the soul, arguing for conditional immortality, a future bodily resurrection, and the ultimate annihilation of the lost on judgment day.*

Weeping and Gnashing of Teeth

FOUR TIMES IN THE Gospel of Matthew we are told that on the day of judgment there will be "weeping and gnashing of teeth" (Matt 8:12; 22:13; 24:51; 25:30). The first, second, and fourth of these passages speak of "the outer darkness" and continue immediately, "*there* (Greek *ekei*) will be weeping and gnashing of teeth." Those who believe in the eternal conscious existence of the lost believe that this weeping will be heard forever in the outer darkness, which they rightly identify with hell. If however we look at the third passage (Matt 24:51), we shall see that no place is mentioned. "There" means "on that occasion." It is at the throne of judgment, as the real nature of the wicked is revealed to them in all its hideousness, in despair and misery because of what they have lost and missed, as they hear the sentence, perhaps through the temporary suffering, which, as we shall see, precedes their destruction, that the weeping and gnashing of teeth are heard.

Both are based on the Old Testament. We find the weeping in Zeph 1:14 and the gnashing of teeth in Ps 112:10. The prophet like the evangelist uses the word "there" and confirms its reference to the day of judgment: "The great day of the Lord is near, it is near, and hasteth greatly, even the voice of the day of the Lord: the mighty man shall cry *there* bitterly." The psalmist confirms that the judgment upon the wicked is extinction: "The wicked shall see it, and be grieved; he shall gnash with his teeth, and melt away; the desire of the wicked shall perish."

Everlasting Punishment

Four times in the New Testament the final state of the wicked is referred to as punishment. First comes the famous phrase at the conclusion of the great judgment scene of the sheep and goats in Matt 25:46: "And these shall go away into everlasting punishment, but the righteous into life eternal." Many have relied on this phrase to support the idea of everlasting conscious suffering of the wicked, reading it as if it said, "everlasting punishing." This is not the meaning of the word. When the adjective *aionios* meaning "everlasting" is used in Greek with nouns of *action* it has reference to the *result* of the action, not the process. Thus the phrase "everlasting punishment" is comparable to "everlasting redemption" and "everlasting salvation," both Scriptural phrases. No one supposes that we are being redeemed or being saved forever. We were redeemed and saved once and for all by Christ with eternal results. In the same way the lost will not be passing through a process of punishment forever but will be punished once and for all with eternal results. On the other hand, the noun "life" is not a noun of action, but a noun expressing a state. Thus the life itself is eternal.

It is this phrase "eternal life" that is here set in contrast to "everlasting punishment." This should warn us that everlasting punishment is likely to mean everlasting death. This is exactly what we find in 2 Thess 1:9, as we shall see. We cannot object that death is not punishment, having been accustomed to use the phrase "capital punishment" all our lives.

The word here translated "punishment" is *kolasis*. A glance at the word in Moulton and Milligan's *Vocabulary* will show how it was used at the time for the pruning or cutting out of dead wood. If that is its meaning here, it reflects Moses' frequent phrase, "shall be cut off from his people." Thus the wicked will be finally cut off from mankind.

The same root occurs again in our second occurrence in 2 Pet 2:9: "the Lord knoweth how . . . to reserve the unjust unto the day of judgment to be punished," or possibly, as we have seen, "to be cut off." The word here is the participle *kolazomenous*. Though the participle is in a present form, our translators were clearly right to render it as a future.

Our third passage is 2 Thess 1:9: "who shall be punished with everlasting destruction from the presence of the Lord and from the glory of his might, when he shall come." This makes it clear that the everlasting punishment of Matt 25:46 is everlasting destruction, and this destruction must be annihilation or personal extinction, since it is destruction from the presence of the Lord. All will agree that the presence of the Lord is everywhere. To be destroyed from the presence of the Lord can therefore only mean to be nowhere. This seems the more probable meaning of the passage, but let us not press it, as it is possible, though we feel less likely, to interpret the presence of the Lord here as the time of his second coming when the everlasting destruction, as we all undoubtedly agree, will take place. The words used here for "shall be punished" are *dikeen tisousin*. They carry the idea of retribution.

Our fourth and last passage is Heb 10:29. The word for "punishment" is *timōria*. It also carries the idea of retribution. The apostle is contrasting the law with the gospel. He says in verse 28 that anyone who despised Moses' law died without mercy and goes on, "Of how much sorer punishment, suppose ye, shall he be thought worthy, who hath trodden under foot the Son of God?" This passage makes clear that death apart from suffering is a punishment. Eternal destruction is a "sorer" punishment. Therefore death (usually by judicial stoning) was a sore one. Now eternal destruction, preceded, as we shall find, by retributive suffering, is indeed much sorer than temporal death. Those put to death under the law will rise again at the end of the world; to judgment it is true, but who knows whether some may not have been, or become at the approach of death, believers at heart, who will therefore rise to eternal life? The terrors and despair of the lost at the throne of judgment, as we find them portrayed in the Bible, cannot be exaggerated.

The Lost in Prison

This seems to be the proper place to introduce the saying of the Lord in the sermon on the mount to be found in Matt 5:25–26: "Agree with thine adversary quickly, whiles thou art in the way with him; lest at any time the adversary deliver thee to the judge, and the judge deliver thee to the officer, and thou be cast into prison. Verily I say unto thee, Thou shalt by no means come out thence, till thou hast paid the uttermost farthing." The parallel passage in Luke 12:58–59 says the same thing in rather different language. It may well have been this passage on which the late Sir Robert Anderson based his description of hell in his book "Human Destiny" as a large prison in which the lost lived forever under restraint, though he rather curiously conceived of them as accepting their destiny. As he was an efficient and important official of police, we can easily understand this idea appealing to him. He evidently shrank from the conception of actual fire and literal torments. Many have felt that this passage justifies the view of the everlasting conscious existence of the lost. But is not the passage a little picture or parable of the wickedness and consequences of lack of forgiveness? Is not the adversary God himself? Then who is the judge and who is the officer? They simply represent figures in the parable. And if so, the prison does the same. In any case can we pit these two isolated passages against what we have seen to be the consistent testimony of the rest of Scripture? What we indeed learn from these sayings is that once condemned the sinner can never hope for restoration. Not only can he never pay the last farthing, but he cannot even pay the first.

Suffering of the Lost

Though Scripture teaches, as we have sought to show, the extinction of the unrepentant sinners in eternal destruction, it does not lead us to think of an instantaneous snuffing out of their lives without exaction of full and complete retribution for wrong done to others by hateful and wicked lives and years of unbroken sin against God. We will select three passages that foresee this suffering.

(a) Obad 15: "the day of the Lord is near upon all the heathen; as thou hast done, it shall be done unto thee: thy reward shall return upon thine own head." Here we find the law of retaliation in force and on reflection we may feel that this is what we should expect.

(b) Rom 2:9: "tribulation and anguish, upon every soul of man that doeth evil."

(c) Luke 12:47–48: here we find that future suffering will vary in degree according to responsibility. Some have been led to believe from the use of the word "servant'" that this passage concerns believers. Apart from the impossibility of such an overthrow of the doctrines of grace the previous verse (46) tells us that it concerns "unbelievers."

We thus learn that included in future punishment is a period of suffering that varies in degree and precedes the fulfilment of the punishment in everlasting destruction. The length of this period of suffering, light or heavy as it may be, is not stated or mentioned in Scripture. Some with the idea of eternal suffering at the back of their minds put it at centuries or even millennia. There are no grounds for doing so.

The Suffering and Death of Christ

It has sometimes been forgotten that we have in history at the center of our faith an open example and illustration of the punishment of sin. The Lord Jesus Christ bore our sins in his own body on the tree (1 Pet 2:24). The use of the phrase "bear his (their) iniquity" several times in the books of Moses proves that to bear our sins means to bear the punishment of them and all Bible-believers will agree that this was actually the case. Now at the time of his passion the Lord Jesus underwent a period of increasing excruciating agony culminating in death. The suffering lasted some hours. There is no reason why we should not take this as the model and example of the final punishment of sin. We are not likely to go far wrong if we conclude that his suffering was the most extreme that will be inflicted on the most defiant and responsible sinner (Judas Iscariot) and comprised therefore in itself, and covered, all lower degrees of desert.

When the Lord Jesus at last died, full satisfaction was made for the sins of the whole world (1 John 2:2), God's holy law was vindicated and all sins potentially or actually atoned for. If he bore the punishment of our sins, that punishment cannot under any circumstances be eternal conscious suffering or misery, for he never suffered this and it is impossible that he could have. Thus the facts of the suffering and death of Christ Jesus prove conclusively that the punishment of sin is death in its natural sense of the deprivation of life. By reason of his deity and the sinlessness of his human nature the Lord could not be held by death. He was in the grave only so long as to prove to the world that he was actually dead and then, as we know and believe, rose to live forever. The unrepentant and unbelieving sinner on the other hand has no escape from death but remains beneath its power eternally.

The Consumption of the Wicked

We will now consider the usage as it bears on our subject of a few Hebrew words with the general meaning of "consume" before bringing our study to an end by an examination of the words used in passages that speak of the destruction of the wicked by the agency of fire.

(1) *Āchal* is the ordinary word meaning "to eat." Its significance for our purpose is that it was often used to express the action of fire. Fire, as we know, consumes, and there is nothing in the Bible to tell us that the eternal fire does not do the same. One of the earliest occurrences of *āchal* with fire is in Num 21:28. (2) *Kālāh* means "to finish." We find it in Isa 1:28: "And the destruction of the transgressors and of the sinners shall be together, and they that forsake the Lord shall be consumed." Again we find it in Ps 59:13: "Consume them in wrath, consume them, that they may not be; and let them know (i.e., let men know) that God ruleth in Jacob unto the ends of the earth." (3) *Suph* means "to bring to an end." It is used of the wicked on the day of judgment in Isa 66:17. It appears again in Zeph 1:2–3 and Ps 79:13. (4) The verb *dāch* means to be extinct. It is used of the end of the wicked probably in Isa 43:17, Ps 118:12 and Job 6:17; and certainly in Prov 13:9; 20:20; 24:20; Job 18:5–6 and Job 21:17.

Before leaving these words with the underlying notion of "consume" it will be interesting to remind ourselves that the common word *āchal* occurs in Exod 3:2 in the account of Moses at the bush, where we are told that the bush burned with fire but was not consumed. This is exactly what many people think will be the case of the lost in hell. We have however never heard of any argument for this doctrine based upon this incident, and with good reason, for not only does the Bible speak consistently again and again of those cast into hell being destroyed and consumed there, but the emphasis that it places upon the supernatural strangeness of the incident of the burning bush suggests that if the Holy Spirit desired us to believe that the same thing is to happen in hell he would have been at pains to make it perfectly clear to us instead of using expressions that would lead us to think that the action of hell fire is identical with the action of fire as we ordinarily know it.

Hell Fire

We now reach our final study, which is an examination of the agency by which the destruction of the wicked will be affected. This is said consistently throughout Scripture to be fire. We shall concentrate on the New Testament, but some preliminary remarks on the Old Testament background must be made.

The ordinary Hebrew word meaning fire is *ēsh*. It occurs about three hundred and fifty times. A glance through a concordance will satisfy us that it bears the same elementary meaning as our own word "fire." It is occasionally used in a figurative sense for something very hot or to describe the wrath of God, as in Lev 13:24; Hab 2:13; Ps 39:3 or Job 31:12. It is used of God himself (Deut 4:24). It is used of the fire that accompanies the presence of God (Deut 5:23), and in this connection it is important to turn to Isa 33:14, where the prophet asks the question, "Who among us shall dwell with everlasting burnings?" Some would reply, "The lost will do so for ever." But that is a wrong answer. The next verse answers the question, "He that walketh righteously, and speaketh uprightly." The sinners and hypocrites (v. 14) are afraid that they cannot do so, and rightly. When they touch the devouring fire, they will be devoured by it. Only the righteous can dwell forever unscathed in the burning fire of God's presence. Hebrew *ēsh* is used in connection with the destruction of the wicked, as in Ps 21:9: "Thou shalt make them as a fiery oven in the time of thine anger: the Lord shall swallow them up in his wrath, and the fire shall devour them."

PART THREE—BIBLICAL SUPPORT FOR CONDITIONALISM

There are two significant occurrences of the verb *lāhat*, which means "to set on fire," "to burn up." The first of these is of great importance. It is found in Mal 4:1: "For, behold, the day cometh, that shall burn as an oven; and all the proud, yea, and all that do wickedly, shall be stubble: and the day that cometh shall burn them up, saith the Lord of hosts, that it shall leave them neither root nor branch." Is not this perfectly plain? How can we read into these words "burn up," "leave neither root nor branch," the conception of everlasting life in conscious misery? Verse 3 confirms the meaning by telling us the result: "Ye shall tread down the wicked, for they shall be ashes under the soles of your feet in the day that I shall do this, saith the Lord of hosts."

The verb *lāhat* is used figuratively in Ps 57:4, though it has nothing in that passage to do with our subject. In Ps 97:3 it speaks again of the destruction of the wicked: "A fire goeth before him, and burneth up his enemies round about."

Greek *Pyr* in the New Testament

The ordinary Greek word for "fire" is *pyr*, corresponding in meaning to Hebrew *ēsh*, Latin *ignis*, and our own *fire*. The Greek and English both stem from a root *pur*, which must have been in use four thousand years ago with the same elemental meaning. The Greek word occurs between forty-seven and fifty-one times in the New Testament, the difference of four being due to possible omissions from our text by what are generally held to be better texts in Mark 9:44–47.

The word occurs twenty times without reference to the second death. The references are as follows: Matt 17:15; Mark 9:22, 49; Luke 9:54; 12:49; Acts 7:30; 28:5; Jas 3:5; 2 Pet 3:7; Rom 12:20; 1 Cor 3:13, 15; Heb 12:29; Rev 8:7; 9:18; 17:16; 18:8; 20:9. More than half of these refer to fire as we know and recognize it, but there are some passages among them at which we should glance. In Mark 9:49 we have fire used as the symbol of fiery trial and persecution with which every disciple must be salted or made acceptable as a living sacrifice to God. In Luke 12:49 fire is used as the symbol of separation between the members of families (vv. 51–53), which was to result by the gospel from the Lord's first coming. In Luke 17:29 we are told of the rain of fire and brimstone that destroyed all the people of Sodom, described in Jude 7, as we shall see, as everlasting fire and symbolic of the eternal fire that will destroy the wicked. The martyr Stephen in his inspired speech refers to the angel who appeared to Moses in the burning bush (Acts 7:30). The fire here is the supernatural fire with which the bush burnt without being consumed, possibly the fire of the presence of God. In 2 Pet 3:7 the apostle speaks of the fire that will destroy the heavens and earth on the day of judgment. We may possibly identify this with the fire of hell or lake of fire. In Rom 12:20 the apostle quoting Prov 25:21–22 uses fire as a symbol of feelings of shame, conviction, and repentance. In 1 Cor 3:13, 15 the fire is symbolic either of the testing fire of judgment at the last day or of earthly tests and trials. Hebrews 12:29 quoted from Deut 4:24 speaks of God himself as fire.

It remains to examine carefully the occurrences of the word *pyr* which relate to the destruction of the wicked. We will divide these into three: (1) those that speak of fire, or unquenchable fire, (2) those that speak of the fire of hell, to which we will add references to hell (Greek *gēnna*) without mentioning fire, eleven in number, and (3) those that speak of the lake of fire.

Unquenchable Fire

(a) Matt 3.10: "every tree which bringeth not forth good fruit, is hewn down, and cast into the fire." What do we naturally expect to happen to a tree that is thrown into the fire? And why should we not expect it in this case also?

(b) Matt 3:12: "he will burn up the chaff with unquenchable fire." The meaning of "burn up" is surely unmistakable. Can it by any trick of imagination be made to mean "preserve alive in everlasting misery"? But many have felt that *unquenchable* fire expresses a special sort of fire that must go on burning forever. Now even if it actually did so, it would not follow that the persons or things cast into it would exist forever without being burned up. But there is no reason to suppose that it does. The idea of unquenchable fire is taken like so much else in the New Testament from the Scriptures of the Old. In Jer 17:27 we read that the Lord will kindle a fire in the gates of Jerusalem that will devour her palaces and *shall not be quenched*. The king of Babylon was the instrument through whom God fulfilled this threat and the palaces were devoured. But is the fire burning now? Of course not. No one in the world could quench it *till it had fulfilled the purpose for which it was kindled*, and then in the course of nature it went out. In Jer 7:20 the Lord says the same thing about his wrath against Jerusalem. Unquenchable fire in Scripture is thus fire that cannot be put out until it has totally devoured what it was kindled to burn up. Such will be the fire that will burn up the wicked.

(c) Matt 7:19: "Every tree that bringeth not forth good fruit is hewn down and cast into the fire." The Lord Jesus here repeats the solemn words of John the Baptist. See (a) above.

(d) Matt 13:40: "As therefore the tares are gathered and burned in the fire; so shall it be in the end of this world." Again can we force "burned" into meaning "exist forever"?

(e) Matt 13:41–42: "they shall gather out of his kingdom all things that offend, and them which do iniquity and shall cast them into a furnace of fire." There is nothing to lead us to expect that those cast into the furnace will be preserved in it as Shadrach, Meshach and Abednego were.

(f) Matt 13:49–50: "the angels shall ... sever the wicked from among the just; and shall cast them into the furnace of fire."

(g) Matt 18:8: "It is better for thee to enter into life halt or maimed, rather than having two hands or two feet to be cast into everlasting fire." This is the first time in the New Testament that we meet with the expression "everlasting fire," which we have discussed above. The expression has been thought to infer the everlasting life of the wicked in misery, just as has the expression "unquenchable fire." But the Bible itself explains its meaning. The apostle Jude tells us (Jude 7) that the fire that destroyed Sodom and Gomorrah was eternal fire (Greek *aionios*, "everlasting," "eternal"). It soon burnt itself out, but it was everlasting in accomplishing a destruction from which the cities have never recovered nor ever will. It was everlasting in its *results*. Such will be the fire that destroys the wicked. The fire by the way of Jude 7 cannot be a fire in which the *inhabitants* of the guilty cities are burning today in another world, because they would not in such a case be "set forth for an example." It must have been the historical fire.

(h) Matt 25:41: "Then shall he say also unto them on the left hand, Depart from me ye cursed, into everlasting fire, prepared for the devil and his angels." Here we have the same everlasting fire and we learn it is prepared for the devil and his angels. Implied in the expression "everlasting fire," as we saw above, is the everlasting destruction of the devil and his angels and of wicked men, agreeable to 2 Thess 1:9. The same thing is stated in Isa 30:33.

(i) Mark 9:44: "where their worm dieth not and the fire is not quenched." This is a description of hell (Greek *gēnna*), which is mentioned at the conclusion of the preceding verse. We will leave the whole clause till we deal shortly with the word *gēnna* and note meanwhile the statement that the fire is not quenched. For this see (b) above.

(j) Mark 9:46: This is identical with (i).

(k) Mark 9:48. This is identical with (i) and (j).

(l) Luke 3:9: see (a) above.

(m) Luke 3:17: see (b) above.

(n) John 15:6: "If a man abide not in me, he is cast forth as a branch, and is withered; and men gather them, and cast them into the fire, and they are burned." We notice that such branches are *burned*. The text does not say, "into the fire, where they are preserved forever in suffering."

(o) Jas 5:3: "the rust of them shall be a witness against you, and shall eat your flesh as it were fire." This passage is clearly expressed in figurative language, but is best thought of as speaking of the fire of hell.

(p) Jude 7: "Sodom and Gomorrah ... are set forth for an example, suffering the vengeance of eternal fire." This is the fire that destroyed Sodom and Gomorrah but we include it here because it explains and illustrates the meaning of eternal (everlasting *aionios*) fire. See (g) above.

(q) Jude 23: "others save with fear, pulling them out of the fire." When we save sinners by the agency of the gospel, we save them from the fire of hell.

(r) 2 Thess 1:7–8: "When the Lord Jesus shall be revealed from heaven with his mighty angels, in flames of fire." This seems certainly to be the fire that accompanies the presence of God. It may be identical with the fire of hell.

(s) Heb 10:27: "a certain fearful looking for of judgment and fiery indignation (Greek *pyros zeelos*, "indignation of fire"), which shall devour the adversaries." Here again the apostle tells us that the adversaries of God will be *devoured* by the fire. But the scheme of natural immortality says that they never will.

(t) Rev 14:9–11: "If any man worship the beast and his image, and receive his mark in his forehead, or in his hand, the same shall drink of the wine of the wrath of God, which is poured out without mixture into the cup of his indignation; and he shall be tormented with fire and brimstone in the presence of the holy angels, and in the presence of the Lamb; and the smoke of their torment ascended up for ever and ever: and they have no rest day nor night, who worship the beast and his image, and whosoever receiveth the mark of his name." We notice here (1) from the context that this is a Reformation message, that is, one of the principles arising from the Reformation and proclaimed by the Reformers; (2) that it is addressed to a certain class of persons. Worship of the beast is the sin of popery. Those who are blinded by popery are those who have refused to receive the love of the truth that they might be saved and to whom God sends strong delusion that they should believe the lie (2 Thess 2:10–11); (3) their torment in fire and brimstone takes place in the presence of the holy angels and in the presence of the Lamb. This is a powerful reason—the first of two—why this cannot be everlasting suffering in hell. Hell is in "outer darkness" (Matt 8:12). It is everlasting destruction *from the presence* of the Lord, not torment in his presence (2 Thess 1:9). This torment may have taken place, or at least been begun, in the history of the world and been manifested in the last plagues (near the climax of which we appear to be living today). See for instance Rev 16:8. However that may be, we may well suppose it to be part of the "tribulation and anguish" (Rom 2:9) that sinners will suffer on the day of judgment. We notice (4) that the smoke of the torment goes up forever and ever. This is the second good reason why the torment here cannot be eternal suffering in hell. The ascent of the smoke shows that the stroke of judgment is over (Gen 19:24, 25, 28; Isa 34:9–10). The torment is the suffering that like that of the Lord Jesus had its climax in death. The ascent of the smoke *forever and ever* proves the judgment to be eternal destruction. In Rev 19:3 we find the smoke of the Babylonish whore going up forever and ever, for the same reason and with the same meaning. There can scarcely be anyone who believes that a great city or ecclesiastical system will exist in conscious torment forever and ever. This is not the meaning of the ascent of the smoke, but something quite different. The torment is eternal torment in the sense of everlasting punishment. We notice that these sinners have no rest day nor night while their suffering lasts nor any restoration from the blackness of darkness forever. This punitive destruction holds no rest for them such as the godly are pictured as having in their graves while they await their glorious resurrection (Rev 14:13; Job 3:17).

Gehenna

In the New Testament alone we find the word *gēnna*, which if it ought to be translated at all is rightly and consistently translated "hell." It occurs eleven times and is identical with the everlasting and unquenchable fire we have just examined. The word is taken from the name of the valley of Hinnom outside Jerusalem where fires were continually kept burning to dispose of the rubbish of the city, including unburied corpses. Hinnom was an abominable place. The idolatrous kings of Judah set up in a high place called Tophet a shrine to the heathen god Moloch at which they burned their children alive in honor of the god, while drums beat loud to drown the screams of the children. The prophet Jeremiah denounced this abominable practice and foretold that Tophet would be destroyed and defiled (see 2 Kgs 23:10; Jer 7:31–32; 19:2, 6; 32:35; 2 Chr 28:3; 33:6).

All references to *gēnna* except the last come from the lips of the Lord Jesus himself. They are:

(1) Matt 5:22: "whosoever shall say, Thou fool, shall be in danger of hell fire." Exact interpretation of this verse is difficult, but it is clear that the Lord is saying that a murderous, angry, or unforgiving spirit makes a man liable to final destruction in hell.

(2) Matt 5:29: here the Lord tells men to separate themselves at all costs from sins of lust so as to avoid being cast into hell.

(3) Matt 5:30: this is identical in meaning with the last.

(4) Matt 10:28: "but rather fear him which is able to destroy both soul and body in hell." Hell means final destruction, not everlasting life in misery.

(5) Matt 18:9: here we have the expression "hell fire" (Greek *teen gēnnan tou pyros*). The verse says the same thing as Matt 5:29 (2 above).

(6) Matt 23:15: "when he is made, ye make him twofold more the child of hell than yourselves." The reference is to a proselyte made by the Pharisees; a child of hell means one destined to go there.

(7) Matt 23:33: "Ye serpents, ye generation of vipers! How can ye escape the damnation of hell?" The Lord is addressing the scribes and Pharisees. To escape the damnation of hell means to escape being condemned to hell. The obstinate self-righteousness of the Pharisees kept them from repenting and believing in Jesus.

(8) Mark 9:43–44: here we find hell identified with the unquenchable fire with the added description, "where their worm dieth not and the

fire is not quenched." Verse 43 is identical in meaning with Matt 5:30. We are aware of course that some texts omit verses 44 and 46 altogether, but the threefold warning of verses 44, 46, and 48 is so full of point and seems to be so much stronger in the context from a purely literary point of view that we will assume for our purpose here that the right readings lie behind our A.V. text. It has often been supposed that the words of verses 44, 46, and 48 describe an everlasting life of suffering and misery in hell. Even if they described a life of conscious suffering there, which we deny, nothing is said about its eternity. But it is often forgotten that the words are a quotation from Isa 66:24. There in the last verse of the great prophet's book in a context where he is describing the world to come, we read, "And they [that is, the redeemed] shall go forth, and look upon the carcases of the men that have transgressed against me; for their worm shall not die, neither shall their fire be quenched; and they shall be an abhorring unto all flesh." We may regard the going forth and looking as taking place on or immediately after the day of judgment, perhaps continually during its course after the condemnation of the wicked. The unique use of the word "carcases" in this connection need not create difficulty. It is not likely to be intended as a literal description of the lost at the time of their being cast into hell. Our friends who believe in natural immortality and everlasting life in hell are probably less likely than we are to regard it as literal and will agree with us that it is not. Surely the whole verse (Isa 66:24) is expressed in terms describing the valley of Hinnom, of which it is a perfect picture. Fires were continually burning there to consume the rubbish of the city and all defilement. Carcasses were consumed by the flames, or, till they were reached by the flames, lay there devoured by worms. In the fire we see eternal destruction and in the worm the suffering that precedes it. Thus the quotation by the evangelist of the prophet's description of Hinom and the taking over in the New Testament of the name of Hinnom to express and describe hell gives us a clear picture of hell as the bonfire and rubbish heap of creation, where everything that defiles (Rev 21:27), including of course wicked men, is burned up and utterly destroyed out of existence in the flames. Can we extract any other meaning from the evangelist's words after finding that they are a direct quotation from the prophet without breaking the unity of the Old and New Testaments?

(9) Mark 9:45–46: see no. 8.
(10) Mark 9:47–48: see no. 8.

(11) Jas 3:6: "the tongue is a fire . . . and it is set on fire of hell." This is the only reference to hell outside the Gospels of Matthew and Mark. Like much else in the epistle of James it is difficult. Some have thought that hell here means the devil, but there seems no biblical warrant for this. Obviously the fire here is in no sense literal. If we are inclined to think that the fire of hell is burning today in another world, and that somehow the tongue is in touch with it, we abandon at once the actuality of the fire of hell. It could only be symbolic. But fire as the agent of destruction of sinners is spoken of so often in Scripture that we do not get the impression that it is a symbol, and a vague symbol at that. Perhaps the most proper way of regarding the apostle's statement in this verse is to think of it as indicating a very fierce and dangerous fire, so fierce that it can only be compared to the fire of hell.

The Lake of Fire

There remain five passages in the closing chapters of the Apocalypse in which the unquenchable and everlasting fire of hell is described as the lake of fire. These are:

(a) Rev 19:20. Here we read that at the great battle of the last day the beast and the false prophet were taken and cast alive both of them into the lake of fire that burns with brimstone. Now the beast is the great Roman empire and the papacy as its last manifestation and the false prophet is the ecclesiastical Roman hierarchy. It will be seen at once that great political and ecclesiastical systems can neither suffer torments nor remain alive and conscious in the lake of fire. It is quite clear that only their utter extermination can result. That they are cast in alive means that they were cut off in the height of their activities. We have here a clear proof that the lake of fire is the agency of utter destruction. The statement here agrees with that of Dan 7:2.

(b) Rev 20:10: "And the devil that deceived them was cast into the lake of fire and brimstone, where the beast and the false prophet are, and shall be tormented day and night for ever." Quite strictly speaking this verse might be said to be outside our scope because it is not concerned with human beings. At the same time it is an important verse and clearly bears upon our argument. We have already found the annihilation of the devil foretold in Ezekiel 28:19 and here we see the fulfilment. This lake of fire is the everlasting fire prepared for his destruction (Matt 25:41).

The dependent sentence speaks of the beast and the false prophet (Rev 19:20). Some have concluded from the word "are" that the beast and the false prophet will be still existing in the lake of fire when the devil is cast into it, which is after an interval of a thousand years (Rev 20:2, 3, 7), but careful readers will note that the word "are" is in italics, which shows that it does not occur in the original Greek. The preceding main clause demands that the words "had been cast" (not "are") should be supplied. The beast and the false prophet had ceased to exist a thousand years previously. Our A.V. text continues "and shall be tormented." This conceals the fact that the Greek verb *basanistheesontai* is plural and refers to all three: devil, beast, and false prophet. Many have used this verse and Rev 14:10 to sustain the view of eternal conscious misery for the wicked in hell. This verse is clearly connected with Rev 14:10, which gives us the clue to its interpretation. There we read of the smoke of the torment going up forever and ever and we saw from the Old Testament passages on which the words are based that the torment ends in everlasting destruction (see above). The meaning here must clearly be the same, or we should have an intolerable inconsistency. Here it is expressed by the verb instead of the noun. To be tormented forever and ever means the same thing as the smoke going up forever and ever, that the torment culminates in everlasting destruction. "Torment" here is used in the same sense as "everlasting punishment," that is, torment with everlasting results. This could apply to the devil. The expression "tormented for ever and ever" can be more easily understood by comparing it with the expression "saved for ever and ever," which can be said of the godly both in Greek and English. This does not mean that they are being saved forever, but that they are once saved with an eternal result. Thus to be tormented forever means to be tormented with the result of everlasting destruction.

(c) Rev 20:14: here we find death and the grave cast into the lake of fire. This can mean nothing but their utter annihilation and proves to us the function of the lake of fire.

(d) Rev 20:15: here we find all the wicked cast into the lake of fire. The previous verse has shown us conclusively that this means their complete extinction.

(e) Rev 21:8: sinners have their part in the lake of fire, which is here and in verse 14 (c above) defined and explained as the second death. The word "death" has in Scripture its natural meaning of the extinction of life and we have seen that there is every reason to conclude that when used in this verse the word has its natural meaning.

Thus we have seen that the devil, the wicked oppressive systems, death and the grave, and all wicked men will on the great day be totally destroyed out of God's creation. Indeed all evil will be destroyed. This adds point and meaning to the apostle's great statement in 1 Cor 15:28. Universalists have looked to this text (for want of a more definite passage), but it will not sustain their theory. However, as long as we hold that the wicked live forever in conscious misery in hell and especially if we hold what seems to be the most terrible aspect of that view, that they continue forever to sin in hell, this word of the apostle's raises grave difficulties. While sinners live and continue to sin, how can God be all in all? But when we come to realize the teaching of the Bible that the devil, sin, death, wicked men, and all suffering will be exterminated forever out of God's creation in the lake of fire, the apostle's statement lights up with golden glory and it is easy to see that on that great day and for the eternity that follows it God will be all in all.

9

New Testament Teaching on Hell

E. EARLE ELLIS

Following two years of service in the U.S. Army, Edward Earle Ellis (1926–2010) spent his next several years preparing for a career in law. But in a crisis moment in his life, spurred by the words to the hymn by Isaac Watts, "When I Survey the Wondrous Cross," Ellis' passion for law was replaced with a passion for knowing God and teaching his Word. He earned his MA and BD degrees in 1953 from Wheaton College Graduate School, and received his PhD in 1955 from the University of Edinburgh. He taught at The Southern Baptist Theological Seminary, Bethel Theological Seminary, New Brunswick Theological Seminary, and finally, Southwestern Baptist Theological Seminary, where he served as Research Professor of Theology, and Scholar in Residence, until his death in 2010. Highly awarded and esteemed, colleague Gerald Hawthorne called Ellis "unquestionably conservative and evangelical," able to "correct the mistaken in whatever traditional views have long been held by evangelicals," yet with a "clear vision of what one must affirm in order to be called an 'evangelical.'" [1]

The traditional view of hell as eternal conscious torment was not, in the mind of Ellis, one such evangelical essential. At their 1997 triennial conference, the Tyndale Fellowship for Biblical and Theological Research featured presentations addressing various issues within the broader topic of eschatology. The main papers presented were subsequently published in the book, Eschatology

---

1. Son, *Ellis*, 12.

in Bible & Theology: Evangelical Essays at the Dawn of a New Millennium
*(Downers Grove, IL: InterVarsity, 1997), which included Ellis' essay, "New
Testament Teaching on Hell." Writing his essay as a memorial to conditionalist John Wenham, Ellis highlights the diversity of thought on hell amongst the
patristic and intertestamental writings, then argues for conditional immortality and the annihilation of the wicked using both the Old and New Testament
(primarily the latter, as indicated by the title of the essay), concluding that resurrection unto immortality is a gift that will be given only to the saved.*

OF THREE VIEWS ADVOCATED in the patristic church, universal salva-
tion is excluded by Scripture. But is the "everlasting punishment" of the wicked an unending process of suffering or an extinction of their being that has an everlasting effect? The former view, reflecting the influence of Platonic philosophy, was present in early Judaism. But the latter better accords with the biblical teaching on the nature of man as mortal and of death as the wages of sin. Immortal being is God's gift only to those who belong to Jesus Christ.

One's understanding of the biblical teaching on the destiny of those outside Christ will probably be governed by the answer given to three antecedent biblical questions. Is man by nature mortal or immortal? Is he both an individual and a corporate being or an individual only? Is death as "the wages of sin" (Rom 6:23) an extinction of being or is it continuing existence in separation from God? For this topic, as for others, biblical anthropology is an essential presupposition for understanding biblical eschatology.

Patristic Writers

Since the early centuries of the church three views on the destiny of the wicked have been advocated,[2] views that may be termed (1) universal salvation, (2) everlasting punishment as a process, i.e., of suffering or tor-
ment, and (3) everlasting punishment as an effect, i.e., of extinction or annihilation. In the patristic church, Origen (c. AD 185–254) was the primary representative of the first view and Augustine (AD 354–430) of the second. Ignatius (c. AD 35–110), Justin Martyr (c. AD 100–165), Arnobius (d. 303–330), and Athanasius (c. AD 296–373) are prominent

2. Cf. Plumptre, "Eschatology," 189–97. For a classification of early Christian writers, see Pétavel, *Problem*, 495f.

PART THREE—BIBLICAL SUPPORT FOR CONDITIONALISM

examples of conditional immortality, that is, immortality given only to those in Christ, and of its corollary, a punishment that is everlasting in its effect, i.e., an extinction of being.

In an early writing,[3] Origen expresses the view that all things will ultimately be brought into subjection to God (1 Cor 15:25) by being "restored" (ἀποκατάστασις, cf. Acts 3:21) to perfection with the resultant salvation of every person, i.e., universalism.[4] He builds his theory not only on the principles of "the free will of man and the goodness of God" (Kelly) but also on the views of the Greek philosophical schools,[5] including the assumption of a Platonic body/soul dualism in which the soul is either immortal or destined for immortality with God.[6]

Augustine, appealing largely to Matt 25:41–46 and opposing Origen's interpretation, argues that the destiny of the wicked is an everlasting process of suffering of both body and soul.[7] He bases his argument on an initial assumption, following the Platonists, that the human soul is

---

3. *Orig. Prin.* 1.6; ANF 4:260–62. This work was written during Origen's Alexandrian period, i.e., before AD 231. Cf. Quasten, *Patrology*, 2:57.

4. For a critique cf. Pétavel, *Problem*, 277–312. A view similar to Origen's may be reflected in Barth, *Christ and Adam*; critiqued by Bultmann, "Adam and Christ." For a contemporary advocate of universal salvation cf. Moltmann, "The End of Everything"; Moltmann, *Coming*, 235–55: "Christ's death on the cross [is] the foundation for universal salvation" (254). But where is that in the Scriptures? From a biblical perspective any view of universal salvation founders (1) on the many judgment texts that exclude such an interpretation (e.g., Isa 66:22f.; Dan 12:2; Matt 12:31f.; 25:46; 2 Thess 1:6–9), (2) on the facts that the term "all" may mean, e.g., "all kinds" (cf. Rom 11:32) and not necessarily "every individual," and (3) that "to reconcile" (ἀποκαταλλάξαι, ἱλάσκεσθαι) an enemy, i.e., to remove the enmity, is accomplished for believers by the death of Christ (Col 1:20) and for unbelievers by their own death. Cf. Bavinck, *Reasonable*, 358f.; Berkouwer, *Work of Christ*, 256–60; Morris, *Apostolic Preaching*, 125–33; Stott, *Cross of Christ*, 197–202.

5. Cf. Chadwick, *Origen*, x–xiii; Harnack, *Dogma*, 377ff.

6. *Against Celsus*, 7.32; ANF 4:623–24. Cf. Kelly, *Doctrines*, 469–74, esp. 473f. Athenagoras (*Ath. Res.* 13.1; ANF 2:156) appears to be the first Christian writer to describe man as made up of an "immortal soul" (ἐκ ψυχῆς ἀθανάτου) and a body. Cf. Barnard, *Athenagoras*, 124f. Before he was converted, Athenagoras had been a philosopher supporting Middle Platonism (37–51). Cf. also *Diogn.* 6; ANF 1:27. (c. AD 200).

7. *City of God* 21; NPNF 2:452–78. Augustine simply asserts that the soul was created immortal (6:12; NPNF 2:121). However, he had predecessors, e.g., Tertullian (*Treatise on the Soul* 4, 22; ANF 3:184, 202), who disagreed with Plato's view that the soul is preexistent, but nonetheless accepts this Greek philosopher's conception of its immortality and "the substance which [man] derived from God himself" (*Against Marcion* 2:5; ANF 3:300) with the consequence, apparently, that the wicked will suffer forever (cf. *The Shows* 30; ANF 3:91). Cf. Pétavel, *Problem*, 250f.

immortal by nature. As a previous adherent of Manichaeism and then of Platonism, he regarded Neoplatonism as the philosophy closest to Christianity.[8] With his great influence the Augustinian view became dominant throughout the Western church.

The view designated conditional immortality, with its corollary, the annihilation of the wicked, is represented by a number of patristic writers.[9] Since this fact is perhaps less well known, a few quotations may be useful. Ignatius, who regarded union with Christ as "the medicine of immortality" (φάρμακον ἀθανασίας),[10] writes that "if [God] were to imitate us according to how we act, we would no longer exist" (μιμήσμταί καθὰ πράσσομεν, οὐκέτι ἐσμέν).[11] He implies that God's judgment would mean the destruction of our being.

Justin Martyr is more explicit:

> God delays causing the confusion and destruction (κατάλυσιν) of the whole world, by which the wicked angels and demons and men shall cease to exist (μηκέτι ὦσι), because of the seed of the Christians.[12]
>
> Thus some which have appeared worth of God never die; but others are punished (αἱ κολάζονται) so long as God wills them to exist and to be punished.... For those things which exist after God, or shall at any time exist, these have the nature of decay (φύσιν φθαρτήν), and are such as may be blotted out and cease to exist.... For this reason souls (ψυχαί) both die and are punished.[13]

---

8. *City of God* 8.5; *NPNF* 2:147. Cf. Markus, "Augustine," 342–46, 359ff.; Pressensé, "Augustinus," 217.

9. Especially the earlier writers. Cf. further Fudge, *Fire That Consumes* (2011), 253–59; Pétavel, *Problem*, 229–45; Constable, *Future Punishment*, 237–326, esp. 325; White, *Life in Christ*, 416–25. Pace Crockett, "Metaphorical View," 65f. Patristic writers cannot be said to favor the Augustinian view of everlasting torment because they use biblical phrases like "everlasting punishment" (2 Clem. 6:7, Lightfoot, *Fathers*, 88; *Mart. Pol.* 11:2; *ANF* 1:41. Cf. Matt 25:46), "everlasting fire" and "fire that is never quenched" (*Mart. Pol.* 11:2, 2:3; *ANF* 1:41, 39. Cf. Jude 7; Mark 9:47f. = Isa 66:24). After all, it is precisely the meaning of these phrases that is the question at issue.

10. *Ign. Eph.* 20; *ANF* 1:58. *1 Clem.* 35; *ANF* 1:14 similarly describes "life in immortality" (ζωὴ ἐν ἀθανασίᾳ) as a gift of God to believers.

11. *Ign. Magn.* 10; *ANF* 1:63. The apodosis clause in a condition contrary to fact is only occasionally in the present tense (cf. Mark 9:42) and often drops the ἄν. Cf. Blass et al., *Greek-English Lexicon*, 523; Robertson, *Grammar*, 1014.

12. *Second Apology* 7; *ANF* 1:190.

13. *Dialogue with Trypho* 5; *ANF* 1:197. Those who regard the soul as immortal are

Irenaeus is equally explicit on man's mortality and his attainment of immortality only in Christ:

> And [God] laid down for [Adam] certain conditions: so that, if he kept the command of God, then he would always remain as he was, that is, immortal; but if he did not, he would become mortal, melting into the earth, whence his frame had been taken.[14]

> How, again, can he be immortal, who in his mortal nature did not obey his Maker?[15]

> [Souls and spirits] had a beginning ... but endure as long as God wills that they should have an existence and continuance ... [God] imparts continuance for ever and ever (*in saeculum saeculi*) on those who are saved.[16]

> [But] they shall wish that they had been burned with "fire" (cf. Isa 9:5) [is said of] those who believe not on Him. ... [For] those who after Christ's appearing believed not on Him, there is a vengeance without pardon in the judgment.[17]

Theophilus of Antioch (c. AD 190), speaks similarly:

> Man was neither mortal nor immortal by nature ... but was able to receive both (δεκτικὸν ἀμφοτέρων). If he [kept] ... the command of God, he would receive immortality as a reward from Him and would become [like] God, but if he ... [disobeyed] God, he would be responsible for his own death. ... Everyone who performs [God's commands] can be saved and, attaining to

---

called Platonists. *Dialogue* 80; *ANF* 1:239 identifies as heretics those "who say there is no resurrection of the dead, and that their souls, when they die, are taken to heaven." Justin's pupil, Tatian (*Address to the Greeks* 13; *ANF* 2:70), also argues that the soul is mortal. Cf. Pelikan, *Shape*, 11–29.

14. *Demonstration of the Apostolic Preaching* 15. Translation of Pelikan, *Shape*, 104. Cf. Froidevaux, *Prédication apostolique*, 54; Robinson, *Irenaeus*, 83. Cf. Gen 3:19. But see Irenaeus, *Against Heresies* 2.34.2; *ANF* 1:411: "Nevertheless [souls] endure, and extend their existence into a long series of ages (*in longitudinem saeculanim*) in accordance with the will of God their Creator."

15. *Against Heresies* 4.39.1; *ANF* 1:522–23. Otherwise: Wingren, *Irenaeus*, 204–207, who is quite misleading on this question.

16. *Against Heresies* 2.34.3; *ANF* 1:411.

17. *Demonstration of the Apostolic Preaching*, 56.

the resurrection, can "inherit imperishability" (ἀφθαρσίαν) (*ad Autolycum* 2, 27).[18]

At the end of the third or the beginning of the fourth century, Arnobius, one of the last early apologists, presents a view of conditional immortality similar to these second-century writers. He observes rightly that God has no obligation or necessity to save anyone[19] and writes:

> [The death] which is seen by the eyes is *only* a separation of soul from body, not the last end—annihilation: this, I say, is man's real death, when souls which know not God shall be consumed in a long-protracted torment with raging fire . . . [20]

> [T]he souls of men are of a neutral character . . . subject to the law of death, *and are* of little strength, *and that* perishable . . . they are gifted with immortality, if they rest their hope . . . on God Supreme, who alone has power to grant such *blessings*.[21]

Arnobius has been criticized as "an immature Christian"; unjustifiably since we have no knowledge of his thought apart from his treatise against the pagans. In any case, he is only one among a number of mostly earlier Christian writers who espoused conditional immortality, that is, immortality only for the righteous in Christ. Athanasius' essay *On the Incarnation of the Word*[22] sounds remarkably like these earlier writers:[23]

---

18. Cf. Grant, *Theophilus*, 69ff. Cf. Matt 19:17, 25; Phil 3:11; Heb 11:35; 1 Cor 15:50, 53.

19. *Against the Heathen* 2.64; *ANF* 6:458. Cf. Frend, "Arnobius," 122, who thinks that Arnobius "shows little trace of Christian theology": but see *ANF* 4:409–10; Moule, "Arnobius." However, Arnobius shows a knowledge of the apostolic writings, defends them, perhaps the Gospels, against pagan criticism (1.54–58; *ANF* 6:428–29), cites at least one text verbatim (2.6; *ANF* 6:435. Cf. 1 Cor 3:19) and alludes to other biblical passages. But he makes little use of Scripture for his argument, probably because his "vast range of learning" (*ANF* 6:408) is focused on a scathing critique of paganism in terms of its own views and practices.

20. *Against the Heathen* 2.14; *ANF* 6:440.

21. Ibid. 2.53; *ANF* 6:454.

22. The translations are dependent in part on those of Thomson, *Athanasius*, 142–85, esp. 184f., 274–77; Lawson, *Athanasius*, 29f., 96. Cf. also Kannengiesser, *Athanase*, 276–79, 340f., 468f.

23. Some regard him as inconsistent on this issue since Athanasius, *Against the Pagans* 32–33, speaks of the soul as "immortal" (ἀθάνατος). But, like Irenaeus, he may mean no more than that the soul does not die with the body. See above, note 12. Otherwise: *NPNF* 4:32–33.

> For the transgression of the commandment was making [men] turn back again according to their nature; and as they had at the beginning come into being out of non-existence, so were they now on the way to returning, through corruption, to non-existence (εἰς τὸ μὴ εἶναι) again. If having then a nature not to exist (τὸ μὴ εἶναι), they were called into existence by the presence (παρουσία) and mercy of the Word, it followed that . . . because they turned to [evil] things that have no being (εἰς τὰ οὐκ ὄντα), they also were deprived of everlasting existence (τοῦ εἶναι ἀεί). . . . For indeed man is by nature mortal in that he was created from nothing.[24]

> [As Christians] according to the mortality of the body we are dissolved (διαλυόμεθα) only for the time that God has ordained for each in order that we may be able "to obtain a better resurrection."[25]

Athanasius concludes his treatise with a reference to Christ's second coming when he will bestow on believers "resurrection and incorruptibility" (τὴν ἀνάστασιν καὶ τὴν ἀφθαρσίαν) and will assign those who have done evil to "everlasting fire and outer darkness" (πῦρ αἰώνιον καὶ σκότος ἐξώτερον).[26] In the light of his earlier comments that man apart from Christ is on his way back to nonexistence, he appears to view the divine fire of judgment as accomplishing and climaxing that effect:

> Thus joined to [the saints] in the fellowship of life (τῇ ἀγωγῇ τῆς συξήσεως), one may escape the danger that threatens sinners and the fire [that comes] on them at the day of judgement . . .[27]

Both Arnobius and Athanasius build their arguments more on philosophical than on biblical foundations. Although they presuppose from their Greek philosophical background a body/soul dualism, they do not from that infer the "soul's" immortality, but only that its life extends in some way beyond that of the body.

---

24. *De Inc.* 4, 20–26.
25. Ibid., 21.5ff. Cf. Heb 11:35.
26. Ibid., 56.3.
27. Ibid., 57.3.

Intertestamental Evidence

Among the intertestamental writings of Judaism are the Qumran texts, the Old Testament Apocrypha and some pseudepigraphal apocalyptic writings; the last are less easy to date and are largely post-first-century in origin or include post-first-century Christian interpolations.[28] Like the patristic literature and the Apocryphal New Testament, these documents also reflect one or other of the two viewpoints, i.e., everlasting suffering[29] and annihilation.[30] Also, like the patristic writers, they exhibit in part a body/soul dualism rooted in Platonic philosophy.[31] The Qumran texts, like the Sadducees[32] and the Old Testament,[33] speak of the whole man as mortal[34] and as perishing at death, and, like the Old Testament, they also

---

28. The only Jewish apocalyptic pseudepigrapha that can be dated with confidence before the first century AD are parts of *1 Enoch*. Fragments of the eleven manuscripts of *1 Enoch* appear at Qumran from the first (1–36), third (72–82), fourth (83–90), and fifth (91–108) sections of the Ethiopic text. There are no fragments from the section, the Book of Parables (*1 Enoch* 37–71). Cf. Milik, *Enoch*, 5ff., *passim*; Knibb, *Enoch*, 2:6–15. See below, n. 49.

29. Judith (16:17), apparently alone among the Old Testament Apocrypha, expresses this view, i.e., that "in the day of judgment" God will take vengeance on Gentiles who attack his people, "giving fire and worms to their flesh and they shall cry in consciousness forever" (ἐν αἰσθήσει ἕως αἰῶνος). Cf. also *4 Macc.* 12:12; perhaps 9:9. See below, note 39.

30. E.g., *1 Enoch* 98:10: "You are ready for the day of destruction. And do not hope that you will live . . . rather you will go and die" (Knibb); cf. 90:25ff.; 97:1. Also 4Q418 69:7f.: "Those who seek the truth will rise for the judgment. . . . All the crazy at heart will be annihilated, and the sons of iniquity will be found no more" (Martinez).

31. In first-century Judaism Philo and the Pharisees believed that "the soul" was immortal. Cf. Philo, *opificio mundi* 135: Man "was created at once mortal and immortal, mortal with respect to his body and immortal with respect to his mind"; Josephus, *Antiquities* 18.14; *Wars of the Jews* 2.162–3: "The Pharisees [say] . . . every soul is imperishable" (ἄφθαρτον) . . . and those of the wicked are punished with an everlasting vengeance" (ἀιδίῳ τιμωρίᾳ); Meyer, "φαρισαῖος," 21; Meyer, *Hellenistisches*. Cf. Hammer, *Sifre*, 307: "man, whose soul is from heaven and whose body is from the earth" (Sifre 306 on Deut 32:2).

32. Cf. Acts 23:8; Josephus, *Wars of the Jews* 2.154–66; *Antiquities* 18.16; Strack and Billerbeck, *Kommentar*, 1:885f. (on Matt 22:23); Schürer, *Jewish People*, 2:391f.; 2:411. The Sadducees were under Hellenistic influences and on this question were more Epicurean than Old Testament. Cf. Josephus, *Antiquities* 10.277f. with 13.173 and Josephus, *Wars of the Jews* 2.164f.; Mishnah, *Sanhedrin* 10:1; Meyer, "Σαδδουκαῖος," 46f.

33. E.g., Pss 6:5; 115:17; see below, n. 40.

34. Cf. 1QS11:20–22; 1QH 3:24; 10:3; 12:25–31; Flusser, "Dead Sea Sect," 262, cf. 254, 257; Mansoor, *Hymns*, 84–89.

affirm his resurrection at the Last Day.[35] In this respect they are closer to biblical perspectives, both Old Testament[36] and New Testament.[37] But neither the Qumran writings nor the Old Testament Apocrypha, nor the largely post-first-century Jewish apocalyptic[38] and rabbinic writings are of central importance; they are neither appealed to nor (with one exception) cited by the New Testament. And it is, I think, a fundamental error in method to interpret the New Testament primarily from Jewish apocrypha and pseudepigrapha or (as the History of Religions school did) from the views of the surrounding paganism, even from pagan views that had infiltrated sectors of Judaism.

More important than views of the different Jewish parties is the teaching of canonical Scripture, which, rightly understood, is for biblical Christianity the infallible revelation of God from which all Christian doctrine must be vetted. The issue for evangelicals, then, is one of biblical interpretation, and to that question we may now turn.

Old Testament Witness

The primary background for understanding the New Testament's teaching on the punishment of the wicked is the background to which it appeals. That is, the Old Testament Scriptures that were received as canonical authority by first-century Judaism[39] and that, with the possible exception of Esther, were identical with the Old Testament canon received by Protestants and Jews today.

The Old Testament displays distinct conceptions of death as the punishment for sin.[40] It depicts the death state and sphere, i.e., שְׁאוֹל (Sheol = ᾅδης, Hades), as a kind of mass grave, six feet under, over which God has power to deliver by resurrection, but with which he has no relationship

---

35. 4Q418 69:7f. ("Sapiental Work A"); 4Q521 12 ("Messianic Apocalypse"); 1QH 3:19–22; 6:29f., 34; cf. 4:21f.; 11:12; 18:25–29; Charlesworth, "Resurrection Texts"; Puech, "Messianism," esp. 246–253; Black, *Scrolls*, 142, 190f. Otherwise: Ringgren, *Qumran*, 148–51.

36. See below, notes 43–46, 52, 54–61.

37. See below, notes 92, 93. For the rabbinical writings see below, note 49.

38. *Pace* Harmon, "Conditionalism."

39. Cf. Ellis, *Old Testament*, 36–50; Beckwith, *Old Testament*, 274–323; Leiman, *Hebrew Scriptures*, 131f., 135.

40. E.g., Gen 2:17; 3:17ff.; Ezek 18:4.

(Isa 14; Ezek 31–32).[41] Despite some metaphorical and symbolic scenes of conversation among the maggots,[42] the Scripture represents the departure into Sheol as the end of individual being, a returning to the common earth[43] and "virtual annihilation."[44] While one may continue to "live" in one's name or progeny,[45] viewed as a corporate extension of one's own soul,[46] there is no longer any personal life or being. The "spirit [that] returns to God who gave it" (Eccl 12:7) is not, as Platonists read it, a part of the individual's personality, much less his essential ego, but rather the "spirit of life" (Gen 7:22; cf. 2:7) that God grants and, at death, takes back (e.g., Job 34:14f.). Man's end is "like water spilt on the ground which cannot be gathered up again" (2 Sam 14:14). Death levels him with all other dying life: man and beast, righteous and wicked, wise and foolish.[47] Sheol is then both the natural end of all mortal creatures and also God's judgment on the disobedient Adamic race.

Anthropologically, the Old Testament views the human "personality [as] . . . an animated body, not (like the Greek) . . . [as] an incarnated soul."[48] It knows no body/soul dualism and has no Platonic conception of an immortal soul with an after-death experience different from the body. Under the influence of Greek mythology and philosophy, this changes later in the thought of some Pharisaic rabbinic tradition,[49] of Jewish[50] and

41. E.g., Job 7:9; Pss 6:5; 30:9. Cf. Ellis, "Life," esp. 698; Tromp, *Primitive Conceptions*, 129–40; Pedersen, *Israel*, 1:460–70.

42. Ezek 31–32; Isa 14:4–11; cf. Luke 16:19–31.

43. Gen 3:19; 25:8; 37:35; Deut 31:16; Job 3:13ff.; 10:9; 17:13–16; Pss 6:5; 49:12; 144:4; 146:4; Eccl 2:14; 3:19ff.; 9:10; 12:7.

44. Johnson, *Vitality*, 93. Cf. Ellis, "Life," 697f.

45. Ps 72:17; Isa 66:22.

46. Cf. Pedersen, *Israel*, I, 254ff.

47. Eccl 3:19ff.

48. Robinson, *Doctrine of Man*, 27.

49. Cf. Meyer, *Hellenistisches*, 25–32, 44–69; (note 21); the texts cited in Strack and Billerbeck, *Kommentar* (note 22), 2:222–34 (on Luke 16:19–31); 4:1016–65. All in all, the rabbinic literature affirms an extended judgment of the unrighteous in *Gehenna*, followed by their annihilation. Cf. e.g., Mishnah, *Eduyoth* 2:10; *Tosefta Sanhedrin* 13:4: "The Israelites . . . and Gentiles who sinned go down to *Gehenna* and are judged there. . . . And, after twelve months their souls perish, their bodies are burned, *Gehenna* absorbs them, and they are turned into dust under the feet of the righteous, as it is written . . . (Mal 4:3)." Cf. Weber, *Jüdische* 390–398: "Therefore, by God's judgment, the nations (*Völkerwelt*) will be delivered to annihilation through the fire of *Gehenna*. In this way the earth, henceforth in the sole possession of Israel and freed from the ungodly, can be renewed and become the abode of everlasting life" (398).

50. Apart from parts of *1 Enoch* the Jewish apocalyptic pseudepigrapha are very

Christian apocalyptic pseudepigrapha[51] and of some patristic literature. Here the real, immaterial personality, the soul, continues after the physical body dissolves into dust. The Old Testament, however, views man as a unity and pictures the whole person as going into the grave.[52]

What then is the hope of the godly and the special judgment of the wicked? The Old Testament hope is the resurrection of the whole person from Sheol. Contrary to a widespread scholarly tradition,[53] a resurrection hope was not a late-appearing conception, since it is found in pre-exodus Egypt (J. H. Breasted; A. H. Sayce)[54] and may have been appropriated from there and reformulated under inspiration by Israel's prophets.[55] In Egypt, it underlay the careful embalming practice, the placing of grain in the tomb and even the burial of Pharaoh's ship alongside the tomb so that in a future resurrection he could use it again to sail the Nile.

---

probably post-first century. In any case they and early Christian pseudepigrapha contain views of body/soul anthropology and of the after-death state of the wicked that are heavily influenced by pagan Greek philosophical and mythological conceptions. Cf. Bauckham, "Hell"; Himmelfarb, *Tours*; Dieterich, *Nekyia*. See above, note 28.

51. ÆFN1 Everlasting torment of the wicked is reflected in, e.g., the *Ascension of Isaiah* 1:3; 10:8ff. (perhaps) and the Ethiopic *Apocalypse of pseudo-Peter*, 7–10. (Further, cf. Himmelfarb, *Tours* [note 40], 8–40; Turner, *History of Hell*, 83–88). One of several "Apocalypses" of pseudo-Peter, it may be dated to the later second century if it is the "Apocalypse of Peter" commented on by Clement of Alexandria (cf. Eusebius, HE 6, 14, 1) and mentioned in the Muratorian Canon; but see Theron, *Tradition*, 113n (on the Muratorian Canon). On the other hand, the apocryphal *Acts of Paul*, 8, 3, 24–27, and *Acts of Peter* (Vercel.), 17, middle, apparently assign the wicked to annihilation.

52. Pss 30:3; 33:19; 88:3; 89:48. See above, note 43. Cf. Ellis, "Life" (note 31), 697f.; Eichrodt, *Old Testament*, 2:214f.

53. E.g., Schürer, *Jewish People*, 2:391f., 411; von Rad, *Old Testament*, 1:405ff.; 2:350. This tradition appears to rest in part on reading Old Testament texts with philosophical preconceptions of the ego's survival of death (e.g., Rad, *Old Testament*, 1:405ff. on Ps 73:23–28) and, in part, on a nineteenth-century evolutionary pattern applied to Old Testament thought in which "resurrection" was placed late on the scale. Consequently, where "resurrection" was admitted, the texts were dated late; where the texts were dated early, a "resurrection" exegesis of them was rejected. It was the merit of Michael Dahood to show the historical and exegetical fallacy of the pattern. See below, note 56.

54. Cf. Breasted, *History of Egypt*; Breasted, *Ancient Egypt*, 55–61, 288ff.; Sayce, *Ancient Egypt*, 170: "the doctrine of the resurrection of the body became an integral part of the Osirian faith."

55. It was apparently also present elsewhere in the ancient Near East. Cf. Smick, "Bearing," who concludes that "some notion of resurrection from the dead was a part of [pre-Abrahamic] Sumerian mythology" (21).

In the Psalms, some of which are among the most ancient Old Testament literature, the hope of resurrection is repeatedly expressed, as Michael Dahood, Derek Kidner, and others have argued.[56] The resurrection also, according to Jesus,[57] underlies God's exodus declaration that he is the God of dead Abraham, a declaration implicitly affirming that he would resurrect Abraham, since "[God] is not the God of the dead."[58] Paul voices the same thought when he teaches that "if the dead are not raised ... those who have fallen asleep in Christ have ceased to exist" (ἀπώλοντο, perished, 1 Cor 15:18) and, in Rom 4:17, where he equates the resurrection of the dead with the calling of non-being into being.[59] In the Old Testament, resurrection is implicitly affirmed throughout in God's power to deliver one from Sheol, but it is explicitly expressed as God's purpose in comparatively few passages in Job, Psalms, Isaiah, and Daniel.[60] Equally, a resurrection, i.e., resuscitation of the wicked, raised for punishment, is present explicitly only in Daniel and perhaps Isaiah.[61] For the Old Testament, then, the assurance of future life does not lie in the idea that some part of the individual survives death, but in the firm

---

56. Kidner, *Psalms*, 1:74, 86, 90; 2:263, 466f. Cf. Pss 16:9ff. (Acts 2:26f.); 17:15; 49:12, 14f.; 73:23–27; 139:18; Dahood, *Psalms*, 1:106, *passim*. From a careful study of the relationship of the biblical psalms to North West Semitic data (and of their differences from the psalms of Qumran), Dahood concluded not only that the biblical psalter was pre-exilic (3:xxxiv–xxxvii) but also that these ancient psalms contain "a deep and steady belief in resurrection and immortality" for the righteous (3:xii–Iii; *cf.* 1:xxxvi). Although his exegesis can be faulted in some respects, Dahood's method and analysis were sound and appear to mark a permanent advance in the research. Cf. Tromp, *Primitive Conceptions* (note 31), 124 (on Isa 26:19), 184 (on Ps 3:6); Smick, "Bearing." Otherwise: Kraus, *Psalms*, 2:91ff., 517, who rejects any expectation of resurrection from Sheol in these Psalms and, following G. von Rad, interprets Ps 73:24 to anticipate an after-death communion with God in "a completely different realm of life" (1:93). But this contradicts all Old Testament depictions of death and Sheol and appears to import Platonic conceptions into the text.

57. Cf. Luke 20:27–40, esp. 37f. par; Ellis, *Luke*, 234–37.

58. Matt 22:32 par.

59. Cf. Käsemann, *Romans*, 123: "the resurrection of the dead [in Rom 4:17] ... deserves to be called a creation out of nothing and presents the eschatological repetition of the first creation."

60. E.g., Job 19:26; Pss 16:8–11; 49:14f.; Isa 25:8; 26:19; Ezek 37; Dan 12:2. Cf. Baldwin, *Daniel*, 204f. Cf. also Jonah 2:1–10 with Matt 12:40.

61. Dan 12:2; Isa 66:24, expounded and applied by Jesus to his hearers re: the unquenchable fire of the final judgment (Mark 9:42–48). It is clearly taught in the New Testament, e.g., John 5:28–29; Acts 24:15; 2 Cor 5:3, 10; Heb 11:35; cf. Phil 3:11 (ἐξανάστασις); Rev 20:5f. Cf. Ellis, "II Corinthians," esp. 219–22.

hope that God will raise from death those in covenant relationship with him.

New Testament Teaching

The New Testament teaching on the punishment of those outside Christ rests upon and arises from the Old Testament teaching on the nature of man and the nature of death. The Scriptures, both Old and New Testament, represent individual personality as a complex and totally mortal monism, a unity that can be viewed from different perspectives, but that cannot be broken into separately existing parts.[62] The biblical view is compatible with an outer/inner distinction[63] or even a matter/thought or matter/will distinction, as long as both aspects are recognized as mortal and as a part of the present fallen creation and thus subject to the natural death process. But it is incompatible with an anthropological dualism in which one part, i.e., the soul or spirit, is considered to have immunity from the processes of the present natural order and thus to be exempt from death, i.e., from a cessation of existence. This kind of dualism[64] has departed from a biblical understanding to a conception rooted in Platonic philosophy, a reading of the New Testament with glasses ground in Athens, resulting in a reconceptualization and redefinition of all the New Testament terms and concepts used for the punishment of the unrighteous. It thereby excludes *a priori* the meaning (in an active sense) of extinction of being, i.e., annihilation, or (in a reflexive or passive sense) of cessation of being.

The New Testament is quite clear about immortality: only God "has immortality" (ἀθανασία, 1 Tim 6:16). It states that among mankind only

62. This may be illustrated by Jesus' interchange with the Scripture scholar at Mark 12:30–33: "'You shall love the Lord your God with your whole heart and . . . soul and . . . mind (διανοίας) and strength' (ἰσχύος); and the scribe replied, 'Well said, teacher . . . [for] to love him with one's whole heart and . . . understanding (συνέσεως) and . . . strength . . . is much more than burnt offerings.'" It is clear that the whole person from the perspective of his inner-self is meant and that the variation in terminology is a matter of indifference. See below, note 63.

63. Cf. Ellis, "Sōma," 135: "Like the Old Testament and unlike a Platonic body/soul or body/spirit dualism, both the inward and outward aspects of the person refer to physical being."

64. It is reflected in the philosophically oriented work of Cooper, *Life Everlasting*, and it seems to underlie Gundry's *Soma*, esp. 159f. But see Köberle, "Das griechische," 133–42.

those in Christ will "put on immortality," and they will do so individually only at their bodily resurrection at the second coming, i.e., parousia of Christ (e.g., 1 Cor 15:22f., 52, 53f.). Paul teaches that this transformation affects the conquest and defeat of death, which is the punishment for sin (1 Cor 15:54–57; cf. Rom 5:12, 18f.; 6:23). The New Testament similarly applies and restricts other terms, like "everlasting life" or just "life"[65] to those in Christ. In this context one may now examine the New Testament terms and concepts used for the ultimate punishment of the wicked.[66]

In the New Testament, hell is the translation of two terms, *Hades* (ᾅδης = Sheol), which, with one possible exception, continues the Old Testament meaning of "the grave,"[67] and *Gehenna* (γέεννα = גיא הנם *gehinnom*). For the purposes of this essay, hell ordinarily refers to *Gehenna*.[68] It is used by Jesus in his exposition of Isa 66:24 (Mark 9:42–48), an eschatological context that very probably refers to the day of final judgment. It is depicted in terms of the garbage dump in the valley of Hinnom on the south side of Jerusalem, "where their worm does not die and the fire is not quenched" (Isa 66:24).[69] Although hell cannot be equated with the analogy, it is represented by it as the ultimate end, an end as outcast, refuse, suffering (for those thrown out there alive), and decay. As hell is used elsewhere by Jesus, it ordinarily has similar connotations of God's final punishment of the wicked on the last day of this age. As such it seems to presuppose, e.g., in Matt 23:15, 33, a resurrection, that is, resuscitation of the unrighteous for judgment.

The New Testament uses analogies other than the Jerusalem dump for the punishment of the wicked on the last day.[70] John the Baptist and

---

65. E.g., Matt 19:29; 25:46; Luke 10:25; John 3:15f.; Acts 13:46ff.; Rom 2:7. On "life" cf. Matt 7:14; John 5:29; Acts 11:18; 2 Cor 5:4; 1 Pet 3:7.

66. The meaning of terms and phrases is not the whole of exegesis, but it is the essential starting point from which any sound exegesis must proceed.

67. Matt 11:23 (= Luke 10:15 [Capernaum]); 16:18 (gates of death); Acts 2:27, 31 (Ps 16:10f.); 1 Cor 15:55 א², Aᶜ (Hos 13:14); Rev 1:18; 6:8; 20:13f. (death and the grave). Luke 16:23: "He was buried in Hades" (א* lat Mcion). Here the scene is similar to Isa 14:9ff., but it is closer to later Greek apocalyptic/mythological perceptions in the picture of bodily torment. See below, note 88.

68. The term occurs twelve times in the New Testament, all but one (Jas 3:6) in the teaching of Jesus. Cf. Matt 5:2, 29f.; 10:28; 18:9; 23:15, 33.

69. Cf. 2 Kgs 23:10. For rabbinic and Jewish apocalyptic pseudepigraphic views cf. Strack and Billerbeck, *Kommentar* (note 22), 4:1029–1118; Bauckham, "Hell," 382–85.

70. See below, under the heading, "New Testament Terms Used for the Fate of Unbelievers."

Jesus compare that punishment to a number of nonhuman objects: burned-up chaff or tree or weeds or branch (Matt 3:12; 7:19; 13:40; John 15:6); a destroyed house, bad fish discarded, an uprooted plant, a chopped down tree (Matt 7:27; 13:48; 15:13; Luke 13:7). Jesus also uses human analogies: the unrepentant unbelievers on the day of judgment, i.e., at the coming of the Son of Man, will be like those drowned in the flood, and those burned up at Sodom, and Lot's wife reduced to salt (Luke 17:27, 29, 32). They will be like wicked tenants destroyed, the rejecter ground to powder, the evil servant cut to pieces (Matt 21:41, 44; 24:51); like the Galileans killed by Pilate, those killed by a falling tower, rebels slain (Luke 13:2, 4; 19:14, 27). On these analogies the punishment of the wicked will be a life-destroying act with a permanent and unrecallable effect.

The destiny of the wicked is also compared by Jesus to a process of punishment: a debtor held in prison, those thrown out of the house into darkness and weeping (Matt 8:12; 22:13; 25:30). But it is not said that the process is without end.

Nouns, other than hell, that describe the destiny of unbelievers also may involve a process such as an undefined vengeance (ἐκδίκησις),[71] or punishment (κόλασις, τιμωρία),[72] or divine wrath (ὀργή).[73] Perhaps "fire" might be included here, but the purpose and effect of fire is either to purge and refine or, in this context, to destroy utterly although pain may accompany the disintegration.[74]

Other nouns for the judgment of the unrighteous connote obliteration. They include annihilation (ἀπώλεια),[75] destruction (ὄλεθρος),[76] death (θάνατος),[77] end (τέλος),[78] disintegration (φθόρα).[79] Verbs used in

---

71. Luke 18:7f.; 2 Thess 1:8; Heb 10:30f.

72. Matt 25:46; Heb 10:9.

73. Matt 3:7; John 3:36; Rom 1:18; 2:5, 8; 3:5; 5:9; 9:22; Eph 2:3; 5:6; Col 3:6; 1 Thess 1:10 (2:16); 5:9; Rev 6:17; 11:18; 16:19; 19:15.

74. Matt 5:22; 13:42, 50; 25:41; Mark 9:47f.; Luke 17:29f.; 2 Thess 1:8; Heb 10:27; 2 Pet 3:7; Rev 11:5; 18:8; 19:20; 20:9f., 14f.; 21:8.

75. Matt 7:13; John 17:12; Acts 8:20; Rom 9:22ff.; Phil 1:28; 3:19; 2 Thess 2:3; 1 Tim 6:9; Heb 10:39; 2 Pet 2:1.

76. 1 Thess 5:3; 2 Thess 1:9 (1 Tim 6:9).

77. Rom 1:32; 6:21ff.; 7:5; 8:6; 1 Cor 15:21f.; 15:56; 2 Cor 2:16; 7:10; Jas 1:15; 5:20; 1 John 5:16; Rev (2:11); (20:6); 20:14; 21:8.

78. Rom 6:21f.; 2 Cor 11:15; Phil 3:19; 1 Pet 4:17.

79. Gal 6:8; 2 Pet 1:4; 2:12.

this context can also have a connotation either of process[80] or of end of being.[81] Of course, for all of these terms one can find an instance where the meaning, annihilation, does not apply. Augustinians, with their presupposition that the individual's essential being cannot cease to exist, present such an instance and suppose that it can be applied to the biblical contexts. But if asked what Greek or Hebrew term would connote annihilation, they offer none, at least none that appear in Scripture. They have decided the question by their presupposition and will be persuaded by no linguistic nor exegetical argument.

New Testament texts on the destiny or punishment of the wicked often have an accompanying adjective, everlasting or age-lasting (αἰώνιος). The term αἰώνιος should not be translated "eternal" because that word has philosophical connotations, a contrast of time with eternity, that has no place in Scripture. The Bible presents man totally as a temporal creature whom God relates to, in both salvation and judgment, totally in time and history, this age and the age to come.[82] For the wicked, Scripture speaks of an everlasting sin (ἁμάρτημα, Mark 3:39), everlasting punishment (κόλασις, Matt 25:46), everlasting judgment (κρίμα, κρίσις, Heb 6:8; Mark 3:25a), everlasting fire (πῦρ, Matt 18:8; 25:41; Jude 7), and everlasting destruction (ὄλεθρος, 2 Thess 1:9).

For the destiny of the righteous, the New Testament uses the same adjective: everlasting judgment (κρίμα, Heb 6:2).[83] Cf. everlasting salvation (σωτηρία, Heb 5:9), everlasting redemption (λύτρωσις, Heb 9:12), everlasting life (ζωή, Matt 25:46). In Matt 25:46 Jesus places together both the destiny of the righteous and that of the cursed:

> Then they will go away into everlasting punishment (κόλασιν),
> but the righteous into everlasting life.

---

80. E.g., (torment): βασανίζειν (Mark 5:7f.; cf. 1:24); (Rev 14:10); (20:10); φθείρειν, διαφθείρειν, καταφθείρειν (disintegrate): 1 Cor 3:17; (2 Cor 4:16); Rev 11:18; 2 Pet 2:12; ἐσθίειν (eat, consume): Heb 10:26f.; κολάζειν (punish: 2 Pet 2:9).

81. E.g., ἀποθνῄσκειν (die, be dead): cf. John 8:24; Luke 20:36; John 11:26; ἀπόλλυναι (perish, dissolve, come to an end, lose): Matt 10:28, 39; 16:25; Luke 13:3; 17:27, 29; 20:16; John 12:25; Rom 2:12; 1 Cor 10:10f.; 15:18; (2 Thess 2:10); (Heb 1:11); (Jas 4:12); 2 Pet 3:5ff.; Jude 5–7; (ἐψ)ολοθρεύειν (cut off, destroy): Acts 3:23; Heb 11:28.

82. Cf. Cullmann, *Time*; Cullmann, *Salvation*.

83. Delitzsch, *Hebrews*, I, 272: "κρίμα αἰώνιον is the final judgment, deciding forever the blessedness of the righteous and the damnation of the wicked (Acts xxiv.25)." That is, it is a one-time point action with an everlasting effect.

PART THREE—BIBLICAL SUPPORT FOR CONDITIONALISM

The two destinies are represented as co-extensive, but they leave two questions unexplained. (1) What is the punishment? (2) Are the two destinies everlasting processes of "everlasting living" and "everlasting punishing" or are they point actions, a one-time dispensing of life and dispensing of punishment that have an everlasting effect? On the second question, similar texts help us to understand that the latter alternative is the proper interpretation of Matt at 25:46. When Jude 7 refers to Sodom undergoing the judgment of "everlasting fire" it does not mean that Sodom is ever burning, but that the effect of the burning lasts forever. When Hebrews speaks of "an everlasting salvation" (σωτηρία αἰωνία, 5:9) or "an everlasting redemption" (αἰωνία λύτρωσις, 9:12) accomplished by the sacrifice of Christ "once for all" (ἐφάπαξ 9:12; cf. 7:27; 10:10), it is clear that it does not mean an everlasting process of saving or redeeming, but rather a one-time act of salvation and redemption that has an everlasting effect. The same is true of the expression "everlasting judgment" (κρίμα αἰώνιον) in Heb 6:2. As Delitzsch pointed out long ago, the phrase refers to the final judgment at Christ's second appearing (Heb 9:28) that decides forever the blessedness of the righteous and the damnation of the wicked.[84]

Only one passage in the New Testament speaks of a punishment of "everlasting torment," and it refers to the punishment of non-human figures, "the devil ... the beast and the false prophet" (Rev 20:10), in a vision-revelation full of highly symbolic scenes. If the passage is taken literally, it appears to contradict the teaching at Heb 2:14 that Jesus will destroy (καταργεῖν) the devil.

The most important and frequent terms for the punishment of sin are death (θάνατος) and destruction or annihilation (ἀπώλεια) and their corresponding verbs.[85] How did this kind of language come to be understood by the later patristic and the medieval church to imply everlasting suffering? The change very probably came about, as Harnack argued, from the fusion of the gospel with Platonic philosophy,[86] especially by the Alexandrian school of Clement and Origen, which resulted in "the transformation of the ecclesiastical tradition into a philosophy of religion."[87] This fusion promoted in the church a dualistic Platonic anthropology

---

84. See above, note 73.
85. See above, notes 65, 67, 71.
86. Harnack, *Outlines*, 155.
87. Harnack, *Dogma*, 2:319–380. Cf. Eusebius, *Historia Ecclesiastica* 6, 37, 1; Lilla, *Clement*, 15, 173–81, 229.

that shifted the Christian hope and the judgment of God from the parousia of Christ and the resurrection of the dead to the departure of the soul to heaven or hell at death.[88] Probably influenced also by the gnostics, it redefined redemption from a redemption of matter to a redemption from matter. With its acceptance of the philosophical dogma of the immortal soul, it paved the road to the doctrine of universal salvation (Origen) or of an everlasting dualism of good and evil (Augustine), the kingdom of God above and the continuing hell below.[89]

Conclusion

The New Testament's teaching of resurrection to immortality as God's gift only to those belonging to Jesus Christ[90] defines its understanding both of salvation in Christ and of God's judgment on those outside Christ. In the case of the latter, it represents, as a good number of writers have recognized,[91] a judgment affecting the annihilation of their being. This judgment will be God's act on the last day of this age when the "just and unjust,"[92] the living and the dead raised to life, will stand before Jesus Christ to receive his verdict, "each according to what he has done in the (natural, Adamic) body."[93] For the impenitent it will involve "weeping

---

88. In some Jewish pseudepigrapha (Bauckham) and rabbinic writings (Billerbeck) the punishment of *Gehenna* ("hell") begins already in hades ("hell") before the resurrection, as it does in the parable told by Jesus, the rich man and Lazarus (Luke 16:19–31). Cf. Bauckham, "Hell," 384f.; Strack and Billerbeck, *Kommentar*, 4:1023–26. Jesus uses a well-known story as an illustration, however, not to give a preview of life after death. Cf. Ellis, *Luke*, 201–6. See n. 57 above.

89. *Pace*, Blocher, "Everlasting Punishment," who makes the intriguing argument that those in hell no longer sin and that their cries are only in recognition and remorse that they had earlier rejected God. But as an Augustinian-Calvinist, Blocher should recognize that if their remorse is a "godly sorrow" it is the product of the Holy Spirit in his work of redemption; if only a remorse that they were caught and judged, that remorse continues to be sin.

90. John 5:28f.; 1 Cor 15:22f., 53ff.; 2 Tim 1:10; cf. Matt 25:46; Mark 10:30 par.; John 6:40; Rom 2:7; 6:23; 1 Pet 1:4.

91. Cf. Atkinson, *Life and Immortality*; Stott in Edwards and Stott, *Essentials*, 312–29; Green, *Evangelism*, 69f.; Guillebaud, *Judge*; Hughes, *Image*, 398–407; Pinnock, "Finally Impenitent"; Wenham, "Conditional Immortality." Cf. also the literature cited by Garrett, *Systematic Theology*, 2:786–807.

92. Acts 24:15; cf. Luke 13:28f.; John 5:28f.; Heb 9:27.

93. 2 Cor 5:10; cf. Matt 25:31–46; Rev 20:11–15; 21:5–8.

and gnashing of teeth,"[94] a sense of loss and pain proportionate to God's just recompense to each,[95] and it will culminate in "the second death"[96] in the "lake of fire,"[97] an utter destruction and extinction of existence.[98] "Judgment Day" will be a somber, awesome, and universally panoramic occasion, in which all mankind and the hosts of angels and archangels will see and will recognize God to be "both righteous and the One who counts righteous" those who have faith in Jesus who, as a propitiation, bore their "everlasting punishment" on the cross of Calvary.[99]

God's last word is not judgment, but salvation. It is the magnificent biblical teaching of resurrection to immortality[100] and everlasting life in "a new heavens and a new earth."[101] At that wonderful time the whole of God's creation will be in perfect harmony and the former "Silent Planet"[102] will resonate with God's praise and prospects. And all evil in God's universe, including all evil creatures, will have passed into nothingness and "shall not be remembered, nor come into mind" anymore.[103]

New Testament Terms Used for the Fate of Unbelievers

Verbs

ἀποθνῄσκειν = מות (die, be dead): cf. John 8:24; Luke 20;36; John 11:26.

ἀπόλλυναι = אבד (perish, lose, dissolve, destroy, come to an end): Matt 10:28, 39; 16:25; Luke 13:3; 17:27, 29; 20:16; John 12:25; Rom 2:12; 1 Cor 10:10f.; 15:18; (2 Thess 2:10); (Heb 1:11); (Jas 4:12); 2 Pet 3:5ff.; Jude 5–7.

βασανίζειν (torment): (Mark 5:7f.; cf. 1:24); (Rev 14:10); (20:10).

διαφθείρειν = תחש (disintegrate): (2 Cor 4:16); Rev 11:18.

94. Matt 8:11f.; cf. 22:13f.; 24:51 Q; 25:14, 30; Luke 19:11, 27; Rev 18:9f.
95. Luke 12:40, 46ff.
96. Rev 2:11; 20:6, 14; 21:8.
97. Rev 20:10–15; cf. Matt 5:22; 13:40–43, 49f.; Mark 9:47f. par.; John 5:6; Heb 10:26f.; 2 Pet 3:7–13.
98. Matt 7:13f.; 2 Thess 1:7ff.
99. Isa 53:4–12; Luke 23:33; Rom 3:25f.; 1 Pet 2:24.
100. 1 Cor 15:53ff.
101. 2 Pet 3:13; cf. Isa 65:17; 66:22.
102. Cf. Lewis, *Silent Planet*.
103. Isa 65:17; cf. 2 Pet 3:13; Rev 21:4.

ἐσθίειν (eat, consume): Heb 10:26f.

(ἐξ) ὀλεθρεύειν = כרת, דדש (destroy) (cut off, destroy): Acts 3:23; Heb 11:28.

καταργεῖν (abolish, waste, destroy): 2 Thess 2:8; 2 Tim 1:10; Heb 2:14.

καταφθείρειν (disintegrate): 2 Pet 2:12.

κολάζειν (punish): 2 Pet 2:9.

φθείρειν (disintegrate, corrupt): 1 Cor 3:17.

Nouns

ἀπώλεια = אבד (destruction, annihilation, ruin): Matt 7:13; John 17:12; Acts 8:20; Rom 9:22ff.; Phil 1:28; 3:19; 2 Thess 2:23; 1 Tim 6:9; Heb 10:39; 2 Pet 2:1; 3:7, 16.

ἐκδίκησις (vengeance, recompense): Luke 18:7f.; 2 Thess 1:8; Heb 10:30f.

ὄλεθρος (destruction, death): 1 Thess 5:3; 2 Thess 1:9; (1 Tim 6:9)

γέεννα = גיא הנם (hell): Matt 5:22, 29, 30; 10:28; 23:15, 33; Mark 9:47f. (Isa 66:24); Jas 3:6.

κόλασις = לושכמ (punishment, a cutting off): Matt 25:46.

ὀργή = אף (wrath [of God]): Matt 3:7; John 3:36; Rom 1:18; 2:5, 8; 3:5; 5:9; 9:22; Eph 2:3; 5:6; Col 3:6; 1 Thess 1:10; (2:16); 5:9; Rev 6:17; 11:18; 16:19; 19:15.

θάνατος = מות (death): Rom 1:32; 6:21ff.; 7:5; 8:6; 1 Cor 15:21f.; 15:56; 2 Cor 2:16; 7:10; Jas 1:15; 1 John 5:16; Rev (2:11); (20:6); 20:14; 21:8.

πῦρ = שא (fire): Matt 5:22; 13:42, 50; 25:41; Mark 9:47f.; Luke 17:29f.; 2 Thess 1:8; Heb 10:27; 2 Pet 3:7; Rev 11:5; 18:8; 19:20; 20:9f., 14f.; 21:8.

τέλος = כלה (end): Rom 6:21f.; 2 Cor 11:15; Phil 3:19; 1 Pet 4:17.

τιμωρία (punishment): Heb 10:9.

φθόρα = תחש (disintegration, decay): Gal 6:8; 2 Pet 1:4; 2:12.

Adjectives

αἰώνιος — αἰών = עוֹלָם (everlasting, age-lasting) cf. eternal.

Modifying:

A. ἁμάρτημα (sin): Mark 3:29 κρίμα (judgment): Heb 6:2.
    ὄλεθρος (destruction): 2 Thess 1:9.
    κόλασις (punishment): Matt 25:46 κρίσις (judgment):
        Mark 3:29a.
    πῦρ (fire): Matt 18:8; 25:41; Jude 7.

B. Compare

1. Ps 24:7 (everlasting temple doors and gates); Deut 35:15 (everlasting hills); 1 Sam 27:8 (everlasting nations); 1 Chr 15:2 (everlasting levitical priesthood); Prov 22:28 (everlasting landmark). Rom 16:25; 2 Tim 1:9; Titus 1:2 (everlasting times, χρόνοι).

2. Matt 25:46 (everlasting life); Heb 5:9 (everlasting salvation); 6:2 (everlasting judgment); 9:12 (everlasting redemption).

   Process or Effect?

Analogies

A. Inanimate Objects
   1. Burned up chaff (Matt 3:12), weeds (Matt 13:40), tree (Matt 7:19), branch (John 15:6).
   2. Uprooted plant (Matt 15:13), chopped down tree (Luke 13:7), bad fish thrown away (Matt 13:48).
   3. House destroyed by hurricane (Matt 7:27).

B. Human Life
   1. Wicked tenants destroyed (Matt 21:41).
   2. Rejecter ground to powder (Matt 21:44).
   3. Evil servant cut to pieces (Matt 24:51).
   4. Galileans killed by Pilate (Luke 13:2).

5. Men killed by falling tower (Luke 13:4).
6. Those drowned in the flood (Luke 17:27).
7. Those burned up at Sodom (Luke 17:29; Jude 7).
8. Lot's wife turned to salt (Luke 17:32).
9. Rebels slain (Luke 19:14, 27).
10. Debtor's kept in prison (Matt 5:26; 18:34f.).
11. Those thrown out of party into darkness (Matt 22:13), cf. Matt 8:12.
12. Worthless servant thrown out of house into the dark (Matt 25:30).

10

Does Revelation 14:11 Teach Eternal Torment?

RALPH G. BOWLES

Ralph G. Bowles is a biblical scholar and theologian who has served as a priest in the Anglican Church of Australia since 1979, ministering to parishes in Sydney and Brisbane. Shaped by the evangelical, Reformed tradition of the Anglican Church, he has received, among other degrees, a Bachelor's in Divinity from London University, and a Doctorate of Ministry from San Francisco Theological Seminary.

Bowles published an article in Evangelical Quarterly *73:1 entitled, "Does Revelation 14:11 Teach Eternal Torment? Examining a Proof-text on Hell." In it, he closely examines one of the texts most frequently cited as support for the traditional view of hell as eternal torment. Based on the text's chiastic structure, its immediate context, the wider context of John's Apocalypse, and the whole Bible's teaching concerning the final destiny of the lost, Bowles concludes that, far from lending support to the traditional view of hell, Revelation 14:11 serves as compelling evidence in favor of conditional immortality and the annihilation of the unsaved.*

THE BELIEF THAT GOD's final judgment of the unsaved will lead to a state of eternal, conscious, tormenting punishment is firmly entrenched in the doctrinal traditions of the Christian church, and is regarded widely as one of the defining pillars of conservative evangelical orthodoxy. While it is seldom explicitly enunciated from pulpits, or even in written gospel presentations, it is still held by most evangelicals as an essential element of faithful biblical belief. It is a doctrine that is believed usually out of duty, not affection, due to a conviction that it is scriptural. Charles Hodge called it "a doctrine which the natural heart revolts from and struggles against, and to which it submits only under stress of authority."[1]

Evangelicals have been accustomed to attacks on this doctrine from liberal critics, who propose an alternative universalism of salvation. In recent years, however, the doctrine of eternal torment has come under questioning again from within the evangelical camp. An alternative, long-held interpretation of the texts, called "conditional immortality," has been put forward as a better expression of the biblical teaching.[2] The conditional immortality view teaches that God will finally and fully bring his enemies to judgment. This will involve the penalty of his wrath against sin and the absolute destruction and removal of his enemies—the extinction of evil.[3] The reemergence of conditionalism in our day has raised the alarm of some evangelical theologians, who detect an attempt to "gag" God's Word and dilute the truth.[4] (It is also worth noting that the conditionalist doctrine is not always correctly understood; it is often confused with annihilationism—the belief that God simply ends the existence of the unsaved without any particular judgment. For example, B. Milne's textbook on Christian doctrine misunderstands the conditionalist position in this way.)[5]

Here is the crucial statement:

> And the smoke of their torment goes up for ever and ever; and they have no rest, day or night, these worshippers of the beast

---

1. Hodge, *Systematic Theology*, 3:870.

2. For example: Edwards and Stott, *Essentials*, 312–31; Wenham, *Enigma*, 68–92; Fudge, *Fire That Consumes*; Hughes, *Image*, 398–407; Pinnock, "Conditional View."

3. For convenience, this article will refer to "traditionalist" to mean those who hold the eternal torment interpretation of final punishment, and "Conditionalist" to refer to those who hold the position of the judgment and final, absolute destruction of the wicked.

4. Carson, *Gagging*, chapter 13; Packer, "Eternal Punishment."

5. Milne, *Know the Truth*, 274.

and its image, and whoever receives the mark of its name. (Rev 14:11 RSV)

This text is regarded by both traditionalist and conditionalist interpreters as one of the strongest texts in support of "eternal torment." In almost all presentations of the eternal torment theory of "hell," Rev 14:11 is cited in the manner of a proof-text, for its apparently clear statement of the endless, conscious torment of the enemies of God.[6] P. Barnett observes that the third angel "proclaimed that the wine of God's fury, the cup of his wrath, and everlasting torment awaits those who worship the beast and its image."[7] R. H. Mounce asserts that those who worship the beast and bear his mark "are to drink the wrath of God and endure eternal torment in fire and brimstone."[8] D. A. Carson cites it as the first of three passages "that are peculiarly difficult for annihilationists."[9] Even the late John Wenham, who held the conditionalist view, acknowledged that "Revelation 14:11 is the most difficult passage that the conditionalist has to deal with.... Certainly, on the face of it, having no rest day or night with smoke of torment going up for ever and ever, sounds like everlasting torment."[10]

The traditional interpretation offers what seems to be the obvious meaning of the text—a depiction of endless tormenting punishment by God. No alternative interpretations are offered by traditional commentators, probably because the surface meaning seems incontrovertible and has the support of the dominant doctrinal tradition of interpretation about "hell." So Rev 14:11 is usually cited without exegetical discussion, in the manner of a proof-text.

It is easy to see why this particular verse is invoked to support this concept. Three elements of the verse suggest the idea of a judgment involving eternal torment: (a) the worshippers of the beast and its image are "tormented" with fire and sulfur in the presence of the angels and the Lamb; (b) this torment appears to continue forever as the fire

---

6. For example, see Milne, *Know the Truth*, 276, where he claims that Rev 14:11 clearly contradicts "annihilationism."

7. Barnett, *Apocalypse*, 118.

8. Mounce, *Revelation*, 274.

9. Carson, *Gagging*, 525. The term "annihilationist" may be misleading if it conveys the impression that conditionalists merely believe in cessation of existence. In fact, they hold to God's penal judgment of sin and the final penalty of destruction in the full, strongest sense of the word.

10. Wenham, *Enigma*, 87.

burns without consuming ("the smoke of their torment rises for ever and ever"); and (c) after this torment is mentioned, their condition is described as one of "no rest, day or night," suggesting that their suffering is unremitting in its eternal duration. When this verse is read through the interpretative grid of eternal torment, it strongly confirms it. This verse also provides some of the key terms and images for the traditional doctrine of hell (torment, fire burning forever, smoke rising, no rest day or night).

The Conditionalist Interpretation of Revelation 14:11

However, an alternative interpretation of this text has been offered (or revived) recently by conditionalist writers, challenging the view that eternal torment is intended in this text. This conditionalist interpretation takes seriously the biblical background and referencing symbolism for this description of judgment in Rev 14:11. It is an attempt to unfold the meaning of the text, albeit in a way that contradicts the dominant evangelical doctrinal tradition.

On the conditionalist view, the three elements of the text are patient of a different construction.

(a) The judgment of God by fire and sulfur is "a cipher for total destruction at Sodom and Gomorrah and thereafter (Gen 19:23, 28; Deut 29:23; Job 18:15–17; Isa 30:27–33; 34:9–11; Ezek 38:22ff.)."[11] The biblical image of judgment by fire and sulfur is a picture of decisive destruction and obliteration—not a picture of enduring torment.

(b) "The smoke of their torment" that ascends forever is a certification and memorial of this accomplished destruction, just as the smoke that Abram saw rising from Sodom pointed to the finality of its destruction (Gen 19:28). The background to Rev 14:11 is to be found in this picture of Sodom's destruction and to the oracle of Edom's destruction in Isa 34:10ff. "Isaiah says 'its smoke will rise forever,' telling us that Edom's destruction is not only certain (not quenched) and complete (smoke rising) but also irreversible. The desolation will be unending."[12]

---

11. Fudge, "Final End," 331.
12. Ibid., 330.

(c) The torment experienced in the presence of the angels and of the Lamb refers to the moment of judgment, not to the eternal state.[13] What continues after their tormenting judgment and destruction is the sign of their extinction—the rising smoke; this is the same picture that is found in Genesis 19 and Isaiah 34. Revelation 14 is here giving us another picture of the fall of God's enemies, similar to the depiction of Babylon's fall in Revelation 18, whose inhabitants suffered torment in their final judgment (Rev 18:10) and whose smoke is viewed as the sign of the city's destruction—a past tense reality: "what city was like the great city?" (Rev 18:18).

This conditionalist reading has been challenged recently by D. A. Carson. He notes the strong force of "forever and ever," and discounts the allusion to Isa 34:10 as having a "typological reference" similar to Sodom and Gomorrah in Jude 7.[14] He draws attention to the crucial statement "they have no rest day or night" as invalidating the idea of completed destruction. If this is a picture of a completed destruction, "why then," counters Carson, "does John insist that the lost 'enjoy no rest day or night,' after the smoke of their completed destruction is said to be ascending?"[15] Conditionalist writers have taken this comment (no rest, day or night) to refer to the uninterrupted suffering of the followers of the beast while it continues, without implying that it will continue forever.[16] Carson claims that this explanation is weak. He makes a strong argument at this point, one that has been felt by conditionalist interpreters. The sequence of the statements in Rev 14:11 (torment, smoke, restless suffering) does seem to pose a serious exegetical problem for the conditionalist view by indicating a continuing, perpetual tormenting judgment.

Within this key text on hell, therefore, there are two elements that are patient of either interpretation. "Tormented with fire and sulfur" may describe an eternal torment, or the painful moment of destructive judgment. "The smoke of their torment that goes up forever" may depict the evidence of a continuing, eternal suffering in God's judgment, or it may be the sign and memorial of a completed destruction ("nothing left but

13. Edwards and Stott, *Essentials*, 318.

14. This begs the question of what kind of judgment is indeed typified by Sodom and Gomorrah in the biblical tradition. Do Jude and other writers like Isa 34:10 use the picture of absolute destruction to typify an ongoing conscious punishment of God's enemies? The punishment of "eternal fire" at Sodom left no enemies behind.

15. Carson, *Gagging*, 525.

16. Fudge, *Fire That Consumes* (2011), 243.

the smoke," as we might say after the bushfire has gone through). It is the third element of Rev 14:11 (no rest day or night), then, that provides the real strength of the traditional exegesis. It is held to convey the unremitting nature of the punishment that continues forever in God's presence. This interpretation of this clause is based on its position in the sequence of elements, as Carson's comment indicates. A closer examination of this key text is needed.

The Meaning of Revelation 14:11

There are four grounds for preferring the conditionalist interpretation of this text about final judgment: (a) the literary structure of the unit itself (Rev 14:9–11); (b) the immediate context of Revelation 14; (c) the wider context of the Revelation to John; (d) the general teaching of Scripture about the final judgment of the wicked.

The Literary Structure of the Unit, Revelation 14:9–11

A closer examination of this passage indicates that the traditionalist reading of this clause ("they have no rest, day or night") as indicating eternal torment may be mistaken. The clue is found in the Old Testament text that is cited allusively here (Isa 34:9, 10). Careful attention should be given to John's use of the oracle against Edom in Isa 34:8–17. R. Bauckham observes that "Isaiah 34:8–17 is a major source for John's oracle against Babylon . . . and also supplies the imagery of the judgement of the worshippers of the beast (Rev 14:10b–11: Isa 34:9–10a). . . . Clearly John read Isaiah 34 as a key prophecy of the eschatological judgement of all the nation, led in their opposition to God's kingdom by Rome (Edom)."[17] In this Isaianic passage, the destruction of Edom in the prophet's vision has the same three elements that are found in Rev 14:11 (judgment by fiery sulfur; a quenchless judgment "night and day"; and a smoke that goes up forever), but the order is slightly different. In Isaiah 34 the order is: (a) fire and sulfur; (b) ceaseless, quenchless punishment; and (c) smoke ascending forever. This is a natural order for a depiction of destruction—the judgment descends in fiery force, unremitting and quenchless while it destroys Edom, and then all that is left is the sign of the destruction—the

---

17. Bauckham, *Prophecy*, 318.

smoke, a memorial of God's wrath executed against his enemy. There is a clear sequence in Isa 34:8ff. that begins with judgment (34:9) and ends with utter desolation and death: "none shall be there, and all its princes shall be nothing" (34:12). There are no living Edomite enemies of God left standing. "The poetical figure of a perpetual furnace of burning pitch and ever-ascending smoke conveys the idea of perpetual desolation, but not at all of endless life in pain."[18]

In Rev 14:10–11 we encounter the same three elements found in Isa 34:9–10, but the order of the description is different: (a) fire and sulfur; (b) smoke ascending forever; (c) no rest day or night. Why does John, in alluding to Isa 34:9–10, reverse the order of the second and third elements of the description? Traditionalists may say that he wants to change the Old Testament picture of annihilating divine judgment into a depiction of eternal, endless torment, but this conclusion may be premature, a case of dogmatic tradition short-circuiting exegetical enquiry.

Examination of the whole paragraph (Rev 14:9–11) suggests another possible explanation for this unusual sequence of the description. The change in the sequence of the description in Rev 14:11 may be due to an inverted parallelistic structure—not a doctrine of endless torment. In the New Testament, when the normal order of a description departs from a linear sequence, it may be a sign of the presence of a structure such as chiasmus (inverted parallelism)—a literary device that consists of a series of two or more elements followed by a presentation of corresponding elements in reverse order.[19] D. A. Carson notes the presence of such complex inverted parallelisms in Scripture: "It has often been shown that those who spoke Semitic languages commonly framed chiasms as part of their speech patterns."[20] An inverted parallelistic structure can be found in Rev 16:6, 7.

To see how John has structured this description of judgment against the worshippers of the beast, it is necessary to examine the whole unit, Rev 14:9–11. It can be set out in its inversion as follows:

---

18. Constable, *Future Punishment*, 60.
19. Man, "Chiasm." Also, Lund, *Chiasmus*.
20. Carson, "Approaching the Bible," 13.

(A) If anyone worships the beast and its image, and receives a mark on his forehead or on his hand, (9)

    (B) he also shall drink the wine of God's wrath, poured unmixed into the cup of his anger, (10a)

        (C) he shall be tormented with fire and sulfur in the presence of the holy angels and in the presence of the Lamb. (10b)

        (Ci) And the smoke of their torment goes up for ever and ever, (11a)

    (Bi) and they have no rest, day or night, (11b)

(Ai) these worshippers of the beast and its image, and whoever receives the mark of its name. (11c).

This pattern conforms to the recognized structure of introverted parallelisms in the Bible. This structure has been described thus: "There are stanzas so constructed that, whatever be the number of lines, the first line shall be parallel with the last; the second with the penultimate; and so throughout, in an order that looks inward, or to borrow a military phrase, from flanks to centre."[21] Using the marks of this figure listed by K. Bailey, it is possible to trace the structure of Rev 14:9–11. The climax of the unit is found in the center (the tormenting destructive judgment by God's fire). There is a turning point in the passage, with a significant shift or movement in the second half (the tormenting judgment moves to completion). The beginning and the end of the unit are usually distinctly identified by identical verbal inclusion (the worshippers of the beast, etc.).[22]

It is the literary structure of Rev 14:9–11 that provides the explanation of the meaning of the judgment and its elements. The crucial key to understanding phrases or sentences is found by matching them with their corresponding items in the whole structure.[23] The introverted parallelism of Rev 14:9–11 shows us that the final element in the depiction of judgment is the smoke rising after the judgment has been completed, as is the case in Isa 34:9, 10. The *climactic* element is in the central position

---

21. Jebb, *Sacred Literature*. London: n.p., 1820. Cited in Bailey, *Poet and Peasant*, 45.

22. Bailey, *Poet and Peasant*, 74.

23. Ibid., 74–75.

in this structure—the tormenting judgment that destroys utterly. The other two elements in the inversion refer to the intense experience of the judgment as it happens; it's a full strength outpouring of God's wrath that leaves no rest or break while it is unfolding. We can see that the phrase "no rest, day or night" is logically prior to the rising smoke. The meaning can be seen by observing the corresponding member of the inverted parallelism. "No rest day or night" is another way of saying that God's wrath is poured out in full strength when the judgment is operating; it is quenchless, unremitting and overwhelming. In modern warfare terms, it is the equivalent of intense, day and night, bombing; there is no break until it obliterates the enemy. The meaning of Rev 14:11 is in harmony with the passage in Isaiah 34 that lies behind it.

The Immediate Context of Revelation 14

It is a mark of illegitimate proof-texting to fix a meaning on a verse without regard for its context. The traditionalist interpretation usually overlooks the context of Rev 14:11. On closer examination, there is a strong disconfirmation of the "eternal torment" theory lying nearby in this section of the Revelation to John.

The traditional reading of Rev 14:11 ignores the crucial fact that this verse is part of a warning of the coming judgment on God's enemies, which is then followed by a description of the actual judgment in Rev 14:14–20. In 14:6–13 the impending final judgment of God is announced, and when the three angels complete their warnings of the great judgment to come (including 14:9–11), there follows in Rev 14:14–20 a description of this final harvest judgment. There are verbal and imagery links in this depiction of the judgment, with the warning proclamation of Rev 14:9–11. In the divine judgment, the vines of the earth (the wicked) are thrown into "the great winepress of the wrath of God." This echoes the words of Rev 14:10: "he himself shall also drink of the wine of the wrath of God." The actual description of this final judgment is a vivid, gruesome picture of utter death and dissolution, not of endless torment: "the winepress was trodden outside the city, and blood flowed from the winepress as high as a horse's bridle, for one thousand six hundred stadia" (Rev 14:20). We look in vain in the description of the final judgment to find a picture of eternal, conscious torment. There is torment certainly, and great distress in the awesome judgment of God, but it ends in the decisive dissolution and obliteration of the enemies of God. The conditionalist interpretation of Rev 14:11 fits the immediate context much better than the eternal torment reading. There is no tension between the terms of the proclamation of final judgment in Rev 14:9–11 and the description of final judgment in Rev 14:14–20. The traditionalist reading has a tension between the eternal torment supposedly predicted in Rev 14:11 and the picture of final annihilating destruction that follows in Rev 14:14–20.

The Wider Context of the Revelation to John

What does this book indicate will be the nature of the divine judgment on the wicked? D. Powys has noted that Revelation "has very little that touches on the subject of the fate of the unrighteous."[24] The Revelation to John seems to make use of recapitulation in its series of visions about divine judgment.[25] There appear to be a number of parallel descriptions of the final judgment of God upon his enemies (Rev 6:12–17; 11:15–18; 14:6–20; 16:17–21; 17:1–19:5; 19:6—20:21). There are connections between this passage in Revelation 14 and other descriptions of judgment. The angel of Revelation 14 proclaims the coming judgment on Babylon (14:8), and this judgment is described at length in Rev 18:1—19:3. The judgment proclaimed on God's enemies by the angel in Rev 14:9–11 is revisited again in an extended treatment in Rev 19:17—20:10. The blessedness of the dead who die in the Lord announced in Rev 14:12–13, is recounted in expanded form in Rev 20:11—21:8. The Revelation to John has many descriptions of divine judgment, including a number of accounts of the final judgment.

Judgment is pictured repeatedly in the language of final, decisive destruction, not ongoing torment. There are other references in Revelation to this judgment announced in Rev 14:11. The same image and expression ("the smoke rises up forever and ever") is used in Rev 18:18 and 19:3. This description is parallel and equivalent in topic and language to the picture in Rev 14:11. The fate of Babylon there shows us that the rising smoke does not indicate a continual burning, since it is expressly stated that "Babylon" is obliterated. Babylon is destroyed but her smoke continues to rise, a perpetual reminder of her destruction in the judgment of God's wrath. There is no suggestion that Babylon is defeated

24. Powys, *Hell*, 364.
25. Page, *Powers*, 218.

while her inhabitants are imprisoned and suffering. If the picture in Revelation 18 and 19 is of a completed destruction, then surely the same is on view in the earlier depiction of the final judgment in Rev 14:6–11. When God's judgment falls, it is intense and terrible in its effect. Another parallel description of the judgment of Rev 14:9–11 is found in Rev 6:12–17. Revelation 14:9–11 depicts the pouring out of God's wrath of judgment day, in a similar portrayal to that found in Rev 6:12–17. While in Rev 6:12–17 we do not find a completed description of final judgment, we do have a vivid depiction of God's enemies suffering the intense wrath of God in full strength: "Fall on us and hide us from the face of him who is seated on the throne and from the wrath of the Lamb! For the great day of his wrath has come and who can stand before it?" (Rev 6:16–17).[26] The clause "they have no rest day or night" is a description of the moment or process of divine judgment, one among the many found in the Revelation to John; it is not a description of the eternal state of the judged.

What other passages in this book suggest an eternally conscious tormenting judgment for the enemies of God? For a book that is filled with depictions of the final judgment of God over his enemies, Revelation is strangely lacking in detail about any ongoing, endless conscious punishment. There are, in fact, only two verses that can be cited in support of this theory (Rev 20:10 and 14:11). Strange as it may sound to those accustomed to think of the eternal torment interpretation as indubitable biblical truth, there is no definite picture or statement of ongoing, eternal conscious punishment of the unsaved in either of these texts. Revelation 14:11 is under challenge in this article as not applicable, and in Rev 20:10 it is the destiny of the supernatural enemies of God that is on view. The exegesis of Rev 20:10 calls for serious examination. As W. J. Dumbrell observes on Rev 20:11–15: "Note that John does not reveal the nature of the judgement of the unsaved."[27] The fate of the devil, the beast, and the false prophet in Rev 20:10 should be considered in the light of background text such as Dan 7:11–12 in which the destruction of the anti-God beast is depicted. Allowance should be made for the use of hyperbole in Rev 20:10. The traditional interpretation of 20:10 imposes a literal meaning on this verse, in a context (20:1–10) that abounds in symbolic elements. Apart from this text, there is no indication of eternal torment, and much evidence of final destruction.

26. Hendriksen, *Conquerors*, 35–36.
27. Dumbrell, *Order*, 343.

The General Biblical Teaching of Scripture on the Destiny of the Unsaved

A final test of any exegetical interpretation is the analogy of faith—how it fits with the general teaching of Scripture on this subject. A full consideration of the wider Scriptural teaching on the fate of the unsaved is beyond the scope of this article. A few comments about how this interpretation relates to the wider biblical tradition may be offered.

The conditionalist interpretation of final judgment has a strong amount of biblical connections to commend it. It is worth noting how the conditionalist reading demonstrates a considerable harmony with the scriptural linkages of background passages such as Genesis 19 and Isaiah 34. We have already drawn attention to the background of this passage in Isaiah 34. It is recognized that Isa 34:1–17 is a picture of the universal judgment of God. Edom symbolizes in Isaiah what Babylon does in Revelation—the ungodly, persecuting world, the adversaries of the people of God. Edom typifies "the Lord's eschatological foe."[28] Isaiah 34 depicts the day of the Lord's vengeance (34:8), after which his enemies are obliterated, leaving a wasteland without human inhabitant. (It is worth noting that this oracle against Edom is introduced as an instance of the "ban" of destruction (34:1–2), for the "ban" is also term of utter destruction and annihilation.)

There may be another level of harmony between Isaiah 34 and Revelation 14—a harmony of literary device and style. There is a case for detecting in Isaiah 34 an inverted parallelistic structure similar to that of Rev 14:9–11, in which Isa 34:8 is the central statement. The frame sections are exhortations to hearers to listen and note the plan of God (34:1; 6–17). The second and penultimate sections both describe the utter destruction by God of his enemies (34:2–3; 11–15). The third and fifth sections describe this supernatural judgment on Edom in two alternative images: a sacrificial sword from heaven (34:4–7), and a judgment of fire and sulfur raining from heaven in a quenchless destruction, until nothing remains (34:11–15). To read Isaiah 34 sequentially is to posit a description of two judgments on Edom. It seems better to view it as a double, inverted parallel description of the same eschatological judgment by God. The conditionalist reading of Rev 14:9–11 brings it into harmony with its Old Testament connections.

---

28. Motyer, *Isaiah*, 268.

The interpretation of the biblical images of judgment is another area of interest. Traditional eternal torment proponents argue that the New Testament writers employ such Old Testament background and imagery in a new, metaphorical, typological way. All the biblical motifs of destruction are thus construed in the New Testament's theology to be metaphors of continued existence in ruin. This point should be challenged, since it involves a direct reversal of the imagery in meaning. Henry Constable made this point a century ago: "Every one of its [Scripture's] images points not to the preservation of being in any state, whether good or evil, but to the utter blotting, out of existence and being, and identity."[29] The conditionalist reading of Rev 14:9–11 does not require that this imagery and symbolism of final judgment be totally reversed in sense. Destruction means destruction. If the Old Testament judgments are to be read typologically, then at least the antitype should not contradict the type. It is a strange fulfilment of the type of a destructive, annihilating judgment in the Old Testament, to become read as a metaphor for ongoing existence in ruin.

Another issue is what the New Testament teaches about the final judgment of the unsaved. As F. F. Bruce observed: "The New Testament answer to this question is much less explicit than is frequently supposed."[30] There certainly is a definite lack of clear didactic exposition of the eternal torment doctrine in the New Testament. It is an interesting exercise to search for clear systematic exposition of this doctrine in the apostolic writings; it is very hard to find. If we want to take these biblical pictures of judgment and destruction and interpret them to teach judgment and ongoing torment, we need to be able to point to clear didactic passages in the New Testament to support such a reading.

Individual Biblical Texts and our Doctrinal Grids

Despite J. I. Packer's claim that Conditionalist interpreters attempt to evade the natural meaning of "some dozens of relevant passages," (which he sees as a prime case of "avalanche-dodging,") the number of key texts is quite few.[31] H. Guillebaud believed that "apart from four or five passages, there is not even an appearance of teaching everlasting torment

---

29. Constable, *Future Punishment*, 71.
30. F. F. Bruce, "Foreword to First Edition." In Fudge, *Fire That Consumes*, xi.
31. Packer, "Eternal Punishment," 12.

in the Bible."[32] The doctrine of eternal torment actually rests on just four "core" texts that appear to teach it plainly or strongly (Matt 18:34, 35; Mark 9:43–48; Rev 14:10, 11; Rev 20:10). For each of these core texts, there are cogent and consistent conditionalist exegetical interpretations. Other passages appear to support it only by the way they are linked and construed.[33] Most of the texts about judgment and destruction can be read consistently with the conditionalist interpretation.

It should concern all Bible students to note how few proof-texts can be cited in support of eternal torment, how much weight is placed on two texts from the Revelation to John (14:11; 20:10); and how other core texts come mainly from parables of Jesus. We are usually wary of interpreters who base their doctrines on proof-texts drawn from the Revelation, or from the parables of Jesus, without the control of didactic passages. It is hard to escape the conclusion that the theory of eternal torment stands on a very narrow exegetical base, and that the texts that control the interpretative grid are few, and come from the most symbolic of biblical books.

The debate on "hell" will be assisted if all contributors focus their thoughts on the few "core" texts upon which the two views rest. Both interpretations have texts that are difficult to reconcile and both have texts that seem to give strongest support.[34] In this debate about a doctrine of immense seriousness, evangelicals should seek to anchor all their beliefs in sound exegetical work on specific texts.[35]

---

32. Guillebaud, *Judge*, 12.

33. This is true of Matt 25:41, 46, which does not teach eternal torment clearly at all, despite repeated claims of traditionalist interpreters. The nature of the eternal punishment is not described, and it is set in contrast to eternal life as an opposite, not a parallel, destiny—the opposite of life. The "eternal fire" mentioned in Matt 25:41 is described elsewhere in Matthew as a consuming fire, not a tormenting one (Matt 3:12). There is no evidence in Matthew's Gospel of a tormenting fire of endless divine punishment.

34. The eternal torment interpretation faces a contradictory text with the most famous, classic "hell" text: Isa 66:24. In this verse, cited by Jesus in Mark 9:43–48, the final destiny of God's enemies is depicted as death. The undying worm and everburning fire do not torment live enemies, but consume the bodies of slain enemies. B. Webb comments: "As it stands, it seems to depict annihilation rather than eternal torment. The bodies are dead." (Webb, *Isaiah*, 251.) There is no clear, deeper extension of meaning in the New Testament citation of Isa 66:24.

35. The eternal torment interpretation is lacking in clear biblical textual exposition. D. A. Carson puts forward the concept of the eternal impenitence and ongoing sin of the unsaved, but is unable to cite one relevant text to support this rationale

It is not easy for Bible readers to assess the general biblical teaching on this subject, because the eternal torment interpretation has been a controlling doctrinal grid. Each text, once it is locked into a grid, serves to govern our perception of other texts, acting like a filter to alternative exegetical indicators. Carson reminds us that "the interpreter's theological grasp, his or her 'systematic theology' . . . may be faulty at many points, but it may be very difficult to spot the faults. The reason is that this synthesis, this systematic theology, itself becomes a controlling grid by which to interpret Scripture, under the guise of serving as the analogy of the faith."[36] In this case, the doctrine of eternal torment, applied as an interpretative grid, compels a particular, metaphorical view of all the texts that deal with "death" and "destruction" as the ultimate penalty for sin. It is hard for those texts that do indeed speak of "destruction" to be heard over the noise of this doctrinal grid.

All doctrines will have some texts that appear to be contradictory. Some will be seen as confirming the interpretation. Many texts can be seen to be consistent. But some texts function as core passages to the interpretation. These core texts are those small number of passages on which the argument is truly resting. The "avalanche" of eternal torment texts is an illusion created by linking texts that do not strongly support the idea into an eternal torment interpretative grid.[37]

Most texts can be fitted into either doctrinal grid as consistent texts. This may be illustrated in the doctrine of final judgment by considering those texts that present the pain and distress that accompany God's judgment. Both interpretations of "hell": (a) relate these texts to the final destiny of the unsaved; (b) teach that God's judgment will involve a painful penalty; (c) recognize that there will be a resurrection to judgment; but (d) differ on how these texts are related to other passages in their sequence and logic.

How can we approach the canonical checking of our interpretations, if it is hard to spot the faults of our grid? The first step is to ascertain upon which particular texts our doctrine actually rests; in the case of eternal torment, it may be a smaller number than we realize. Then these texts need to be closely examined, apart from the straitjacket of a dogmatic

---

for endless torment. The only verse he cites is, on his own admission, inapplicable (Carson, *Gagging*, 533).

36. Carson, "Approaching the Bible," 15.

37. D. A. Carson has shown how most doctrines are constructed by linking texts into an interpretive grid; Carson, *Fallacies*.

grid. The traffic between our doctrinal grid and the specific exegesis needs to be two-way; the exegesis must be allowed to correct the grid.

The interpretation outlined in this article seeks to show that the actual teaching of this Scripture (Rev 14:11) does not clearly and unambiguously endorse the traditional grid of eternal torment through which it is usually read. Instead, the text is patient of other plausible interpretations. This study of one verse demonstrates the importance of checking the doctrinal grid that we bring to particular texts such as Rev 14:11. The conditionalist treatment shows what a different result is produced when a familiar "hell" proof-text is approached without the eternal torment doctrinal grid.

Conclusion

Revelation 14:11 has been for centuries a core proof-text for the eternal torment doctrine of hell. This paper suggests that this text does not support this theory of an eternally enduring conscious tormenting punishment of his enemies by God. Rather, it describes in graphic terms, along with comparable passages, the awesome moment or process of penal judgment by God that issues in their complete, eternal extinction from his new creation.

This crucial text, then, does not describe some kind of eternal torment in the fires of hell, but rather a different picture of "hell," awesome and somber in its own way. It is a frightening reminder that those who find themselves in the camp of God's enemies will face finally his full wrath in a devastating, painful and judicial judgment that will destroy them utterly and completely. This interpretation in no way removes from the New Testament, nor from this passage, the concept of God's wrath against sin and evil-doers. The conditionalist interpretation does not in any way reduce or remove the doctrine of "hell" as God's final judgment of the unrighteous.

The traditional interpretation of hell as eternal torment is a doctrine that is unpleasant even for many of its proponents. It is seldom taught and probably seldom given much critical reexamination. It is not a doctrine that we like to talk about. When it is challenged, "orthodoxy" springs up to protect it, like an anti-bandit shield at a bank. The conditionalist interpretation will serve exegetes well by showing that there is another paradigm for viewing this issue. Let us open up some two-way traffic between our doctrinal grid and actual texts. Let us allow these texts to speak for themselves.

This issue should not be avoided or neglected. Unlike some other exegetical and theological issues, the question of "hell" concerns central issues of our gospel message. Christians offer people a hope of salvation, and it is surely supremely important to convey to them clearly and unambiguously what lies ahead for them if they decline the offer of forgiveness through the work of Christ. To speak to people about matters of such consequence demands of all Bible students a serious attention to what the Word of God actually teaches—apart from revered and old interpretations. It may be that the Lord does indeed threaten the unsaved with a judgment of eternal torment, but this fact is not taught—certainly not clearly and incontrovertibly taught—in Rev 14:11.

11

The General Trend of Bible Teaching

HAROLD E. GUILLEBAUD

Harold Earnest Guillebaud (1888–1941) was an Anglican archdeacon, missionary, and translator of the New Testament. After completing his studies at Cambridge he embarked on missionary work in Rwanda for eight years before returning to England to take a position as curate at St. Paul's in Cambridge. He would later return to Africa in 1936 to translate the Bible into Kirundi, and to write a book on Runyarwanda Grammar and Syntax. Some of his other works include Some Moral Difficulties of the Bible *and* Why the Cross?

*It was during his three-year hiatus in England, however, that Guillebaud was introduced to conditionalism by hearing Basil Atkinson preach at Holy Trinity Church. This would spurn Guillebaud to write his own work exploring conditionalism—*The Righteous Judge*—and although Guillebaud finished his work before returning to Rwanda, it was not published until after his death just five years later.*

THE FOREGOING STUDY OF the word "eternal" has given results that are decidedly against theories of the Ultimate Restoration of the lost. But neither Matt 25:46 nor any other text containing the word "eternal" can be used either as proof of the doctrine of everlasting torment, or as decisive evidence against it. On the other hand, there are certain passages, not more than four in all (Matt 18:34, 35; Mark 9:43–48; Rev

14:10–11; 20:10), the first obvious meaning of which does seem to point to an everlasting continuance of conscious suffering in hell for those who are sent there. But before considering whether this first obvious meaning of these passages is necessarily the true meaning, it is well to see what is the general teaching of the New Testament on this subject apart from them . . .

Separation from God: Penal Suffering

Some texts emphasize the separation from God of those who are condemned at the Judgment. "Depart from me, ye that work iniquity" (Matt 7:23; cf. Luke 13:27). The same thought is expressed by "the outer darkness" (Matt 8:12; 22:13; 25:30). Compare also Jude 13 "wandering stars, for whom the blackness of darkness has been reserved forever." Here, however, the thought may not be exclusion from God only, but also the end of existence: the wandering stars are extinguished in eternal night. Second Peter 2:17, which omits the figure "wandering stars" also omits "forever."

Other texts speak of suffering, but without any indication of duration. The "outer darkness" texts quoted above contain the terrible phrase "there shall be the weeping and gnashing of teeth." The same phrase occurs also in Matt 13:42, 50; 24:51; Luke 13:28. In none of these texts is there any statement that the suffering will continue forever, and indeed, as we shall see presently, the first two rather suggest the contrary. The parable of the Rich Man and Lazarus seems to refer to the time between death and the judgment. It is, therefore, outside the scope of this book, and we shall not discuss it.

Paul, who generally speaks only of "destruction" or "perdition" as the fate of the wicked, in one place uses the words "tribulation and anguish" (Rom 2:9).

Penal suffering, therefore, certainly forms a part of Bible teaching about the doom of the lost, but there is no statement that this suffering will continue forever.

Then there are those passages that speak of fire. Again it is to be noticed that none of the texts that speak of fire say the lost will suffer eternally in it. The nearest approach to such a statement is the mention of the "eternal fire" (Matt 18:8; 25:41), the meaning of which, from the analogy of Jude 7, may be "the fire which destroys forever," even as the fire from heaven destroyed Sodom and Gomorrah forever. But see the discussion of this phrase in the previous chapter.

But we can go further than this. The main emphasis in the texts that speak of fire is on the destructive rather than the tormenting effects of the fire. John the Baptist says of the Lord Jesus that "he will gather his wheat into the garner, but the chaff he will burn up with unquenchable fire" (Matt 3:12, Luke 3:17). The Greek word rendered "burn up," like its English equivalent, is a strong word implying total destruction, and chaff is utterly destroyed by fire. The word "unquenchable" means simply "that which nothing and no one can quench," which cannot be prevented from accomplishing its destructive purpose. But there may be the further thought that, after it has completed the destruction, it continues forever as a memorial of the wrath of God. In any case it can hardly be intended to reverse the meaning of "burn up" by suggesting an eternally *uncompleted* process of burning.

The wicked are compared by John the Baptist and our Lord to a tree that is hewn down and cast into the fire (Matt 3:10; 7:19). So also John 15:6: "If a man abide not in me, he is cast forth as a branch, and is withered; and they gather them, and cast them into the fire, and they are burned." It is the destruction of what is worthless that the imagery suggests, not endless torment of living beings. Twice in the Epistles the destruction of the wicked by fire is spoken of: "A fierceness of fire which shall devour the adversaries" (Heb 10:27); "the revelation of the Lord Jesus from heaven with the angels of his power in flaming fire, rendering vengeance to them that know not God, and to them that obey not the gospel of our Lord Jesus: who shall suffer punishment, even eternal destruction from the face of the Lord and from the glory of his might" (2 Thess 1:7–9).

In fact there are only three places in the New Testament where the fire of hell is clearly and unmistakably associated with penal suffering. In Matt 25:41 the condemned are told to "depart . . . in to the eternal fire which is prepared for the devil and his angels," and it is said later, "And these shall go away into eternal punishment." We have seen that the usage of the word "eternal" at least permits, and we would say supports, the view that the "eternal fire" inflicts a punishment that is eternal because it finally destroys. In the other two places, though penal suffering is indicated, the destruction of what is worthless is the more prominent idea. In the parable of the Tares we read, "As, therefore, the tares are gathered up and burned with fire; so shall it be in the end of the world" (Matt 13:40). Our Lord adds that the Son of Man will send forth his angels, and they shall cast the wicked into the furnace of fire, "there shall be the weeping and gnashing of teeth." And in verses 47–50 of the same chapter, the parable of the Drag Net tells how the fishermen gather the good fish into vessels, and cast away the bad. "So shall it be in the end of the world: the angels shall come forth, and sever the wicked from among the righteous, and shall cast them into the furnace of fire: there shall be the weeping and gnashing of teeth." These terrible words do make quite clear that the destruction is not immediate, and that the purpose of the fire is not to consume only. But they do not remove the impression of the imagery that the wicked are compared to the worthless weeds that are thrown into the fire to be burned up, and to the worthless fish that are thrown away to be got rid of. Penal suffering comes into the application of the parables, for a death by fire is necessarily a very awful death, but it surely is not the main point, or it could not be so entirely lacking in the imagery of the parables themselves.

But what of the lake of fire in the book of Revelation? It is mentioned four times (19:20; 20:10, 14; 21:8). The second of these is among the four passages we are reserving for later consideration. Revelation 21:8 ends with these words, "Their part shall be in the lake that burneth[1] with fire and brimstone, which is the second death." The term the Seer is explaining here is not the second death, but the lake of fire. Compare "seven horns and seven eyes, which are the seven Spirits of God" (v. 6), and "bowls full of incense, which are the prayers of the saints" (5:8), and "for the fine linen is the righteous acts of the saints" (19:8). It is clear that the horns and eyes, the bowls of incense and the fine linen are symbols that are explained in the second half of each clause. So here the lake of fire is the symbol, and the second death that which explains it. Revelation 20:14 is more ambiguously expressed, "Death and Hades were cast into the lake of fire. This is the second death, even the lake of fire." But comparison with 21:8 shows that the meaning is, "This symbol, the lake of fire, is the second death." But if the "second death" is the explanation of the symbol "the lake of fire," this explanation should surely have its natural meaning, and so the suggestion of these phrases is that the second death is indeed

---

1. The same strong word is used in the Greek, as that which is translated "burn up" in Matt 3:12.

very awful death, a fiery death, but, nevertheless, ultimately death, death of the soul as well as the body (Matt 10:28).

Death, Destruction, Perish

We have seen that the majority of those texts which speak of the fire of hell seem to lay the main emphasis on the destroying and consuming function of fire, even where the thought of suffering is not absent. Now we must consider those texts that use such words as "destruction," "perdition," "consume," "perish," for the doom of the lost. In our Lord's own teaching these are Matt 10:28, "Fear Him which is able to destroy both soul and body in hell"; Matt 21:44, "He that falleth on this stone shall be broken to pieces, but on whomsoever it shall fall, it will scatter him as dust"; Luke 13:3, "Except ye repent, ye shall all in like manner perish" (it is possible, but not at all likely, that our Lord means bodily death here); Luke 19:27, "These mine enemies, which would not that I should reign over them, bring hither and slay them before me"; and John 3:16 (which may be the inspired comment of the Evangelist rather than the direct words of the Lord), "God so loved the world that he gave his only begotten Son, that whosoever believeth in him should not perish, but have eternal life."

In the Acts not much is said that bears on future punishment. Peter says to Simon Magnus, "Thy money perish [lit. be for perdition] with thee" (8:20); the rejecters of the gospel "perish" (13:41); they "judge themselves unworthy of eternal life" (13:46); their blood will be on their own heads (18:6). Compare Paul's words to the elders of Ephesus, "I am pure from the blood of all men" (20:26), meaning that he had given his witness faithfully, so that none would perish through his default.

In the Epistles, future punishment is almost invariably referred to in terms of death and destruction. Penal suffering is mentioned twice only: "tribulation and anguish" (Rom 2:9), and "affliction" (2 Thess 1:6). There is no suggestion in these passages that the suffering will be everlasting, but in 2 Thess 1:9, Paul speaks of eternal destruction, the meaning of which we have considered above. Those who are without Christ in this life are four times spoken of as "they that are perishing" (1 Cor 1:18; 2 Cor 2:15; 4:3; 2 Thess 2:10). Other striking expressions are, "the wages of sin is death" (Rom 6:23); "if ye live after the flesh, ye must die" (Rom 8:13); "whose end is perdition" (Phil 3:19); "hurtful lusts, such as drown men in destruction and perdition" (1 Tim 6:9); "sin, when it is full grown, bringeth forth death" (Jas 1:15); "the day of judgment and destruction of ungodly men" (2 Pet 3:7).

Summary of Teaching So Far Considered

The general trend of the Bible teaching so far considered, is that those whom God condemns at the final judgment will be separated forever from him, and sentenced to a very awful "second death." But just as in the language of this world a "terrible death" means a death accompanied by suffering and horror, but yet is quite definitely the end of life, so the texts so far considered supply no reason why the second death should not be the end of existence, although it will be a terrible death, a death by fire, whatever the "fire" may mean. The fire is spoken of chiefly as that which burns up or devours those whom God has rejected as unfit for the gift of eternal life. The fact that they must suffer in the process of destruction is undoubtedly a part of the Bible teaching, but it is less prominently or frequently stated than the fact that their doom is destruction. Throughout the Epistles, from Romans to Jude, there is only one passage which refers to future punishment without using some word meaning "die," "destroy," or "perish," and that one (Rom 2:9) speaks of "tribulation and anguish," but without any suggestion that it is eternally continued.

The Meaning of "Death" and "Destruction"

We are well aware of the reasons which have been put forward to show that such words as "death," "destruction," and the like are capable of a meaning other than the end of existence. They are, and we have no thought of disputing it. For example, those who reject Christ are said to be "dead in trespasses and sins" even in this life (Eph 2:1, and see Luke 9:60): they have life, but not true life. So also the Greek words rendered in the active "destroy" and in the passive "perish" or "be lost," and this verb and the derived nouns are quite often used with reference to a ruined and useless condition of a person or thing.

But it is possible to press this fact too far, true as it is. It is not denied that, if it were clear beyond question from Bible teaching elsewhere that the doom of the lost will be everlasting torment, it would be quite possible to understand "death," "destruction," and the like, as meaning a wretched and ruined existence. But we have now considered the whole body of Bible teaching on this subject, except four passages, and the weight of the evidence has been against everlasting torment rather than for it. Moreover the context generally indicates clearly enough when those words are to be understood in this secondary sense. The disciples say, "to what purpose hath this waste of the ointment been made?" (Mark 14:4), where "waste" represents the word elsewhere rendered "perdition." But the context indicates plainly the sense in which the word is used. The same is true of "Leave the dead to bury their own dead" or "dead in trespasses and sins." But there is no context to suggest that "whose end is perdition" (Phil 3:19), or "a fierceness of fire which shall destroy the adversaries" (Heb 10:27) are intended to mean an eternity of conscious torment, rather than the destruction of which they appear to speak. And this is true not only of the context of the texts themselves, but also there is no positive evidence for everlasting torment in the whole of the Epistles from Romans to Jude. The nearest approach to an exception is the phrase "eternal destruction" in 2 Thess 1:9; but . . . the meaning of other similar phrases, such as "eternal judgment," "eternal salvation," and "an eternal sin," does not at all support the view that "eternal destruction" means an eternally continued process of destruction.

Seeing then that the Epistles are the chief source from which all, or nearly all, Christian doctrines are derived, it is very strange that, if the true doctrine the Word of God intends us to receive is that of everlasting torment, there should be no clear statement of it anywhere in the Epistles, but that they should always use terms that seem on the face of them to point to the end of existence. We have seen that in our Lord's teaching the greater number of his sayings point in the same direction, and only in two of his sayings (or three, if Matt 25:41, 46 be counted) is there even any appearance of teaching everlasting torment. Is not this a strong reason for hoping the first impression given by those two sayings, which we have not yet considered, will be found not to be the true meaning; as we have seen reason for believing in the case of the verses in Matthew 25?

Is the Scripture Ambiguous?

Dr. Agar Beet in *The Last Things* put forward with great learning and ability the view that, as between endless torment and the ultimate ending of existence, the teaching of the Bible is ambiguous. Neither view is ruled out, neither can be held to be definitely proved from the Bible. Dr. Beet builds this theory on what we regard as the secondary meaning of the words "death," "destruction," "perdition," and the like, which for him is the essential meaning. He says that these words certainly do not of themselves mean endless torment, but neither on the other hand do they mean ultimate extinction of existence. "Destruction" or "perdition," he says, means utter and final ruin, but indicates nothing as to what becomes of the ruined person or object: it is compatible with either a continued miserable existence, or a cessation of existence, but it proves neither. So, also, "death" in his view is the deprivation of all that makes life worth living, but not necessarily the end of existence, though it might be, if there were other conclusive evidence, which, however, he says there is not. In sum, he holds that God has not seen fit to reveal to us clearly and certainly what the ultimate fate of the wicked will be, beyond the fact that it will be irretrievable and utter ruin.

On this theory the present writer has three observations to make. First, although we grant freely that words such as "destroy" or "death" quite frequently have the meaning of "ruin" or "deprivation of good life," yet we cannot admit that this is any but a secondary use, the primary sense being "deprive of existence" and "end of existence." And there are definite reasons that show the use of these words in the New Testament, as applied to future punishment, is not so vague and indeterminate as Dr. Beet supposes. Here are two of these reasons.

1. The terms "life" and "death." Put together these three facts. (a) There is no statement in the Bible that all men are immortal, but on the contrary a definite statement that only God has immortality; (b) there are many express statements that eternal life is the gift of God through Jesus Christ; (c) Paul says that "the wages of sin is death." Surely the natural suggestion of these three facts taken together is that death means not only the deprivation of a happy existence, but what it naturally should mean in human language, the end of existence. This natural suggestion is not in itself final proof, but we submit that it is *prima facie* evidence, which requires something definite on the other side to overthrow it. In other words, "death" is not merely neutral, it has a strong bias in the direction of the end of existence.

2. The term "destroy." The Greek word is very often used in the sense of "ruin," and we do not deny that it can be ambiguous. But we deny that

this word is always or generally ambiguous, as applied to future punishment in the New Testament.

Dr. Beet says we must not put too much weight on the one metaphor of the destruction of vegetable matter (i.e., chaff, weeds, and branches) by fire. But we submit that the life of any living thing is necessarily ended by fire, unless God supernaturally provides otherwise: therefore, where fire is in question, the verb "destroy" is not ambiguous at all, but definitely implies the ending of life. It would be ridiculous to say that any living thing was thrown into the fire to be "ruined." God is able to destroy soul and body in hell (Matt 10:28). Now hell is a place of fire: the word Gehenna is rarely used without some mention of fire in the context. To destroy in hell means to destroy by fire. So also again, when the writer to the Hebrews says that fire shall devour the adversaries (10:27), the natural meaning of the words is certainly that their life will be ended, and of course not their bodily life alone, but body and soul, as our Lord said. Only one thing would upset this conclusion, and that is definite evidence that all souls are immortal, and therefore cannot be destroyed (in the full sense of the word) even by fire. But there is no such evidence, as Dr. Beet acknowledges.

Our second observation is that if the words "death" and "destroy" are used in a neutral sense of "ruin," and prove nothing either way as between endless torment and ultimate extinction, this ambiguity must have been deliberately intended by God. We should have to suppose that the inspiring Spirit did not reveal to the apostles any more exact information about the fate of the condemned than that it would be a final ruin. If Paul, for instance, had known that they would suffer in torment for all eternity, it is incredible that he should have been content to use terms by which he meant nothing more definite than "ruin," or an ambiguous "death," which could be understood equally well as endless misery or the cessation of existence. But as regards the Lord Jesus, who knew all the facts of the other world, we should be compelled to suppose that he deliberately used ambiguous language.

This takes us straight to our third observation, which is that Dr. Beet's theory must logically issue in ruling out endless torment as quite incredible. The Lord Jesus certainly knew the full truth. If that truth were that the condemned would ultimately come to the end of their existence, then his use of terms that men have misunderstood, largely through the influence of a theory of immortality of the soul, which he did not teach, is natural enough. But if the truth were endless torment, what then? If God is really going to punish those who reject salvation with endless torments, it is unbelievable that he should not have inspired his apostles to tell men so in unmistakable terms, while there is still time for repentance. It is also unthinkable that his Son, foreseeing so awful a fate for the impenitent, should have contented himself with veiled hints that fall far short of warning them in advance. The advocate of the traditional theory is here on far stronger ground than Dr. Beet, for the former interprets our Lord's words as giving very distinct warnings of this awful fate, and he maintains that he did this in his love and pity, if so be that men might be warned in time.

Indeed this theory of Dr. Beet rules out endless torment in two ways. First it enormously increases the moral difficulty of believing that God could punish his creatures with endless torment, by adding the supposition that having formed this purpose he deliberately refrained from warning men clearly what he intends to do. Secondly, the doctrine of endless torment is by common consent so dreadful, that only a deep conviction that the teaching of the Bible cannot honestly be explained otherwise, can make it possible to believe that God could punish so. Such a doctrine cannot be accepted at all as a mere "perhaps." If there is doubt, the doubt must be resolved on the side of the more merciful theory.

The Four Excepted Passages

We now approach the study of the four passages, which we reserved to the last on the ground that they have the appearance of being exceptions to the general trend of Scripture teaching, in that the first impression which they give is in favor of the doctrine of everlasting torment. Two of the four are sayings of our Lord (Matt 18:34, 35; Mark 9:43–48), and two are found in the book of Revelation (Rev 14:10, 11; 20:10). In the consideration of these passages there are two things to be borne in mind.

First, they are as much the Word of God as any other Scripture, and nothing whatever can justify a dishonest wresting of their meaning. But, secondly, we are entitled to take into account the general sense of the teaching of the Bible itself on this subject, and to study them with this in mind. The second of these considerations does not by any means nullify the first. Perhaps the best way of making clear what we mean by taking into account the general sense of Scripture is to illustrate from another case where this has to be done.

The first impression the parable of the Unjust Steward makes on many people is that our Lord is represented as commending a dishonest action. It is of course incredible that he can really have done so, but the question might arise whether the report of his words had that meaning, in which case it could not be a true report. But in all our Lord's recorded teaching elsewhere there is nothing whatever to give any ground for supposing that those who reported his words and acts would imagine him capable of commending dishonesty. Indeed in the words that immediately follow the parable itself, he is represented as inculcating the necessity of a faithful use of money entrusted to us. This fact legitimately supplies a very strong presumption against the truth of that first impression of his words in the parable of the Unjust Steward. This presumption would not justify any twisting of words into a forced meaning, but it does suggest a close examination of the words used and their connection with their context. When this is done, it is seen that so far from being a commendation of dishonesty, the parable is a lesson on the wise and faithful use of money by the Christian.

In the same way, the seeming discord between the four passages we are now about to study and the general sense of Scripture teaching on the subject elsewhere creates a strong presumption that the first impression these passages give is not their true meaning, and suggests the need of a very careful study of them in order to get below the surface, and make sure, as far as we can, that we understand the real intention of the words.

The parable of the Unmerciful Servant ends with the words, "And his lord was wroth, and delivered him to the tormentors, till he should pay all that was due. So shall also my heavenly Father do unto you, if ye forgive not every one his brother from your hearts." We may take together with these words another saying in Matt 5:26: "thou shalt by no means come out from thence (from prison), till thou have paid the last farthing." This saying indeed states nothing about torment, and, taken by itself, could not fairly be considered to suggest it: but those who believe that everlasting torment is proved by other evidence would naturally interpret this saying in conformity, for the prison is a metaphor that might cover much.

The debt owed by man to God is evidently a symbol of sin, and to pay that debt to the last farthing can mean nothing less than to suffer the full penalty that sin deserves. But when can the sinner pay in full the penalty due to his sin, represented in figures by the enormous sum of two million pounds (Matt 18:24), *and be free*? The only possible answer is, Never. One indeed paid it for him in full, but if he rejects him, he can certainly never pay it himself.

So far all is clear. But neither of these sayings can be made into evidence for everlasting torment without assuming something that is not said in either case, namely that the existence of the sinner must continue forever. The illustrations used by our Lord do not suggest such a thing. A prisoner who never comes out of prison does not live there eternally. The slave who was delivered to the tormentors till he should pay two million pounds would not escape from them by payment, but he would assuredly die in the end: why should not the same result be at least a possibility in the application? The only thing that could rule out the possibility would be the definite certainty that no human soul can ever die in the full sense of the word. But it has been shown that there is no scriptural evidence for this idea, unless it be in the doctrine of everlasting torment itself, which would then need to be proved by independent evidence, or the reasoning would be circular.

Therefore the conclusion with regard to both these parabolic statements is that their main teaching is the impossibility of the sinner ever satisfying the divine justice and so becoming free, but that though they would agree with the doctrine of everlasting torment, if that were established elsewhere, they cannot of themselves prove it.

Mark 9:43–48

In this, the most terrible of our Lord's saying about future punishment, we are warned against clinging to anything that may cause us to stumble. Though it be as dear or seemingly necessary to us as a hand or foot or eye, it must be given up, for it is better to enter into life without it, than with it to be cast into hell, into the unquenchable fire, "where their worm dieth not, and the fire is not quenched." The first impression made by these words is that of unending torment. They suggest a process of corruption and burning, which is perpetually continuing and never completed. And as it is generally regarded as an axiom that neither the soul nor the resurrected body can ever come to an end, the assumption is made that these words are pictures of perpetual conscious suffering, whether purely spiritual, or both spiritual and physical.

But we must observe that our Lord is drawing his imagery from Isa 66:24. Now it would not be true to say that, when Old Testament texts are quoted in the New Testament, they are always used in exactly the sense they have in their Old Testament setting. But there is always a presumption that a quotation has the same meaning as in its original context, and the words should not be interpreted differently in the two places without good reason.

In Isa 66:24 the prophet, who had been speaking of the final destruction of the enemies of Jehovah at Jerusalem, says, "And they [those who come to worship] shall go forth, and look upon the carcasses of the men that have transgressed against me: for their worm shall not die, neither shall their fire be quenched: and they shall be an abhorring unto all flesh." Here the picture is of a miraculously protracted destruction of *corpses*. We may say indeed that such a picture must be ideal and symbolic, and so no doubt it is, but symbolic of what? Is it a natural interpretation of symbolism to make the perpetually protracted destruction of dead bodies symbolize the perpetual torment of living souls and bodies? There seems no adequate reason for supposing that our Lord intended so to change the meaning of the prophet's words when he adopted them.

The words "they shall be an abhorring to all flesh" point to the effect of the judgment. The spectacle of corpses (which of course cannot suffer) in a perpetual process of corruption and burning would create horror and loathing in all who beheld, so in the fulfilment of the symbol we can see a perpetual memorial of the righteous wrath of God, and of his judgment against sin. May not this be the key to the meaning of our Lord's words in Mark 9?

It is clear that there will be penal suffering, for that which goes into the fire in the first instance will be alive, and therefore must suffer: "rather than having thy two hands to go into hell, into the unquenchable fire . . . rather than having two eyes to go into hell." But the question is what is meant by the added words "where their worm dieth not, and the fire is not quenched"? The comparison with the text of Isaiah seems to show that our Lord is warning those who cling to evil that their fate will be not only to perish by fire, but to become thereafter an eternal memorial of God's judgment. Like the chaff and the weeds and the dead branches, the wicked will be utterly destroyed as by fire, but the awful picture of corpses consumed by the undying worm and the unquenchable fire symbolizes that by some means there will be a perpetual memorial of that destruction that the wrath of God against sin will have achieved. Our Lord's words no more suggest the perpetual existence of human beings in conscious torment than the corpses in Isaiah's picture suggest such a thing.

It will be said that by this interpretation our Lord's warning is deprived of most of its awfulness. It is true that it is deprived of that element that has made the words so terrible a burden on the faith and conscience of those who humbly accept his authority. But to say that what remains is not so very dreadful seems to us strange blindness! Death by fire is a very terrible thing in this world, and in the timeless conditions of eternity it is only to be expected that which corresponds to death by fire would be far more dreadful, even though death in the fullest sense were the ultimate issue. Moreover, even in this life it is a strong human instinct to desire to leave behind some honorable memorial of ourselves. We all regard the death penalty as enormously increased in horror when it is accompanied by shame and the handing down of an evil memory. Jude evidently considered that the severity of the judgment on Sodom and Gomorrah was immensely increased by the fact that they were not only destroyed, but destroyed by "eternal fire"; i.e., by fire that made them a perpetual desolation, and an eternal memorial of God's judgment on atrocious wickedness. The contrast God puts before us in his Word is between eternal life with him in glory, and the destruction of soul and body by the fire of his wrath followed by an eternal memorial of dishonor (see Isa 66:24; Dan 12:2).

If the above interpretation of Mark 9:43–48 is right, there is no word of the Lord Jesus Christ that teaches endless torment. There are indeed only three sayings of his that have even the appearance of teaching it; this passage in Mark, the saying at the end of the parable of the Unmerciful Servant (Matt 18:34, 35), and the saying about eternal fire and eternal punishment (Matt 25:41, 46). His other sayings can only be understood in that sense, if the interpretation is influenced by the belief that it is impossible that any soul should really die.

Far be it from us to minimize the dreadful severity of his words. He spoke of an outer darkness, where there shall be weeping and gnashing of teeth; his comparison of the condemned to weeds thrown into the furnace to be burned up indicates a final rejection and a terrible end; the imagery of the undying worm and unquenchable fire indicates that in and after their destruction the wicked will be a perpetual memorial of God's just judgment, instead of being, as they might have been, to the eternal praise of the glory of his grace (see Eph 1:6; 2:7). His words leave, as far as can be seen, no ray of hope that the mercy which the condemned have rejected here will ever be offered to them hereafter. But in all this there is no word to say that their suffering will be prolonged to all eternity, and even in Mark 9:43–48 the imagery is taken from the destruction of corpses that cannot feel.

Revelation 14:10, 11

"If any man worshippeth the beast and his image . . . he also shall drink of the wine of the wrath of God . . . and he shall be tormented[2] with fire and brimstone in the presence of the holy angels, and in the presence of the Lamb: and the smoke of their torment goeth up for ever and ever (Greek, unto ages of ages); and they have no rest day and night,[3] they that worship the beast and his image, and whoso receiveth the mark of his name."

These words are very terrible. The Redeemer (for the title "the Lamb" refers to his redeeming death) will himself command and approve the dreadful punishment of those who have rejected him and his redemption, and deliberately chosen the service of his enemy. The people spoken of are those who deliberately take the devil's side in the supreme contests of good and evil, when the issues are perfectly plain. But are we to understand that the torment will continue forever and ever? This is certainly the first impression given by the words. But let us examine more closely the two clauses that give that impression. The words "they have no rest day and night" certainly say that there will be no break or intermission in the suffering of the followers of the beast, while it continues: but in themselves they do not say it will continue forever. The words "the smoke of their torment goeth up unto ages of ages" do at first appear to say this, but this is not at all necessarily the meaning. In considering Mark 9:43–48 we say that the meaning there is that there will be a perpetual memorial of the righteous judgment of God, which will continue after it has achieved the destruction of the wicked. May not "the smoke of their torment" that "goeth up unto ages of ages" be just exactly this? When men were burned at the stake, the smoke of their torment would continue to rise long after the torment itself had ceased. So also we read in Rev 19:3 that the smoke

---

2. Matt 5:25, 26 speaks of imprisonment, but not of torment.

3. The phrase "day and night" is transferred from earthly to eternal conditions: it is used elsewhere of the praises of the redeemed . . . (Rev 4:8; 7:14, 15).

of the burning of "Babylon" goes up unto the ages of the ages. Whatever Babylon may be, the imagery here is of a burning city, and we know how the smoke of a burning city would continue to rise long after the last inhabitant had perished. May it not be that what can happen for some hours or days on earth is pictured here as happening through the ages of eternity? Evil shall be destroyed, God shall be all in all,[4] but the awful memorial of his righteous judgment and his final victory shall always remain as a testimony to angels and to men.

Revelation 20:10

"The devil that deceived them [the nations] was cast into the lake of fire and brimstone, where are also the beast and the false prophet; and they shall be tormented day and night unto the ages of the ages."

The word "are" is not in the Greek, and it is probable that instead of "are" should be supplied "had been cast"; see Rev 19:20 where it is said that the beast and the false prophet were "cast alive in to the lake of fire." But this makes no real difference to the sense, for in 20:10 it is said that "they," i.e., the beast and the false prophet as well as the devil, shall be tormented forever and ever. But between Rev 19:20 and 20:10 "a thousand years had intervened" (20:2, 7–10), no doubt a symbolic period, but surely representing a very long time. The lake of fire had held the beast and the false prophet for a thousand years, or whatever that symbol represents, without destroying them, and then after this they were to be tormented unto the ages of the ages.

But it is impossible in any case to build on this one verse the awful doctrine of the endless torment of all the lost, for the simple reason that it does not refer to human beings (or at any rate not to ordinary human beings) at all, but to the devil, the beast, and the false prophet. Many people understand the beast and the false prophet as institutions or abstractions, such as the apostate Christianity of Rome, or the anti-God spirit that is so prevalent in our own day. These interpretations would make this verse particularly difficult to understand. But even if the beast and the false prophet should be individual human beings, they are incarnations of Satan, filled with his spirit, and endowed by him with supernatural power (2 Thess 2:8–10; Rev 13:2, 3, 11–15). Their fate, therefore, is no sort of indication of the fate of ordinary human beings.

---

4. 1 Cor 15:28.

It may be said that Matt 25:41 shows that human beings who go to hell will share the devil's fate. But the statement that they go "into the eternal fire prepared for the devil and his angels" does not at all necessarily mean that they remain alive in that fire as long as the devil would.

But does Rev 20:10 really mean that the trinity of evil powers will be tormented for all eternity? There is a statement elsewhere that should make us pause before corning to a final conclusion in this matter. The strange prophecy about the King of Tyre in Ezekiel (28:11–19) contains a number of statements that could not apply to any human being, and the only being in the universe whom they would fit is Satan: see especially verses 13–16. There is apparently a mingling of type and antitype here. The King of Tyre is denounced and threatened, but the prophet recognizes behind him a power mightier than he. Of this dread being, who was once "the anointed cherub that covereth" and was in Eden the garden of God, it is said "thou art become a terror, and thou shalt never be any more" (verse 19) . . . the same prophecy that had been applied to the city of Tyre in Ezek 27:36. Paul's statement in 1 Cor 15:28 that God shall be all in all seems impossible to reconcile with the eternal existence of the devil, even in hell. Now in addition we have this definite statement in Ezekiel that the devil shall "never be any more," which seems to mean that his existence shall come to an end.

We must reconsider Rev 20:10 in the light of these facts as well as of the general trend of Bible teaching on future punishment. It must be admitted that New Testament usage elsewhere is against interpreting "unto the ages of the ages" as meaning anything short of endless eternity. Outside the book of Revelation it occurs seven times, always in ascriptions of praise to God, such as "to whom be glory for ever and ever." In Revelation itself it occurs twelve times: three times in ascriptions of praise: four times of God who "liveth for ever and ever" (4:9, 10; 10:6; 15:7); once of the reign of God and Christ (11:15); once of the reign of his saints (22:5); and in 14:11; 19:3 and the present verse in connection with judgment. But these facts, however important are not finally conclusive. When this phrase is applied to the life of God or to the praise his people will render to him in eternity, it must mean forever without end, because God himself can never end, and he has given eternal life to his redeemed. But although the expression must mean a terribly long time, or what corresponds to such a thing in the timeless state, its meaning may well be limited to its context when it is applied to a being of whom it is said elsewhere that he is not absolutely eternal. If it be said that this is a juggling with words, we may reply that a legal document is not considered to be dishonest when it uses the term "in perpetuity" of an earthly transaction, although we all know that the world itself is not absolutely eternal.

In conclusion, we desire to disclaim dogmatic certainty on this tremendous question. It does seem to us that the general trend of Bible teaching on future punishment points to destruction in the sense of the ending of conscious existence, though the process of destruction will involve penal suffering, which in certain cases, notably that of the devil, may be awfully prolonged. And we believe that the explanations given above of the four apparent exceptions to the general teaching of Scripture are legitimate and consistent with reverence and honesty. But we acknowledge that, especially with regard to Rev 20:10, there is a margin of uncertainty. All we can say is that, if the verse does really mean that absolutely endless torment will be the fate of the devil and the evil power inspired by him, a tremendous problem arises as to the eternity of evil, with regard to which we could only wait for further light till we know as we are known.

The Unquenchable Fire

There is an explanation of the words "their fire is not quenched" (Isa 66:24, cf. Mark 9:48), which is different from that given above, but may possibly be the true meaning. Jeremiah wrote, "If ye will not hearken unto me ... then will I kindle a fire ... and it shall devour the palaces of Jerusalem, and it shall not be quenched" (Jer 17:27). Jeremiah cannot have meant that Jerusalem would be destroyed by a fire that would burn forever, for certainly this did not happen, and elsewhere Jeremiah looks forward to the restoration of God's people. He meant that the fire would burn until it had accomplished its purpose, no one would be able to put it out. It is possible then that the words in Isaiah "their worm shall not die, neither shall their fire be quenched" were meant in a similar sense. The worm would corrupt, and the fire would burn, until God's purposes were satisfied, but not necessarily forever. If so, the same explanation would be valid in Mark.

This explanation is mentioned as showing how untrue it is that there is no honest alternative to everlasting torment in the explanation of Mark 9:43–48. But the present writer prefers the explanation given above. It agrees better with Rev 14:11, "The smoke of their torment goeth up for ever and ever"; also Jer 17:27 does not suggest any supernatural extension of the ordinary time required for fire to destroy a city, it merely says that the fire would not be quenched (till it had done its work). But in Isaiah it is otherwise: "From one new moon to another, and one sabbath to another, shall all flesh come to worship before me, saith Jehovah. And they shall go forth, and look upon the carcasses of the men that have transgressed against me: for their worm shall not die, neither shall their fire be quenched." The prophet evidently meant some supernatural extension of the time ordinarily required for burning dead bodies, and, as he was using the language of symbol, it seems more likely that an eternal memorial of God's wrath was meant (as in Rev 14:11) than the meaning should be, as in Jeremiah, that the fire should not be quenched till it had done its work.

12

Claims about "Hell" and Wrath

ANTHONY C. THISELTON

Anthony Thiselton is Professor of Christian Theology at the University of Nottingham. A fellow of the British academy, Thiselton has degrees from the University of Sheffield (PhD) and the University of Durham (DD). As a priest in the Church of England, he has served on eight committees of General Synod, the Doctrine Commission, and as a member of the Crown Nominations Commission. He is perhaps most well known as a scholar of hermeneutics and the theory of interpretation; his texts The Two Horizons: New Testament Hermeneutics and Philosophical Description *and* New Horizons in Hermeneutics: The Theory and Practice of Transforming Biblical Reading *remain perennial standards in the hermeneutics classroom.*

In this chapter from his book, Life after Death, *Thiselton clarifies that his view is not to be equated with the immediate destruction of the dead, which constitutes a denial of resurrection of the unjust or any future judgment of God.*

THIS LANGUAGE IN MATTHEW, Mark, and Luke certainly seems to underline the concept of some serious losses that those who advocate a universalist theory of salvation must face. But many argue, as Powys does, that this loss denotes not everlasting punishment, but sheer destruction. We shall consider shortly whether destruction must be instant, but it certainly is not everlasting. Meanwhile, Powys declares, "Destruction is the most common way of depicting the fate of the unrighteous within the Synoptic Gospels."[1] As to other references to "hell," he cites C. S. Lewis as observing, "The Dominical utterances about Hell, like all Dominical sayings, are addressed to the conscience and the will, not to our intellectual curiosity."[2]

Not everyone is convinced by this. The Evangelical Alliance Commission concludes, "The New Testament . . . implies some duration of punishment," though "John, Paul and the other letters refer mainly to perishing, destruction, and death."[3] On Paul, Powys similarly concludes, "Existential human experience rather than . . . prospective divine action" is the main point in such passages as Rom 1:18–32.[4] Romans 9:22 speaks of "objects of wrath that are made for destruction" (Greek, *skeū orgēs katērtismena eis apōleian*). But here there appears to be no hint of eternal torment, only of destruction. The Fourth Gospel has no reference to Gehenna, torment, or fire. Usually, if John touches on the fate of unbelievers, it is said that willful refusal to recognize Christ results in (or is the fruit of) blindness and disobedience, and leads to perishing or death. Clearly the unbeliever will somehow participate in the resurrection, but will then be condemned (John 5:29). Believers, by contrast, "will not perish, but have eternal life" (John 3:16); will cross from death to life (5:24); will "never perish" (10:28); and will "never die" (11:26). First John is similar: believers "passed from death to life" in contrast to the loveless who "remain in death" (1 John 3:14). A reference to "punishment" occurs in 4:17–18; but usually it is a matter of life or death (5:16).

A closer investigation of Paul shows that he never speaks of "hell," but regularly of death (Greek, *thanatos*): "The wages of sin is death" (Rom 6:23); "The message about the cross is foolishness to those who are perishing" (1 Cor 1:18; Greek, *apollymenois*). We shall consider "wrath" shortly, and in the next chapter "judgment" (Greek, *katakrima* and cognate terms). "Destruction" (Greek, *apōleia*), occurs in Rom 9:22; Phil 1:28; 3:19; 1 Thess 5:3; 2 Thess 1:9. Only one passage seems to support the traditional Augustinian view. In 2 Thess 1:8–9, Paul (some would say a Pauline associate) declares, "Those who do not obey the gospel of our Lord Jesus Christ . . . will suffer the punishment of eternal destruction, separated

1. Powys, *"Hell,"* 284.
2. Lewis, *Pain*, 107; cf. Powys, *"Hell,"* 295.
3. Hilborn, *Hell*, 51.
4. Powys, *"Hell,"* 310.

from the presence of the Lord, and from the glory of his might." But "eternal destruction" (Greek, *olethron aiōnion*) still means "destruction," even if "eternal" refers to its quality.

Admittedly, as we have seen, John Chrysostom does understand the reference to refer to "hell," and argues, "It is not temporary."[5] Perhaps he means "not reversible." For although Frederick Danker interprets *aiōnios* to mean "pertinent to a period of time without beginning or end" or "without end," in this context *olethros*, he states, usually means "a *state* of destruction, ruin, death" (my italics), so that it is the *state* of destruction that will not end.[6] Abraham Malherbe translates it "eternal ruin," but adds, "It does not mean annihilation."[7] He relates it to 1 Cor 5:5; Phil 1:28; *Pss. Sol.* 2:31, 34; Heb 6:2; and Matt 18:8; 25:41. Many patristic commentators, he notes, interpreted *apo-* temporally; others saw it as equivalent to *ek*. But Malherbe sees it as causal; bringing ruin by his presence. It seems to be more serious than a straightforward cessation of existence.

Such questions reintroduce more broadly theological ones. *If "hell" means separated from all that is good in the presence of God, can we conceive of the human entity still existing by virtue of its own life?* Paul Tillich, one of the most metaphysical theologians of the twentieth century, makes two comments about "hell." First, it underlines "the seriousness of the condemning side of the divine judgement, the despair in which the exposure of the negative is experienced."[8] But, second, he cannot conceive of a dualism or split in the divine nature that allows for a realm of darkness, disobedience, and ruin to co-exist forever by his sustaining power. Splits in the nature of reality are for him demonic, and render the nature of an enduring hell absurd. This would not be a stark problem if "destruction" was thought to be the main description of the fate of unbelievers. Hebrews speaks of "those who are destroyed" (Heb 10:39); 2 Pet 3:7, 9, 16 also speak of "destruction." Revelation uses this term (Rev 11:18); but it also refers to torment (14:9–11); "the second death" (2:11); torment forever (20:10); and the lake of fire or burning sulfur (21:8). Daniel 12:2 speaks of "everlasting contempt."

---

5. *Homilies on 2 Thessalonians*, Hom. 2 and 3; *NPNF*, ser. 1, vol. 13, 384–85
6. Danker, *Lexicon*, 33–34 on *aiōnios* and 702 on *olethros*.
7. Malherbe, *Thessalonians*, 402.
8. Tillich, *Systematic Theology*, 435.

The Evangelical Alliance Commission, however, seems to label everyone who advocates the "cessation of life" view as a *"conditionalist."*[9] We must consider this problem. "Conditionalism" means the theory of *conditional immortality;* i.e., *immortality does not depend on innate human capacity, but is conditional upon God's gift of immortality or resurrection.* Although the Evangelical Alliance Commission and textbooks of this persuasion claim that the notion begins with the early church fathers, it was first a clear inference from Paul's teaching about the resurrection. Paul insists that resurrection is a gift of God, as much as justification by grace through faith alone. *It is a mistake to identify absolutely with annihilationism and the total nonexistence of hell*, as the Evangelical Alliance Commission and many traditional conservative writers suggest.[10] But *nowhere in the New Testament is resurrection due to innate capacity of human beings.* "Annihilationism" is widely taken to mean extinction or annihilation immediately after death. The unbeliever, on this basis, will know nothing of "the Last Things" except only this-worldly experience of dying, and "hell" would become an empty concept. Numerous books and debates offer only the two extremes of immediate extinction or everlasting torment. We reject both of these alternatives.

---

9. Hilborn, *Nature of Hell*, 52.
10. Ibid., 60–67; Berkhof, *Systematic Theology*, 690–92.

PART FOUR

Philosophical Support for Conditionalism

The "problem of hell" is depicted in various ways in the philosophical literature.[1] Traditionally, analysis of hell has centered on the question of its justice and whether a loving, merciful God would truly send anyone there to suffer for eternity. This is to view the problem as a question of *fairness*. The most common manifestation of this characterization is the *proportionality objection*—the claim that justice requires punishment to fit the crime and that finite human sin could never warrant eternal conscious torment.

But there are other characterizations of the problem. The *marred new creation objection* argues the eternal flames of hell cast a dark shadow over the new heavens and earth, either because in God's victory he is never finally rid of sin, evil, and suffering, or the perpetual existence of sin and rebellion undermines God's sovereignty, or because the eternal weeping and gnashing of teeth of the damned (presumably some of whom are friends and relatives) detracts from the blessedness of the saved.

There are also objections levied against the *suffering* found in hell. Of particular note is the *pointlessness objection*.[2] It has been argued that on the traditional view those in hell suffer pointlessly, for there is no hope for them to be restored to God or rehabilitated in their character. For what reason does God keep alive those in hell? The claim that the eternal suffering of the damned gives glory to God strikes most as barbaric (at worst) or undignified of the loving, merciful God found in the Scriptures (at best). Surely the God of such ingenuity and compassion we see displayed in the Scriptures could find a less injurious way of bringing himself glory.

Historically these charges were perhaps not as forceful due to the assumption of the inherent immortality of the soul. If souls *must* live forever, then of course God has to put them somewhere and so hell becomes a logical necessity. But these questions gain new force with modern theology's rejection of the soul's inherent immortality as an unbiblical thesis.

1. Buenting, *Problem*, 1.
2. Kvanvig, *Problem*, 3.

PART FOUR—PHILOSOPHICAL SUPPORT FOR CONDITIONALISM

Yet the defender of the traditional view of hell is not left without possible responses to these objections. A common rejoinder to the proportionality objection is what has been named the *status argument*. This is the idea, originating from medieval thinkers, that the seriousness of a crime is relative to the status and dignity of the one who is affronted. Since God's dignity is of infinite value, presumably sin is worthy of infinite punishment. And against the pointlessness objection there is the response, which began with Thomas Aquinas, that those in hell *continue to sin forever* and thus must continue to be punished. Both of these responses will come under scrutiny in the readings of this section.

So the literature abounds with debate over the traditional view of hell (and various modified traditional views), on the one hand, but it is also ripe with debate over the likelihood of *universalism* on the other hand. (Conditionalism itself has received far less discussion.[3]) Among the key issues concerning universalism is the question of *retributive versus restorative punishment*—but the question of what sort of punishment is hell brings up the more fundamental question of whether hell is punishment at all. The majority of conditionalists would answer *yes*, annihilation is retributive punishment dealt out as judgment against the wicked—perhaps appealing to Rom 6:23: "the wages of sin is death." Taking this route the conditionalist, like the traditionalist, will need to account for how the infinite punishment of eternal death is proportional to finite human sins.[4] But retributive justice is not intrinsic to the conditionalist view itself, as cessation of being could be seen as a natural consequence of disconnection from God, the very source of being. Or, as one of the following authors will argue, perhaps annihilationism is consistent with restorative justice after all, so that attacking retributive justice would not necessarily favor universalism.

Conditionalism, then, holds the philosophical middle ground between the traditional view and universalism. If arguments against

3. A notable exception, critical of annihilationism, is Brown and Walls, "Annihilationism."

4. However there is an asymmetry here since the annihilationist, unlike the traditionalist, appeals to a punishment of cessation of existence rather than a punishment requiring an eternal maintaining of existence. The annihilationist could point out that God has no *obligation* to allow the wicked to live forever (see Swinburne's chapter in this book). We must beware that the question of proportionality presupposes a "right" to exist on behalf of the wicked. Surely God has made no promises to the wicked to cause their lives to endure in the next age. In this sense the "punishment" of extinction could include the removal of the sheer grace of life.

universalism are successful—for instance that humanity's gift of free will entails the possibility some will never be reconciled to God—and if traditionalism fails to account for why God would keep alive the wicked, punishing them forever and ever, even in light of his new creation, then conditionalism readily suggests itself as a solution to the problem of hell.

13

Is the Soul Immortal?

PHILIP E. HUGHES

Philip Edgcumbe Hughes (1915–1990), New Testament scholar and theologian, was an Anglican clergyman and editor of The Churchman *from 1959 to 1967. After serving as tutor and vice principal of Tyndale Hall, a conservative evangelical Anglican college in Bristol, England, Hughes came to America to teach at Columbia Theological Seminary, Westminster Theological Seminary, and Gordon-Conwell Theological Seminary. Some of his works include commentaries on Hebrews, the Second Epistle to the Corinthians, and his magnum opus on the doctrine of man,* The True Image: The Origin and Destiny of Man in Christ.

At the end of The True Image, *Hughes takes to task the notion of the immortality of the soul by weighing it against the biblical revelation and he insightfully illuminates the connections between this doctrine and that of everlasting punishment. Human immortality, for Hughes, is a gift of grace from God "who alone is immortal" (1 Tim 6:16). For a human to "assert his own independent self-sufficiency is to deny his own constitution and thus to dehumanize himself."*

CALVIN'S OPPOSITION TO THE opinion that in physical death the soul dies together with the body and in the intermediate state sleeps a sleep of death was consonant with and indeed required by his belief in the immortality of the human soul. Thus he maintained that his affirmation

185

"that the soul, after the death of the body, still survives, endued with sense and intellect," was identical with the affirmation of "the immortality of the soul."[1] In support of the doctrine of the soul's immortality he cited a number of biblical texts: first of all, Christ's saying in Matt 10:28, "Do not fear those who kill the body but cannot kill the soul; rather fear him who can destroy both soul and body in hell," on the basis of which he had good reason for concluding that the soul survives the death of the body. But it is difficult to see how he could derive an argument for the immortality of the soul from this saying, since it would seem, quite to the contrary, to imply the soul's mortality: that God can destroy both soul and body must surely mean that the soul is destructible. Nor do other places adduced by Calvin necessarily point to the immortality of the soul, namely, John 2:19, "Destroy this temple, and in three days I will raise it up," which refers, as the Apostle explains, to "the temple of his body"; Luke 23:46, "Father, into thy hands I commit my spirit" (cf. Ps 31:5), and Acts 7:59, "Lord Jesus, receive my spirit," where Jesus and Stephen respectively, while suffering physical death, entrust their souls to God; John 19:30, Jesus "gave up his spirit," to the same effect; 1 Pet 3:19, which states that Jesus "went and preached to the spirits in prison," but which, as it is one of the most difficult and most widely controverted passages in the New Testament, not least as regards the identity of these "spirits," cannot safely be held to support belief in the soul's immortality; Eccl 12:7, "The dust returns to the earth as it was, and the spirit returns to God who gave it"; and Luke 16:19ff., which speaks of the state after death of the rich man and Lazarus.

These references are given in Calvin's early work opposing the doctrine of soul-sleep, but there is no indication of any subsequent change of mind on his part. In the *Institutes* some of the same passages of Scripture are cited and man's soul or spirit is defined as "an immortal yet created essence, which is his nobler part." Calvin also argued that in men's fallen state "the light has not been so extinguished in the darkness that they remain untouched by a sense of their own immortality," and, further, that the human conscience "is an undoubted sign of the immortal spirit," indeed that "the very knowledge of God sufficiently proves that souls, which transcend the world, are immortal."[2] There is, however, a

---

1. Calvin, *Psychopannychia*, 427. The Westminster Confession, 32:1, assigned to the souls of men "an immortal subsistence."

2. Calvin, *Institutes*, 1.15.2; 1:184.

strangely Platonic ring to assertions, both in the *Psychopannychia* and in the *Institutes*, about the soul being "freed from the body," about the body "weighing down the soul" and being "the prison of the soul," about the soul being "set free from this prison" and "loosed from these fetters" when we "put off the load of the body"[3]—even if it is impossible to doubt that Calvin intended this phraseology to be understood in the Pauline context of the conflict in the believer between flesh and spirit (Gal 5:17), not in the Platonic sense of a radical dualism between soul and body. Commenting on 1 Cor 15:43, for example, he observed that "our body is now, indeed, subject to mortality and ignominy, but will then [after the resurrection] be glorious and incorruptible."[4]

The passages quoted by Calvin indicate that the human soul survives physical death, not that it is in itself immortal. The notion of the inherent immortality of the soul, it is true, has been generally accepted in the Christian church, and this is certainly a factor to be taken into account. The question of primary importance, however, is that of its compatibility with the biblical revelation. A consideration that has weighed with many defenders of this notion is the widespread conception of the soul's immortality in numerous different cultures and religions throughout the course of history, or at least the intimation of the continuation of existence beyond the grave. But this suggests an innate awareness that death is not the end of the story, indeed that man is answerable to God who is the source of his life, rather than a proof of personal or collective immortality (cf. Heb 9:27; 4:12f.). Another argument that has been advanced is that by reason of his creation in the image of God man must participate in the excellencies attributed to God, of which everlasting existence is not the least; and this has been said therefore to require the postulation of human immortality.[5] Man's formation in the image of God does indeed imply his possession of life in a manner that transcends that of other animate creatures; but it cannot mean the possession of life in the same sense as that in which God possesses it, if only because God possesses

---

3. Calvin, *Psychopannychia*, 432, 433, 443. *Institutes*, 1.15.2; 1:184. Similarly, Calvin, *Corinthians*, ad loc., explained the "groaning" mentioned in 2 Cor 5:4 as arising from the knowledge of Christians that "they are here in a state of exile from their native land" and "shut up in the body as in a prison," with the consequence that "they feel this life to be a 'burden' because in it they cannot enjoy true and perfect blessedness" and "are unable to escape from the bondage of sin otherwise than by death."

4. Calvin, *Corinthians*, 50.

5. Gregory of Nyssa, *The Great Catechism*, 5; *NPNF* 2.5:479.

life absolutely, from eternity to eternity, whereas man possesses it derivatively and subject to the good pleasure of his Creator. The immortality of man or of the human soul is not then a necessary conclusion from this premise. It has also commonly been argued either *a priori* that the immortality of the soul demands the everlasting punishment of the wicked as well as the everlasting blessedness of the redeemed, or *a posteriori* that the endless punishment of the wicked as well as the endless blessedness of the redeemed demands the immortality of the soul.[6]

What may be deduced from the biblical revelation? First of all, that man as originally created was both potentially immortal and potentially mortal. In close association with this is his having been created potentially sinless, but also potentially sinful. The possibility of his sinning involved the possibility of his dying, just as the possibility of his not sinning involved the possibility of his not dying. As we have remarked earlier, this does not mean that man was originally created in a state of neutrality between righteousness and sinfulness and between living and dying; for, on the contrary, his creation in the divine image, which is the bond of his personal fellowship with his Maker, placed his existence quite positively within the sphere of godliness and life. His loving and grateful concurrence with the will of God, who is the source of his life and blessedness, would have ensured the continuation of his existence in unclouded blessing as he conformed himself to that image in which he is constituted. It was by his rebellion against his Creator that he passed from a positive to a negative relationship and brought the curse upon himself. His death, which is the sum of that curse, is also the evidence that man is not inherently immortal.

To contend that only the human soul is innately immortal is to maintain a position that is nowhere approved in the teaching of Scripture, for in the biblical purview human nature is always seen as integrally compounded of both the spiritual and the bodily. If this were not so, the whole doctrine of the incarnation and of the death and resurrection of the Son would be despoiled of meaning and reality. Man is essentially a corporeal-spiritual entity. God's warning at the beginning, regarding the forbidden tree, "In the day that you eat of it you shall die," was addressed to man as a corporeal-spiritual creature—should he eat of it, it was as such that he would die. There is no suggestion that a part of him was undying and therefore that his dying would be in part only. The immortality,

---

6. See, e.g., Augustine, *City of God* 6.12; *NPNF* 1.2:121.

accordingly, of which the Christian is assured is not inherent in himself or in his soul but is bestowed by God and is the immortality of the whole person in the fullness of his humanity, bodily as well as spiritual. This immortality, unearned by us, has been gained for us by the incarnate Son who, by partaking of our human nature in its fullness, both bodily and spiritual, and by dying our death, nullified the power of the devil and removed from us the fear and the sting of death (Heb 2:14f.; 1 Cor 15:55f.). Our new life in Christ, which includes our ultimate resurrection to life and immortality, is owed entirely to God and his grace. *It is God who alone has immortality* and thus who alone may properly be described as immortal (1 Tim 6:15–17; Rom 1:23). And it is for us to confess, as did the Apostle, that by virtue of God's purpose and grace "*our Savior Jesus Christ has abolished death and brought life and immortality to light through the gospel*" (2 Tim 1:9f.). The immortality that was potentially ours at creation and was forfeited in the fall is now really ours in Christ, in whom we are created anew and brought to our true destiny.

In his comments on 1 Tim 6:16 Calvin made it plain that he did not regard immortality as inseparable from human nature or from the essence of the soul. "I reply, when it is said, that God alone possesses immortality," he wrote, "it is not here denied that he bestows it, as he pleases, on any of his creatures." To say God alone is immortal is to imply that he "has immortality in his power; so that it does not belong to creatures, except so far as he imparts to them power and vigour." This means, further, that "if you take away the power of God which is communicated to the soul of man, it will instantly fade away." Thus Calvin concluded that "Strictly speaking, therefore, immortality does not subsist in the nature of souls . . . but comes from another source, namely, the secret inspiration of God."[7] The question that remains unanswered in the position represented by Calvin is this: if it is granted that immortality is a gift imparted by God and, further, that the being to whom it is imparted would "instantly fade away" were God's power to be removed, what grounds are there for concluding that immortality is a permanent gift that will not under any circumstances be removed, and accordingly that no rational being will ever relapse into nonexistence, or, in other words, suffer destruction? It is a conclusion that (as we shall see) seems to rest largely on the supposition that the endless bliss of the redeemed requires to be balanced by the endless punishment of the damned.

7. Calvin, *Timothy*, 168.

There is good reason, we believe, for suggesting that the issue of the soul's immortality, in the sense that it is an endowment that will under no circumstances be removed, calls for some reconsideration in the light of biblical truth. We have objected that the survival of the person, or the soul, in the intermediate state between death and resurrection does not necessarily imply its everlasting survival. What God has brought into being he can also destroy. The New Testament foresees "a resurrection of both the just and the unjust" (Acts 24:15; John 5:29), when the latter "will go away into eternal punishment, but the righteous into eternal life" (Matt 25:46). This final separation will take place "when the Lord Jesus is revealed from heaven"; for it is then that those "who do not know God" and "who do not obey the gospel of our Lord Jesus" will "suffer the punishment of eternal destruction and exclusion from the presence of the Lord and from the glory of his might" (2 Thess 1:7–9). This punishment is also described as being "thrown into the eternal fire" (Matt 18:8) or "into hell, where their worm does not die and the fire is not quenched" (Mark 9:44, 47; cf. Matt 3:12), and as causing weeping and gnashing of teeth to those on whom it comes (Matt 13:36ff., 49f.; cf. 8:12; 22:13; 24:51; 25:30).

In the Apocalypse of St. John the ultimate doom of the devil, the beast, the false prophet, and all their followers whose names are not found written in the book of life, together with "Death and Hades," is to be cast into the lake burning with fire and brimstone (Rev 2:11; 19:20; 20:6, 10, 14f.; 21:8). The imagery of this destruction, which is called "the second death," reflects the judgment that overtook Sodom and Gomorrah. It is recorded that "the Lord rained on Sodom and Gomorrah brimstone and fire from the Lord out of heaven, and overthrew those cities, and all the valley, and all the inhabitants of the cities," and that "the smoke of the land went up like the smoke of a furnace" (Gen 19:24–28). The fate of these cities was seen as a warning and a typification of the final judgment of the wicked. Thus in Rev 14:10–11 it is said that the beast and his worshippers "shall be tormented with fire and brimstone ... and the smoke of their torment goes up forever and ever." It was a warning meanwhile of the devastating judgment that was ready to burst upon other civilizations in the course of history—for example, Babylon, regarding which Jeremiah prophesied that "as when God overthrew Sodom and Gomorrah and their neighbor cities, says the Lord, so no man shall dwell there, and no son of man sojourn in her" (Jer 50:40); and even the people of Israel, whose apostasy, Moses warned, would render "the whole land brimstone and salt, and a burnt-out waste, unsown, and growing nothing, where no grass can sprout, an overthrow like that of Sodom and Gomorrah, Admah and Zeboiim, which the Lord overthrew in his anger and wrath" (Deut 29:23). And St. Peter gave the admonition that God "by turning the cities of Sodom and Gomorrah to ashes condemned them to extinction and made them an example to those who were to be ungodly" (2 Pet 2:6).

The terrible fate of the cities of the plain is thus a paradigm not only of the divine retribution that obliterates cities and communities but especially of the final judgment of the world by which the destroyers of the earth will be destroyed and the creation purged of all defilement (Rev 11:18; 21:8, 27); for "the heavens and earth that now exist have been stored up for fire, being kept until the day of judgment and destruction of ungodly men" (2 Pet 3:7). Then what cannot be shaken will remain; but meanwhile we must constantly remember the importance of living godly lives, "offering to God acceptable worship, with reverence and awe, for our God is a consuming fire" (Heb 12:27–29; 2 Pet 3: 11–13).

In St. Jude's brief letter these same cities are said to "serve as an example by undergoing a punishment of eternal fire" (Jude 7). Even though this was not the final judgment, the obliterating fire is described as *eternal* fire. The reason for this, no doubt, is that it was *divine* fire, the fire of judgment sent by the Lord; for obviously in the case of these cities the fire was not eternally endured by their inhabitants. It was fire that struck and left devastation from which no restoration could follow. This consideration may reasonably raise the question whether the eternal and unquenchable fire of the final judgment (Matt 8:18; Mark 9:44) will be eternally endured by those who are consigned to it. Is this what is meant by "everlasting punishment" (Matt 25:46) and by the assertion regarding those who suffer it that "the smoke of their torment goes up forever and ever" (Rev 14:11)? Such terminology can certainly bear the inference that the torment of the damned in hell will be endlessly continued; and this inference has been thought, as we mentioned, to provide an appropriate balance for the doctrine of the everlasting life which, as is universally agreed, the redeemed are to enjoy without end or term. It is a balance on which, for example, Augustine insisted. Referring to Matt 25:41, he exclaimed: "What a fond fancy it is to suppose that eternal punishment means long continued punishment, while eternal life means life without end!" Both destinies, he maintained, "are correlative—on the one hand punishment eternal, on the other hand life eternal"; consequently, to say that "life eternal shall be endless, punishment eternal shall come to an end, is the height of absurdity."[8]

The logic of this interpretation is sound enough so long as it is *punishment* that is spoken of as being endless. But, as we have seen, the ultimate contrast (as was also the original) is between everlasting *life* and everlasting *death*, and this clearly shows that it is not simply synonyms but also antonyms with which we have to reckon. There is no more radical antithesis than that between life and death, for life is the absence of death and death is the absence of life. Confronted with this antithesis, the position of Augustine cannot avoid involvement in the use of contradictory concepts, for the notion of death that is everlastingly endured requires the postulation that the damned be kept endlessly alive to endure it. Thus Augustine was forced to argue that for those in hell "death will not be abolished, but will be eternal,"[9] and that "the living bodies of men hereafter will be such as to endure everlasting pain and fire without ever dying";[10] and he depicted the wicked as everlastingly doomed to "drag a miserable existence in eternal death without the power of dying."[11] It would be hard to imagine a concept more confusing than that of death, which means existing endlessly without the power of dying. This, however, is the corner into which Augustine (in company with many others) argued himself.

By way of further illustration we will turn to a famous sermon preached by another notable Christian divine of a more recent period, Jonathan Edwards, who described the endlessness of God's wrath in the following terms:

> It would be dreadful to suffer this fierceness and wrath of Almighty God one moment; but you must suffer it to all eternity. There will be no end to this exquisite horrible misery. When you look forward, you shall see a long forever, a boundless duration before you ... and you will absolutely despair of ever having any deliverance, any end, any mitigation, any rest at all. You will know certainly that you must wear out long ages, millions of millions of ages, in wrestling and conflicting with this almighty merciless vengeance; and then when you have so done, when so many ages have actually been spent by you in this manner, you

8. *City of God* 21.23; NPNF 1.2:469.
9. Ibid., 21.3.1; NPNF 1.2:453.
10. Ibid., 21.5.2; NPNF 1.2:456.
11. *Enchiridion*, 111; NPNF 1.3:273.

will know that all is but a point to what remains. So that your punishment will indeed be infinite.[12]

It is only right to point out that, while they firmly believed in the endless torments of hell, Augustine was intent on refuting the notion that future punishment would lead at last to universal restoration (universalism), which was connected with the philosophy of the Platonists and the thought of Origen, and that the purpose of Edwards in this sermon was compassionately to urge his hearers to flee from the wrath to come and all its terrors by taking refuge in the redeeming grace of the gospel.[13]

The difficulty (if such it is) of equating everlasting death with everlasting existence was compounded in the case of Augustine by reason of the fact that he took the unquenchable flames of eternal fire to be meant in a literal sense. In facing the question how it would be possible for resurrected persons of body and soul to be kept from being consumed by these flames he invoked the support of scientific fact, as he thought it to be, that certain lower creatures, and in particular the salamander, "can live in the fire, in burning without being consumed, in pain without dying."[14] It was decidedly shaky support, however, because the naturalists known to him of his own and earlier periods reported this competence of the salamander with skepticism as a traditional or legendary notion. But in any case the supposed ability of the salamander was irrelevant, because it is not a capacity shared by human beings with salamanders, and Augustine had perforce to resort to the hypothesis that in the flames of hell the wicked would in this respect become salamander-like: "Although it be true," he wrote, "that in this world there is no flesh which can suffer pain and yet cannot die, yet in the world to come there shall be flesh such as now there is not, as there will also be death such as now there is not."[15]

---

12. Edwards, "Sinners," 11.

13. Thus Edwards, "Marks," 538, wrote: "The gospel is to be preached as well as the law, and the law is to be preached only to make way for the gospel, and in order that it may be preached more effectually. The main work of ministers is to preach the gospel.... So that a minister would miss it very much if he should insist so much on the terrors of the law as to forget his Lord, and neglect to preach the gospel; but yet the law is very much to be insisted on, and the preaching of the gospel is like to be in vain without it.... Some talk of it as an unreasonable thing to fright persons to heaven; but I think it is a reasonable thing to fright persons away from hell.... Is it not a reasonable thing to fright a person out of a house on fire?"

14. *City of God* 21.9.2; *NPNF* 1.2:461.

15. Ibid. 21.3.1; *NPNF* 1.2:453.

Augustine, in short, found it necessary to introduce a change in the meaning of *death* if his belief in the endlessness of the torment of hellfire was to be sustained; and this is a necessity for all who understand eternal destruction in this way, whether or not they consider the flames of hell to be intended in a literal sense. Such persons can indeed claim to be in good company; but they should be aware that their interpretation is open to serious questioning. Apart from the fact that it involves a drastic change in the meaning of death so that, in this eschatological perspective, it signifies being kept alive to suffer punishment without the power of dying, some other considerations must be taken into account.

First of all, because *life* and *death* are radically antithetical to each other, the qualifying adjective *eternal* or *everlasting* needs to be understood in a manner appropriate to each respectively. Everlasting life is existence that continues without end, and everlasting death is destruction without end, that is, destruction without recall, the destruction of obliteration. Both life and death hereafter will be everlasting in the sense that both will be *irreversible*; from that life there can be no relapse into death, and from that death there can be no return to life. The awful negation and the absolute finality of the second death are unmistakably conveyed by its description as "the punishment of eternal destruction and exclusion from the presence of the Lord" (2 Thess 1:9).

Secondly, immortality or deathlessness, as we have said, is not inherent in the constitution of man as a corporeal-spiritual creature, though, formed in the image of God, the potential was there. That potential, which was forfeited through sin, has been restored and actualized by Christ, the incarnate Son, who has "abolished death and brought life and immortality to light through the gospel" (2 Tim 1:10). Since inherent immortality is uniquely the possession and prerogative of God (1 Tim 6:16), it will be by virtue of his grace and power that when Christ is manifested in glory our mortality, if we are then alive, will be superinvested with immortality and our corruption, if we are then in the grave, will be clothed with incorruption, so that death will at last be swallowed up in victory (1 Cor 15:51–57; 2 Cor 5:1–5). And thus at last we shall become truly and fully human as the destiny for which we were created becomes an everlasting reality in him who is the True Image and the True Life. At the same time those who have persisted in ungodliness will discover for themselves the dreadful truth of Christ's warning about fearing God, "who can destroy both body and soul in hell" (Matt 10:28).

Thirdly, the everlasting existence side by side, so to speak, of heaven and hell would seem to be incompatible with the purpose and effect of the redemption achieved by Christ's coming. Sin with its consequences of suffering and death is foreign to the design of God's creation. The renewal of creation demands the elimination of sin and suffering and death. Accordingly, we are assured that Christ "has appeared once for all at the end of the ages to put away sin by the sacrifice of himself" (Heb 9:26; 1 John 3:5), that through his appearing death has been abolished (2 Tim 1:10), and that in the new heaven and the new earth, that is, in the whole realm of the renewed order of creation, there will be no more weeping or suffering, "and death shall be no more" (Rev 21:4). The conception of the endlessness of the suffering of torment and of the endurance of "living" death in hell stands in contradiction to this teaching. It leaves a part of creation which, unrenewed, everlastingly exists in alienation from the new heaven and the new earth. It means that suffering and death will never be totally abolished from the scene. The inescapable logic of this position was accepted, with shocking candor, by Augustine, who affirmed that "after the resurrection, however, when the final, universal judgment has been completed, there shall be two kingdoms, each with its own distinct boundaries, the one Christ's, the other the devil's; the one consisting of the good, the other of the bad."[16] To this it must be objected that with the restoration of all things in the new heaven and the new earth, which involves God's reconciliation to himself of *all things*, whether on earth or in heaven (Acts 3:21; Col 1:20), there will be no place for a second kingdom of darkness and death. Where all is light there can be no darkness; for "the night shall be no more" (Rev 22:5). When Christ fills all in all and God is everything to everyone (Eph 1:23; 1 Cor 15:28), how is it conceivable that there can be a section or realm of creation that does not belong to this fullness and by its very presence contradicts it? The establishment of God's everlasting kingdom of peace and righteousness will see the setting free of the whole created order from its bondage to decay as it participates in the glorious liberty of the children of God (Rom 8:21).

Fourthly, the glorious appearing of Christ will herald the death of death. By his cross and resurrection Christ has already made the conquest of death, so that for the believer the fear and sting of death have been removed (Heb 2:14f.; 1 Cor 15:54–57), the passage from death to

---

16. *Enchiridion* 111; *NPNF* 1.3:273.

life is a present reality (John 5:24), and the resurrection power of Jesus is already at work within him, no matter how severely he may be afflicted and incommoded outwardly (2 Cor 4: 11, 16). We do not yet see everything in subjection to the Son (Heb 2:8); but nothing is more sure than that every hostile rule and authority and power will finally be destroyed, including death itself. Hence the assurance that "the last enemy to be destroyed is death" (1 Cor 15:24–26). Without the abolition of death the triumph of life and immortality cannot be complete (2 Tim 1:10). This is the significance of *the second death*; it will be the abolition not only of sin and the devil and his followers but also of death itself as, in the final judgment, not only will Death and Hades give up their dead for condemnation but Death and Hades themselves will be thrown with them into the lake of fire (Rev 20:13–15). Hence the clear promise that "death shall be no more" (Rev 21:4).

Though held by many, it is it is a hollow contention that if the death sentence pronounced at the final judgment against the unregenerate meant their annihilation the wicked would be getting off lightly and would be encouraged to regard the consequence of their sin without fear. (It may be interposed that far more does the expectation of the never-ending torment of finite creatures raise the question of the purpose that might be served by such retribution.) There is altogether no room for doubting that, first, at the last judgment God will mete out condign punishment in accordance with the absolute holiness of his being, and, second, the Scriptures allow no place whatsoever to the wicked for complacency as they approach that dreadful day when they will stand before the tribunal of their righteous Creator. This ultimate day of the Lord is depicted as a day of indescribable terror for the ungodly, who will then be confronted with the truth of God's being, which they had unrighteously suppressed and experience the divine wrath which previously they had derided. They will then learn at first hand that "it is a fearful thing to fall into the hands of the living God" (Heb 10:31). There is nothing light or laughable in the terrible scene witnessed by St. John in his apocalyptic vision: "Then the kings of the earth and the great men and the generals and the rich and the strong, and every one, slave and free, hid in the caves and among the rocks of the mountains, calling to the mountains and the rocks, 'Fall on us and hide us from the face of him who is seated on the throne, and from the wrath of the Lamb, for the great day of their wrath has come, and who can stand before it?'" (Rev 6:15–17).

The horror of everlasting destruction will be compounded, moreover, by the unbearable agony of *exclusion*. To be inexorably excluded from the presence of the Lord and from the glory of his kingdom, to see but to be shut out from the transcendental joy and bliss of the saints as in light eternal they glorify their resplendent Redeemer, to whose likeness they are now fully and forever conformed, to be plunged into the abyss of irreversible destruction, will cause the unregenerate of mankind the bitterest anguish of weeping and wailing and gnashing of teeth. In vain will they have pleaded, "Lord, Lord, open to us!" (Matt 25:11f.; cf. 7:21–23). Too late will they then wish they had lived and believed differently. The destiny they have fashioned for themselves will cast them without hope into the abyss of obliteration. Their lot, whose names are not written in the Lamb's book of life, is the destruction of the second death. Thus God's creation will be purged of all falsity and defilement, and the ancient promise will be fulfilled that "the former things shall not be remembered or come to mind" as the multitude of the redeemed are glad and rejoice forever in the perfection of the new heaven and the new earth (Isa 65:17f.; Rev 21:1–4).

14

Divine Justice

Henry Constable

Henry Constable (1816–1891), a graduate of the University of Dublin, was ordained an Anglican priest in 1850 by archbishop of Dublin, Richard Whately. Whately and Constable are two names among several of those who advocated conditionalism in the nineteenth century, which "saw a revival of conditionalism that swept across national, linguistic, and denominational lines."[1]

Of nineteenth-century books defending conditionalism, Constable's Duration and Nature of Future Punishment, *published in 1868, may be the best known today, having been printed in at least six editions and influencing readers around the world. In this excerpt from Constable's book, he addresses a common traditionalist response to objections based on the seeming injustice of eternal torment, namely that God's justice is inscrutable, and examines the issue's impact on the traditional view of hell.*

WE NOW APPROACH A very solemn question—the question of divine justice. We approach it with the deep reverence that becomes a creature when he scans and judges the conduct of his maker, but also with the confidence that becomes one who is invited by his maker to this inquiry. It is indeed said that we are not able to judge God's ways and this no doubt is often true. It is true, however, only of those dealings of his

---

1. Fudge, *Fire That Consumes* (2011), 338.

with which we are imperfectly acquainted, or which, from their nature, are above our comprehension. The present subject belongs to neither of these categories. Future punishment is a matter fully placed before us. No question occupies a more distinct position than it does in divine revelation. We are clearly told its cause and its nature; we are told to ponder and study it. We are not treated as children incapable of forming an opinion of what is just or unjust in God. If we were thus incapable, a large portion of Scripture would be useless and meaningless. Called upon in God's Word to love, respect, and confide in him, and *having his entire conduct towards men*, whether just or unjust, *brought to our view, in order to produce these feelings in us*, we are thus *viewed by God himself as capable of judging of his character*, of his love, his mercy, his wisdom, his justice, and his judgment. He does not thus merely regard us as capable, but he has directly appealed to us to judge his conduct towards us, admitted his creature's scrutiny as the exercise of a right—and this not merely in the case of his faithful people, but even of those who were alienated from him. Abraham was not rebuked when he judged a certain supposed line of conduct unworthy of the God in whom his trust was placed.[2] Rebellious Israel, misjudging God's dealings from ignorance and prejudice, are invited to look fairly at it and see if indeed God's "ways are not equal."[3] Christ allows to the generation of his day the power of judging rightly, and only on such a supposition could they lie under their deep guilt.[4] "The law of justice in our hearts," it has been well observed, "is only a reflection of God's perfect justice."[5] In the human breast there is a true sense of what is just, and God not only allows it, but insists upon its exercise towards himself. He has told us his character. He challenges us to bring any line of conduct attributed to him to the test. In the question of future punishment we have the highest case on which any tribunal shall have ever sat, and we may be sure that the judge of all the earth will do right, not merely in his own eyes, but in those of all his intelligent creation: of the angels who stand round his throne; of the redeemed who rejoice in their acceptance; of the very damned who listen to their sentence.

But we are often told that, while no doubt God's conduct towards sinners will one day appear to the redeemed and even to the lost to have

2. Gen 18:23–25.
3. Ezek 18:29.
4. Luke 12:57.
5. Girdlestone, *Dies Iræ*, 170.

been just, yet that we must be content to wait until it shall so appear. This life is to pass away, the hour of resurrection must come, the throne of judgment must be set, the guilt of the lost be displayed, the everlasting sentence be passed, *and then,* the redeemed and the lost alike will see that God's ways were just. Not so, we reply. God appeals to us *now* to judge. He places before us his character *now*, in order that we may judge. It is *now* that our conduct is to be affected, our fears aroused, our respect gained, our love won, for the God and Father of our Lord Jesus Christ. It is *now* that misapprehension of him will tell with power; it is now that a correct judgment is to save the soul. When the judgment is set, and the sentence passed, *it is too late.*

But they who tell us to *wait in faith* wholly miscalculate the real position of the question before us. *They suppose faith in God is to sustain the mind against the appearance of injustice in God's dealings with men.* They reverse the mode of God's own proceeding. They suppose faith first to exist, and this faith is to withstand and subdue all that may appear unjust. The exact opposite to this is the way in which God deals with man. *He has come to an unbelieving and alienated world and put his character before them to win their fear, their repentance, and their love.* We judge from our little stand point, taught from infancy to believe in God, to believe that he can do no wrong, to attribute any appearance of wrong on his part to our ignorance, to put down all injurious judgment of him as unbelief and sin. With all our training at our mother's knee, from our teacher's lips, from that pulpit where man claims to speak in the name of God, we yet know how the *Christian heart and judgment* mourn, stumble, are perplexed, stand aghast, at the *justice* that is proposed to them as *the justice of God*. But it was not thus that the question was first presented, or that the human mind was won to submission. *It was to a world of unbelievers* that God was proposed as a God of justice, as well as of pity and of love. To this world, which had no faith, God was proposed for acceptance. God's character and conduct were placed before it to *win* its faith and its love. So it is even now. So it is to a great extent even in so-called Christian lands; it is so wholly in heathen lands. God's character and conduct are to win faith, not to be sustained by faith against appearances. The missionary tells the unbeliever what kind of God the God of the Christian is, to convert the unbeliever to the faith. Can we wonder that the answer of the heathen to our messages should be, "We cannot, and will not, believe in a God of whom you affirm such outrageous wrong"?

We arrange the matter as God has arranged it. God's conduct, whether past or future, is *to win* man's respect, faith, and love, and not to be hardly and with difficulty palliated, excused, defended, *tolerated*, through man's faith. We are to come not merely to the truthful child at our knee, to the modest youth in our school, to the admiring disciple listening to our words, but we are, and may, and ought, to come to the incredulous skeptic, the profligate sinner, the hard stern man, to the poor heathen outside our pale, the outcast Pariah, the cultivated Brahmin, the followers of Confucius, and say to one and all, "Here is *our* God, the God and the Father of our Jesus Christ. Give him your love; give him your faith; give him your obedience and your fear. *His character demands it at your hands.*" It is thus we will propose the grand question of the divine justice in the treatment of sinners. We will not wait for the day of judgment to propose it. We propose it when it ought to be proposed: in the day of salvation. We ask the human heart for its verdict. We say that judged by human judgment—that of believers and unbelievers alike—the punishment that the theory of Augustine supposes God will inflict is *infinitely too great*, and we are therefore to reject it as untrue, because it is wholly unworthy, not merely of a merciful Father, but a just God.

Before we put our question of just or unjust, we must first refer plainly to the punishment itself. We will not attempt to describe it in our own words. We will merely give a few passages descriptive of it from writers who hold the view.

Here is an extract from a little book entitled *The Child's Path to Glory*, published at Birmingham, and which has passed through at least seven editions:

> There is nothing but misery in hell. You would never more have one moment's ease; for there is nothing but pain and torment there. Put together all you can think of that is miserable, and painful, and terrible, and it is all nothing to what is prepared for those who go there; and that not for an hour, or a day, or a year, but *for an eternity*. The lost souls who live in that horrible pit *wish to die*, but they are not able; for God says, "Their worm dieth not." The frightful and cruel devil may torment them as much as he pleases—they are made strong to bear it.

Here is the account given by the famous Jonathan Edwards of America: "imagine yourself to be cast into a fiery oven, all of a glowing heat, or into the midst of a glowing brick-kiln, or of a great furnace, where your pain would be as much greater than that occasioned by accidentally touching a coal of fire, as the heat is greater. Imagine also that your body were to lie there for a quarter of an hour, full of fire, as full within and without as a bright coal of fire, all the while full of quick sense ... O then, how would your heart sink, if you thought, if you knew, that you must bear it forever and ever!"[6] Here is the description of hell by the celebrated preacher Mr. Spurgeon:

> Only conceive that poor wretch in the flames who is saying, "O for one drop of water, to cool my parched tongue!" See how his tongue hangs from between his blistered lips! How it excoriates and burns the roof of his mouth, as if it were a firebrand. Behold him crying for a drop of water. I will not picture the scene. Suffice it for me to close up by saying, that the hell of hells will be to thee, poor sinner, the thought that it is to be forever. Thou wilt look up there on the throne of God, and it shall be written "forever!" When the damned jingle the burning irons of their torments, they shall say "forever!" When they howl, echo cries "forever!"
>
> "Forever" is written on their racks,
> "Forever" on their chains;
> "Forever" burneth in the fire,
> "Forever" ever reigns.[7]

These are very horrifying descriptions. *We* turn with unmitigated loathing from the idea that a scene such as is depicted above ... is to go on to eternity. But others, who do not agree with us in our view of future punishment, are almost, if not altogether, as much disgusted with them as we are. The ablest and purest minds that still cling desperately to the Augustinian theory cannot endure such descriptions, and will not allow that they represent the hell in which they believe. They gravely reprobate the horrors that were so dear and familiar to the Middle Ages, and that are still urged in all their minute and terrible detail by preachers and writers, Protestant and Romanist. They do not think them *true* descriptions of hell. They think that they exaggerate its terrors.

    We do not ourselves enter into the question whether the descriptions of future punishment in Scripture are literal or figurative, because we do not think the solution of the question to be really *of any consequence*.

---

6. As quoted in Miller, *Jonathan Edwards*, 160.
7. Spurgeon, *Sermons*, 189–90.

Scripture tells us there will be a worm, a fire, darkness, etc.; but it does not seem to take any trouble to explain whether it speaks literally or figuratively. But whichever view be taken of its language, it must commend itself to reason that *the punishment signified is in either case equally terrible though different in character*. If there be a literal fire consuming, and a literal worm gnawing, we know the exact pain produced: if the fire and the worm be figurative, they are figurative of a pain and suffering such in intensity as would be produced by the literal agents. Nothing then is really gained by rejecting the literal view or by changing the *bodily pains* of which they chiefly speak *into suffering and anguish of the mind*. If the descriptions of Scripture are figures they are at the same time *true figures*: if they are not to be understood literally they must yet be understood as giving us the *truest and best ideas possible of the real anguish and misery of hell*. On no hypothesis can we understand hell as other than a scene where pain and anguish, mental or bodily, or both, of the most intense and terrible nature, are endured by all who have any existence there. Hell cannot by any artful handling of words, by any skillful manipulation of phrases, be toned down into a place other than of the most fearful kind. Descriptions, such as Christ has given, are not to be by us withdrawn as too terrible. He has spoken of "unquenchable fire" and the undying "worm," and we may not, and ought not, to withhold these terrible images from the mind. The real question is, not whether they are literal or figurative, but whether the pains they point to and portray are pains to be endured forever, or which sooner or later produce a destruction of the sentient being, from which there is no recovery.

Literal or figurative, then, the descriptions we have above quoted from various Augustinian writers are substantially true, if the Augustinian theory is true. Between them and us there is a wide difference indeed; for we hold that these are *consuming and destroying agents*, reducing the living to death, and removing even the appearance of that which has become dead and loathsome. But between those who hold the descriptions of Scripture as literal, and those who hold them to be figurative, there is no difference of any material kind. Both believe in anguish of the most terrible nature as continuing throughout eternity. Nor can we well see how they can refuse the additional idea that this anguish must go on increasing throughout eternity as the despair of any end grows blacker and blacker.

Such then, according to the Augustinian theory, is to be the eternal future of myriads of creatures framed and fashioned by God. Such descriptions, be they literal or be they figurative, are, according to their teaching, *true of every being placed in hell*. They picture the eternity not only of fallen angels and men who rejected the gospel, but of the multitudes who never heard the name of the Father and the Son. If the "second death," and "everlasting destruction," and "perishing," of the wicked, be what the theory of Augustine teaches, the ignorant heathen endure it as well as the rejecter of the gospel, for they who "have sinned without law shall perish" as they who sinned in the law,[8] and the men of Tyre, Sidon, and Nineveh must appear in the judgment as well as the generation that listened to the words of Christ.[9] Eternal agonies are the "*few stripes*" that Augustine's theory has provided for the most ignorant offender.[10] Are eternal agonies a just punishment for *any*, be they servants who knew or were ignorant of their master's will? We will take the latter case first.

We will take the case of some poor islander a remote Pacific isle. Steeped in densest ignorance was his mind from the day he was cast a helpless infant upon this dark world, to the time he sunk back still more helpless in death. No lesson of virtue, of moderation, of purity, had ever cast its light on him. What should he know of justice who only saw the strong oppressing those who were weaker than they? What should he know of purity who in the women of his tribe or nation had never seen one who had even a faint idea of woman's highest grace? How was religion in his case to give him some higher holier, lovelier notions than he could learn from his fellow man? Religion! The gods whom he worshipped—if indeed he worshipped any—were gods to whom rites of cruelty and impurity were a pleasing incense!

We do not say of such a man that he has *no* guilt. We do not believe that any one gifted with reason has ever lived *a life free* from guilt. Even where no revelation of true religion kept fully before the human mind the sense of right and wrong as in the sight of God; even where no distorted ray of tradition still kept up some rude sense of the essential difference of some from other actions; even in the darkest age and the remotest corner where a humanity sees only a society as degraded as itself; even *there* the pain and suffering which evil inflicts, through one man upon another,

8. Rom 2:12.
9. Matt 11:22; 12:41.
10. Luke 12:48.

keeps alive the sense of right and wrong in the lowest type of the human mind.

The savage has indeed never heard such lessons as the gospel teaches in its every page, of a God who loves his enemies, and so urges upon children, to be "tender-hearted, forgiving another, even as God for Christ's sake hath forgiven you."[11] The savage has never, in his experience or in the dim tradition of his tribe, conceived of such a man as Jesus of Nazareth, who, in all his aims, had none for self, but all for his Father and his brethren. But, in his smoking homestead, his slaughtered children, his wife carried captive to another's lust—in scenes such as these, and by acts such as these, some sense of right and wrong produced by the sense of injury and loss is kept alive, and where there is the sense of right and wrong there is the capacity of offending and the claim for punishment from God.

But how is such a man's guilt to be estimated, to be weighed in the scales of justice, to be adjudged its fitting recompense? We have the divine words for saying that this man's guilt is *small*. The judgment of reason is confirmed by that of God. A favorite proposition of our Augustinian opponents, though by no means so favorably regarded now as it used to be, is that "All sin is of an infinite nature, and requires endless conscious suffering as its only suitable punishment." But what says God, and God's Son, of the sins of heathen men? Do we find Jesus Christ, who came down from heaven to tell us his Father's mind, talking the scholastic jargon which our modern preachers have learned from the ingenious brain-twisting of the Middle Ages? We do not. What does he say of sins such as we have spoken of? Speaking even of Jews, who had so much fuller light than heathen men possess, he yet declared that if he had not "come and spoken unto them they would not have had sin."[12] While of the dark heathen sinner he said, "he that knew not his Lord's will, and did commit things worthy of stripes, *shall be beaten with few stripes*."[13] And thus we find from the highest authority that the sins of the heathen are light, and that the punishment they shall feel shall be also light—*a few stripes*. They are the words of Christ. And is hell, according to Augustine's theory, a place of few stripes to any placed therein? Is a life of endless agony, of despair growing more despairing as eternity rolls on and still

11. Eph 4:32.
12. John 15:22.
13. Luke 11:48.

brings no relief, no prospect of a close—is this a just punishment for the offences of heathen? Is this the Christian man's explanation of the *"few stripes"* of Christ his master? A few stripes! Why if Methuselah had been multiplying the figures of arithmetic from the time he could calculate till he reached his 969th year he could not have arrived at any appreciable part of the sum of the stripes which the Augustinian theory would inflict on the sinners of the heathen.

Away then with this diabolical doctrine which shocks all our sense of justice and casts bitter contempt upon the merciful words of Christ. Is a life of endless agony, ever increasing, what Jesus meant by a *"few stripes"*? God forbid that we should dare thus to tamper with his words. The heathen offender will know of no such hell as Mr. Spurgeon . . . and President Edwards . . . have depicted. When the Red Indian of the American forest, or the dusky child of the remote Pacific isle, wakes up at the solemn resurrection and hears judgment pronounced against him for willful offense against such dim light as he possessed, it will not be condemnation to a place where he is to suffer agony while the redeemed of Christ enjoy their endless life. The Lord has told us so, and we believe him.

Our view needs no vindication, does not compel us to keep it discreetly in the background, and does not reduce us to subterfuge to escape its consequences. It does not force us to advance arguments we feel to be unworthy of a child, or faintly to defend the justice of a procedure that our heart whispers to us is only worthy of a devil's conception. By it, the next life's dealings with the sinner will but follow the analogy of this. He who scans the course of nature may from it anticipate that future course which revelation opens to our view. *According to it God's ways with the sinner are equal.* They are severe, but they are just. They are full of awe, but they can be contemplated with calmness. They show the aware of a justice in whose consequences we can rejoice. Its issue is eternal death. If it brings the sigh of sadness over a lost soul, it brings also the deep full breathing of infinite relief. "The wicked," says Locke, "had no right to demand their existence, and so no right to demand its continuance." We require neither the "purgatory" of Augustine, nor the "universal restoration" of Origen—man's desperate refuges from the hell he has himself conceived. Looking on the calmed face of death, we will say, "It is well." The woes, the agony, the despair, of life, are passed away from its features with the sin that produced them.

15

Divine and Human Punishment in the New Testament

CHRISTOPHER D. MARSHALL

Christopher Marshall is the head of the School of Art History, Classics and Religious Studies at Victoria University of Wellington. His expertise is in ethics—both theoretical and applied—and New Testament theology, with an emphasis in the Anabaptist tradition. Marshall remains active in promoting peacemaking and justice and he was the recipient of the 2004 International Community Justice Award. His book Beyond Retribution *was named in the American Academy of Parish Clergy's list of "Top Ten Books for Parish Ministry Published in 2001," nominated for the Grawemeyer Award in Religion in 2002, and included among the list of "Outstanding Academic Titles" by the book review journal* Choice *in 2003.*

For Marshall, God's justice is in no way constituted by retribution or vengeance upon sinners, but is rather a "restorative and reconstructive justice, a saving action by God that recreates shalom and makes things right." In light of this he suggests the notion of restorative punishment, which is "the pain of taking responsibility" for one's personal actions and their consequences. When applied to the final end of the wicked, their punishment is the lack of connection with God, and connection with him, Marshall reminds us, is necessary for existence; this "punishment" is self-inflicted and merely allowed by God out of respect for free will rather than retributively dealt out by him.

PART FOUR—PHILOSOPHICAL SUPPORT FOR CONDITIONALISM

MOST REFERENCES TO DIVINE judgment in the New Testament are eschatological in reference. The wrath of God upon sin, partially reflected in historical experiences, is definitively located at the close of history, "the day of wrath, when God's righteous judgment will be revealed" (Rom 2:5). This conviction permeates New Testament literature from beginning to end. Indeed, the canonical narrative closes with this announcement: "See, I am coming soon; my reward is with me, to repay according to everyone's work" (Rev 22:12, 18–21; cf. 11:18).

There is no uniform conception of final judgment and its consequences to which all New Testament authors subscribe.[1] They speak selectively and allusively about realities that, by definition, lie beyond human experience and knowledge, each author giving emphasis to different aspects of the traditions he draws upon and employing a diversity of terms, images, and genres in doing so. Nevertheless, a sufficient number of common or similar convictions merge in their writings to give us reasonable insight into how, in broad terms, they understood eschatological judgment. At the end of the age, all people, both the living and the dead, both "the righteous and the unrighteous,"[2] will appear before the judgment seat of God or Christ,[3] where each will receive "recompense for what has been done in the body, whether good or evil."[4] A separation will occur. The righteous will depart into eternal life.[5] For them there will be "rewards" or "prizes" or "treasure in heaven."[6] The wicked, however, "will go away into eternal punishment (*kolasin aiōnion*)."[7] In the Gospels, Jesus speaks frequently of "Gehenna,"[8] or the place of outer

---

1. According to Reiser, *Judgment*, 162, "The coexistence of what, from a logical point of view, are mutually exclusive eschatological conceptions, a situation apparently regarded as unproblematic—this is characteristic of Jewish and to a great extent of Christian intellectual history."

2. Acts 24:15; cf. Luke 13:28–29; John 5:28–29; Heb 9:27.

3. Rom 14:10; 2 Cor 5:10.

4. 2 Cor 5:10; cf. Matt 25:31–46; Rom 2:6–11; Rev 20:11–15; 21:5–8.

5. Matt 7:14; 19:29; 24:46; Luke 10:25; John 3:15–16; 5:29; Acts 11:18; 13:46–47; Rom 2:7; 2 Cor 5:4; 1 Pet 3:7; cf. Heb 5:9; 9:12.

6. Mark 9:41; 10:21, 28–30; Matt 5:12, 46; 6:1–6, 16–21; 10:41; 19:28–29; 20:1–16; 24:46–47; 25:21, 23; Luke 6:23, 38; 12:33–34; 14:12, 14, 15; 18:28–30; cf. 1 Cor 3:5–15; 4:4–5; 2 Cor 5:10; Phil 3:12–16; Col 3:24–25; Eph 6:8–9.

7. Matt 25:46; cf. Mark 3:28–29; 9:42; 12:9; 14:21; Matt 5:26; 10:15, 28, 33; 11:20–24; 12:31–32, 36–37; 13:30, 41–42; 18:35; 25:41, 46; Luke 12:47; 13:9, 22–30; 16:23–31; 18:7–8; 19:27; 23:41; John 3:36; 5:28–29; cf. Matt 3:7/Luke 3:7 (John the Baptist).

8. Cf. C. Milikowsky, "Gehenna."

darkness and unquenchable fire where there will be "weeping" (signifying misery or fear) and "gnashing of teeth" (denoting anger or frustration) by those excluded from salvation.[9] He also indicates that judgment will fall not just on individuals but on cities and nations as well.[10] Many other New Testament texts speak of the eternal loss the wicked will face, which is described variously as an experience of "wrath,"[11] "vengeance,"[12] "repayment,"[13] "tribulation and distress,"[14] "fire,"[15] and, most often, of "destruction," "death," or "disintegration."[16] Particularly graphic is 2 Pet 2:9, which speaks of the unrighteous being "kept under punishment (*kolazomenous tērein*) until the day of judgment."[17]

Now, inasmuch as retributive justice consists in proportionate recompense according to deserts, the New Testament descriptions of final judgment as a matter of God assessing and recompensing human works,[18] sometimes with the suggestion that there will be varying degrees of reward or punishment depending on merit,[19] could easily be understood to

---

9. Mark 9:42–48; Matt 5:22, 29–30; 8:11–12; 10:28; 13:41, 42, 50; 18:8–9; 22:13; 23:15, 33; 24:51; 25:30; Luke 12:4–5; 13:28–29; cf. Jas 3:6.

10. Matt 10:15; Matt 11:21–24/Luke 10:13–15; Matt 21:43–44; 23:35–38.

11. Matt 3:7; Luke 21:33; John 3:36; 1 Thess 1:9–10; 5:9; 2:14–16; Rom 2:1–11; 3:5; 4:15; 5:9; 9:22–23; 12:19–21; Eph 2:3; 5:6; Col 3:6; Rev 6:16–17; 11:18; 14:10, 19; 15:1, 7; 16:1; 16:19; 19:15.

12. 2 Thess 1:6–10; Heb 10:28–30; Jude 7; cf. Rom 12:19; 1 Thess 4:6; Luke 18:7–8.

13. Rom 12:19; 2 Thess 1:6; 2:9–12; Rom 6:23; cf. 1 Cor 3:17; Gal 6:7–8; Rom 1:27, 32.

14. Rom 2:9; 2 Thess 1:6.

15. Matt 5:22; 13:42, 50; 24:41; Mark 9:47–48; Luke 17:29–30; 2 Thess 1:8; Heb 10:27; 2 Pet 3:7; Rev 11:5; 18:8; 19:20; 20:9–10, 14–15; 21:8.

16. Destruction, death (*olethros*): 1 Thess 5:3; 2 Thess 1:9 (1 Tim 6:9); death (*thanatos*): Rom 1:32; 6:21–23; 7:5; 8:6; 1 Cor 15:21–22; 15:56; 2 Cor 2:16; 7:10; Jas 1:15; 1 John 5:16; Rev 2:11; 20:6; 20:14; 21:8; annihilation, ruin, destruction (*apoleia*): Matt 7:13; John 17:12; Acts 8:20; Rom 9:22–24; Phil 1:28; 3:19; 2 Thess 2:3; 1 Tim 6:9; Heb 10:39; 2 Pet 2:1; 3:7, 16; decay, disintegration (*phthora*): Gal 6:8; 2 Pet 1:4; 2:12; end (*telos*): Rom 6:21–22; 2 Cor 11:15; Phil 3:19; 1 Pet 4:17.

17. The text could be construed to mean either that the unrighteous will be punished before the day of judgment, in some intermediate state (so NRSV), or that the unrighteous will be punished on the day of judgment. See Bauckham, *Jude*, 253–55.

18. This theme pervades both Old and New Testaments. See, e.g., Pss 9:8–21; 37:9, 33; 58:12; 62:10, 13; Job 34:11; Prov 10:16; 24:12; Eccl 12:14; Isa 3:10–11; 59:18; Jer 17:10; 25:14; 32:19; Lam 3:64; Hos. 4:9; Rom 2:1–16; 14:7–12; 1 Cor 3:10–17; 4:1–5; 5:1–5; 6:9–11; 9:24–27; 11:27–34; 2 Cor 5:9–10; Gal 5:19–21; 6:7–10; Col 3:25; Eph 6:8; 1 Tim 5:24–25; 2 Tim 4:14.

19. See, e.g., Mark 10:29–30; Luke 12:47–48; Matt 10:15; 11:22, 24; 12:40; 1 Cor

teach that divine justice is essentially and ultimately retributive justice. More worrisome is that the doctrine of final damnation could be taken to mean that the God we are to imitate is finally vindictive, not forgiving; that salvation is, ultimately, the achievement of coercive power, not of self-surrendering love; that punitive pain is an everlasting reality, not a remedial or restorative mechanism. Any such implications, if applied to criminal practice today, would have disastrous results. Nor is this merely a hypothetical concern. Throughout Christian history, the fear of being consigned to hell by a truly merciless God has fueled and justified all manner of horrific violence. It is a short step from denying the future existence of one's opponents after death to denying their right to exist before death. Moreover, for centuries the use of torture to convert heretics and infidels was considered justifiable, even merciful, since it would serve to deliver them from eternal torture in hell. Thus, as Hans Küng explains,

> All who were worthy of damnation, destined for hell, were opposed with the sword, with torture and continually with fire, so that by the death of the body here below the soul might perhaps be saved for the hereafter. Forced conversions, burning of heretics, Jewish pogroms, crusades, witch hunts in the name of a religion of love, cost millions of lives (in Seville alone in the course of forty years four thousand persons were burned by the Inquisition).[20]

The most prolonged and sadistic forms of public execution were employed both to serve as a foretaste of God's judgment to come and to afford victims the chance to influence their eternal destiny by their manner of endurance. Judicial judgment and eternal judgment were mutually related, as Michel Foucault explains:

> The eternal game has already begun: the torture of the execution anticipates the punishments of the beyond; it shows what they are; it is the theater of hell; the cries of the condemned man, his struggles, his blasphemies, already signify his irremediable destiny. But the pains here below may also be counted as penitence and so alleviate the punishments of the beyond: God will not fail to take such a martyrdom into account, providing it is borne with resignation. The cruelty of the earthly punishment will be deducted from the punishment to come: in it is glimpsed the promise of forgiveness. But, it might be said, are not such

---

15:41; Eph 6:8.

20. Küng, *Eternal Life*, 136. See also Moltmann, *Today's World*, 59–60.

terrible sufferings a sign that God has abandoned the guilty man to the mercy of his fellow creatures? And, far from securing future absolution, do they not prefigure imminent damnation; so that, if the condemned man dies quickly, without a prolonged agony, is it not proof that God wishes to protect him and to prevent him falling into despair? There is, therefore, an ambiguity in this suffering that may signify equally well the truth of the crime or the error of the judges, the goodness or the evil of the criminal, the coincidence or the divergence between the judgment of men and that of God. Hence the insatiable curiosity that drove the spectators to the scaffold to witness the spectacle of sufferings truly endured; there one could decipher crime and innocence, the past and the future, the here below and the eternal. It was a moment of truth that all the spectators questioned: each word, each cry, the duration of the agony, the resisting body, the life that clung desperately to it, all this constituted a sign.[21]

Such potentially negative implications of biblical teaching on eschatological punishment need to be faced squarely at this point in our investigation. Yet the relevant exegetical data is so massive, the theological and philosophical issues entailed so profound, and current opinion on them so diverse, that there is no way to deal adequately with them in a few pages. What I intend to do is to clarify why the doctrine of eternal damnation is problematic for notions of restorative justice, then identify several reasons for questioning whether eschatological judgment really does amount to a scheme of strict retributive justice.

A Hell of a Problem

The idea that human history will climax in a definitive act of judgment, followed by the destruction of sinners or their consignment to hell,[22] can-

21. Foucault, *Discipline*, 46.

22. Considerable confusion is caused by the fact that the term "hell" has been used in English translations to render two different Greek terms in the New Testament with different referents. The term "hades," which occurs eleven times (Matt 16:18; 11:23; Luke 10:15; 16:23; Acts 2:27, 31; Rev 1:18; 6:8; 20:13–14), usually designates the realm of the dead (roughly equivalent to sheol in the Old Testament), whereas the term "Gehenna," which occurs twelve times (Mark 9:42–48; Matt 5:22, 29–30; 8:11–12; 10:28; 13:41, 42, 50; 18:8–9; 22:13; 23:15, 33; 25:30; 24:51; Luke 12:4–5; 13:28–29; cf Jas 3:6), designates the place of final punishment for the wicked (although hades in Luke 16:23 includes torment). Furthermore, the popular notion of hell as the home of Satan is not linked directly in the New Testament with hades (though cf. Rev 20:10, 14) or

not be regarded as a minor or incidental theme in Christian faith, for two main reasons. One is the sheer weight of biblical material that suggests otherwise. The theme is frequent in the teaching of Jesus,[23] particularly in Matthew's Gospel,[24] and widely attested elsewhere in the New Testament. The idea of eschatological condemnation explains what believers have been saved from, as well as what the wicked are destined for, and the threat of final loss is sometimes appealed to as a sanction for righteous behavior in the present.[25] The other reason has to do with theodicy. The biblical conception of God as all-powerful, all-knowing, and perfectly good requires ultimate vindication in the face of present sickness, sin, suffering, and death. The doctrine of the Last Judgment offers the hope that the results of human wrongdoing will be rectified, that people who have suffered unjustly will be recompensed, and that the wicked who have escaped justice in this life will face it in the next. Intuitively most people know that without final judgment, there can be no ultimate justice.

So the notion of final judgment has fundamental importance to Christian belief. Yet it would be false to make it central. The heart of Christian proclamation is the good news of the dawning of God's kingdom, of Christ's conquest of sin and death, and of the renewing work of the Holy Spirit. References in the New Testament to the positive benefit of salvation here and now far outweigh references to the negative consequences of damnation in the future.[26] There are some graphic references to damnation in the Gospels, but Jesus was no hellfire preacher. As Küng points out, "Nowhere does he show any direct interest in hell. Nowhere does he reveal any special truths in regard to the hereafter. Nowhere does he describe the act of damnation or the torments of the damned.

Gehenna. It is linked, if at all, with the "abyss" (Luke 8:31; Rev 9:1, 11; 20:1, 3; but cf. Rom 10:7, an Old Testament quotation in which "abyss" is synonymous with "hades/sheol"—cf. Ps 71:20; 107:26). The "gates of hades" in Matt 16:18 is probably better taken as a reference to death and destruction than to demonic powers, though this is disputed.

23. According to Reiser, *Judgment*, 303–4, more than 25 percent of the traditional discourse material of Jesus in the Synoptic tradition is concerned with the theme of final judgment. In the layers of the tradition, some 35 percent of the oral discourse in Q, 22 percent in Mark, 28 percent of the oral discourse material in Luke's special material, and a massive 64 percent of the discourse material in Matthew's special material is concerned with judgment.

24. See Charette, *Recompense*, esp. 119–61.

25. On warrants and sanctions in New Testament ethics, see Keck, "New Testament Ethics."

26. See Marshall, "Salvation."

... The heart of his message, which is meant to be the *eu-angelion*—not a threatening but a joyous message—lies elsewhere."[27] In his careful historical study *Jesus and Judgment*, Marius Reiser demonstrates the pervasiveness of the theme of judgment in the preaching of Jesus, yet he finds the heart of Jesus' message in his announcement of salvation:

> Jesus' preaching was sustained by the conviction that the repentance of the individual and of the whole nation should not so much aim at avoiding catastrophe as at gaining God's salvation. ... The central focus of his speech and action is not judgment and the way to avoid it, but the reign of God and how to gain it; it is not fear of judgment that should move Israel to repentance, but the fascination of the reign of God. Therefore his message could not be better summarized than in Mark 1:15. But when it met with rejection, Jesus had to point to the reverse side of the medal.[28]

That said, references to judgment and damnation still abound in the New Testament, and they pose profound problems, both philosophical and moral, for Christian belief. The problems are keenest for the traditional understanding of *hell as a place of everlasting, conscious torment*, which has long been considered the clear teaching of Scripture. Not only is its biblical basis highly questionable,[29] but the very idea of the damned

---

27. Küng, *Eternal Life*, 133–34.

28. Reiser, *Judgment*, 255; cf. 315.

29. There is only one clear reference to eternal torment in the New Testament (Rev 20:10). Not only does this refer to nonhuman figures (the devil, the beast, and the false prophet), which themselves represent evil systems rather than individuals, but it is highly symbolic language that is not intended to be taken literally. This is especially so since elsewhere we are told that God will destroy the devil (Heb 2:14), and John himself decodes the symbol of the lake of fire as being "the second death" (20:6, 14; 21:8; cf 2:11). In all other references to pain associated with judgment, such as wailing and gnashing of teeth (e.g., Matt 13:42, 50; Luke 13:28) and torment (Luke 16:24; Rev 14:10–11; 18:7, 10, 15), there is no clear indication that it is considered everlasting in nature. The texts may refer, for example, to a temporary experience of pain prior to final judgment, or to the reaction of the condemned to the passing of a verdict against them. (Note how in Rev 14:10 the holy angels and the lamb are present during the torment.) Or they may simply be figurative depictions of the horror of final loss. Images of "unquenchable fire" (e.g., Matt 3:12; Mark 9:43, 48) and "undying worms" (Mark 9:48; cf Isa 66:24) are also not meant to imply unending torture. Instead, they underline the fact that nothing can prevent the agents of destruction from completing their work, which is total obliteration (cf. Heb 10:27; 12:29). In every case the evocative and metaphorical nature of apocalyptic and parabolic language must be allowed for. The overwhelming weight of biblical data favors annihilation or destruction as the fate of

being kept in a state of perpetual pain depends on two propositions that are, in the long run, insupportable.

The first proposition is that redemption can be considered complete even though sin and suffering continue forever in hell. If immortality is not a "natural" property of the human soul, if all life is a gift of God (1 Tim 6:16; Acts 17:25–29; John 5:21), if nothing exists apart from the word of God (Rom 11:36; Col 1:17; Heb 1:3), then the wicked who live forever in hell can do so only because God actively sustains them in existence, despite their predilection for corruption and even though there is no hope for their repentance and restoration. This results in the impossible scenario where, on the one hand, God's conquest of sin and death is deemed complete (1 Cor 15:28), where all things have been reconciled to God (Col 1:20), where every tear has been wiped from every eye, and mourning and pain have been ended forever (Rev 21:4), and God has become "all in all" (1 Cor 15:27), yet where, on the other hand, there is one corner of God's dominion where sin, suffering, and rebellion continue to exist, sustained by nothing less than the creative activity of God. The finality of God's victory over evil is fatally compromised by the notion of eternal existence in hell. One way around this objection is to propose that God's ultimate triumph depends not on the eradication of all evil but only on its definitive subjection to God's purposes. The continued existence of the wicked, now totally subservient to God's rule, serves positively to advertise God's final supremacy. But this will not do. The biblical writers never deny God's continuing sovereignty over evil, and their vivid pictures of ultimate redemption go well beyond the forcible subjection of evildoers to portray the total extinction of all evil. Indeed, it must be this way, for it is not God's power that needs vindicating but God's goodness, and God's sovereign goodness cannot be reconciled with the eternal persistence of evil. As Norman Krauss explains, "The power and right to punish evil cannot vindicate God's goodness. Vengeance and everlasting retribution do not undo or redress the wrong that has been done. Retribution is no substitute for restitution."[30]

The second insupportable proposition concerns the reason why the wicked are kept alive by God in hell. The traditional answer is that the residents of hell are sustained in existence in order to be punished

---

the wicked. Of the burgeoning literature on this, see Fudge, *Fire That Consumes*; Ellis, "New Testament Teaching on Hell"; and Prestidge, *Destiny*.

30. Krauss, *God Our Saviour*, 213.

retributively for their earthly sins, which is deemed necessary to vindicate God's justice. The problems with this explanation are manifold. One major problem relates to the matter of just desserts, the fit between the punishment and the crime. What human wrongdoing could possibly justify infinite punitive pain? Surely, on the principle of proportionality, for infinite punishment to be deserved, an infinite amount of harm must have been caused by sinners within the temporal limits of their earthly, finite existence. But is this the case? Is it even possible for a finite creature to cause infinite harm to God or to God's creation?

One common reply is to argue that human guilt is proportional to the status of the party offended against and to the amount of harm *intended*, not just to the severity of the actual harm done. Since God is an infinite being, and the intention of sinners is to reject in principle the rule of that being, sin against God is infinitely serious and merits infinite punishment.[31] Moreover, this calculation applies to every sin, even the smallest infraction (otherwise, some arbitrary measure of seriousness would be required) and to every sinner (even to atheists, who have no conscious intention of rejecting the rule of a God they do not believe exists). However, as J. L. Kvanvig shows, the "status argument" is philosophically flawed.[32] Certainly it does not apply in the earthly criminal realm. Killing an infant is no less serious than killing an adult; robbing a homeless street kid is no less immoral than robbing a wealthy person of high social status. Arguably it is morally more repugnant to harm a weaker party than a stronger one. That the situation is different with an ontologically superior being—namely, God—must simply be asserted as self-evident; it cannot be logically proven. Similar problems exist with regarding every sin as equally meriting infinite punishment and with viewing all human wrongdoing as an intentional rejection of God's rule.

Another solution to the problem of disproportionate punishment is to suggest that the impenitent in hell, by consistently refusing God, repeatedly sin and therefore merit ongoing punishment. D. A. Carson proposes that "at the end hell's inmates are full of sin. They hate and attract retribution, they still love only themselves and attract retribution, they are neither capable of nor desirous of repenting, and attract retribution."[33] This has been deemed "perhaps the strongest argument

---

31. For recent statements of this view, see Peterson, "Stott"; and Dixon, *The Other Side*.

32. See especially Kvanvig, *Problem*, 25–66.

33. Carson, *Gagging*, 534.

used by traditionalists."[34] But it is hardly satisfying. By rendering the activity of sinning an unending reality, this proposal seriously diminishes God's ultimate victory over evil and its effects, as mentioned above. Moreover, to suggest, as Carson and others do, that God wills the continuous punishment of sinners in order to glorify his holy justice is surely to remake divine justice in our own image, to view it as a tit-for-tat payback procedure that spirals on forever and ever.

As well as the problem of disproportionate deserts, there is also the problem of justifying eternal suffering as the penalty. What morally defensible motive can God have (and even God cannot be exempted from moral assessment)[35] for inflicting everlasting pain, least of all a God who "does not willingly afflict or grieve anyone" (Lam 3:33), a God whose "anger is but for a moment; but [whose] favor is for a lifetime" (Ps 30:5)? In the human realm the deliberate infliction of pain on another party is considered to be an intrinsic evil, unless it is deemed essential for the achievement of some greater good that will benefit the one who suffers. In the case of eternal torment, however, there is no greater good to be achieved; there is no future value that compensates for the pain of the present. "From God's side," says Walter Moberly, "there is no credible motive for inflicting retributive suffering on a really incorrigible sinner. . . . Deliberately to prolong a man's existence to all eternity in a condition of abject terror and demoralization, is unthinkable. To desire torture for torture's sake is admittedly diabolical and belongs only to the pathology of a diseased mind."[36] Because the pain of hell leads nowhere, because there is no benefit for those who endure it, Kvanvig aptly describes hell as "paradigmatic . . . of truly pointless, gratuitous evil."[37] Substituting mental

---

34. Gray, "Destroyed," 16.

35. Some argue that eternal suffering must simply be accepted as a theological fact despite its moral problems, and that it is wrong for a mere creature to subject God to moral scrutiny. However, if God is the author of morality, God's own actions must ultimately be shown to conform to the moral principles God imposes on humanity. If something must be called good because God does it, when by every criterion of morality such an action is evil, then all standards of morality collapse, and ultimately there becomes no way to differentiate between God and the devil. Furthermore, if God is beyond all moral judgments, so that nothing God does could ever be said to be bad, then it should also be true that nothing God does can ever be said to be good or just or praiseworthy. It is true that God's ways are higher than ours (Isa 55:9), but they are *higher*—not lower—than ours!

36. Moberly, *Punishment*, 343.

37. Kvanvig, *Problem*, 9.

anguish, such as remorse, frustration, and disappointment, for physical pain, as most contemporary advocates of eternal suffering do, does nothing to ease the problem. Pain is pain, whether suffered in mind or body, and the more that eternal torment is viewed as remorse and regret, the more it resembles the repentance that God seeks and ought therefore to terminate the punishment! It has even been argued that the very notion of eternal remorse or regret is meaningless and impossible. Moberly suggests that a person who is so incurably wicked as to be consigned to hell would, by definition, lack the requisite conscience, moral insight, and self-awareness to feel guilt or remorse, or to recognize his or her suffering as deserved punishment. If any of those requisites existed, the person would be redeemable, and God would never abandon a potentially curable person to hell. Accordingly, "the notion of endless retributive and unredemptive punishment must be pronounced unthinkable. It is unthinkable because it combines elements that are really contradictory."[38]

What all this means is that it is impossible to justify morally the imposition of eternal suffering on human beings for their limited wrongdoings in this life. The argument that doing so is necessary to vindicate God's justice, and that this is the greater good that outweighs the sufferings of hell, is of no help. If to sustain someone in endless pain is immoral and unspeakably cruel, it cannot be a work of justice, and there is no logical reason why endless retribution is necessary to uphold God's justice. For this reason, and because a substantial body of exegetical evidence favors it, an increasing number of interpreters argue that the final judgment of the wicked consists of *their annihilation, not their endless suffering*. That is, to punish the wicked, God withdraws the gift of life, and they cease to exist; they are literally "destroyed." [39] Such punishment is still "eternal" (Matt 25:46; 2 Thess 1:9), but it is eternal in consequence or character, not in duration.[40] Annihilationism faces fewer moral difficulties than

38. Moberly, *Punishment*, 329–67 (quote from 339). See also Moberly, *Suffering*, 102–21.

39. See, e.g., Matt 10:28; Rom 2:12; 9:22; Phil 1:28; 3:19; 1 Thess 5:3; 2 Thess 1:9; 2 Pet 3:7, 9; Jas 4:12.

40. The word "eternal" is used in both a qualitative and a quantitive sense in the Bible. It is sometimes urged that if eternal life in Matt 25:46 is everlasting in duration, so too must be eternal punishment. But "eternal" in both phrases may simply designate that the realities in question pertain to the future age. Furthermore, inasmuch as life, by definition, is an ongoing state, "eternal life" includes the idea of everlasting existence. But punishment is a process rather than a state, and elsewhere when "eternal" describes an act or a process, it is the consequences rather than the process that are

eternal suffering, but it still encounters the problem of how an eternal punishment can be regarded as a just and proportionate recompense for temporal, finite sins. An eternity of nothingness is as much an infinite penalty for finite sin as an eternity of pain. As Kvanvig puts it, "Nothing is to be gained in responding to objections to a penal theory by substituting metaphysical capital punishment for metaphysical life imprisonment."[41] Retributive punishment remains God's final word, whether it takes the form of eternal incarceration or irreversible execution, and God still suffers a staggering loss of the beings created in his own image.

Two other main options exist. One is to deny the outcome of damnation altogether, whatever its nature, in favor of *universal salvation*. Some critics reject the thought of hell entirely; others see it as a theoretical possibility that will never be realized; still others, like Jürgen Moltmann, suggest that Jesus' own sufferings exhausted and destroyed the torments of hell.[42] Certainly there is a clear theme in New Testament teaching that anticipates the reconciliation of all things to God (see further below). In light of this, and in view of what we know about the expansiveness of God's love, it is quite appropriate for Christians to hope fervently for the universal redemption of all humankind, especially since this is evidently something God personally desires (1 Tim 2:4; 2 Pet 3:9). But the repeated emphasis in Scripture on the possibility of eternal loss warns against superficial optimism, as does the stubborn reality of human freedom. We cannot glibly assume that, even given the choice, every person would freely choose union with God over final separation from God. Some people, through the practice of evil, may become so resistant to surrendering themselves in love to God that the very thought of eternal intimacy with God would seem excruciatingly painful.[43] The other, more promising option is to find *nonretributive categories* for explaining the doctrine of final judgment. For it is when hell is viewed as a matter

---

everlasting (e.g., Heb 6:2, "eternal judgment"; Heb 9:12, "eternal redemption"; Mark 3:29, "eternal sin"; 2 Thess 1:9, "eternal destruction"; Jude 7, "eternal fire"). Eternal punishment is therefore something that is ultimate in significance and everlasting in effect, not in duration.

41. Kvanvig, *Problem*, 68. For a helpful summary of the debate between traditionalism and annihilationism, see Gray, "Destroyed," 14–18.

42. Moltmann, "The End of Everything," 263–64; Moltmann, *Today's World*, 142–45.

43. For a philosophical critique of universalism, see Kvanvig, *Problem*, 73–96. For an exegetical and theological critique, see the references in note 60 below.

of penal retribution that most of the moral and philosophical problems outlined above emerge.

A Nonretributive Approach to Eschatological Judgment

The doctrine of final damnation is, as we have seen, usually explained in terms of God's retribution on human sin. Yet when measured against the retributive canon of just desserts, the punishment imposed is hard to justify, since it seems out of all proportion to the crime that occasions it. This is especially true if the punishment is understood as eternal torment, but is also the case if it is understood as destruction or annihilation. This calls into question whether the New Testament theme of eschatological judgment is best viewed as an exercise in strict retributive justice. Several considerations, I suggest, point in a different direction.

In the first place, it is important to affirm the priority of God's love in judgment as well as in redemption. The long-standing practice of appealing to heaven as proof of God's love and to hell as proof of God's justice is simplistic and misleading.[44] There is no contradiction between God's love and God's justice. Throughout the biblical story, God's basic orientation to humanity is one of self-giving love, with God conforming the demands of his holiness to those of his steadfast, redemptive love. "God's justice is his love in action," N. T. Wright explains. "God's love is the driving force of his justice."[45] While it may include punitive recompense for wrongdoing, God's justice is larger than retribution and is ultimately satisfied by healing and restoration, not by punishment. From this it follows that even the eschatological condemnation of the wicked at the Last Judgment must flow ultimately from the restorative love of God, not from the demands of retributive justice. It is out of undying love for every human being, not out of a need to exact retribution, that God declares eternal judgment on the impenitent.

This important—though paradoxical—insight serves to preserve not only the unity of God's nature but also the initiative or sovereignty

---

44. See Kvanvig, *Problem*, 107–12. On the origins of this tradition, see Bonda, *One Purpose*, 1–44. Moberly, *Punishment*, 361, aptly dismisses the doctrine of double predestination, in which most of the human race are created to be "vessels of wrath" to display God's justice, as "a moral monstrosity" and "a heresy more deadly than any other, because more dishonouring to God and striking more fatally at the root of the whole idea of God which Christ came to teach and to embody in action."

45. Wright, *Saint Paul*, 110–11.

of God's action. For retributive justice is inherently reactive rather than proactive or creative in character; it is a response to something that has already happened. If final judgment is wholly retributive in character, it is compelled by something external to God: the existence of sin. If it is an expression of divine love, it issues from something within God's own being—namely, God's love for humanity and God's commitment to see human beings realize their potential. That potential is union with God. To enjoy such union, people must participate in God's perfection. This requires their full and free cooperation, a willing submission to God that cannot be coerced. Some may shrink from such surrender and choose instead radical separation from God. Out of love for them, God must honor their freedom of choice. It would be unloving and unjust to force them against their will to take up eternal residence in God's kingdom, which for the stubbornly impenitent would be an experience of hell.

It is true, however, that the idiom employed in the New Testament to depict final judgment includes notions of wrath, vengeance, and punishment, even of torment (Luke 16:23, 26; Matt 18:34), beating (Luke 12:47–48), drowning (Mark 9:42), and being cut in pieces (Matt 24:51/ Luke 12:46). But it is crucial to recognize, in the second place, the figurative, parabolic nature of the language used to describe realities that, *ex hypothesi*, lie outside human experience. The diversity, grotesqueness, and mutually exclusive nature of the images used to depict hell (pitch darkness yet eternal fire, destroyed bodies yet ever-feeding maggots, and so on) corroborates the metaphorical, hyperbolic nature of such discourse. The same applies to images of reward and punishment. The basic thought is that earthly actions have eschatological significance and will receive appropriate recognition from God. But a wide range of images and metaphors from the world of human relations are used to express the process of assessment and its outcome. God has a treasury, keeps books, hires and fires, pays wages, harvests crops, herds animals, hands down sentences, scourges slaves, gives rewards, refines metal, confers prizes in athletic contests, holds feasts, bestows inheritances, and so on. Such language, says Jerome Quinn, is "figurative and connotative rather than denotative and literalistic."[46] Notions of reward or repayment are simply commercial metaphors for the intensification of relationship with God granted to the redeemed. (What greater reward could there be?)[47] To envisage some kind of quantifiable material benefits is to miss

46. Quinn, "Merit," 88; cf. 84.
47. On sayings that seem to suggest degrees of reward in heaven, see Blomberg,

the metaphorical reference of the language and to imply that something can be added to the bliss of knowing God. Conversely, the metaphors of judicially imposed punishments and torments for the condemned—wailing and gnashing of teeth—capture the loss and sheer horror involved in being excluded from relationship with God. (What greater punishment could there be?) To imagine some kind of cosmic torture-chamber where the lost suffer endless or prolonged retribution is to miss the figurative, apocalyptic nature of these utterances, as well as the paraenetic or pastoral intention behind them. While Jesus uses graphic imagery to visualize Gehenna, he does not relish or welcome the damnation of the wicked but portrays it precisely in order to avert it. In his careful study Reiser identifies "one important point" at which Jesus differs from the apocalyptic texts of Judaism:

> The depictions of judgment in early Jewish texts are quite often dictated by an unconcealed hatred and thirst for revenge: the hatred of the pious against the godless, of the righteous against the wicked, of the tortured against the torturers. In these texts, the eschatological judgment brings not only righteous punishment for sinners, but also serves for the final satisfaction of those who, against all obstacles, remained true to God and God's law. ... Nothing of that can be found in the preaching of Jesus. His words about judgment are not inspired by hatred of sinners, but solely by love for them. In fact, he has come especially to call them to the eschatological banquet.[48]

So, although the metaphors of reward and punishment may suggest carefully calculated retribution, their intended referent is personal and relational, and, as Stephen Travis points out, "there cannot be genuine retribution in the context of personal relationships."[49] People's individual destinies consist either of an intensification of their relationship with God or of an alienation from him. "To talk freely of punishment in the sense of retribution," Travis says, "is to distort the Christian message and encourage misunderstanding. To speak of relationship or lack of relationship with God is to get to the heart of the matter."[50]

"Degrees"; and Travis, *Judgment*, 142–54.
  48. Reiser, *Judgment*, 321–22.
  49. Travis, *Judgment*, 44.
  50. Ibid., 169.

Thirdly, while human works are subjected to divine assessment, the fundamental criterion of judgment is not external action but one's overall character and direction of life. Human works are evaluated inasmuch as they are the fruit of character and the essential manifestation of our relationship with God, however unconscious that may be (cf. Matt 25:31–46; Rom 2:12–16). Put otherwise, a person's basic orientation to the goodness that is God is displayed concretely in how one lives one's life, especially in how one treats other people. This in turn determines how one responds to a direct encounter with the manifestation of God's goodness in the person of Jesus, so that one's relationship to Jesus may serve as a measure of character, and vice versa.[51] This is why the New Testament divides humanity into only two groups, the saved and the lost, rather than into endless gradations based on varying merit.[52] The fact that judgment is based on personal character and relationship to God undermines any notion of strict retribution. God is not some kind of heavenly certified accountant who carefully calculates appropriate repayment for each individual's deeds, but a God who does "not count their trespasses against them" (2 Cor 5:18), a loving parent who "does not deal with us according to our sins, nor repay us according to our iniquities," but instead, remembering "that we are dust," a God who has "compassion for his children" (Ps 103:6–14). Jesus' parables insist that God's will to

---

51. There are at least four main criteria mentioned in the New Testament for a positive outcome at judgment: (1) one's treatment of others (e.g., Luke 10:25–37; Matt 19:16–19; Matt 5:22; 25:31–46); (2) one's good works in general (e.g., Matt 7:15–23; 12:36; 25:14–30; Luke 19:11–27; John 8:51; Rom 2:7–10; 2 Cor 5:10; 2 Thess 1:8; Eph 5:6; 1 John 2:17; Heb 5:9; Rev 2:23; 22:12; 20:12); (3) one's intrinsic character (e.g., Matt 18:3–4; 23:5–12; Gal 5:19–21; Eph 5:5); and (4) one's relationship to Christ (e.g., Mark 8:34–38; 10:21; Luke 13:34–35; 19:41–44; John 3:36; 6:40, 47, 51; 20:31; Acts 2:21; Rom 10:10–13; 1 Cor 15:22–23; 2 Tim 2:10–11; Heb 2:3; 10:29) or to God (Luke 10:27–28; Jas 1:12; 2:5; 2 Thess 1:8). No contradiction exists between these four criteria. In several sayings, for example, "works" and "relationship to Jesus" are brought together as the basis for judgment (e.g., Luke 6:46–49/Matt 7:24–27; Luke 12:8–9/Matt 10:32–33; Luke 13:25–27; Matt 7:21–23; 25:10–12). Like different facets of a diamond, each criterion gives expression to the same thing: a commitment and conformation of character to what is known of God's will.

52. Jesus sees two ways lying before people (Matt 7:13–14; Luke 13:23–24), each with eternal significance. In the Gospels Jesus frequently divides people into two groups with two destinies: children of the kingdom and children of the evil one (Matt 13:38); children of light and children of this world (Luke 16:8); the wise and the foolish (Matt 7:24–27; 25:1–13); sheep and goats (Matt 25:31–46); those who acknowledge him and those who deny him (Luke 12:8–9); those who enter life and those thrown into hell (Mark 9:42–48). Paul also sees only two destinies before people (e.g., Rom 2:1–11; 1 Cor 1:18).

redeem far outweighs his need to pay exact recompense for sins. In the parable of the workers in the vineyard, Jesus shows that those who think of God in terms of strict distributive or retributive justice fundamentally misunderstand God (Matt 20:1–16; cf. Matt 22:1–16; Luke 15:11–32; 18:9–14). Similarly, Paul, recognizing that a strictly retributional scheme would doom all humanity, insists that justification is a gift of pure grace (Rom 3:23–24; cf. Eph 2:8–10), not the outcome of a quid pro quo justice. For no matter how good our life or how many our good deeds, we can never merit or deserve the "reward" of salvation. The frequent use of the slave-master metaphor in the New Testament rules out all possibility of deserved reward, for any benefit that a first-century slave received from a master was never merited but was pure favor (Luke 17:7–10). Our relationship with God transcends all notions of just desserts, for it is transfused by unmerited grace.

In the fourth place, while the eschatological loss suffered by the impenitent may be regarded as the penalty of sin, and hence a punishment, it is not strictly retributive. Retributive punishment implies the external, secondary imposition of penalties in proportionate recompense for deeds done. But there is little hint of varying severities of punishment;[53] the lost are typically treated as a single category who suffer the same fate. As C. W. Emmet observes, "There are in the Gospels no 'poetic justice' parables, no limelight scenes of sensational punishments of evil-doers or dramatic vindication of virtue. There is no hint of any special doom on the Herods, Pilate, or the priests as individuals."[54] Furthermore, and crucially, the punishment in question—exclusion from relationship with God[55]—is not externally imposed by God but is the inherent, inevitable

---

53. In certain sayings Jesus speaks of "greater condemnation" or a "worse fate" awaiting those who have had greater knowledge and opportunity (Mark 12:40/Luke 20:47; Matt 10:15/Luke 10:12–14; 11:22–24), and in Luke 12:47–48 he speaks of lesser and greater beatings. Some take this as indicating degrees of punishment in hell depending on merits (e.g., Carson, *Gagging*, 533; Blomberg, "Eschatology," 6). But these sayings are intended to underscore divine impartiality; God will take into account the opportunity and circumstances of people in determining judgment. This is not the same as teaching "grades of punishment." The reference in Luke 12:47–48 is part of the scenery of the parable and teaches, if anything, the principle that responsibility is commensurate with endowment and opportunity. Moreover, can one meaningfully speak of degrees of unending pain? Does not the endless duration of the pain render any relative measures of severity both arbitrary and meaningless?

54. Emmet, "Retribution," 2:518.

55. Matt 25:46; 2 Thess 1:9; cf. Phil 1:23; 2 Cor 5:8; 1 Thess 4:17; 5:10.

climax of the character of evil itself. Sin leads by inner necessity to death (Rom 6:25; cf. 1:32), and ultimate salvation implies the final negation of sin and evil. God's respect for human freedom and personality means that God cannot force those who choose evil to become good. If the wicked freely resist God's healing grace offered in some definitive self-disclosure by God to them, then they will suffer the same negation of God's presence suffered by all else that is evil. But in truth the punishment suffered is self-inflicted, not retributively imposed; the impenitent "bring swift destruction upon themselves" (2 Pet 2:1; cf. Luke 19:22; Acts 13:46). Since they choose to remain on "the road that leads to destruction" (Matt 7:13), the only possible outcome is the complete eradication of their being ("their end is destruction," Phil 3:19). That God allows this to occur has nothing to do with wreaking vengeance or retribution on sinners. As Miroslav Volf says, "God will judge, not because God gives people what they deserve, but because some people refuse to receive what no one deserves; if evildoers experience God's terror, it will not be because they have done evil, but because they have resisted to the end the powerful lure of the open arms of the crucified Messiah."[56] Judgment flows from the outworking of God's loving justice that works to make all things right for the benefit of sinners and to invite, but not coerce, their participation.

For this reason, we noted earlier that the notion of *everlasting existence* in hell separated from relationship with God is impossible to sustain, since existence itself requires connection with God. Many thinkers still do argue for hell as a continuing state of self-incarceration, captured in C. S. Lewis's celebrated proposal that the doors of hell are locked from the inside, often combined with the thought that those in hell have become so devoid of moral consciousness that they have ceased to be personal beings. Kvanvig proposes a "composite view of hell" that combines the possibility of continued existence with the logical necessity of annihilation. He characterizes hell as "a journey beyond death toward annihilation, but with the possibility that the journey is never completed." Some people may be unfitted for heaven yet unready to make the kind of free, rational choice for annihilation that God, in his love, must honor, and they may therefore exist for an extended—perhaps an eternal—period in hell.[57] If such a scenario is to be envisaged, then God's attitude to those

---

56. Volf, *Exclusion*, 298. Notwithstanding this quote, it should be noted that Volf refuses to shrink from affirming the essential violence of God's final judgment; see 275–306.

57. Kvanvig, *Problem*, esp. 107–33, 136–61 (quote from 168). Cf. Spanner, "Is Hell Forever?"; Cheetham, "Temporal."

on the journey must be one of still seeking their reform and restoration, perhaps hoping their experience of pain will become penitential. Yet the proposal is deeply problematic, for God's endless patience becomes the cause of the endlessness of sin and suffering. The overwhelming evidence of the New Testament is that final judgment entails an irrevocable decision for life or death, for eternal union with God or definitive separation from God.

All this suggests that the retributive language and imagery of the New Testament do not a retributivist theology make. And yet—and this is the fifth point—retributional words and metaphors are still deliberately employed by the New Testament writers in discussing final judgment. This is partly because of the communicative power of such images, and partly because retributive terminology safeguards important theological truths. It attests, on the one hand, to human culpability and to the fact that human works are serious, consequential, and weighty matters. To choose between good and evil in this life has transcendent significance. On the other hand, it prevents the notion of self-imposed judgment degenerating into an impersonal, deistic cause-and-effect mechanism that operates apart from God's moral will. This cannot be so, for God is personal, sin is a personal affront to God, and the cause-and-effect process operates only because God personally enables it to operate. Retributivist categories safeguard God's personal and sovereign involvement in dealing with evil and the discriminating character of divine justice. Ultimately it is *God* who secures the triumph of righteousness and the destruction of sin, and God's dealings with human beings are never arbitrary or capricious. In practice, however, divine judgment works itself out nonretributively inasmuch as God "gives people up" to experience the consequences of their own free choices.

One final point remains to be made. I have argued so far that the idea of eschatological judgment does not operate on the basis of strict retributive justice, that the loss suffered by the impenitent is self-chosen, even if it entails God's active acceptance of their choice. But is all this enough to solve our problem? Does not biblical teaching on the definitive destruction of offenders at the Last Judgment, even if we view it more as a matter of metaphysical suicide than divinely imposed capital punishment, still remain an obstacle for a thoroughgoing, Christian philosophy of restorative justice? In one sense the answer is Yes. Hell is nothing if it is not a problem! But there are two good reasons not to exaggerate the dilemma unduly.

One has to do with the unique and truly definitive nature of final judgment. In all other situations where offenders are dealt with, an appeal can be made to some remaining goodness within them, however residual, to promote restoration. By contrast, anyone who is destroyed at the eschatological judgment will have become so totally identified with all that is evil that nothing remains of their personality to be restored. The utter uniqueness of this situation precludes using it to avoid a commitment to restoration in every other situation we face; if God works for restoration up until the very last moment, so too must we. It also precludes using the Last Judgment as a justification or paradigm for corresponding human action in present history, as happened during the Inquisition, for example. To the contrary, God's prerogative of final judgment challenges and critiques—rather than underwrites and validates—violent human retribution on wrongdoers (Rom 12:19–21). "God is not needed to create guilt or to punish," Albert Camus once said. "Our fellow-men suffice, aided by ourselves. You were speaking of the Last Judgment. Allow me to laugh respectfully. I shall wait for it resolutely, for I have known what is worse, the judgment of men."[58]

As well as the issue of uniqueness, it is also crucial to recognize the limited, fragmentary nature of our knowledge about ultimate realities and resist dogmatic assertions about the inescapability of hell for all but a righteous minority. Certainly we must reckon with the possibility of eternal loss for some of God's creatures. It is affirmed throughout the New Testament, not least by Jesus himself, and it would be foolish to assume that he was making idle threats. The battle between good and evil is deadly serious, and habituating oneself to evil in this life is fraught with eschatological danger. But alongside warnings of eschatological separation lies a string of New Testament texts that proclaim the universal efficacy of Christ's atoning death (1 John 2:2; Heb 2:9), the all-inclusive reach of God's mercy (John 12:32; Rom 11:32–36; 1 Tim 4:10; Titus 2:11; Jas 2:13), the eventual confession of Christ's lordship by every human tongue (Phil 2:10–11; Rev 7:9), and the final restoration of the entire created order to the divine intention (Rom 8:18–27; 1 Cor 15:22–28; Col 1:19–20; Eph 1:9–10—cf. Acts 3:21). "Therefore, just as one man's trespass led to condemnation for all," Paul writes, "so one man's act of righteousness leads to justification and life for all" (Rom 5:18; cf. 1 Cor 15:28). How these two biblical themes—one that envisages two alternative, co-existing destinies,

---

58. Camus, *The Fall*, 81.

and the other that anticipates the uniting of all things in Christ—are to be reconciled is impossible to say.[59] Most interpreters weaken the universalist theme to mean not the reconciliation of literally all things to God but the reconciliation of all remaining things after the wicked have been removed from the scene. Salvation extends to all kinds of things and to all classes of people, but not to all individuals.[60] Others weaken the judgment theme, perhaps construing the depictions of hellfire as indicative of a painful but purgatorial encounter with God after death,[61] or perhaps, like Jan Bonda, envisaging a time beyond eternal destruction when God gives life and justification to the dead.[62] Maybe a humble agnosticism is the wisest option. How the destruction of all wickedness and the redemption of all things are both to be affected is known only to God. For our purposes, the point to notice is that God's final word is not retribution but restoration, the recreation of heaven and earth so that sin, suffering, sickness, and death are no more. "And the one who was seated on the throne said, 'See, I am making all things new'" (Rev 21:3–5).

---

59. See Boring, "Universal Salvation."

60. See, e.g., Wright, "Towards a Biblical View"; and Wright, "World-Wide Community."

61. Küng, *Eternal Life*, 137–39, cf. 211–13; Moberly, *Punishment*, 365–67.

62. "The judgment of the godless will not be the end," says Bonda. "All who are lost will one day come to conversion and return to the father, the God of love; *together with* the church they will kneel and join in their hymn of praise for the salvation he extends to all in the name of Jesus" (*One Purpose*, 228).

16

A Kinder, Gentler Damnation?

Nigel G. Wright

Nigel Wright is the former lecturer of Christian Doctrine and Principal at Spurgeon's College in London, from which he retired in 2013 after twenty-one years of academic service to the college. Having been ordained as a Baptist minster for over forty years, Wright has served as the Baptist Union president (2002–3) and been involved with the Baptist World Alliance. He is a Fellow of the Royal Society of Arts, the Higher Education Academy, and the Royal Historical Society.

In his work The Radical Evangelical, *Wright sees himself as partitioning out middle ground between fundamentalism and liberalism, thereby creating theological space for the modern evangelical. His project taken as a whole veers from the center of the evangelical spectrum, however, and lands Wright on the "left" side of many issues within evangelicalism. His consideration of the doctrine of hell demonstrates how varied are the instances of conditional immortality, which hail from all corners of evangelicalism—not just from those with a highly conservative view of Scripture making solely exegetical arguments.*

Wright contends it is God's love—not his wrath, nor his justice—that is to be taken as primary when considering the doctrine of hell. He takes to task those who claim fallen, finite humans are in no position to scrutinize God's desired form of punishment. "The root question here," he writes, "concerns whether there is a true revelation of God in Christ." It is Christ's imaging of

God that enables us to understand God's heart of justice. Even so, theological liberals will find no comfort in Wright's conclusions, as even in spite of his critique of traditionalism he maintains hell is "no soft option, no kinder, gentler damnation."

Hell as Eternal Torment

IT IS NOT THE general concept of "hell" but its content that is here contested. There are forms of self-imposed or humanly created hell, the way our sins isolate us from other people, for instance. The Bible refers to more than this, however, and does so in a way that cannot be brushed aside. Hell is interpreted by evangelicals to be the ultimate destiny of the impenitent, a state of eternal, conscious torment. Nothing less is adequate retribution for human sin. To downplay hell is seen as reducing the gravity of sin and the offense it causes to God.

Plainly there are difficulties here. We are asked to believe that a finite quantity of sin committed in time is rightly recompensed by an infinite quantity of torment in eternity. This seems to fly in the face of the principle of proportionality.[1] By what scale of justice does finite sin, however horrendous, deserve infinite recompense? The standard response to this employs a feudal argument based on the person of the overlord: it is the infinite worth of the divine person offended that constitutes the infinite culpability of the sin. Human sinners are thus rendered liable to judgment of eternal duration because of the one against whom they have sinned. When the further objection is raised that this denies all human understandings of justice, we are told that God's justice is other than fallen human justice and what to us appears unjust may in fact in God's eyes be just.

As cast, however, this discussion leans in the wrong direction. The ultimate reality about God is not the iron logic of his justice and his laws but the illogical extravagance of his love. God's essence is not wrath but love. Wrath is a temporary manifestation of his holy love, but not the last word. Some, of course, insist that human ideas of divine love are hopelessly sentimental. The holy God is true love and is free to save or damn human beings without compromise to his loving nature. Others object

---

1. Exod 21:23–4; Lev 24:20; Deut 19:20. These much misused "eye for eye, tooth for tooth" sayings are not intended to legitimate vengefulness but to establish the idea of proportional and maximum punishments.

that this places divine love in a category that is gratuitous rather than gracious. Yet a doctrine of hell might be grounded in the love of God[2] by insisting, in my view quite rightly, that love does not ultimately override the will of the one who is loved. It can draw, persuade, and seek to win another, but it cannot coerce the response of love. If human beings harden themselves against divine love they may well come to the point of no return, to a state of self-willed inability to do other than resist God's love ... So with hell: the creation of free persons by the personal and loving God who seeks and enables free response cannot exclude the possibility of final loss.

Conditional Immortality

Final loss of the impenitent is not, therefore, incompatible with the love of God; rather, its possibility is a deduction from it. This still offers us no help in assessing the claim that hell consists in everlasting torment. Eternal loss and eternal torture are hardly the same thing. The former might be defensible, but what about the latter? If it is believed that the human soul is inherently immortal, that it never ceases to exist but must endure eternally either in heaven or in hell, a concept of eternal torment might be inevitable. In this sense hell could be a state of metaphorical burning, being consumed by remorse, regret, and the accusations of conscience after having received the vision of God that makes it absolutely clear what eternal love and beauty have been forfeited.

Yet it is hard to conceive of the redeemed enjoying eternal blessedness while being conscious of other human creatures in torment, many of whom will have been related to them in life. To argue that final judgment dissolves earthly bonds of connection, so that the anguish of the lost is no longer felt by the redeemed, is a convenient argument but a somewhat callous and not particularly convincing one. And how could we live in a new heaven and a new earth in which God is all in all[3] if in some part or dimension of that new creation there are creatures in torment?

The question in this argument concerns what is meant by the "immortality of the soul." This doctrine is well represented in the Christian tradition but many would agree that it owes more to Hellenistic philosophy than to the Hebrew background of Christianity. Often the term

2. Kvanvig, *Problem*, 130, 135–61.
3. 1 Cor 15:28.

seems to denote the belief that the soul is able to outlive the body and that physical death is not the same as personal extinction. That the essence of human beings is not destroyed by physical death is certainly taught in the New Testament.[4] But this scarcely constitutes "immortality" in the stronger sense of being "incapable of dying." In fact, Jesus spoke about the one who is able to destroy both body and soul in hell.[5]

All would agree that in the absolute sense only God has immortality.[6] Whatever "immortality" is given to human beings is therefore derivative and relative. Since the New Testament clearly considers the enduing of *mortals* with immortality as an eschatological reality at the coming of Christ,[7] this suggests that they do not possess immortality even in a relative sense until and unless they attain that condition; consequently, both physically and spiritually they are capable of extinction, even if spiritual extinction does not coincide with physical death. This view is sometimes known as "conditional immortality," since immortality is made dependent upon a new divine act of transformation.

This discussion heightens the difficulty of the doctrine of hell. If human beings are not inherently immortal then the only way they can suffer eternal torment is if they are eternally sustained in being by God. God therefore deliberately maintains potentially millions or even billions of human creatures in being in order to be tormented and does so because in their limited space and time they have offended against his person. It is extremely difficult to square this with the God of compassion and justice whom we encounter in and through Jesus Christ. The two visions of God bear no resemblance to one another. It helps not at all to argue that God's standards of justice are different from our own, since the obvious riposte is that such a God is inferior to human beings. If human beings would not do to their worst enemies what God, according to some, purposes to do to creatures whom he loves, then this kind of God is not worth believing in and it is hard to blame people who find it impossible so to do.

In fact the argument is unconvincing that God's justice is so far removed from human justice. Certainly, human perceptions of justice are distorted. Comparative studies show how they differ from social context to social context. But the root question here concerns whether there

4. E.g., 2 Cor 5:8.
5. Matt 10:28.
6. 1 Tim 6:16.
7. 1 Cor 15:53.

is a true revelation of God in Christ. If the only God who exists is the Christlike God who loves his enemies, the Father of Jesus Christ, it becomes impossible to believe in an inscrutable, hidden God who is other than what we see in Christ. Jesus did not deny the human sense of love and justice and its potential as an analogy for imaging God. He argued that God was so much more loving and more just than that. So: "If you, then, though you are evil, know how to give good gifts to your children, *how much more* will your Father in heaven give good gifts to those who ask him!"[8] God's standards of justice and fairness are not less than the human, but so much more.

Reconstructing Hell

Hell is that reality created by the very being of the holy God when in the future he fills all things and makes himself directly present in every part of his creation. Tradition speaks of the "four last things," heaven and hell, death and judgment. But when it comes down to it, there is only one last thing and that is God himself, the Alpha and the Omega,[9] the first and the last.[10]

The present age is one in which God has created space for human beings, for their lives to run their course. We are called to seek God and to find him, but might also resist and reject him. In the end we meet with God and there is no escaping him. It is this final encounter that spells heaven or hell. For the finally impenitent sinner who has resisted all the works of God to draw him or her out of themselves and to himself, this encounter means destruction, as it nearly did for Isaiah who on seeing the holy God cried out "Woe is me! For I am *disintegrated*" (the literal meaning of the Hebrew).[11] It is inevitable that this be so, for this is the only way the person who rejects God can experience God.

Hell is not a place of eternal conscious torment in fire but an ultimate, final encounter with God. The lost do not simply cease to exist when they die physically; they are not quietly liquidated after the judgment when they have been restored to conscious and personal existence. The torment of hell consists in beholding God at the last, looking upon

8. Matt 7:11.
9. Rev 1:8.
10. Isa 44:6.
11. Isa 6:5.

his beauty, majesty, and infinite love and knowing that through one's own deliberate fault all of this has been made forfeit and lost. In short, hell is the *infinite loss of God*. Here is the moment of truth in the feudal idea that our sin against God's infinite person constitutes our infinite sin, yet it is now reversed. Our loss is as great as is God himself, since his eternal purpose has been to be our God and to become all in all to us.

Yet this infinite loss is forced upon no one. It is self-selected. As C. S. Lewis put it: "There are only two kinds of people in the end: those who say to God, 'Thy will be done,' and those to whom God says, in the end, 'Thy will be done.'"[12] This by no means lessens the horror of hell. Rather, it clarifies in what this horror consists: not in fire, sulfur, and burning, even throughout eternity, but in refusing and therefore losing the God who has love for us as his very being. Once more, our theology is personally and relationally defined not as torment in some eternal concentration camp, but as a falling out of the hands of the one who loves us. The horrific images of fire or darkness capture something of the tragedy and pain, but ultimately the loss of God who is the source and ground of all life provides no way in which any creature could continue to be.[13]

Enough has been said to show that this is no soft option, no kinder, gentler damnation, but a destiny to avoid, for God's sake and for our own.

---

12. Lewis, *Divorce*, 72.
13. Matt 8:12.

17

The Future of the Totally Corrupt

RICHARD G. SWINBURNE

Richard Swinburne is Emeritus Nolloth Professor of the Philosophy of the Christian Religion, University of Oxford; Emeritus Fellow of Oriel College, Oxford; and Fellow of the British Academy. He is a leading philosopher of religion, arguing persuasively for the rationality of the basic Christian doctrines using the tools of analytic philosophy. Swinburne is well known for his trilogy on the philosophy of theism: The Coherence of Theism *(1977),* The Existence of God *(1979), and* Faith and Reason *(1981).*

This chapter comes from a later work, Responsibility and Atonement *(1989), in which Swinburne turns to examine and justify the Christian notions of moral responsibility, forgiveness of sins, and how atonement is possible. The possibility of moral and character formation is central to his thesis and once applied to both saint and sinner alike, the question inevitably arises, what should God do with persons whose character is wicked and who have not benefited from Christ's atonement? Here Swinburne outlines the reasoning behind heaven and hell.*

Significantly, Swinburne is a foremost modern defender of the substance dualist view of human persons—that humans are essentially immaterial souls, embodied.[1] *His commendation of the conditionalist view, therefore, serves as a reminder to those evangelicals who associate conditional immortality with*

---

1. See Swinburne, *Soul*.

an exclusively physicalist view of persons, or with the denial of a conscious intermediary state ("soul sleep"), that conditionalists hold to a variety of views regarding human constitution. For Swinburne, however, the conditionalist view flows naturally from the understanding that God has created human beings as rational souls, capable of making free will decisions and thereby forming their characters over time.

Soul and Body

MAN CONSISTS OF SOUL and body. What makes me me is not this body, for it is conceivable that each part of it be replaced (gradually, or at a stroke) and yet I continue to have experiences. So there must be another part of me, the essential part that makes me me, and to which I give the traditional name of soul. It is the soul that is the initiator of intentional action and is the subject of conscious experience, and is the vehicle of character (i.e., to which beliefs and desires belong). The soul may not be able to function without a body in the normal course of things, but God could give it a new body or keep it temporarily in being without a body. In considering now how a good God who seeks man's eternal well-being in friendship with himself will deal with men of various kinds, I phrase the question (since their earthly bodies will be destroyed) in terms of how he will deal with souls of various kinds. A soul deprived of its body would, however, have no way of expressing itself or influencing the world, and no way of acquiring knowledge of it, and no instrument to give it the energy to organize its mental life. Of course, God could give to a soul new ways of expressing itself and acquiring knowledge and energy from some other source, to enable it so to act. But, as it is at the moment, many of the kinds of desires to act and beliefs about the world that we have acquired during our lives are of a kind naturally expressed and derived through bodily means—viz., many of our desires are desires to do things with our bodies, and many of our beliefs about objects are beliefs about how sensorily they look or feel, viz., about how they present themselves to eyes or hands. Human souls seem fitted for human bodies. For this reason alone I am inclined to accept the normal Christian view that God will give eventually to such souls as he keeps in being after death new bodies, and any continuing existence of the soul without a body is a temporary state. The primary concern of this book is, however, with the most general moral issues, and so the primary concern of this chapter is with whether a good God would keep men in existence after death, and the quality of the kinds of belief and desire which he would give to men (e.g., whether he would give them desires for the good, and true beliefs about what is good) and whether he would satisfy their beliefs and desires. The issue of whether any life after death would be an embodied life seems a relatively subsidiary issue, and so not one to which I shall devote further argument.

During men's life on earth their characters are formed; and, given that he has free will, each man is the final determinant of his own character—though circumstances make it harder for some than for others to form a good character. At the end of life souls are of various kinds.

The Future of the Totally Corrupt

First, there is the totally corrupt (or wicked) soul whom we left at the end of the last chapter. He has allowed there to form in himself a strong desire to resist awareness of the good. How will a perfectly good God deal with him?

Perhaps God could remove from this soul the desire to resist awareness of the good, resensitize it to the good. However, I suggest that it would be wrong of God so to do. He who seeks man's eternal well-being in friendship with himself would respect man's free choice and not force his friendship upon him. In giving to men the gift of free will, a creator is, I suggest, under an obligation not to use force to change it when men's choices are not to his liking. A good God who made creatures with a choice of pursuing the good or pursuing the bad would allow those creatures to become what they deliberately, persistently, and freely in all aspects of their behavior choose to be. Like a good parent, he would, of course, encourage his children to follow one way rather than another; but in the end he would allow them the consequences of their choice, to become the sort of person they choose to become.

Although a good God could *allow* a man to become totally corrupt; it would surely be wrong of him to *make* an agent who began life with a vision of good eliminate that vision and lose his soul. Surely no good God would take back from a man that most precious of gifts, the gift of the ability to make or mar himself as a person. Christian tradition has been divided over whether God reprobates, i.e. predestines to damnation, any man. For the reason given I side with those who claim that he does not;

that a man can only damn himself. Since any who do damn themselves will have had an initial vision of a good, and a capacity to choose it freely, they will have been given God's gracious help, enough of it to avoid damnation if they choose (though grace of varying amounts, making it easier for some than for others). Augustine and his classical Protestant successors must be numbered among those who hold that God does reprobate; so, too, alas, must St. Thomas Aquinas.[2] But there is a strong tradition before Augustine, and a firm Catholic tradition after Duns Scotus culminating in the clear implication of a firm declaration of the Council of Trent, that God does not reprobate.[3]

What would a good God do with such a totally corrupt being as we have described? This corrupt being has sinned against his creator, and made no atonement for his sins, nor helped others to atone for theirs. He has destroyed his God-given capacity for moral awareness and choice and left himself as an arena of competing desires. He certainly deserves punishment, and God has a right to punish him (and the more his guilt is subjective, as opposed to objective, the greater the punishment deserved). And it is perhaps good that God should exercise that right if, in order to provide men with a disincentive to sin, he has vowed previously that he will punish sinners. We saw in the last chapter how the threat of the pains of hell can be a valuable means to get men to pursue the good, ultimately for better reasons. But God, being good, would not punish a sinner with a punishment beyond what he deserved; and I suggest that, despite majority Christian tradition, literally everlasting pain would be a punishment beyond the deserts of any human who has sinned for a finite time on earth.[4] To punish a man with such punishment would be horribly vindictive, and a good God would not be that.

On the other hand, what is the point of keeping a totally corrupt being alive? He has lost the center of his being. There would be no point in giving him the "vision" of God, for he could not enjoy it. As I noted in the last chapter, the wicked cannot be happy in doing actions or experiencing states whose value arises from their moral goodness. Moral goodness is so central to what God is that only one who valued that would wish to

2. *Summa Theologica* 1a. 2ae. 23.3.
3. Denzinger, *Sources*, 1556. See also the Second Council of Orange (ibid., 400). The post-fifth-century Greek tradition was, of course, largely uninfluenced by Augustine. St. John Damascene is therefore to be numbered among those who deny reprobation (see Tixeront, *Dogmas*, iii., 478).
4. For careful discussion of this point, see Adams, "Hell."

adore God. For the totally corrupt there must be the *poena damni* (i.e., damnation), the penalty of the loss of the vision of God, a penalty of far greater importance than any *poena sensus* (i.e., punishment by means of painful sensations, which I shall call in future sensory punishment), as Augustine, himself a firm advocate of eternal sensory punishment for the wicked, pointed out. The *poena damni* is a loss of good, not an inflicted evil; and it is not so much a punishment inflicted from without as an inevitable consequence of a man allowing himself to lose his moral awareness. Annihilation, the scrap heap, seems an obvious final fate for the corrupt soul. There is an obligation on God not to punish anyone beyond what he deserves, and that, I have suggested, involves an obligation not to punish a man who has sinned on earth with everlasting sensory punishment. But there is no obligation on God to keep any man alive in a world to come. Yet should he keep the totally corrupt man alive forever, my argument suggests that he will give him only those pleasures whose enjoyment involves no recognition of the moral goodness of what is enjoyed. That the wicked have permanently a status quite other than that enjoyed by the blessed (their subsequent pattern of life, if any, would not be a very good one) seems a crucial central point of the great biblical parables of judgment such as the parable of the sheep and the goats. As Augustine himself put it in response to criticism of his own stern doctrine: "This perpetual death of the wicked, then, that is their alienation from the life of God, shall abide forever, and shall be common to them all, whatever men, prompted by their human affections, may conjecture as to a variety of punishments, or as to a mitigation or intermission of their woes."[5]

The New Testament writings seem to me ambiguous on the issue of whether the punishment of the wicked is an everlasting sensory one. They are fairly unanimous that the end of life marks a permanent division between the good and the wicked, and hence the fate of the wicked is αἰώνιος, not unreasonably translated "everlasting." And they claim that the wicked shall be thrown into a fire; this is sometimes described as αἰώνιος, but sometimes rather as ἄσβεστος, "unquenchable." But all that the latter implies is that the fire will leave nothing of the wicked unburnt; and indeed, if we take such talk literally, and suppose the wicked to be ordinary embodied men, the consequence of putting them in such a fire will be their elimination. St. Paul in one place talks of the fate of the

5. *Enchiridion*, 112–13; *NPNF* 3:273.

wicked as "eternal destruction from the face of the Lord."[6] There are even occasional passages that seem to imply that the division of the sheep and goats is only a temporary one. For example, there is the warning to men to be reconciled quickly with their adversaries lest they be thrown into prison: "You shall by no means come out from there until you have paid the last penny."[7] As John Hick comments, "Since only a finite number of pennies can have a last one, we seem to be in the realm of graded debts and payments, rather than of absolute guilt and infinite penalty."[8] St. John sometimes seems to suggest that sin is its own punishment.[9]

However, most Christian theologians of subsequent centuries have had a fairly definite doctrine of eternal sensory punishment of the wicked. The best-known exception was Origen, who claimed that all men would eventually be saved, and his view remained to exert a considerable influence over the next three centuries. Gregory of Nyssa advocated Origen's view, and Gregory Nazianzen toyed with it. St. Basil acknowledged that most ordinary men of his day believed that the sufferings of hell were only of finite duration;[10] and St. Augustine acknowledged the diversity of opinions on this matter that were current in his day.[11] Augustine, however, was firm in his own belief in the eternal sensory punishment of the wicked, and Pope Pelagius I declared that the wicked "will burn without end."[12, 13]

Medieval thinkers, however, were united in supporting the view that the wicked would undergo an eternal sensory punishment. The First Council of Lyons (AD 1245) declared that those who died without penitence in mortal sin would be "crucified forever in the fires of eternal hell."[14] Aquinas, however, claimed that this physical punishment was not of infinite intensity; and, like all other thinkers, he also held that it varied

---

6. 2 Thess 1:8.
7. Matt 5:26.
8. Hick, *Death*, 244.
9. See, e.g., John 3:19.
10. St. Basil, *Reg. Brev. Tract.*, 267.
11. *Enchiridion*, 113; *NPNF* 3:273.
12. Denzinger, *Sources*, 443.
13. For references and discussion of the patristic period, see Kelly, *Doctrines*, 473f. and 483ff.; Tixeront, *Dogmas*, ii., 193–99, 331–47; and the discussion (in connection with the different topic of Purgatory) in Goff, *Purgatory*, ch. 2.
14. Denzinger, *Sources*, 839.

PART FOUR—Philosophical Support for Conditionalism

in intensity for different sinners.[15] Protestant reformers stoutly defended eternal sensory punishment. But the last two centuries have, of course, witnessed a large-scale rejection of this view, at least among Protestants and Anglicans.

I suspect that one factor that influenced the Fathers and scholastics to affirm eternal sensory punishment was their belief in the natural immortality of the soul. Even if God could eliminate a soul (and some of their arguments have the consequence that he could not), it would in their view require an action of God of a quite extraordinary supernatural kind to eliminate a soul.[16] The extinction of the wicked was therefore seldom entertained as a possibility open to God. The only possibilities being eventual everlasting happiness or everlasting misery, it was not totally unnatural that the Fathers and scholastics should hold everlasting misery to be the fate of the wicked—for the other options would involve God not taking the wicked free choice of the wicked seriously. Today we think that conservation in existence rather than elimination is what requires special divine action, and so there is in our view an obvious alternative to eternal punishment to which God could consign the wicked—he could eliminate them.

---

15. See *Summa Contra Gentiles* III. 145 and *Summa Theologica* 1a. 2ae. 87.3. ad 4.

16. See Aquinas, *Summa Contra Gentiles* II. 55 and 79; and the discussion of arguments such as his in Swinburne, *Soul*, 305f.

PART FIVE

Historical Considerations

ADHERENTS TO THE TRADITIONAL view of hell sometimes claim that Jesus' words concerning hell and final punishment would have been nearly universally understood by his first-century Jewish listeners as promising eternal torment for the lost. Robert Morey, for example, writes, "it was the general belief of the Jews that eternal [conscious] punishment awaited the wicked."[1] Douglas Jacoby relates, "I still hear people say that all Jews in New Testament times believed in eternal torment," but, he says, "this is not accurate."[2] Indeed, as noted by Francis Chan and Preston Sprinkle, "While some [first century Jews] believed that the wicked would be annihilated, others believed that hell is a place of never-ending punishment."[3] Edward Fudge concurs, "When Jesus came upon the scene, and during the century that followed, diverse, conflicting ideas circulated among the Jews."[4] Even Eldon Woodcock, who says conditionalism divests Jesus and the Bible of their truthfulness and divine authority,[5] acknowledges that there were competing views among Jesus' contemporaries concerning personal eschatology.[6]

Further, traditionalists also sometimes allege that for the next few hundred years the Christian church was virtually unanimous in their belief in the unending torment of the lost. Junius Reimensnyder wrote in 1880 that *"with a unanimity almost absolute* . . . the pious fathers of the first three centuries held as a fundamental, fixed, and settled article of the Christian faith . . . the *endless duration* of the future punishment of the wicked."[7] A century later, William Crockett made the blanket statement, "During the time of the early Apostolic Fathers, Christians believed hell

---

1. Morey, *Afterlife*, 127.
2. Jacoby, *Heaven and Hell*, 98.
3. Chan and Sprinkle, *Erasing Hell*, 55.
4. Fudge, *Fire That Consumes* (2011), 120.
5. Woodcock, *Hell*, 9.
6. Ibid., 95–96.
7. Reimensnyder, *Doom Eternal*, 15–16.

would be a place of eternal, conscious torment."[8] This is, again, inaccurate. Traditionalist John Walvoord concedes, "It is possible to provide almost endless quotations from the early Fathers up to modern theologians who believe in [the traditional view] and who do not," leading him to admit that "there has been diversity of opinion from the beginning."[9] Steve Gregg explains, "The earliest Christian writings, after the New Testament, were not explicit as to the precise fate that awaits sinners after the resurrection and final judgment,"[10] and upon examining several of the ancient texts, he concludes that "all three views of hell were prevalent, existing side-by-side from the second century onward . . ."[11]

In the chapters that follow, two religious historians examine ancient Jewish and Christian writings concerning final punishment. The first author surveys extra-biblical, contemporaneous Jewish references to "Gehenna" and concludes that when Jesus used the word, his hearers would have recalled the Old Testament's corpse-filled valley of Hinnom, as the term hadn't yet developed into a toponymous reference to the place of eschatological final punishment, let alone one of eternal torment. The second author explores the writings of the earliest Christians following the close of the canon, coming to the conclusion that there was diversity of opinion concerning the nature of final punishment, and that among them were several prominent conditionalists.

---

8. Crockett, "Metaphorical View," 65.
9. Walvoord, "Literal View," 14.
10. Gregg, *Hell*, 112.
11. Ibid., 130.

18

The Development of Gehenna between the Old and New Testaments

KIM G. PAPAIOANNOU

Kim G. Papaioannou earned his BA double-majoring in religion and history, and an MA in religion, from Newbold College, England, and later received a PhD in theology from Durham University. He served as a Master's and Doctoral Program Director and taught as a Professor of New Testament at AIIAS, Philippines, before moving to Cyprus to pastor a local congregation, a role in which he had previously served in Northern Ireland and in Greece.

Papaioannou's PhD advisor was Professor Loren T. Stuckenbruck, a prominent scholar of early Jewish and Christian literature. Papaioannou's doctoral dissertation, "Places of Punishment in the Synoptic Gospels," examined the development of traditions about the afterlife and final punishment among early Jews and Christians, a topic he expands upon in his recently published book, The Geography of Hell in the Teaching of Jesus. The following excerpts from Papaioannou's book discuss the development—or lack thereof—of Gehenna in Jewish writings between the Testaments.

PART FIVE—HISTORICAL CONSIDERATIONS

Non-Biblical Jewish Literature

IT IS OFTEN TAKEN for granted that the next step in the development of a Gehenna tradition [after its original use in the Old Testament] is to be found in the various Jewish writings dating from the third century BC to the second AD. R. H. Charles in his monumental study on Jewish and Christian eschatology reconstructed this development with considerable detail. He argued that in the earlier Old Testament books the concept of Gehenna is to be found only in embryonic form and that it begins to develop only with some passages in Isaiah (30:33; 50:11; 66:24) and in Daniel (12:2), which he dated no earlier than the third century BC and very likely to the second.[1] Originally, Gehenna is envisaged as referring to the immediate punishment of apostate Jews and in the second century it broadens to include the final abode in the next world. By the first century it slowly began to include other nations as well.[2] The corporeal nature of the punishment begins to recede to the background, as the sufferings were now believed to affect only the soul.

Charles' detailed analysis is interesting but today rather outdated. Further inquiry into the composition of Jewish "Apocrypha" and "Pseudepigrapha," as well as into some of the Old Testament books referred to by Charles, throws his chronological sequence into serious doubt. Nonetheless, the notion that this body of Jewish writings does indeed represent the next step of development of a Gehenna tradition is widely accepted. With these thoughts in mind it is useful to take a look at the evidence.

LXX

The Roman numerals LXX are used as an abbreviation of the word "Septuagint," which in turn designates the translation of the Hebrew Scriptures into Greek. The story of the translation as expressed in the Letter of Aristeas[3] hardly represents events as they happened. Nonetheless, it is usually accepted that the Hebrew Scriptures began to be translated into Greek after Alexander the Great's conquests that made Hellenistic influence

---

1. Charles, *Future Life*, 161–163, 244, 272, 474–75.
2. He cites Judg 16:17; SE 1 *En.* 48:9; 54:1, 2; 62:12, 13.
3. According to the *Letter of Aristeas*, King Ptolemy Philadelphus (c. 285–244 BC) called on seventy-two Jewish scholars—six from each tribe—to translate their Scriptures into Greek for the king's library in Alexandria.

dominant in the Middle East. The translation began with the Pentateuch, probably in the third century BC and continued with the other writings. It was presumably done primarily for the large Greek-speaking Jewish community of Alexandria. Today there are many different manuscripts extant with considerable variations in reading and a critical text of the complete LXX Old Testament has yet to be worked out.[4]

In the discussion of the Ge-hinnom passages above [not reprinted here] it was noted that the LXX closely parallels the Masoretic and the few instances where the Greek gives a slight difference in emphasis are discussed in the relevant footnotes. This may suggest that the translators did not feel the need to expand on the description of Ge-hinnom, as may have been the case had there been a well-developed tradition associating the toponym Ge-hinnom with eschatological punishment, as in the New Testament and later Jewish writings. That such a tradition had not yet developed is suggested by the way that the LXX renders the name of this valley.

The three different ways in the Hebrew text noted above of referring to Ge-hinnom, are translated into a number of Greek forms. We have, for example, φάραγξ Ὀνομ, Εννόμ or Εννώμ,[5] φάραγξ υἱοῦ Εννομ,[6] πολυάνδριον υἱοῦ Εννόμ,[7] Γαι Οννόμ,[8] ἐν Γαιβενθόμ,[9] Γαμβέ Εννόμ,[10] Γεβανέ εννόμ,[11] Γαιεννα,[12] νάπης Σοννόμ,[13] γῆ Βεεννόμ,[14] and νάπης υἱοῦ.[15]

---

4. There are four important critical editions of the LXX: Swete's, the Cambridge LXX, Rahlfs, and Göttingen. The first two follow Codex Vaticanus (B). Swete's critical apparatus is rather limited; the Cambridge is much more complete but, sadly, by 1940, when the project came to a halt, only half the LXX had been published. Rahlfs 1935 edition is based on the three main Codices, Vaticanus, Alexandrinus, and Sinaiticus. Possibly the most important edition is the Göttingen LXX. Unlike the other three, it does not rely on one codex. Rather, the text is a result of careful assessment of all available texts.

5. Josh 15:8 A and B respectively, and Neh 11:30 (S).
6. Jer 7:31, 32 (B).
7. Jer 19:6 (B).
8. Josh 18:16, (A).
9. 2 Chr 28:3 (B).
10. 2 Chr 28:3 (A).
11. 2 Chr 33:6 (B).
12. Josh 18:16.
13. Josh 18:16 (B).
14. 2 Chr 33:6 (A).
15. Josh 18:16 (A).

Of these, Γαιεννα bears closest relation to the form of "Gehenna" of the New Testament and it is used in a text without any religious or eschatological implications. The large number of variations in translating the Hebrew would suggest that there had not developed a fixed tradition that would conjure up images of divine punishment.

Apocrypha and Pseudepigrapha

In the "Apocrypha" and "Pseudepigrapha" there are several references to Gehenna.[16] After noting the relevant passages, I shall consider the degree to which they provide a background to the Synoptics.

In *4 Ezra* 2:29 and 7:36 we have two references. The former offers some advice in order that "your sons will not see Gehenna" which is reserved as a fate for the nations (2:28). The context is of a judgment after a bodily resurrection, since 2:29 refers to the sons of the righteous who "sleep" in the hiding places of the earth—i.e., are dead in their graves. *4 Ezra* 7:36 makes mention of the "pit of torment that will appear ... the furnace of Gehenna[17] [that] will be made manifest." *4 Ezra* is composite in nature. B. Metzger suggests that it was written between AD 100 on the basis of a supposed reference to the destruction of Jerusalem in 3:1, and 120 on grounds that a Jewish work would hardly have found its way into Christian circles (as *4 Ezra* did), after the Bar-Kosiba rebellion.[18] Stone questions attempts to date the work on internal evidence. It must have been written, however, well before AD 190 since it is quoted by Clement of Alexandria in a non-extant Greek form,[19] which in turn, Stone maintains, was a translation of a Hebrew original.[20] The work was probably composed in Palestine and bears a close resemblance to the later book *2 Baruch*. It wielded considerable influence on later writers. As chapters

---

16. In looking at the references to Gehenna in the Apocrypha and Pseudepigrapha, I have used the indexes of Charles, *APOT*, and Charlesworth, *OTP*. In general, we should keep in mind that the extant texts for most of these writings are considerably later than the actual composition and often show evidence of later additions. It is thus difficult to determine whether the word "Gehenna," when it occurs, was part of the original or subsequently interpolated.

17. "Gehenna" in the Latin, Syriac, Ethiopic, and Georgian versions, but "fire" in the Arabic 1 and 2 and the Armenian versions (Stone, *Ezra*, 203).

18. Metzger, *OTP*, 1:520.

19. Greek fragments published are translations from the Latin (Stone, *Ezra*, 5).

20. Stone, *Ezra*, 9–10.

1–2 are later Christian additions (including the 2:29 reference to Gehenna) *4 Ezra* proper begins with chapter 3. *4 Ezra* therefore furnishes us with only one possible authentic reference, 7:36: here Gehenna is a furnace and a place of torment for the wicked, in contrast to Jeremiah where it is a place of annihilation in a battle.

In *2 Baruch* there are two references: 59:10 and 85:13. In the first instance God shows to Moses "the mouth of Gehenna" among many other places, paradise included. Gehenna is the locale where the wicked will be tormented in the coming judgment, according to their wickedness (54:21). Then God will blot them out (54:22). In the second instance, the writer makes reference to the way of fire, and the path, which leads to Gehenna where there is no repentance.[21] *2 Baruch* is dated after the destruction of the temple in AD 70, possibly around or after 100.[22] For chapters 1–77 there is only one manuscript in Syriac, whereas for the last nine (78–86) there are several. The last nine chapters are not part of the original composition but later additions. Some of the 85:13 manuscripts do not contain the word Gehenna at all.[23]

In the *Ascension of Isaiah* there are two texts: 1:3 and 4:14. The first makes a passing reference to the "torments of Gehenna." The second describes the return of the Messiah, after a short reign on earth by Beliar and his hosts. As the Messiah arrives from heaven, the saints leave their human bodies behind and their souls ascend to meet him (4:17). In contrast, Beliar, his hosts and all the wicked are to suffer the torments of Gehenna where they will be "consumed" and "will become as if they had not been created" (4:18). There is thus a contrast between the righteous who move to a higher level of immaterial existence and the wicked who suffer annihilation in their body. The significance of the *Ascension* for early Judaism is marginal, however. Whereas initially this book was considered to be a collection of three separate compositions, containing both Jewish and Christian material,[24] more recent research suggests that the whole composition is Christian in origin.[25]

In *3 Enoch* 44:3 and 48D:8 there are two more references to Gehenna. The work is Jewish and extant, though in different forms, in several

---

21. Charles, APOT, 1:470–526; cf. Klijn, OTP, 1:652.
22. Klijn, OTP, 1:616–17.
23. *l* reads "to the glowing coals" while *c* "to the realms of death."
24. Knibb, OTP, 1:143–76.
25. Carey, "Ascension," 65–78.

PART FIVE—HISTORICAL CONSIDERATIONS

manuscripts. It is attributed to rabbi Ishmael of Palestine who died in AD 132 shortly before the Bar Kosiba rebellion. However, as P. Alexander indicates,[26] it is a pseudepigraphon of much later composition, which might contain some early traditions. In 43:1–3 the patriarch Enoch is first shown the immaterial and pre-existent souls of the righteous in heaven in the presence of God. Then in chapter 44 he is shown the souls of the wicked carried by the angels Zaariel and Samkiel to be tortured in Gehenna with rods of iron. There follow some terrifying descriptions of the faces of the wicked turning green and their souls being black, but eventually they are purified (44:5). In 48D:8 Gehenna has been in existence since Creation week.

In the *Apocalypse of Abraham* 15:6 the visionary, while flying on a pigeon, sees a light in which "a fiery Gehenna was enkindled." Again the fires of Gehenna are presumed to have existed from ancient times. Abraham sees a crowd of wicked people suffering there, from which one may infer that the whole body is thrown into its fires. The *Apocalypse of Abraham* in its current form is Christian, but derives from a Jewish work. It is dated towards the end of the first century AD. It was probably composed in Hebrew, though now it is extant only in Slavonic versions from the fourteenth to the seventeenth centuries.[27]

In the *Greek Apocalypse of Ezra* 1:9 there is one brief mention of Gehenna. Despite its mention however, the writer envisioned eschatological punishment as occurring in the valley of Jehoshaphat (3:5ff.), thus showing a preference for the motif of Joel 3:1ff. The context of the punishment is the final judgment of the wicked in bodily form, and the result is their total annihilation. The *Greek Apocalypse of Ezra* is dated anywhere from AD 150 to 850.[28]

Among the *Sibylline Oracles* there are three references—1:104, 2:292, 4:186. J. Collins has dated the Jewish Oracles from 30 BC to AD 250 though most likely at the turn of the era, while the Christian portions after AD 70.[29] Book 3 is considered to be the earliest, while Books 1, 2, and 4 could not have been composed before the end of the first century AD.[30] This is the *terminus post quem*—the earliest possible dating. 1:104

26. Alexander, OTP, 1:226.
27. Rubinkiewicz, OTP, 1:681–705.
28. Stone, OTP, 1:561–579.
29. Collins, OTP, 1:331. Geffcken, *Komposition*, 49, has dated both Jewish and Christian Oracles in the third century.
30. Books 1 and 2 must have been written after Theophilus wrote towards the end

describes how the "Watchers" were noble but nevertheless "went to the dread house of Tartarus ... to Gehenna, of terrible, raging, undying fire." The tradition of the noble "Watchers" who became corrupt is old and described in detail in the Book of Watchers (1 Enoch 1–36—hence BW), where the "Watchers"[31] are angelic beings—the fallen "sons of God" of Genesis 6:1.[32] The names Tartarus and Gehenna, however, do not appear in any of the 1 Enoch books, and so have been introduced by the pseudo-Sibyl, or derive from another tradition. It is not clear if the mention of "undying fire" of 1:104 should be understood to imply that the suffering continues forever. 2:292 is much clearer. The writer envisions angels who will throw the wicked into Gehenna.[33] There are detailed descriptions of the suffering, and the wicked will "call death fair ... [but] it will evade them" (2:307). In contrast, 4:186 says that those who have sinned by impiety, "a mound of earth [will] cover, and broad Tartarus, and the repulsive recesses of Gehenna." The punishment of Gehenna comes after a conflagration that burns everything and turns it to ashes (4:171–78). There follows a general bodily resurrection (4:181, 182) and then the wicked suffer their fate. The mound of earth suggests that Gehenna functions as a near equivalent for the grave, suggesting the annihilation of those thrown into it.

Last but not least is the testimony of 1 Enoch. This early and very influential collection of books deals to a considerable extent with the eventual fate of the righteous and the wicked. The word "Gehenna" does not occur but there are a number of allusions to lakes or valleys of fire, possibly in the environs of Jerusalem. Two of the more important come from the Similitudes (1 Enoch 37–71—hence SE), which is the only portion of the book not found at Qumran and whose date has been a matter of considerable debate.[34] The first occurrence (54:1–6), describes the

---

of the first century, for they show an awareness of his work. Book 4 must have been written after AD 80 because it makes reference both to the destruction of Jerusalem in AD 70 and the eruption of Vesuvius in AD 79. On the dating see Schürer, History, 3:632–43.

31. ἐγρήγοροις (egrēgorois) עיר (see Stuckenbruck, "Glossaries"), 42.

32. Cf. SE 1 En. 69; AA 1 En. 86–88; Jub. 5; 2 En. 18:7; T. Reub. 5:6–7; T. Naph. 3:5.

33. For Christian redaction on book 2 see Kurfess, APOT 2:703–45.

34. The question of the date of the Enochic Similitudes has not been settled. Some would argue in favor of an early date on two premises: (a) a possible reference (56:5–7) to the Parthian invasion of Palestine in 40–37 BC, and (b) possible relation to some New Testament texts. The first premise cannot stand, both because the reference is very vague and also because while the Similitudes view the coming of the Parthians

punishment of Azazel and his hosts in a deep valley.[35] The name of the valley is not given. SE *1 Enoch* 54 and 56 are set within the context of a long vision. In chapter 52 Enoch is carried off "in a wind vehicle" to the west (52:1), and sees "a mountain of iron, a mountain of copper, a mountain of silver, a mountain of gold, a mountain of colored metal, and a mountain of lead" (52:2). The valley in question is located in another direction of the compass (54:1). It is called the "Abyss of complete condemnation" (54:5), and contains "imprisonment chains" for Azazel and his hosts (54:4). The second reference comes in 56:1–4. It is not clear if the valleys of SE *1 Enoch* 54 and 56 are identical; however since that second valley is also called an "abyss" suggests that they are. In the valley of 56, Azazel, the evil angels and everything associated with them come to an end and are not "henceforth ... reckoned" (56:4). While the valley(s) in question is/are said to be located on the face of the earth (54:1), the mention of metal mountains and the comparison of the valley(s) to an abyss connote a cosmic, rather than Judean geographical setting. This, coupled with the absence of a place name for the valley(s), makes any attempt to associate these passages with Ge-hinnom conjecture.[36]

There is, however, one passage in BW *1 Enoch* that is early in date and appears to be relevant.[37] The text in question is 27:1–2 where an accursed valley is mentioned.[38] The righteous are said to inhabit a

---

("Persians") as a disaster, generally the Jews welcomed it. The second premise is also precarious—if there is any relation between the Similitudes and the New Testament, the influence could be either way. The fact that the Similitudes were not found in Qumran could suggest a date later than AD 68. Milik, *Enoch*, 91–98, considers the Similitudes a Christian composition and dates them in the late third century AD. The SNTS Seminar on the Pseudepigrapha that met in Paris in 1979 overwhelmingly came out in favor of a first century AD date. See, Knibb, "Date," 345–59; Charlesworth, "Seminars," 315–23; Mearns, "Dating," 360–69, "Date," 118–19.

35. Black, "Eschatology," 1–10.

36. Cf. my comments on *1 En.* 90:20–27 below.

37. Indeed, Montgomery, "Holy City," 33, calls this passage "the earliest evidence" for the association of hell with the valley of Hinnom.

38. Charles, *Enoch*, 57. Isaac's translation of the Ethiopic text (OTP, 27), reads: "For what purpose does this blessed land ... (have) in its midst this accursed valley?" Extant Greek Manuscripts (primarily Panopolitanus) phrase the question slightly differently: "and why is this valley accursed?" In the Ethiopic, Enoch expresses surprise that the accursed valley is located in the midst of the blessed land. In the Greek, he expresses surprise at the very existence of an accursed valley. The Ethiopic would thus be more in harmony with the existence of developed traditions of punishment in a valley. The relevant Aramaic phrase is not extant in Qumran ultimately leaving the issue of which version is more authentic, in the balance.

mountain (Mount Zion?) from where they see the wicked suffering under the judgment of God. This reference is often quoted as a forerunner to the Gehenna motif in the New Testament.[39] However, this association remains uncertain. In discussing the Old Testament material above, we noted that divine punishment in Ge-hinnom was only one of several punishment-in-a valley motifs. While it is plausible that BW *1 Enoch* 27:1–2 reflects the Ge-hinnom texts of Jeremiah, it is equally plausible that it reflects thematically similar texts like Joel 3:1–3 in which the location of punishment is the valley of Kidron or Tyropoeon.[40] Whatever the meaning, however, the fact that the word "Gehenna" is not mentioned indicates that the name of the valley had not here become a by-word for the punishment God in the sense it appears in the Gospels.[41]

This brief overview of Gehenna in the "Apocrypha" and "Pseudepigrapha"[42] has yielded only a few early texts of possible relevance: *4 Ezra* 7:36, *2 Baruch* 59:10, *Apocalypse of Abraham* 15:6 and possibly the three texts in the *Sibylline Oracles*. However, these are all dated after AD 70, toward the end of the century or even later. We have also observed a

39. Davies and Allison, *Matthew* 1:514.

40. In this respect, it is appropriate to comment on AA *1 En.* 90:20–27, which Davies and Allison, *Matthew* 1:514, also consider a reference to Gehenna. The writer sees a fiery Abyss located "at the right hand of the house" (90:27—presumably the temple), "in the middle of the ground" (90:26), and into which, the sinners are thrown. The compass direction of the right hand depends on the direction the writer was facing. If he was facing north, the valley would be the Kidron; if south, then Tyropoeon. If the reference to the Abyss in the "middle of the ground" refers to the middle of Jerusalem, then it would be a reference to the Tyropoeon that dissects the city. It could definitely not be Ge-hinnom, because Ge-hinnom is located on the opposite side of the city from where the temple stood.

41. Nickelsburg (*Enoch*, 318–19) assumes the valley of Hinnom is intended here though he admits the concept of an eschatological Gehenna flourished later. He draws a parallel between the righteous "seeing" the suffering of the wicked as expressed in the Ethiopic text of 27:3a, and a similar motif in the LXX of Dan 12:2 and Isa 66:24 of which, at least the later, he believes pictures the valley of Hinnom. He also sees the valley of Hinnom in AA *1 En.* 90:26 in the "abyss" that is opened in the center of the earth. In the absence of a clear reference to the valley of Hinnom in these texts and in light of the absence of evidence for the contemporary use of Gehenna as a byword for punishment, Nickelsburg's association is forced.

42. Charles would add the *T. Mos.* 10:10 where in the Latin we find the word *terramos*. Charles, who took a special interest in Gehenna, thought that behind *terram* lay the Greek γῆ (*gē*) which, in turn, transliterated the Hebrew גּיְא (*ge*) (supposedly short for Ge-hinnom). Obviously such a reconstruction is highly speculative and is further undermined by the fact that the Hebrew גּיְא and the Greek γῆ have a different meaning.

move away from corporeal punishment to punishment that involves the soul, as well as a move away from annihilation of the wicked to Gehenna as a place of fearful torment, often everlasting.

Other Early Jewish Writings

When looking at other Jewish documents, one is struck by the lack of references to Gehenna. The Dead Sea Scrolls are completely silent. The relevant texts of Jeremiah are absent from the biblical manuscripts. More conspicuous is the absence of the word in the *War Rule*. Since this document portrays an eschatological battle between the "sons of light" and the "sons of darkness" Ge-hinnom would be the natural locale for such a battle. The complete absence of any reference suggests that, at least within the community of Qumran, the Ge-hinnom texts of Jeremiah did not exert a strong influence.

Philo and Josephus are also silent on Gehenna as a place of punishment. Nonetheless, in Josephus there could be references to the valley without the use of the name. In "War of the Jews" VI.8.5, he refers to Jewish soldiers who, while being pursued by the Romans, run to the valley "which is below Siloam." The pool of Siloam was located near the spot where the valleys of Kidron, Tyropoeon, and Ge-hinnom met. Likewise, in V.12.2 Josephus describes how the Romans built a wall encompassing Jerusalem, which passed above the valley that is "below Siloam." Finally, in V.12.3 he explains that as the siege of Jerusalem progressed and famine began to take its toll among the inhabitants of the city, the corpses of those who had died were thrown into the valleys below the city walls—presumably including the valley below Siloam. Such references not only undermine the claim that the valley of Ge-hinnom had become Jerusalem's rubbish dump, but also enhance the view that the name Gehenna had not fully developed into a by-word of destruction, at least within Jewish circles.

The Mishnah/Talmud

The Mishnah is a collection of oral traditions and took its final shape sometime in the beginning of the third century AD. This would seem to disqualify it as a witness for the development of the Gehenna motif up to the time of the New Testament save that it contains traditions that purport to go back as early as the third century BC.[43] To what extent such traditions were transmitted accurately is a matter of conjecture, yet our search would be incomplete without brief mention of them. Five references to Gehenna take the form גֵּי־הִנֹּם,[44] four of which are attributed to rabbis who lived well after the first century AD. Nonetheless, in *Pirqe Aboth* 1:5 a reference is attributed to Rabbi Jose ben Johanan who lived during the second century BC. However, it is almost certain that R. Jose's words end with 1:4 and that 1:5 is a much later addition, perhaps by the compiler himself.[45]

The Babylonian Talmud with exegetical comments on the Mishnah, was compiled perhaps as late as the fifth and sixth centuries AD. Similar to the Mishnah, it purports to contain material from rabbis who lived as early as the first century BC. The accuracy of the attributions is open to question given a gap of several centuries. Nonetheless the historical witness of the Talmud is important as we are trying to discern how and when the idea of Gehenna as the eschatological place of punishment developed and gained prominence. The word Gehenna appears well over fifty times, in most instances attributed to rabbis of the third and fourth centuries AD. The earliest attributions would be to Akiba ben Joseph[46] towards the end of the first century AD, to Johanan ben Zakkai[47] well after the middle of the first century, and to the School of Shammai[48] anytime from AD 50 to the Bar Kosiba revolt.

This overview of the Hebrew Bible and the early Jewish writings to the first century AD has provided us with an impressive accumulation of evidence: lack of interest for the toponym Ge-hinnom among the later Hebrew prophets concerned with eschatological punishment; casual references to Ge-hinnom in late historical Old Testament books; absence of exegetical additions and casual transliterations of Ge-hinnom in the LXX, that do not betray a strong Gehenna tradition; and complete silence of such important witnesses as the Dead Sea documents, Josephus, Philo, the early Mishnah and Talmud rabbis and of the early "Apocrypha" and

---

43. Neusner, *Judaism*, 25–28.
44. *Kidd.* 4:14; *Eduy.* 2:10; *Ab.* 1:5; 5:19; 5:20.
45. Herford, APOT, 2:692.
46. E.g. *b. B. Bat.* 10a; *b. Hag.* 15a.
47. *Ber.* 28b.
48. *R. Hash.* 16b; cf. Tosefta *Sanh.* 13:3.

"Pseudepigrapha." None of these observations lead to the conclusion that the evidence supports, or even hints at, a coherent, gradual development of the theme beginning with Jeremiah and continuing down the centuries. On the contrary, what we have is a large and obvious gap. Jeremiah makes reference to punishment in Ge-hinnom having been impressed by very specific events that took place there (the great apostasy of Ahaz and Manasseh and the radical activities of the reforming Josiah) and then the concept lies dormant for centuries. It seems therefore that there is no evidence that Gehenna was a part of common eschatological judgment parlance at any time before the first century AD.[49]

This conclusion is further strengthened by the thematic gap between Ge-hinnom in the Old Testament and Gehenna in later Jewish writings. Ge-hinnom in the Old Testament was a valley in which the apostate Jews would be annihilated in battle, their bodies being left unburied and exposed in shame. Fire plays only a minor role. Despite the eschatological overtones, the language does not have cosmic dimensions. In the "Apocrypha" and "Pseudepigrapha," on the other hand, Gehenna has become a term that signifies an eschatological, often out-of-this-world place. There the wicked, sometimes in their bodies, sometimes only as disembodied souls, are sometimes annihilated but often anguish in fire forever without end. It simply does not make sense to assume that the tradition developed from the simple battle-language of the Hebrew Scriptures to the otherworldly hell of bodies and/or, more often, souls, of the "Apocrypha" and "Pseudepigrapha," all at once. Since there are no extra-biblical Jewish literary works that contain evidence of intermediate steps in the development of the tradition, we have to look elsewhere for the missing links.

Synopsis and Synthesis

Traditionally it has been presumed that the Gehenna language of the Gospels had been inspired by a perpetual fire that was burning in the valley of Hinnom outside the walls of Jerusalem where the city's rubbish was thrown to be consumed. This view, however, has fallen from favor in recent years primarily because there is no documentary evidence earlier than the thirteenth century testifying to the existence of such a dump. It has been, therefore, customary to look to contemporary extra-biblical

---

49. A number of writers have also noted the lack of evidence. E.g., Bailey, "Gehenna," 191; Albright and Mann, *Matthew*, 61–62.

Jewish literature for a possible source of inspiration. I have argued that such an endeavor is wrought with uncertainty owing first to the obvious divergences between them and the Gehenna of the Gospels, and secondly to the likelihood that the references preserved in the Jewish sources represent a later development of a Gehenna tradition. This is evident in that they entail more elaborate and embellished descriptions and that they are found in literary strata decidedly later than the Synoptic Gospels.

Given the inadequacy of the above attempts to locate possible sources for the Synoptic Gehenna, I have suggested that we should look to the Old Testament "judgment" texts that envision God punishing his enemies, be they apostate Jews, Gentiles, or both, in a valley outside Jerusalem. The motif is fairly common and appears in different format in a number of prophecies. The two that seem to have played a determinative role in the Synoptic language are the Jeremiah "valley of Hinnom" prophecies (7:29–34 and 19:1–13) and Isa 66:24. The influence of these texts is visible most clearly in Mark 9:43–48, where the Jeremiah prophecies furnish the name Gehinnom, Hellenized to Gehenna, while Isaiah provides the image of the unquenchable fire and the destroying worm. Indeed, the consuming fire of the LORD surfaces repeatedly throughout both Isaiah (1:31; 5:24, 25; 9:5, 18, 19; 10:16, 17; 30:30, 33; 43:17; cf. Jer 17:27) and the Synoptic Gospels (Matt 3:10–12; 7:19; 13:40, 42, 50; Luke 3:9, 17).

The language of the Gospel of Luke also seems to derive from Isa 66:24. In his sole reference to Gehenna in 12:4–5 it is a place where the corpses of the wicked are thrown to be consumed after they have received their sentence. Luke therefore, most closely reflects Isa 66:24 where the fire and the worms serve to consume the corpses of the enemies of God rather than act as agents of divine punishment.

Gehenna is perhaps the most dominant locale used in relation to the final judgment. The first element that became immediately apparent is Matthew's preference for the term. Matthew refers to Gehenna a total of six times in five different pericopes (5:22; 10:28; 5:29; 18:10; 23:15, 33) in contrast to Mark's three times in one pericope (9:43–48) and Luke's one in one (12:4–5). A similar Matthean dominance is true of the other Day of Judgment locale: the outer darkness where there is weeping and gnashing of teeth. The two testify to Matthew's special interest in the Day of Judgment in contrast to Mark and Luke's more passing references.

A second element conspicuously present in all three Gospels is the emphasis on the body. Of the ten Gehenna texts the body is specifically mentioned in six (Mark 9:43, 45, 47; Matt 5:29; 10:28; 18:8) strongly implied in another (Luke 12:4–5) and not precluded in the remaining (Matt 5:22; 23:15, 33). This emphasis underlines two points. First, the final judgment is preceded by a bodily resurrection of the wicked. Clearly there can be no judgment on the body if the body is not resurrected. Second, the notion that judgment only takes place on corporeal persons intimates that there is no judgment in supposed other forms of existence. The emphasis on judgment on the body therefore precludes any punishment or judgment before the end of time and the Day of Judgment.

A third element is the striking absence of detailed descriptions of torment so common in other Jewish and Christian, contemporary and later, descriptions of the final judgment. Indeed, Gehenna is nowhere in the Synoptics presented as a place of torment. Rather, it is a place of destruction. This is intimated in the motifs that lie behind it. Both the Gehinnom prophecies of Jeremiah (7:29–34 and 19:1–13) and Isa 66:24 that have influenced the Gehenna language of the Gospels depict the destruction rather than the torment of the wicked. It is also evidenced in the Synoptic language used to describe it. It is a place of fire, but not the fire usually associated with hell that torments, but does not consume. Rather, it is the Isaianic fire that burns and consumes as easily and thoroughly as fire consumes chaff, or dead trees (Matt 3:10, 12; Luke 3:9; cf. Isa 1:31; 43:17). The nature of the punishment is vividly brought out in Matt 10:28 where it is compared to temporal death and is found to be more fearful. While temporal death removes life there is still the hope of the resurrection. In contrast the destruction of Gehenna is total and final with no hope of regress because God himself oversees it. The finality of Gehenna is also forcefully presented in Matt 5:22–23 where it is compared to the capital punishment ancient Hebrew courts were entitled to pass on certain offences.

The destructive imagery associated with Gehenna reaches an apogee in Luke 12:4–5. In language reminiscent of Isa 66:24, Luke records it not as a place where destruction is inflicted on the wicked, but rather as the place where the corpses of those already destroyed in the final judgment are thrown to be burned and consumed. Gehenna, therefore, becomes the place of the annihilation of corpses and impurities and as such, brings to a conclusion the punitive work of the judgment.

In light of this emphasis on destruction rather than torment it is no surprise to find the worms of Isa 66:24 in action (Mark 9:43–48). These are not worms that torment as grotesquely presented in later Christian works, but rather the maggots that feed on corpses and the other impurities.

19

Conditionalism in the Early Church

LeRoy E. Froom

LeRoy Edwin Froom (1890-1974) was professor of historical theology at Andrews University, a Seventh Day Adventist minister and historian, and the founding editor of Ministry Magazine. *He served as the first associate secretary of the General Conference, the governing body of the Seventh Day Adventist denomination, in the Ministerial Association from 1926 to 1950.*

*Froom is most known for his two works of historical theology—*The Prophetic Faith of our Fathers *(four volumes published from 1948-1953) and* The Conditionalist Faith of our Fathers *(two volumes published from 1965-1966)—which trace, respectively, the church's understanding of prophecy and conditional immortality throughout its history. In this chapter Froom wields his historian's pen to outline the Apostolic and Ante-Nicene Fathers' stance towards conditionalism.*

Significance of Testimony of Apostolic Fathers

THE TERM "APOSTOLIC FATHERS," coined later, embraces those Christian writers of the subapostolic age who lived nearest to, or whose lives partly paralleled, the last of the apostles. They are usually listed as Clement of Rome, Ignatius of Antioch, the writer of *The Didache* and of the *Epistle of Barnabas*, Hermas of Rome, Polycarp of Smyrna, and Papias.

And to these is sometimes added the writer of *The Epistle of Mathetes to Diognetus* and that of the *Homily of Clement*. The time spread is about the first half of the second century.

The two ways, as they are called, are constantly set forth, and the endings of the ways, life and death—with eternal life and immortality as the gift of God for the redeemed, and restricted to believers; and the contrary doom of death and everlasting destruction for the impenitently wicked. This pattern, or emphasis, is woven consistently throughout the writings of the apostolic fathers, which we now examine.

Clement of Rome—Neither Innate Immortality Nor Eternal Torment

We will now trace what Clement of Rome teaches in the authentic *First Epistle* in regard to immortality and punishment—with perishing, destruction, and death for the wicked, and salvation and life and immortality for the redeemed as the gift of God, for which reward we must wait.

Significant Silences in Clement's Witness

Scholarly Anglican Prebendary Henry Constable rightly calls attention to Clement's "silence on certain points." Clement "never speaks of the *immortality of the soul*,"[1] either in thought or in phrasing, nor of *eternal punishing*, both of which concepts about in later church writers, such as Tertullian (d. c. 240) and Augustine (d. 430). Clement says that man is "mortal";[2] consisting only of "dust and ashes ... his life be but of one day."[3] This is significant. But he is far more than negative.

Immortality a "Gift" of God, to be Sought For

Clement sets forth immortality as one of God's glorious gifts to the redeemed. "Life in immortality," as he phrases it, is a *gift* of God to the righteous. And it is "prepared for such as wait for him." To gain it we must "earnestly strive" for it, "in order that we may share in his promised

---

1. Constable, *Future Punishment*, 168.
2. *1 Clem.* 39; *ANF* 1:15.
3. Ibid., 17; *ANF* 1:9–10.

PART FIVE—HISTORICAL CONSIDERATIONS

gifts."[4] Clement did not believe that the wicked either possessed Immortality by nature or should ever obtain it.

As to *zōē* ("life," or "existence"), Clement likewise uses it only in the sense of existence. He speaks of the "*life of man* which may last but for a day."[5] It is not mere "happiness," or "well-being," as contended by a later school of writers. With Clement, "*righteousness is not life, but the way to life.*"[6] And it is God's will that we should "taste of immortal knowledge,"[7] "the knowledge of immortality."[8]

Death Is Cessation of All Life

Clement presents "death" (*thanatos*) as the lot of all mankind. He sets it forth as the deprivation of life, the cessation of the faculties, the ending of all activities. All men are subject to its claims, except such as Enoch, who was exempted by translation, for, as Clement says, "death was never known to happen to him."[9] But from Abel on to Christ and the martyrs, all suffered death.[10] Christ, as our Savior and substitute, was "brought down to death." Again, "his soul was delivered to death, and he was reckoned among the transgressors, and he bare the sins of many."[11]

And when Clement discusses that death which is the ultimate fate of the wicked, he clearly states that they will ultimately be deprived of all existence, and become nonexistent. He does not refer to a merely spiritual death in sin, or of endless life in everlasting misery, as was later projected by Tertullian and Augustine.

Wicked to Perish, Be Destroyed, Cease to Exist

As to the future punishment of the wicked, Clement uses such terms as *teleutaō* (to "finish," "accomplish," "end"), and thus "to die," as the end or loss of human existence. He goes on to state that death was visited upon

4. Ibid., 35; *ANF* 1:14.
5. Constable, *Future Punishment*, 240. See *1 Clem.* 17; *ANF* 1:10.
6. Constable, *Future Punishment*, 240. See *1 Clem.* 48; *ANF* 1:18.
7. *1 Clem.* 36; *ANF* 1:14–15.
8. Ibid.; *ANF* 1:115, n. 1.
9. Ibid., 9; *ANF* 1:7.
10. Ibid., 4, 16; *ANF* 1:6, 9.
11. Ibid., *ANF* 1:9.

the people of Jericho,[12] and death came to the army of Pharaoh in the Red Sea.[13] That is the death that comes upon all men through sin.

Again and again Clement uses the terms "perish" and "destruction"[14] as the equivalent of "punished with death"[15] for the fate of the wicked. He frequently quotes from the Old Testament—the New Testament was not yet assembled—citing how "transgressors" are to be "destroyed from off the face of" the earth;[16] how the prophet looked for the wicked and "behold, he was not";[17] how evildoers are to be "cut off," along with "the remembrance of them from the earth;"[18] how God will "destroy them," literally they are to be "wiped out," and God will "blot out" even "their name from under heaven."[19] That was Clement's belief. It is sketchy, and not amplified, as with other writers soon to follow. But his witness is consistent and conclusive, and is significant because of its timing.

Ignatius of Antioch—Immortality Solely for Saints; Sinners to Perish

Presumably next in timing among the apostolic fathers comes Ignatius, surnamed Theophorus (d. c. AD 107), bishop of Antioch, who suffered martyrdom by being thrown to wild beasts in the Flavian Amphitheater at Rome during the latter half of Trajan's reign (AD 98–117). He was converted to the Christian faith in maturity, but the rest of his personal life is wrapped in obscurity.

To the Ephesians: Immortality Is "Gift" of Christ

In *The Epistle to the Ephesians* Ignatius expresses consciousness and concern over the approaching latter-day crises lying before the church. Thus: "The last times are come upon us. Let us therefore be of a reverent spirit." He urges the men of Ephesus to "stand in awe of the wrath to come," and

12. Ibid., 12; *ANF* 1:8. Cf. Josh 2; Heb 11:31.
13. Ibid., 51; *ANF* 1:19. Cf. Exod 14.
14. Ibid., 39, 53, 55; *ANF* 1:15, 19, 20.
15. Ibid., 41; *ANF* 1:16.
16. Ibid., 14; *ANF* 1:8. Cf. Ps 2:21–22.
17. Ibid. Cf. Ps 37:35–37.
18. Ibid., 22; *ANF* 1:11. Cf. Ps 34:16.
19. Ibid., 53; *ANF* 1:19. Cf. Exod 32:10.

admonishes, "*Let us be found in Christ Jesus unto the true life.*"[20] We shall see how this continuing theme of *life in Christ* runs as a golden thread throughout his epistles. He refers, for example, in chapter three, to Jesus Christ as "our inseparable life."[21] This he enlarged upon in chapter seventeen by declaring that our Lord was anointed "that he might *breathe immortality into his church.*" He warns against the "prince of this world" leading any "away captive from the life which is set before you." And he asks, "Why do we foolishly perish, not recognizing the gift which the Lord has of a truth sent to us?"[22]

In chapter eighteen Ignatius alludes to the provision of the cross as being "to us salvation and *life eternal.*"[23] And in chapter nineteen he tells of "God himself being manifested in human form for the *renewal of eternal life.* . . . Henceforth all things were in a state of tumult, because he meditated the abolition of death."[24] Then in chapter twenty he interestingly refers to "breaking one and the same bread, which is the *medicine of immortality*, and the antidote to prevent us from dying, but [which causes] that we should *live for ever* in Jesus Christ."[25] Life, eternal life, is his burden.

In all of this Ignatius stresses the fact that the gift of immortality comes only through Christ, whereas death is the inevitable portion of the sinner. He says, in chapter sixteen, that the person who "corrupts by wicked doctrine the faith of God" shall, thus defiled, "go away into *everlasting fire*, and so shall every one that hearkens unto him."[26]

The unquenchableness of the fire does *not*, however, involve the later Augustinian conception of endless existence in torment of all who are cast into it. That dogma of the indefeasible immortality of the wicked as well as the righteous was an innovation not introduced for another century. So, in writing to the Ephesians, Ignatius holds that "immortality" and "eternal life" for the righteous are the exact opposites of "perishing" for the wicked.

---

20. *Ign. Eph.* 11; *ANF* 1:54. (Italics supplied.)
21. Ibid., 3; *ANF* 1:50.
22. Ibid., 17; *ANF* 1:56.
23. Ibid., 18; *ANF* 1:56, 57. (Italics supplied.)
24. Ibid., 19; *ANF* 1:57. (Italics supplied.)
25. Ibid., 20; *ANF* 1:58. (Brackets in original, italics supplied.)
26. Ibid., 16; *ANF* 1:56.

To the Magnesians: Death Is Ceasing to Be

At the very outset of Ignatius' *Epistle to the Magnesians* (in Ionia, Asia Minor) he speaks of Christ as "the constant source of our *life*."[27] He then sets forth the two basic alternatives in chapter five: "Seeing, then, *all things have an end*, these two things are simultaneously set before us—*death* and *life*; and every one shall go unto his own place."[28] And he adds, concerning the "unbelieving," and those Christians "not in readiness to die into his passion," that "his [Christ's] life *is not in us*."[29] In chapter ten he makes the unequivocal statement, "For were he to reward us according to our works, we should *cease to be*."[30] This comports with Ignatius' message to the Ephesians, that when the sinner is rewarded according to his deeds he will then cease to exist. Thus there will be an end of all things—except of those who partake of the proffered life in Christ.

To the Trallians: Life through Christ's Death

In the introduction to his *Epistle to the Trallians* (in Caria, Asia Minor, southeast of Ephesus), Ignatius speaks of Jesus Christ, "who is our hope, through *our rising again to him*," or "in the *resurrection* which is by him."[31] In this new treatise he continues to write in harmony with his previous declarations, as when he states in chapter two, concerning "Jesus Christ, who died for us," that "by believing in his death, ye *may escape from death*."[32] And again in chapter four, "I restrain myself, lest I should *perish* through boasting."[33] And finally, in chapter nine, that as the Father quickened Christ, so "after the same manner his Father will so *raise up us* who believe in him by Christ Jesus, apart from whom we do not possess the *true life*."[34] Life, then, is only in Christ, and those who do not possess this life are to perish.

---

27. *Ign. Magn.* 1; *ANF* 1:59. (Italics supplied.)
28. Ibid., 5; *ANF* 1:61. (Italics supplied.)
29. Ibid., note 3 reads, "after the likeness of His passion."
30. Ibid., 10; *ANF* 1:63. (Italics supplied.) Denniston, *Perishing Soul*, 296–97, renders it, "We are no more" (*ouk etiesmen*).
31. *Ign. Trall.* introduction; *ANF* 1:66. (Italics supplied.)
32. Ibid., 2; *ANF* 1:66. (Italics supplied.)
33. Ibid., 4; *ANF* 1:67. (Italics supplied.)
34. Ibid., 9; *ANF* 1:70. (Italics supplied.)

PART FIVE—HISTORICAL CONSIDERATIONS

Barnabas—Contrasts Eternal Life with Eternal Death

Virtually no scholar ascribes *The Epistle of Barnabas* (c. AD 130–c. 140) to the apostle Barnabas, friend and companion of the apostle Paul. Rather, it is credited to another of the same name. The internal evidence has always been conclusively against the older view. The writer was possibly a Jewish Christian of Alexandria, for the Barnabas epistle is mentioned by Clement of Alexandria and by Origen, also of Alexandria, and its tendency to allegorize fits into the Alexandrian scene.[35]

Life through Christ; Death through Sin

Chapter seven (on "Types of Christ") says that Christ, who is also our judge, was stricken that he might give us life.

> If therefore the Son of God, who is Lord [of all things], and who will judge the living and the dead, suffered, that *his stroke might give us life*, let us believe that the Son of God could not have suffered except for our sake.[36]

Chapter eight ("The Red Heifer a Type of Christ") states "that [through the cross] those believing on him shall *live for ever*."[37] And he adds, in chapter nine, "Who is he that wishes to live for ever? By hearing let him hear the voice of my servant."[38] That is man's part. Then in chapter ten, passing to the various precepts and prohibitions of Moses, Barnabas says, "he means, 'Thou shalt not join thyself or be like to such men as are ungodly to the end, and are condemned to death.'"[39] Next, in chapter eleven, Barnabas speaks of the water of life, the river, and the trees whose leaves never face, and comments, "'and whosoever shall eat of these shall live for ever.' This meaneth: Whosoever, he declares, shall hear thee [Jesus] speaking, and believe, shall *live for ever*." "Whosoever" is unconditional, but assures immortality for all such as hear and heed. In contrast the ungodly are like the "chaff, which the wind sweeps away

---

35. Newman, *Church History*, 1:221–22, says, "We cannot avoid the supposition that the epistle was written by a man who had come under the influence of the Alexandrian philosophy, probably of the earlier forms of Gnosticism as well."

36. *Barn.* 7; *ANF* 1:141. (Brackets in original; italics supplied.)

37. Ibid., 8; *ANF* 1:142. (Brackets in original; italics supplied.)

38. Ibid., 9; *ANF* 1:142.

39. Ibid., 10; *ANF* 1:143.

from the face of the earth."[40] That is the tenor of his paralleling series of contentions.

Death from Sin Involves Destruction

In chapter twelve Barnabas states that it was because of Israel's sins that "they were delivered to death." He then tells how, when Moses stretched forth his hands, victory for Israel resulted, but "when again he let down his hands, they were again destroyed." And why? "That they might know that they could not be saved unless they put their trust in him."[41] That was the condition of their salvation—trust in him, or conditional salvation. Then Barnabas makes this application: "Moses makes a type of Jesus, [signifying] that it was necessary for him to suffer, [and also] that he would be the *author of life* [to others]."[42]

That is, Jesus died to save men consigned to death.

"Eternal Death": Synonym for Second Death

The phrase "eternal death" appears in chapter twenty for the first time as a synonym for the second and definitive death. It is "eternal death with punishment." Here distinction is to be made between punishment by *deprivation of life* and mere punishment by pain through the senses. "Eternal death with punishment" (*meta timōrias*) obviously involves an infliction of suffering preceding death, and the end of being.[43] And this statement by Barnabas is immediately followed by the conclusion, in chapter twenty-one, which opens with:

> It is well, therefore, that he who has learned the judgments of the Lord, as many as have been written, should walk in them. For he who keepeth these shall be glorified in the kingdom of God; but he who chooseth other things [condemned in the previous chapter] shall be *destroyed* [*apoleitai*] with his works. On this account there will be a resurrection, on this account a retribution.[44]

---

40. Ibid., 11; *ANF* 1:144. (Italics supplied.)

41. Ibid., 12; *ANF* 1:144–45.

42. Ibid., 12; *ANF* 1:145. (Brackets in original; italics supplied.) Note 4 reads, "and he shall make him alive."

43. Ibid., 20; *ANF* 1:149.

44. Ibid. (Italics supplied.)

To perish with his works is clearly to exist no more. The *works* are destroyed by coming to an end. Thus also with the *worker* of iniquity.[45]

Summarizing Conclusion concerning the Apostolic Fathers

It has often been asserted that the dogma of the innate immortality of the soul and the eternal torment of the wicked, as later taught by Tertullian and finally established by Augustine, was *always* the position of the early Christian church. But the scholarly investigations of Henry Constable, Anglican Prebendary of Cork, Ireland, led him to reply with positiveness, "We wholly deny it." And after his exhaustive study of the apostolic fathers, Constable declared that they were just as much opposed to the everlasting-torment theories of Augustine as to the theories of Origen and his universal-restoration concept. Here is the key statement of Constable's sweeping conclusion:

> From beginning to end of them [the apostolic fathers] there is not one word said of that immortality of the soul which is so prominent in the writings of the later fathers. Immortality is by them asserted to be peculiar to the redeemed. The punishment of the wicked is by them emphatically declared to be everlasting. Not one stray expression of theirs can be interpreted as giving any countenance to the theory of restoration after purgatorial suffering. The fire of hell is with them, as with us, an unquenchable one; but its issue is, with them as with Scripture, "destruction," "death," "loss of life."[46]

Constable even went so far as to issue this challenge to his contemporaries, which appears in each of the six editions of his major treatise, "We challenge our opponents to controvert our view of them in a single particular."[47] And it should be added that no one during his lifetime, when discussion over the question was rife, ever undertook to disprove his contention.

---

45. "The strong shall be as tow, and the maker of it as a spark, and they shall both burn together, and none shall quench them" (Isa 1:31).
46. Constable, *Future Punishment*, 167.
47. Ibid.

Irenaeus of Gaul—Conditionalist Champion on Western Outpost

We now turn to Irenaeus, of Gaul, most conspicuous and learned conditionalist of the third century, who bore a remarkable testimony in this transition hour. [A]bout AD 178 Irenaeus (c. 130–202), who had been born in Asia Minor, was made bishop of Gaul. He had received a Hellenistic education, but definitely belonged to the West, and became one of the most learned and renowned of the early ante-Nicene fathers.

He had been a pupil of Polycarp of Smyrna, who, it will be remembered, was an avowed conditionalist. This association doubtless influenced Irenaeus' own views on this controverted question.

Wicked Destined to Cessation of Being

Irenaeus seemed to exhaust the expressive vocabulary at his command in denying the immortality of the unsaved. The incorrigibly wicked are consigned to eternal punishment, which, he explains, ends in complete cessation of being or existence; and this results in the end of all evil. The chastisement of the wicked will be eternal in its *effects*, because God's benefits are eternal. His argument, in a sentence, was this: *To be deprived of the benefits of existence is the greatest punishment, and to be deprived of them forever is to suffer "eternal punishment."* This should be borne in mind.

Eternal Continuance is "Bestowed" and "Imparted"

In chapter thirty-three [of Book Two of *Against Heresies*] Irenaeus exposes the fiction and "absurdity of the doctrine of the transmigration of the souls." He says they "never existed in other bodies."[48] Irenaeus tells of the resurrection of the entire man—how "all those who have been *enrolled* for life [eternal] shall rise again, having their own bodies, and having also their own souls, and their own spirits, in which they had pleased God."[49] Irenaeus' climax comes in chapter thirty-four, where he explicitly

---

48. *Against Heresies*, 2.33.5; ANF 1:410.
49. Ibid.; *ANF* 1:411. (Italics supplied.)

declares that "God alone, who is Lord of all, is without beginning and without end," and therefore "unchangeable."[50]

Moreover, "created things" will, he maintains, "endure as long as God wills that they should have an existence and continuance,"[51] and gives "length of days for ever and ever." He declares of such, "It is the Father of all who *imparts* [gives] continuance for ever and ever on those who are saved."[52] As to the "bestowed" life he adds:

> For life does not arise from us, nor from our own nature; but it is *bestowed* according to the grace of God. And therefore he who shall preserve the life *bestowed* upon him, and give thanks to him who *imparted* it, shall receive also length of days for ever and ever. . . . But he who shall reject it, and prove himself ungrateful to his Maker, inasmuch as he has been created, and has not recognized him who *bestowed* [the gift upon him], deprives himself of the [privilege of] continuance for ever and ever.[53]

"Perpetual Duration" Is Unending "Existence"

His argument is amplified and enforced in section four, where Irenaeus asserts that "the soul herself is not life, but partakes in that life *bestowed* upon her by God."[54] And he adds:

> When God therefore *bestows* life and perpetual duration, it comes to pass that even souls which did not previously exist should henceforth endure [forever], since God has both willed that they should exist, and should continue in existence.[55]

That is the declared basis of "the continued duration of the soul."[56]

---

50. Ibid., 2.34.2; *ANF* 1:411.
51. Ibid., 2.34.3; *ANF* 1:411.
52. Ibid.
53. Ibid.; *ANF* 1:411–12. (Brackets in original; italics supplied.)
54. Ibid., 2.34.4; *ANF* 1:412. (Italics supplied.)
55. Ibid. (Brackets in original; italics supplied.)
56. Ibid.

Final Annihilation of the Wicked

Some have claimed that when Irenaeus ... refers to *aiōnion* fire and *aiōnion* punishment, he means *eternal torment*, and not destruction. But such overlook the definitive declarations of Irenaeus' systematic coverage, which show conclusively that by *aiōnion* punishment he did not mean eternal punish*ing*, but rather punishment in the world to come that ends in cessation of being. The *first* death cuts man off from a life of but few years' duration—a life that is due to die. But the *second* death cuts the sinner off from eternal life, and is consequently an eternal death. This is attested by Dr. Philip Schaff, who states Irenaeus' position impressively:

> It is therefore the more remarkable that the doctrine of future eternal punishment was not taught ... so far as we know, nor the doctrine of universal restoration; but on the other hand, the doctrine of the final annihilation of the wicked was clearly taught by so eminent a man as Irenaeus.[57]

And Edward Beecher, after recording a similar conclusion, remarks on the "very great reluctance in the ranks of the orthodox, in modern times, to concede that he was a defender of the doctrine of the annihilation of the wicked."[58]

Dean Frederic W. Farrar likewise adds that Irenaeus—

> uses the phrase "eternal punishment," or "eternal fire," as all use those phrases who accept the Bible; and in one passage he says that "the good things of God, being eternal and endless, the *privation of them* also is eternal and endless." Certainly this passage shows his opinion that the "pain of loss" (as we all believe) may be eternal and endless.[59]

Such was Irenaeus' concept of life, death, and destiny—most explicit of the early church fathers.

---

57. Schaff, *History*, 2:194–95.
58. Beecher, *Retribution*, 198.
59. Farrar, *Mercy and Judgment*, 239–40. (Italics supplied.)

PART FIVE—HISTORICAL CONSIDERATIONS

Arnobius of Africa—Last Ante-Nicene Conditionalist Spokesman

Approximately a century after the martyrdom of Irenaeus, Arnobius (fl. c. AD 297–310), of Africa, called the Elder, one of the bright ante-Nicene lights of the first decade of the fourth century, brought forth a notable confession of his newly espoused Christian faith.

Meets Paganism on Its Own Ground

Arnobius' book, though written before his actual baptism, is a statement of mature convictions. Here on heathenism's own ground he meets the arguments, the taunts and reproaches, brought against Christianity by the stalwarts of paganism. And he not only repels their charges but undertakes to persuade them that Christianity is fully demonstrable by evidence. He does not quote heavily from Scripture, which was largely unknown to his readers—and would not be admitted as evidence by them anyway—so he presents the *facts* of Scripture rather than actual quotations from the text. He seeks to impress them with the fatal weakness and fallacy of their own reasoning, and the folly of polytheism.

A Destruction that Leaves Nothing Behind

After referring to paganism's problem of a soul that is "immortal, everlasting, and without bodily substance," yet being "punished" and made to "suffer pain," Arnobius asks, "But what man does not see that that which is immortal, which *is* simple (note 17: "i.e., not compounded of soul and body"), cannot be subject to any pain; that that, on the contrary, cannot be immortal which does suffer pain?" He then speaks of those who, being cast into the flames, are "annihilated," and "pass away" in "everlasting destruction."[60]

Ultimate "Annihilation" is Man's "Real Death"

Arnobius next declares that according to Christ "theirs [the souls'] is *an intermediate state*"—there are those that "may on the one hand perish if

---

60. *Against the Heathen*, 2.14; ANF 6:439.

they have not known God, and on the other be delivered from death if they have given heed to his threats and proffered favors."[61] Then follows Arnobius' clear definition of man's "*real death*":

> This is man's real death, *this which leaves nothing behind.*[62] For that which is seen by the eyes is *only* a separation of soul from body, not the last end—annihilation: this, I say, is man's real death, when souls which know not God shall be consumed in long-protracted torment with raging fire.[63]

Arnobius clearly distinguishes between the first death and the final death, and declares that in the true, or final, death of the wicked there is "nothing left behind"—absolute destruction after the final death agonies. He warns against the presumption of Innate Immortality. Continuance of life, he holds, is *conditional*.

Athanasius—Then Conditionalism into Eclipse

Athanasius (c. 297–373), bishop of Alexandria and most prominent theologian of the fourth century, is commonly called the "defender of orthodoxy," because of his conspicuous championship of the eternal deity of Christ in the battle over the Godhead, as against the prolonged attacks of Arianism.

In his *De Incarnatione Verbi Dei* ("On the Incarnation of the Word") Athanasius expounds how God the Word (Logos) by his union with human manhood restores to fallen man the image of God, in which he had been created. And by his death and resurrection he met and overcame death and the consequences of sin.

Man Not Created with Perverse Tendencies

Athanasius' introduction in sections one to three begins with the doctrine of creation by the Word, and man's allotted place, followed by the abuse of his high privileges and resultant loss. It portrays how the Father has saved the world by him through whom he first made it.[64] The creation

61. Ibid., 6:439–40.
62. "*Haec nihil residuum faciens.*"
63. Ibid., 6:440.
64. *De Inc.* 1; *NPNF* 4:36.

was out of nothing. And, be it particularly noted, with man created above the rest, but incapable of independent perseverance.[65]

As it was by the Word that man was called from non-existence into being, so by the one fault that forfeited that life he incurred corruption.[66] Having thus incurred ruin, man of himself must sink back into destruction.[67] Only the original Bestower of life, Athanasius held, could now rescue him and restore life.

Creator Must Both Renew and Restore

Athanasius presses the point that, having incurred corruption, none could renew but he who had created man. The Son alone could re-create, suffer for all, and represent all to the Father.[68] So the Word visited this earth and took a body of our nature, and that of a virgin.[69] He took a mortal body, capable of death, uniting it with his deity, that he might stay the corruption of the race. Becoming one with us he clothed us with immortality[70] as a result. Created in the "image" of God, man had fallen away from God.[71] So God restored in us the grace of his image.

That is Athanasius' view of the vicarious, atoning death of Christ on the cross, in its relation to the redemption of man and his resurrection and future life. It reveals a magnificent grasp of the over-all issues and a continuity of treatment that was unsurpassed in his day. On the actual nature and destiny of man Athanasius was at times self-contradictory.[72] It was a transition hour. He sometimes reproduces some of the very

65. Ibid., 3; *NPNF* 4:37.
66. Ibid., 4–5; *NPNF* 4:38.
67. Ibid., 6; *NPNF* 4:39.
68. Ibid. 7; *NPNF* 4:39.
69. Ibid., 8; *NPNF* 4:40.
70. Ibid. 9; *NPNF* 4:40.
71. Ibid., 11; *NPNF* 4:42.

72. Athanasius was an avowed immortal-soulist when he was twenty-one, at the time he wrote his first book, *Contra Gentes* ("Against the Heathen"), about AD 318, and thus seven years before the Council of Nicea in 325. (*NPNF* 4:lxxxvi, 1.) At that time Athanasius expressly declared the soul to be immortal (*Against the Heathen*, 33; *NPNF* 4:21), with power to continue life outside of the body after death (ibid.). But even in this treatise Athanasius says, in his closing paragraph, "Immortality and the kingdom of heaven is the fruit of faith and devotion towards him [God], if only the soul be adorned according to his laws"—and refers to the "prize" of "life everlasting" (Ibid., 47.4; *NPNF* 4:30).

thoughts and phrases of Plato that were openly employed by Athanagoras and Tertullian. But he did not follow with them to their conclusions. He passed over the final destruction. And the semi-conditionalism he voiced was, erelong, drowned out in the swirling tide of Platonism, which in time swept over Christendom. But his was a retarding voice that was heard, and was respect in his day.

PART SIX

Conditionalism and Evangelicalism

With the publication of *Evangelical Essentials* John Stott, in keeping with the evangelical ethos of the primacy of Scripture in doctrinal matters, called for a fresh reexamination of the biblical materials regarding hell: "I do plead for frank dialogue among evangelicals on the basis of Scripture," he wrote. "I also believe that the ultimate annihilation of the wicked should at least be accepted as a legitimate, biblically founded alternative to their eternal conscious torment."[1] In 1989, just one year later, over three hundred and fifty evangelical leaders gathered at Trinity Evangelical Divinity School for the "Evangelical Essentials" conference, in part to discuss the boundary lines of what makes Christian evangelicalism distinct. There J. I. Packer gave a paper that included critique of the conditionalist position, but found to his surprise that the conference was in fact split over the question.[2] As *Christianity Today* reported:

> Strong disagreements did surface over the position of annihilationism ... the conference was almost evenly divided as to how to deal with the issue in the affirmations statement, and no renunciation of the position was included in the draft document.[3]

To be sure, conditionalism remains a minority view within evangelicalism, but it has steadily gained ground within the evangelical camp over the last half a century. As Alan Gomes, professor at Talbot School of Theology has noted, evangelicals can no longer simply wave aside annihilationism via guilt by association with fringe or cultic groups.[4] It is accepted by thoroughbred evangelicals who genuinely disagree over the interpretation of what the Scriptures teach. Because of the irreduc-

1. Edwards and Stott, *Essentials*, 320.
2. Packer, "Annihlationism," 38.
3. *Christianity Today*, June 16, 1989, 60, 63.
4. Gomes, "Evangelicals." It is true that some cultic groups teach annihilationism (e.g., Jehovah's Witnesses), but as Gomes points out, it would be fallacious to reject annihilationism on that basis, especially since such groups also teach doctrines like the inerrancy of Scripture.

ible necessity of biblical interpretation in this debate, voices such as I. Howard Marshall have echoed Stott's plea, urging us to "seek to explore and discuss [the biblical materials regarding hell] irenically and respectfully without accusing one another of heresy or rejecting members of the evangelical family who are questioning whether traditional interpretations of Scripture are really true to Scripture."[5] Likewise, F. F. Bruce, in the preface to Edward Fudge's work, *The Fire That Consumes*, advises that when there is "no unanimity here among people who are agreed in accepting the Bible as their rule of faith ... in such a situation polemic should have no place. What is called for, rather, is the fellowship of patient Bible study."[6]

The following chapters represent the contributions of traditionalists who are respected evangelicals—or in the case of the report from the Evangelical Alliance, a body of evangelicals—*who are not themselves convinced of conditionalism*, but who proceed in this very spirit of evangelical charity. They recognize conditionalists' high regard for Scripture, concern for evangelism, and desire to warn unbelievers of the fearful reality of hell, and they urge for continued dialogue on these issues. For instance, the ACUTE report ("Alliance Commission on Unity and Truth Among Evangelicals") concludes with this commendable counsel:

> We encourage traditionalist and conditionalist evangelicals to pursue agreement on the matter of hell, rather than merely acquiescing in their disagreement. As they do so, we call upon them to maintain constructive dialogue and respectful relationships, even when their differences seem intractable.

---

5. Marshall, *Endorsement*.

6. Bruce, "Foreword," xi. Bruce expressed his own view in a letter to John Stott: "Annihilation is certainly an acceptable interpretation of the relevant New Testament passages.... For myself, I remain agnostic. Eternal conscious torment is incompatible with the revealed character of God." (As quoted in Timothy Dudley-Smith, *John Stott*, 354.)

20

Hell and Evangelical Unity

EVANGELICAL ALLIANCE

The Evangelical Alliance (EA) bills itself as "the largest and oldest body representing the UK's two million evangelical Christians,"[1] officially founded in 1846 under the motto, Unum Corpus Sumus in Christo *("We are One Body in Christ").*[2] *Not to be mistaken as pushing simple ecumenism, following the formation in 1945 of the World Council of Churches, EA warned that "'outward uniformity' should not to be mistaken for . . . 'real spiritual unity.'"*[3] *Today, the EA strives for this sort of unity, working across seventy-nine denominations and 3,500 churches in the UK, and with over 600 million evangelicals worldwide as part of the World Evangelical Alliance.*

The Alliance Commission on Unity and Truth among Evangelicals (ACUTE) was formed by EA in 1993, and "is committed to an ongoing programme of research and publication on theological issues which are of concern to evangelicals."[4] *ACUTE issued its first official statement in response to the controversy surrounding the "Toronto Blessing," a wave of charismatic activity beginning in 1994, and in 1996 issued a paper addressing the question, "What is an Evangelical?" ACUTE tackled "The Nature of Hell" in 2000, concluding*

1. Evangelical Alliance, "About us."
2. Hilborn and Randall, "A Brief History," 1.
3. Ibid., 3.
4. Hilborn, *Hell*, vii.

that "conditional immortality is a significant minority evangelical view," and that "'evangelical conditionalists' have strong evangelical credentials, and have in particular demonstrated a genuine regard for the authority of Scripture," while urging evangelicals "to pursue agreement on the matter of hell, rather than merely acquiescing in their disagreement."[5]

To some extent, the acceptability of both traditionalist and conditionalist views of hell has already been acknowledged within the evangelical constituency. Derek Tidball's influential study of past and present evangelicalism in fact defines this debate as a distinctively evangelical one, which many in the wider church and world would regard as an internal "family" dispute.[6] Likewise, Rob Warner and Clive Calver's recent account of evangelical unity and doctrine acknowledges conditionalists to be an established "evangelical party."[7]

On the other hand, concern has been expressed in certain quarters that conditionalists may be transgressing the boundaries of evangelical orthodoxy. Thus both Anthony Hoekema and John Gerstner provocatively describe the recent growth of evangelical conditionalism as a "revolt," with Gerstner calling its proponents to repent as a matter of urgency.[8] Then again, evangelical conditionalists can be equally passionate in advocating their own position. Indeed, John Wenham, Clark Pinnock, and Robert Brow may fairly be described as "proselytizers" for the conditionalist cause, seeking to "convert" evangelicalism from what they regard as a grossly mistaken doctrine of eternal conscious punishment to one which better reflects the true message of the gospel.[9]

In view of such tensions, it is salutary to assess the relative importance of the traditionalist-conditionalist debate for the contemporary evangelical agenda. More specifically, we need to determine those aspects of the doctrine of hell that evangelicals should regard as primary and non-negotiable, as against those aspects that may be deemed *adiaphora*—that is, secondary concerns over which it is possible to differ with integrity.

---

5. Ibid., 134–35.
6. Tidball, *Who are the Evangelicals?* 152–55.
7. Calver and Warner, *Together We Stand*, 87.
8. Hoekema, *The Bible and the Future*, 265; Gerstner, *Repent or Perish*.
9. Wenham, "Conditional Immortality," 190–91; Pinnock and Brow, *Unbounded Love*, 88, 94.

Of course, the distinction of primary from secondary issues depends to a large degree on how one chooses to define evangelicalism. At present, there is an abundance of studies addressing this matter.[10] All agree that evangelicals are those who believe in a triune God, the incarnation, the sacrificial atonement of Christ, his bodily resurrection and second coming, justification by faith, the supreme authority of the Bible, and the missionary prerogative. Yet differences appear when evangelical authenticity is assessed in relation to issues such as baptismal practice, the ecumenical movement, the ordination of women, biblical inerrancy, evolution, spiritual gifts, the millennium, and, for that matter, the nature of hell. Some writers see one or more of these issues as "primary" rather than "secondary," with lines between essentials and non-essentials being drawn in different places. For others, none of them would warrant separation or breach of fellowship.

Furthermore, the actual criteria for determining whether something is primary or secondary for evangelicals are not always straightforward. For our part, we would suggest that they comprise four interrelated considerations. Listed roughly in order of importance these are: a) doctrinal, b) historical, c) ideological, and d) relational. It will be useful to apply each of these considerations to the current evangelical debate about hell. This will in turn enable us to draw positive conclusions about the debate, and to make recommendations on how evangelicals should deal with the subject of hell. Since the presenting issue for this report is the acceptability or otherwise of conditionalism, we shall focus our assessment on this in particular.

Conditionalism, Unity, and Evangelical Doctrine

The first basis on which evangelicals must establish whether something is either primary or secondary is that of doctrine, and specifically biblical doctrine. The Evangelical Alliance Basis of Faith typifies this priority when it claims as its primary source "the Scriptures of the Old and New Testaments," and takes these Scriptures to be "entirely trustworthy" and "supremely authoritative in all matters of faith and conduct." Given evangelical agreement the Bible's witness to the existence of hell *per se*,

---

10. Some to mention include: Tidball, *Who are the Evangelicals?*; McGrath, *Evangelicalism* and *A Passion for Truth*; Noll, *Evangelical Mind*; Wells, *No Place for Truth*; Thompson, *Saving the Heart*.

the question is whether the Bible depicts this hell so unambiguously as a place of eternal torment that no alternative view could legitimately be deemed "evangelical."

At the very least, our study has confirmed that the main evangelical proponents of conditionalism demonstrate a high regard for the authority of Scripture, and seek to make their case by thorough exegesis of the relevant texts. In this specific sense, there can be little doubt that they are operating as evangelicals. Furthermore, we would go so far as to say that their work has highlighted verses and images that some traditionalists may previously have ignored or even misconstrued. For instance, no one who has studied the work of Fudge or Powys can seriously read the many biblical references to God's "destruction" of the impenitent without considering whether they might in fact denote a final cessation of existence rather than endless conscious perishing.

Of course, it must be admitted that a properly evangelical *intention* to uphold the primacy of Scripture does not necessarily lead to proper evangelical theology. As far as possible, evangelicals seek to make doctrine clear and consistent, since they are those who maintain the Reformation principle of biblical "perspicuity." On the face of it, this would militate against a conciliatory, "both/and" approach to conditional immortality/eternal conscious punishment. After all, it seems illogical to suggest that people could be both annihilated and tormented forever! Having said this, it is worth bearing in mind that both conditionalism and traditionalism rely to some extent on words and images from our present space-time world to portray a destiny that lies beyond that world. We now know, however, that space and time are relative even in the present universe, that time is experienced differently at different velocities, and that visibility is affected by gravity. Against this background, Douglas Spanner has suggested intriguingly that one recently discovered feature of the universe may help to resolve the traditionalist-conditionalist dichotomy. A spaceship traveling into a black hole would be sucked in and annihilated. Yet an observer would continue to see this ship appear to hover about the horizon of visibility, gradually fading but without definite end. Similarly, hell might be experienced as annihilation but observed as continuing punishment, gradually fading from view.[11]

Whether or not Spanner's thesis manages to resolve the present evangelical debate, it should be acknowledged that not *every* doctrine

---

11. Spanner, "Is Hell Forever?" 107–20.

need be utterly clear at the present time, or in our current situation. Especially with respect to the last things, certain details of which are hidden from even Christ himself (Mark 13:32), it may be legitimate to accept some divergence of opinion on these details until God discloses them at the end of the age. For instance, evangelicals have accepted different views on the great tribulation of Matthew 24 and Revelation 6–19, while agreeing that it points to an impending reality. Likewise, they can agree on the genuine horror and godless irreversibility of hell, while nonetheless being prepared to wait until judgment day itself to find out whether it will last forever or not.

Conditionalism, Unity, and Evangelical History

A second way of distinguishing evangelical essentials from non-essentials is through recourse to history. This approach entails looking back to those periods of the church's life when God has invigorated his people through reformation, revival, and renewal. The birth of Protestantism in the early 1500s, the Puritan era, and the Evangelical Revival are obvious reference-points here.[12]

Where the doctrine of hell is concerned, this historical criterion of unity is less favorable for conditionalism. After all, evangelicals did not seriously entertain the eventual extinction of the unsaved until the late nineteenth century, and then did so only in relatively small numbers.[13] Besides, it had been consistently anathematized by the church in the preceding thirteen centuries. At the same time, however, evangelicals are typically cautious about tradition as compared to Scripture, and are wary of appeal to ecclesiastical precedent. One obvious example of the way evangelicals have modified their thinking on a long-established belief is their change of mind on the issue of slavery in the early 1800s. Here was a "doctrine" and practice many evangelicals had advocated, and justified from Scripture, but which came to be seen as misguided, and that evangelicals now would reject out of hand.

As we have seen, some evangelical conditionalists contend that eternal conscious punishment is at least as deserving of theological revision

---

12. Alister McGrath makes illuminating use of the Reformers, for example, as one inspiration for evangelicalism today: *Roots that Refresh*.

13. A charge that the work of Seventh Day Adventist L. Froom seeks to demolish, although at times unconvincingly. Froom, *Conditionalist Faith*.

as was slavery. What is clear, however, is that for evangelicals worthy of the name, revision on this or any other historic article of faith must proceed on the basis of biblical interpretation rather than mere emotion. Here history can help, since the interpretative tradition on a biblical text or doctrine can indicate how heavily the burden of proof lies on those who wish to change things. In the case of conditionalists this burden of proof is considerable, since the traditional view has prevailed for by far the greater part of the church's history. It is consequently incumbent upon them to make their case with humility and respect among traditionalists whose convictions reflect the legacy of Augustine, Calvin, Luther, Wesley, Edwards, and others.

Conditionalism, Unity, and Evangelical Ideology

A number of attempts have been made to describe evangelicalism in terms of a particular worldview or ethos. Although doctrine obviously plays a key part in such definitions, it does not exhaust them, since they usually embrace more behavioral features as well. The best known of these ideological descriptions is the one offered by David Bebbington. This identifies four key characteristics of an evangelical—conversionism (a call to people to be converted), activism (an active faith affecting all of life), biblicism (a commitment to the authority and inspiration of the Bible), and crucicentrism (holding the cross at the center of all life and theology).[14] If we follow this schema, those who hold a conditionalist position would remain within the parameters of authentic evangelicalism. It is clear from the survey we have conducted that they are certainly committed to conversion and mission, to activism in the world, to the Bible as their ultimate authority, and to the centrality of the cross. By this set of criteria, at least, we would have to conclude that those specific details of hell's duration, quality, finality, and purpose that are at issue in the current evangelical debate are comparatively less essential.

Conditionalism, Unity, and Evangelical Relationships

Evangelicals often identify one another not because of any clear outward "badge," but because of what might be called a "family resemblance." We

---

14. Bebbington, *Evangelicalism*.

are part of the same relational network and, although we may differ from one another in many other ways, we recognize and embrace the differences. Whether we talk of there being various tribes of evangelicals,[15] branches of the same tree,[16] colors of the rainbow, or facets of a Rubik's cube,[17] we tend to know "family" when we see them. And when it comes to those who have moved from traditionalism towards conditionalism, the familial ties remain strong. They may differ on the details of hell, yet it is clear that virtually all of those who have defended conditionalism recently have done so as self-professed and well-established members of the evangelical household. Some, indeed, have made enormous contributions to it (e.g., John Stott, John Wenham, Michael Green, and Philip Hughes).

These images of "family" and "tribe" are, of course, also important in Scripture. The people of God, though diverse through time and space, all form part of the same extended community. On this criterion, those who have embraced conditionalism, while disagreeing with the majority, have done so from within the community, and on behalf of the community, and will remain within the community even if it finally rejects their convictions on this specific point.

This four-fold assessment of the evangelical debate on hell crystallizes what has been clear throughout this report: namely, that while the differences between traditionalists and conditionalists are significant and heartfelt, these two groups still have a great deal in common—not only in general terms but also specifically in relation to the fate of the unrighteous.

~

Conclusions and Recommendations

The Bible describes hell as a realm of destruction. Evangelicals, however, diverge on whether this destruction applies to the actual *existence* of individual sinners (eventual annihilation), or to the *quality of their relationship with God* (eternal conscious punishment). Although Scripture frequently presents God's ultimate punishment for sin as "death," the meaning of "death" in Scripture is not confined merely to the cessation of

---

15. As in Calver and Warner, *Together We Stand*.
16. As in Percy, *Words*.
17. As in Tidball, *Who are the Evangelicals?*

earthly life, and is often used to convey long-term spiritual estrangement from God (Matt 7:13, 10:28; John 5:16; Eph 2:1).

Evangelicals diverge on whether hell is eternal in *duration* or *effect*—that is, whether an individual's punishment in hell will literally go on "forever," as a ceaseless conscious experience, or whether it will end in a destruction that will be "forever," in the sense of being final and irreversible. It should be acknowledged that both of these interpretations preserve the crucial principle that judgment is on the basis of sins committed in *this* life, and that when judgment is to hell it cannot be repealed (Matt 25:41–6; Mark 9:43–8; Luke 16:26).

God's purpose extends beyond judgment to the redemption of the cosmos. Evangelicals diverge on whether a place is preserved for hell in this new order of things, but it is important to stress that, either way, God's demands of justice will have been fully and perfectly met by this point (Rev 20:14; 21:4; cf. 22:15).

∼

We recognize that the interpretation of hell in terms of conditional immortality is a significant minority evangelical view. Furthermore, we believe that the traditionalist-conditionalist debate on hell should be regarded as a secondary rather than a primary issue for evangelical theology. Although hell is a profoundly serious matter, we view the holding of either one of these two views of it over against the other to be neither essential in respect of Christian doctrine, nor finally definitive of what it means to be an evangelical Christian.

∼

We appreciate the concerns of some that the influence of conditionalist theology has grown within evangelicalism in recent years, but recognize that the majority of those who have published as "evangelical conditionalists" have strong evangelical credentials, and have in particular demonstrated a genuine regard for the authority of Scripture.

We encourage traditionalist and conditionalist evangelicals to pursue agreement on the matter of hell, rather than merely acquiescing in their disagreement. As they do so, we call upon them to maintain constructive dialogue and respectful relationships, even when their differences seem intractable. To these ends, we commend our report for consideration, discussion, and implementation.

21

Diverse Christian Beliefs about Life beyond Death

ROGER E. OLSON

Roger Olson is Professor of Christian Theology and Ethics at Truett Theological Seminary of Baylor University. He has served as president of the American Theological Society (Midwest Division), as editor of Christian Scholar's Review, *and as co-chair of the Evangelical Theology Group of the American Academy of Religion. He is the author of over fifteen books, including* The Mosaic of Christian Belief: Twenty Centuries of Unity and Diversity *(2002).*

Discussing the "Future of Evangelical Theology" in Christianity Today, *Olson has argued that as a unified historical movement evangelicalism is dead—and has in fact split into at least two "loose coalitions"—but as an ethos it is alive and well. In such a context he suggests a broader view of what constitutes orthodoxy and in his estimation conditionalist theology remains within the "evangelical" fold. Although Dr. Olson is not himself an conditionalist, his historically and culturally informed analysis directs a way forward in the current debate on hell.*

A FINAL AREA OF significant diversity in Christian belief about personal eschatology—life beyond death—has to do with the *nature of hell*. While most Christians throughout history have believed that hell is

PART SIX—CONDITIONALISM AND EVANGELICALISM

everlasting torment of the wicked—whether flames or not—some Christians believe that hell is extinction. This controversial interpretation of hell is known as *annihilationism* and *conditional immortality*. (The two can be distinguished, but they are nearly identical in essence.) Belief that hell will be everlasting, conscious punishment of some kind (not necessarily fire and brimstone) is shared by the vast majority of Christians down through history—Eastern Orthodox, Roman Catholic, and Protestant—and is based on several passages of Scripture including Jesus' own words about Gehenna—a fiery, smoke-filled dump near Jerusalem that Jesus used as an image of the destination of Satan and those who obey him[1]—which Jesus called "eternal fire." Revelation 20 refers to a future "lake of fire" into which death and hades are to be thrown together with all of God's enemies. These are described as a place where they will be "tormented day and night for ever and ever."[2]

Annihilationists—including all members of various Adventist denominations, churches, and organizations—believe that the everlastingness of hell is extinction. That is, persons who are consigned there are punished and shown mercy at the same time; God punishes them by burning them up completely and shows them mercy by allowing them to cease existing as rebellious persons under condemnation. It is God's form of mercy killing and capital punishment. Annihilationism has been embraced by a number of conservative evangelical theologians outside of Adventist circles. Edward Fudge published a book-length study and defense of it in 1982;[3] Clark Pinnock[4] and John Stott,[5] two notable evangelical scholars, have endorsed it (Stott "tentatively"), as has Anglican evangelical theologian Philip Edgcumbe Hughes.[6] The rise of interest in and affirmation of annihilationism has predictably given rise to a reaction; many conservative evangelical theologians have resurrected the old polemical labels of heresy and aberrational teaching to marginalize those evangelicals who would dare to embrace a belief that was once relegated to the sectarian margins of Protestantism. This hardly seems like a valuable expenditure of time and energy. Annihilationism does not strike

1. Matt 18:9; 25:41.
2. Rev 20:10.
3. Fudge, *Fire That Consumes*.
4. Pinnock, "Conditional View."
5. Edwards and Stott, *Essentials*, 314–20.
6. Hughes, *Image*, 398–407.

at the heart of the gospel or even deny any major Christian belief; it is simply a reinterpretation of hell. More importantly, its harsh condemnation by a few fundamentalists should not deter Christians from accepting one another as equally believers in the gospel of Jesus Christ in spite of differences of opinion about the nature of hell. Contrary to what some fundamentalist critics have charged, annihilationism is not tantamount to universalism or *apokatastasis*. It is simply a minority view of the nature of hell, not a denial of hell.

22

Equally Orthodox Christians

BEN WITHERINGTON III

Ben Witherington III received his PhD from the University of Durham and is Professor of New Testament for Doctoral Studies at Asbury Theological Seminary and a member of the doctoral faculty at St. Andrews University. A prolific writer, Witherington has authored over forty books, including The Jesus Quest: The Third Search for the Jew of Nazareth, Invitation to the New Testament: First Things, *and many New Testament commentaries; he has also represented the voice of evangelical academics on many broadcast television and cable news programs.*

Witherington contributes to the Patheos website via The Bible and Culture Blog, from which the following chapter is derived. Witherington's view towards conditionalism could be safely described as "friendly, but unconvinced." His voice is representative of the growing consensus among evangelical scholars that conditionalism is an acceptable alternative to the traditional view of hell.

Hell? No??

DOES THE NEW TESTAMENT teach that 1) there is a hell, and 2) some folks are going there (not necessarily in a handbasket), and 3) they will experience eternal torment once there?

I have put the matter in three parts, because you could answer questions 1) and 2) with an emphatic yes, and in fact say no to 3). Indeed, there is a time-honored tradition of interpreting the NT to say that what happens to the damned is that they are consumed in hell or Gehenna or the lake of fire—pick your favorite moniker—but then, since they are *consumed*, there is no eternal torment. Their suffering does not go on and on forever. And one of the possible implications of interpreting the NT this way is that when we finally get around to the last rodeo, which is to say to the new heaven and new earth, only believers in Christ are left standing on the premises. Now this is certainly not universalism in the typical modern sense of the term; it's not an "all dogs go to heaven" kind of universalism, or a Unitarian kind of universalism. This is, instead, the view that except for those who willfully and knowingly refuse to have any part in Christ and his kingdom, "Love Wins."

I had a student come up to me this week who thought he had resolved the above conundrum and said we need not choose between annihilationism and eternal torment because *for the person in question, the torment is forever, if by forever we mean always until he or she ceases to exist*. This is an interesting spin on the old question and worth considering, especially when you actually do your homework on the Hebrew word *olam* or the Greek equivalent *aeon*.

Olam has been loosely translated "forever" but the problem with this translation, according to my esteemed colleague Bill Arnold in his 1 Samuel commentary, is twofold: 1) In the phrase *berit olam* (loosely "forever covenant" or "eternal covenant") it becomes clear that *olam* actually means a covenant of a definitely long but unspecified duration. In other words, it doesn't exactly seem to be a synonym for our word "eternal," which means infinitely going on into the future. 2) Notice that we have the phrase *olam wu olam* in the OT, loosely translated "forever and ever." Now the phrase *wu olam* is totally unnecessary if in fact *olam* by itself means "forever." In that case, the additional phrase is redundant. And in fact we have the same issue with the word *aeon* in Greek which could be rendered "forever" but it could refer to a specific period of time—an age or aeon. And sure enough we have this same redundancy with a similar Greek phrase. For example in Heb 13:21 (in some mss.) we have the phrase "unto the aeon of aeons." Why exactly would we need the "of aeons" phrase at all, if "aeon" itself means forever in the modern sense? Inquiring minds want to know.

But what exactly does the Bible say about hell?

Let's start with some basic facts. Fact One—the Old Testament says little or nothing about hell. What it does talk about is *sheol*, the land of the dead, which in Greco-Roman thinking has been called hades. For example, in 1 Samuel 28 we hear about Samuel's shade or spirit being called up from sheol to be consulted by the medium of Endor. Samuel is none too pleased about the summons, but he is not depicted as having been in either heaven or hell. He is simply in the land of the dead. This concept of sheol continued on well into the New Testament era, and may well represent what Paul believes about where people have gone who have died, but who are not in Christ. For Christians, of course, Paul says "to be absent from the body is to be present with the Lord" (2 Cor 5), but what about everyone else?

In 1 Corinthians 15, Paul says quite literally that Jesus is raised on Easter "from out of the dead ones," not merely raised from death, though that is true, but raised from out of the realm of dead persons. This suggests that the dead are still out there, and have not yet been consigned to hell.

Indeed, traditionally the Christian idea was that no one is consigned to hell until *after* the Final Judgment—which, in case you're wondering, has not yet taken place! Paul is perfectly clear that the Final Judgment comes after Jesus returns, and there is the *bema seat judgment of Christ* (again 2 Cor 5) before which we all must appear to give an account of the deeds we have done in the body. (Yes, even Christians are accountable for such things.) Thereafter, it would appear, we are assigned to our eternal destinations.

Or consider Revelation 20. Though this is a highly metaphorical and apocalyptic text, it nevertheless suggests the following sequence: 1) the return of Christ; 2) the temporary confinement of Satan; 3) the resurrection of those who are in Christ who will rule with Christ during the millennium; 4) the resurrection from the dead of those not in Christ at the end of the millennium; 5) Satan released, and a final hubbub that leads to Jesus' judgment on Satan and the nations who are sent packing off to the lake of fire, once and for all. So 6) the new heaven and new earth does not emerge until *after* Final Judgment has been done on the earth. And when John says "and there was no more sea" this is metaphorical but means there was no more chaos waters, no more evil in the universe. This may suggest that hell is not "forever and ever amen." But there is other evidence, which can be read in different ways.

Let's be clear that the answer to the first question—is there a hell to be found in the New Testament?—is certainly *yes*. And Jesus is perhaps the one most clear about this. He calls it Gehenna, and he says it's rather like the stinky garbage dump in the Hinnom Valley south of the City of David, and like a garbage dump it's where the worm does not die and the fire never goes out. And there are people expected by Jesus to go there, as the parable of the Rich Man and Lazarus shows in Luke 16. Granted, this is a parable, an extended metaphor, but it is surely referential, and it indicates the rich man is in an unpleasant place and there is no remedy. There is an unalterable divide between the bosom of Abraham and the place where the rich man currently resides in the afterlife. The parable teaches that how we live in this life has consequences for where we end up in the afterlife, and this must be taken seriously.

A good presentation on the implications of this is C. S. Lewis' famous work, *The Great Divorce*.

So far we have seen that the rather clear answers to the questions, is there a hell? and, are some people going there? are yes, and yes.

What about texts that suggest that hell is a place of eternal torment? Yes, there are such texts, and they can be interpreted that way. Perhaps the most famous of these texts is 2 Thess 1:5–10, which should be quoted in full:

> All this is evidence that God's judgment is right, and as a result you will be counted worthy of the kingdom of God, for which you are suffering. God is just: He will pay back trouble to those who trouble you and give relief to you who are troubled, and to us as well. This will happen when the Lord Jesus is revealed from heaven in blazing fire with his powerful angels. He will punish those who do not know God and do not obey the gospel of our Lord Jesus. They will be punished with everlasting destruction and shut out from the presence of the Lord and from the glory of his might on the day he comes to be glorified in his holy people and to be marveled at among all those who have believed. This includes you, because you believed our testimony to you.

Note—there is that word *aeon*, in this case *aeonion* in verse 9, and in the NIV translated "eternal," as above.

Notice several things about this text: 1) The point at which people are punished with everlasting destruction and shut out from the Lord's presence is "*on the day when he comes.*" Not before the return of Christ, but on the day when he returns. This certainly suggests that while lots of people are in the land of the dead just now, none of them are yet in hell. That comes after the final judgment of Jesus. 2) What are we to make of the phrase "eternal destruction"? This has usually been interpreted to mean eternal torment. But note the word "destruction." The phrase seems almost an oxymoron—how can anything be eternally destroyed? If it is destroyed, isn't it done with, over, gone? I agree that this phrase might be interpreted to refer to eternal torment, but this is not perfectly clear. Eternal torment may be the implication of Jesus' parable of the Weeds, which ends by saying, "They will be thrown into a blazing furnace where there will be weeping and gnashing of teeth" (Matt 13:42), but Jesus does not say for *how long*. The fact that the fire doesn't go out in Gehenna does not tell us how long a particular person in Gehenna suffers from it. Second Peter 3:7 similarly talks about the judgment and *destruction* of the ungodly, but it also shortly after this talks about the destruction of the old heavens and old earth, and the author seems to imply that once something is destroyed it is gone. In this case it is replaced by a new heaven and a new earth.

What are the implications of all this? I don't think we can debate that the NT says there is a place we today call hell, and that some people will end up there, because of their own choices and wickedness. Whether they will experience eternal torment is more debatable. My advice, however, is that we abstain from pronouncing a final judgment on any human soul; that is Jesus' job at the final judgment. We simply don't know the outcome of many who are not followers of Christ now.

And here is a final reason for caution—Romans 11 clearly says that when the Redeemer comes forth from Zion he will turn away the impiety of Jacob—that is, says Paul, when Jesus comes back and the dead are raised, "all Israel will be saved," which *at least* means a lot of Jews being saved who currently do not believe in Jesus. Perhaps what Paul means about the second coming in Phil 2:5–11 is that there will come a day when all will recognize Jesus as the Christ and as Lord, at the eschaton, even though many of them don't do that now. But there is a difference between recognizing and embracing the truth about Jesus. The demons recognize the truth about Jesus, but it does not transform them.

What I am more sure of than ever, is that there is no salvation outside of Jesus Christ, and that in the end "every knee will bow and ever knee confess," even those humans or demons who want to have nothing to do with Jesus thereafter. Salvation in the end is *not* just a matter of being forced to recognize the truth—it's about positively embracing and trusting that truth. And there are apparently some who will never ever do that. To them God says, "if you insist, have it your way." Hell is the place where you experience the absence of the presence of God for as long as you continue to exist. Whether there is a time when hell will cease to exist, like the crystal sea of Revelation, equally orthodox persons can debate. Annihilation or destruction of Satan, hell, and its inhabitants is a possible interpretation of the eschatological endgame, but it is also possible hell will go on *olam wu olam wu olam* ("forever and ever and ever"). If the former is true, then the last persons standing are all followers of Christ according to Revelation. Revelation 21:8 seems pretty clear—"But as for the cowardly, the faithless . . . [etc.], their place will be in the lake that burns with fire and sulfur, which is the second death." Even more telling is the statement in Rev 22:15 that states that after the new heaven has landed on the new earth and the new Jerusalem has been set up, "outside are the dogs and sorcerers and fornicators and murderers and idolaters, and everyone who loves and practices falsehood." It would appear from these last two texts that hell still has a future, even after the new heaven and new earth show up at a theater near you. What this suggests is that love, even divine love, does not always win with everyone, not even in the end, and it breaks the heart of God as it should break ours.

Why Annihilationism is Not Universalism

One of my brightest former students asked me about Matt 10:28. Doesn't this text, he asked, favor the view of eternal torment? The text literally reads, "Do not fear those who can kill the body but cannot kill the *psuchen*. Fear rather the one who is able to destroy (*apolesai*) both body and *psuchen* in Gehenna." Here we have yet another stern saying of Jesus about Gehenna. Jesus is making a contrast between what human beings can do to a person (physically kill them) and someone else who can destroy both body and human spirit.

It needs to be remembered that the Greek notion of the inherent immortality of the soul was apparently only believed by the most Hellenized of Diaspora Jews, and Jesus doesn't qualify as such a person, as this very saying proves. Jesus thinks your whole self can be destroyed. The verb *apollumi* means to destroy or kill, and in the middle voice to perish, be lost, be ruined, and even "to pass away." Much depends on what sort of and how strong a nuance one wants to put on the verb here, but in view of the parallel construction it would appear certain that Jesus is referring to someone who can kill, do away, destroy the human spirit, not merely the body, and the place of that destruction is Gehenna.

Let us consider a war scene for a moment. It is one thing to be wounded and suffer a long time or endlessly (throughout the rest of one's life) for it, but it is another thing to be killed or destroyed. These verbs in this verse refer to an end of something, its terminus, not its continuation. Though it is certainly possible to read this text in another way, it would appear to me that this text definitely does favor the annihilationist view of what happens to a person in Gehenna, and it must carry the most serious of weight, as it is a saying of Jesus, warning his own disciples (you will notice it is not a warning to the non-elect or non-disciples, though he could have said the same thing to them presumably).

My good colleague Lawson Stone and I had a good exchange on annihilationism, and one of his objections was that the annihilationist view seems to imply instant extinction (nihilism) and so not really a suffering for one's sins that one committed in this life. I disagreed.

In none of the texts in the NT that might be said to favor annihilationism are we told that one's termination is instantaneous and does not involve a considerable period of suffering. Indeed, from the parable in Luke 16 and several other texts, we would assume that it does involve an agonizing period of suffering. The point is, the suffering doesn't last forever because eventually the person is burned up or destroyed, or his spirit is killed; use whatever language you like.

And here is where it may be well to ask a good question: why would even a holy God, the God of the Bible, require *infinite* suffering for a finite number of earthly sins? Here, I think, Rob Bell is right to ask a question about such a notion. Is that actually fair and just? The OT law of *lex talionis*, which says only a hand for a hand, only a foot for a foot, only a life for a life, suggests a principle of justice that involves proportional and appropriate response depending on the sin committed.

While I certainly believe God is holy, just, and fair, I also believe God is loving, compassionate, and merciful, even to the lost or damned. The issue of the whole character of God is certainly raised when we see, for example, Jesus balancing justice and mercy in the famous woman caught in adultery story (John 7:53—8:11, probably not an original part of the Gospel of John, but I would suggest nevertheless a true story about

Jesus). Do we really want to say the character of the Father is dramatically different from the character of God revealed to us in Jesus his Son? I don't think so. Thus while I think there are a variety of texts, especially from Revelation, which *may* suggest eternal torment of the lost, there are none that I see that *must* be interpreted this way. And I say this after having read a lot of early Jewish apocalyptic literature where there is a lot of gloating of the vindicated and oppressed about the ongoing suffering of the lost. The NT comes across as much less vindictive than that, and indeed even the martyrs under the altar in Revelation are told to leave vengeance, final justice, in the hands of God. And so we should. The rider on the white horse (the Lamb/Jesus) will sort things out in the end and as part of the Last Judgment.

Is annihilationism, then, *any sort* of form of universalism? No, it is not. Let us return to the battlefield imagery. My father fought in WWII for George Patton's army and he saw many destroyed villages at the end of the war in Germany and Czechoslovakia, destroyed by Allied bombers. When he walked into a village and found a few survivors, a few who had been saved through and despite the maelstrom, while the vast majority had been destroyed, he could never have said, "well they all ended up being saved." Of course not. The last persons standing were saved, and none of the last persons standing were destroyed, but this is hardly any form of universalism at all.

In other words, if you believe that Matt 10:28 supports the notion of the lost suffering and then being extinguished or destroyed in Gehenna (see the lake of fire in Revelation), you are not a universalist. You simply believe that the only persons left standing on the promises and sitting in the premises in the new earth, the new Jerusalem, will be saved persons—Jew and Gentile united in Christ, as Paul would put. This in no way denies: 1) justice for sin and wickedness on earth; 2) that only some will in the end be saved, and they are saved on the basis of the atoning work of Christ; 3) that there is suffering in Gehenna, where God allows those who insist on being separated from him forever to have their way. What this view does not necessarily do, in the same way the eternal torment view does, is raise questions about the loving, merciful, compassionate character and proportional response of our God to sin and wickedness and even to the lost.

PART SIX—CONDITIONALISM AND EVANGELICALISM

The Case for Permanent Residence in Hell

Having already made the case that an annihilationist view can be shown to be exegetically defensible and theologically coherent, if you aren't already confused, I am now going to turn around and make the other case, the case for hell being permanent and having some permanent residents. I am going to refrain from calling it eternal torment, since the Bible doesn't really directly use that language but we are going to talk a bit more about everlasting destruction.

What then is the case for their always being a hell with permanent residents, "forever and ever amen"? Firstly, there is what I already pointed out from the very last book of the Bible, loved and loathed by millions precisely because of this sort of subject. Look once again at Rev 22:14–15, the very last reference to "insiders and outsiders" in the entire Bible. What it says is that the blessed have the right to enter the city gates and the right to eat of the tree of everlasting life. The contrast in the next verse is with the outsiders—the "dogs," the sorcerers, the fornicators, the murderers, the idolaters, and "everyone who loves and practices falsehood." There is certainly no suggestion at all that the outsiders listed could become insiders and enter the city gates. No, they are parked outside, looking on from afar, and they are still alive and conscious. This conclusion is simply reinforced in Rev 21:27, which stresses, "But nothing unclean will enter it, nor anyone who practices abomination or falsehood, but only those who are written in the Lamb's book of life."

Let's talk about that last phrase, a very important phrase in Revelation, which should be compared to the simpler OT phrase, "the book of life" (Ps 69:28), which refers to merely physical existence, not everlasting life and could be translated "the book of the living."

Revelation does not tell us how a person gets their name written in the Lamb's book of life, and indeed Revelation warns that your name can be erased from the Lamb's book of life if you commit apostasy, even if it was provisionally in there previously. This is very clear in Rev 3:5 and it comports with the overall theme of Revelation, namely the warning of Christians in Asia Minor who are being persecuted, prosecuted, and even executed, that they need to hold on to their faith to the end, and overcome or conquer in the same way Jesus the Lamb did—by martyrdom, faithfulness even unto death.

Revelation is the canonical book of martyrs, and the stern exhortations to remain faithful clearly enough imply the possibility that this or that Christian might fail to do so. And if they fail to do so, their names can be erased from the Lamb's book of life. Revelation 13:8, 17:8, and 20:15 suggest at a minimum that God has always known, even from before the foundation of the earth, that some folks were never going to respond to him positively, not ever, and that they would end up in the lake of fire. Even allowing for the fact that this book is highly metaphorical and apocalyptic in character, it sounds very clear that in the case of those folks, those who refuse to be saved, that they will never turn and live, and will never be rescued from the lake of fire. In their cases, love does not win. Whatever else one can say about John of Patmos, he certainly doesn't believe in the salvation of every last human being in the end.

Let's go back to a couple of Gospel and Pauline texts now. I am thinking of Matt 25:31–46, the famous parable of the sheep and goats. Bearing in mind this is an extended metaphor, a parable, still it has stark language that has to be seen as referential and taken seriously, even though it cannot be taken literally. Parables don't work that way, not this parable, nor the one in Luke 16 about the rich man and Lazarus. The danger is overpressing the language to give us more information than it intends to give us. Nevertheless, this parable is indeed about the great divide at the final judgment. It uses language very much the same as the language about the Lamb's book of life in Revelation.

The parable of the sheep and the goats says, for example, that the sheep will be addressed as follows: "Come you blessed by my Father, inherit the kingdom prepared for you from before the foundation of the world" (v. 34). God always had a plan for kingdom come, on earth, as it is in heaven, had always planned for it (not the other worldly heaven) to be the final dwelling place of the saved. Our final destination as believers is not somewhere up there, but right now here in the new earth, in the new Jerusalem, after the restoration of all of creation. This is a theme Rob Bell stresses, and he is right to do so. The final state of affairs for believers does not involve disembodied life in heaven.

In this same parable, at verse 41 we hear about those who did not do deeds of charity to whom it will be said, "You that are accursed, depart from me into the eternal fire prepared for the devil and his angels." God was not caught by surprise by the fall of humans and angels, and the corruption of creation. Before it ever happened he had already planned for everlasting redemption as well as everlasting judgment. The parable ends with the words, "And those will go away into everlasting punishment, but the righteous into everlasting life" (v. 46).

This deliberate and clear contrast where the word "everlasting" seems to be used in the same way in both alternative phrases strongly suggests Jesus believes that there is no annihilation of the lost. There is only everlasting punishment. And it is a perfectly fair reading of 2 Thess 1:8–9 to conclude that Paul is saying exactly the same thing. However much the phrase "everlasting destruction" may sound like an oxymoron to our ears, it had to have some definite meaning to Paul, and he expands its sense by adding, "separated from the presence of the Lord and from the glory of his might." Whatever else we may wish to say about hell it involves separation from the presence of the Lord forever, something the parable in Luke 16 also suggests.

So where does this leave us, if a good case, solidly based in Scripture, can be made for either annihilationism or everlasting punishment? Where it leaves me, at least, is that I have to be honest and say, either conclusion is possible, and equally orthodox. This is one of those points where equally orthodox Christians can agree to disagree and should not question each other's orthodoxy because of it.

It is also worth stressing that *both cases rely on highly metaphorical language to make their case,* which is why I would suggest that we back off from being overly dogmatic about our conclusions on this matter. I would also finally like to stress as well that *in neither case are we talking about a scenario in which all persons end up being saved, and in neither case are we talking about anyone being saved who is not in the Lamb's book of life. In both views, Jesus is the only savior for all the world, and having a positive relationship with Jesus in the end is the only way love wins.*

Based on all my work on the theology and ethics of the NT (see *The Indelible Image Vols. 1–2*), if I were a betting man (which I am not), I would bet that probably the annihilationist view is closer to the truth, based on the revealed character of God in Christ as both just and loving. But I don't know that I can be sure about this when the evidence is so imagaic and so metaphorical.

What I do know is that many of our notions of hell are probably out to lunch. As those two texts from the end of Revelation we mentioned at the beginning of this section make clear, exclusion from the new Jerusalem is on the basis of sin, conscious sin—sins of the mind (idolatry and false worship), and sins of the flesh (immorality). The lake of fire is a punishment for those who love their sins and falsehood instead of loving their God and the evidence suggests they could have done otherwise. It is never an unfair outcome when someone goes to hell. Never, for there is no injustice with God ever.

But the emphasis is not placed on the lake of fire, even in Revelation, and that is not the end of the story. The end of the story in Revelation 21–22 is about inclusion in the city of God, the inclusion of "whosoever will" be included. For as the Johannine writer said, "For God so loved the world (not merely the elect, but the world), that he gave his only Son, so that whosoever will believe in him may not perish, but have everlasting life. Indeed, God did not send his Son into the world to condemn the world, but in order that the world might be saved through him" (John 3:16–17). This is a clear revelation of the heart of God who is both loving and just, both merciful and righteous, both compassionate and holy. And we do well to emphasize over and over again that truth enshrined in what my fellow Charlottean, Billy Graham thought was the greatest good news passage ever written. I agree with him. Let us stoke and extol the fires of divine love, not the fires of hell.

APPENDIX

Recommended Reading for Further Study

Conditionalism

1. *The Fire That Consumes* (3rd ed.)—Edward Fudge
2. *Hell: A Final Word*—Edward Fudge
3. *"Hell": A Hard Look at a Hard Question*—David Powys
4. *The Geography of Hell in the Teaching of Jesus*—Kim Papaioannou

Traditionalism

1. *Hell Under Fire*—Christopher Morgan and Robert Peterson (editors)
2. *Erasing Hell*—Francis Chan & Preston Sprinkle
3. *Hell on Trial: The Case for Eternal Punishment*—Robert Peterson
4. *Hell: The Logic of Damnation*—Jerry Walls

APPENDIX

Universalism

1. *The Evangelical Universalist* (2nd ed.)—Gregory MacDonald (pseudonym of Robin Parry)
2. *The Inescapable Love of God* (2nd ed.)—Thomas Talbott
3. *Universal Salvation? The Current Debate*—Robin Parry and Christopher Partridge (editors)
4. *Her Gates Will Never Be Shut*—Bradley Jersak

General

1. *Two Views of Hell*—Edward Fudge & Robert Peterson
2. *Four Views of Hell*—William Crockett (editor)
3. *All You Want to Know about Hell*—Steve Gregg
4. *What's the Truth about Heaven and Hell*—Douglas Jacoby
5. *The Oxford Handbook of Eschatology*—Jerry Walls (editor)

Bibliography

Adams, Marilyn M. "Hell and the God of Justice." *Religious Studies* 2 (1975) 433-47.
Albright, W. F., and C. S. Mann. *Matthew*. The Anchor Bible 26. Garden City, NY: Doubleday, 1979.
Alexander, P. "3 Enoch." *Old Testament Pseudepigrapha*, vol. 1, edited by J. H. Charlesworth, 223-316. London: Danton, Longman and Todd, 1985.
Atkinson, Basil F. C. *Life and Immortality*. Taunton, UK: Phoenix, n.d.
Bailey, Kenneth. *Poet and Peasant & Through Peasant Eyes*. Grand Rapids: Eerdmans, 1983.
Bailey, L. R. "Gehenna." In *The Interpreter's Dictionary of the Bible—Supplement*, edited by George Arthur Burttrick, 184-92. New York: Abingdon, 1976.
Baldwin, Joyce G. *Daniel*. Tyndale Bible Commentary Series. Leicester, UK: InterVarsity, 1978.
Barnard, Leslie. W. *Athenagoras: A Study in Second-Century Christian Apologetic*. Théologie Historique 18. Paris: Éditions Beauchesne, 1972.
Barnett, Paul W. *Apocalypse Then and Now: Reading Revelation Today*. Sydney: Anglican Information Office, 1989.
Barth, Karl. *Christ and Adam: Man and Humanity in Romans 5*. New York: Harper, 1957.
Bauckham, Richard J. *The Climax of Prophecy: Studies in the Book of Revelation*. Edinburgh: T. & T. Clark, 1993.
———. "Early Jewish Visions of Hell." *JTS* 41 (1990) 335-85.
Bavinck, Herman. *Our Reasonable Faith*. Translated by Henry Zylstra. 1956. Reprint. Grand Rapids: Baker, 1977.
Bebbington, David. W. *Evangelicalism in Modern Britain: A History from the 1730s to the 1980s*. London: Unwin Hyman, 1989.
Beckwith, Roger T. *The Old Testament Canon of the New Testament Church*. London: Clowes, 1985.
Beecher, Edward. *History of Opinions of the Scriptural Doctrine of Retribution*. New York: Appleton, 1878.
Berkouwer, Gerrit. C. *The Work of Christ*. Translated by Cornelius Lambregtse. Grand Rapids: Eerdmans, 1965.
Black, Matthew. "The Eschatology of the Similitudes of Enoch." *Journal of Theological Studies* 3 (1952) 1-10.
———. *The Scrolls and Christian Origins: Studies in the Jewish Background of the New Testament*. London: Nelson, 1961.

Blass, Debrunner, et al. *A Greek-English Lexicon of the New Testament.* Chicago: University of Chicago Press, 1957.

Blocher, Henri. "Everlasting Punishment and the Problem of Evil." In *Universalism and the Doctrine of Hell,* edited by Nigel M. de S. Cameron, 283–312. Grand Rapids: Baker, 1992.

Bloesch, Donald G. *The Last Things: Resurrection, Judgment, Glory.* Downers Grove, IL: InterVarsity, 2004.

Blomberg, Craig L. "Degrees of Reward in the Kingdom of Heaven?" *JETS* 35.2 (1991) 26–34.

———. "Eschatology and the Church: Some New Testament Perspectives." *Themelios* 23.3 (1998) 3–26.

Bonda, Jan. *The One Purpose of God: An Answer to the Doctrine of Eternal Punishment.* Grand Rapids: Eerdmans, 1998.

Boring, M. Eugene. "The Language of Universal Salvation in Paul." *JBL* 105.2 (1986) 269–92.

Breasted, James H. *Development of Religion and Thought in Ancient Egypt.* 3rd ed. New York: Harper & Row, 1959.

———. *A History of Egypt from the Earliest Times.* 2nd ed. New York: Scribner's, 1909.

Brown, Claire, and Jerry Walls. "Annihilationism: A Philosophical Dead End?" In *The Problem of Hell: A Philosophical Anthology,* edited by Joel Buenting, 45–64. Farnham, UK: Ashgate, 2009.

Brown, Colin, editor. *The New International Dictionary of New Testament Theology.* 4 vols. Grand Rapids: Zondervan, 1978.

———. "Foreword to First Edition." In *The Fire That Consumes: A Biblical and Historical Study of the Doctrine of Final Punishment,* edited by Edward Fudge, xi–xii. 3rd ed. Eugene, OR: Cascade, 2011.

Buenting, Joel, editor. *The Problem of Hell: A Philosophical Anthology.* Farnham, UK: Ashgate, 2009.

Bultmann, Rudolf. "Adam and Christ according to Romans 5." In *Current Issues in New Testament Interpretation: Essays in Honor of Otto A. Piper,* edited by William Klassen and Graydon F. Snyder, 143–65. New York: Harper, 1962.

Buis, Harry. *The Doctrine of Eternal Punishment.* Philadelphia: Presbyterian & Reformed, 1957.

Caird, George. B. *A Commentary on the Revelation of St. John the Divine.* London: Black, 1966.

Calver, Clive, and Rob Warner. *Together We Stand: Evangelical Convictions, Unity and Vision.* London: Hodder & Stoughton, 1996.

Calvin, John. *Commentary on the Epistles of Paul the Apostle to the Corinthians.* Vol. 2. Translated by John Pringle. Edinburgh: Calvin Translation Society, 1849.

———. *Commentaries on the Epistles to Timothy, Titus, and Philemon.* Translated by William Pringle. Edinburgh: Calvin Translation Society, 1849.

———. *Institutes of the Christian Religion.* Vol. 1, edited by John T. McNeill. 1960. Reprint. Louisville: Westminster John Knox, 2006.

———. *Psychopannychia.* In *Calvin's Tracts,* Vol. 3. Translated by Henry Beveridge. Edinburgh: Calvin Translation Society, 1851.

Camus, Albert. *The Fall.* Harmondsworth, UK: Penguin, 1957.

Carey, G. "The Ascension of Isaiah: An Example of Early Christian Narrative Polemic." *Journal for the Study of the Pseudepigraphic* 17 (1998) 65–78.

Bibliography

Carson, Donald A. "Approaching the Bible." In *New Bible Commentary, 21st century Edition*, edited by Donald A. Carson et al., 1–19. Leicester, UK: InterVarsity, 1994.
———. *Exegetical Fallacies*. Grand Rapids: Baker, 1984.
———. *The Gagging of God: Christianity Confronts Pluralism*. Grand Rapids: Zondervan, 1996.
———. *The Gospel according to John*. Leicester, UK: InterVarsity, 1991.
Chadwick, Henry. *Origen: Contra Celsum*. 1953. Reprint. Cambridge: Cambridge University Press, 1980.
Chan, Francis, and Preston Sprinkle. *Erasing Hell: What God Said about Eternity, and the Things We Made Up*. Colorado Springs, CO: David Cook, 2011.
Charles, Robert. H., editor. *The Apocrypha and Pseudepigrapha of the Old Testament in English*. 2 vols. Oxford: Clarendon, 1913.
———. *The Book of Enoch or 1 Enoch*. Oxford: Clarendon, 1912.
———. *A Critical History of the Doctrine of the Future Life*. London: Black, 1913.
Charlesworth, James H., editor. *The Old Testament Pseudepigrapha*. 2 vols. London: Danton, Longman and Todd, 1983, 1985.
———. "Prolegomenous Reflections towards a Taxonomy of Resurrection Texts." In *The Changing Face of Judaism, Christianity, and Other Greco-Roman Religions in Antiquity*, edited by Ian H. Henderson and Gerbern S. Oegema, 237–64. Studien zu den Jüdischen Schriften aus hellenistisch-römischer Zeit 2. Gütersloh: Gütersloher Verlagshaus, 2006.
———. "The SNTS Pseudepigrapha Seminars at Tübingen and Paris on the Books of Enoch." *New Testament Studies* 28 (1978–79) 315–23.
Charette, Blaine. *The Theme of Recompense in Matthew's Gospel*. Sheffield, UK: Sheffield Academic, 1992.
Cheetham, David. "Hell as Potentially Temporal." *ExpTim* 108.9 (1997) 260–63.
Constable, Henry. *The Duration and Nature of Future Punishment*. 5th ed. London: Kellaway, 1875.
Cooper, John W. *Body, Soul, and Life Everlasting*. Grand Rapids: Eerdmans, 1989.
Crockett, William V. "The Metaphorical View." In *Four Views on Hell*, edited by William Crockett, 43–90. Grand Rapids: Zondervan, 1992.
Cullmann, Oscar. *Christ and Time*. London: SCM, 1952.
———. *Immortality and Resurrection*. New York: Macmillan, 1965.
———. *Immortality of the Soul or Resurrection of the Dead?* London: Epworth, 1958.
———. *Salvation in History*. London: SCM, 1967.
Dahood, Mitchell. *Psalms*. 3 vols. Garden City, NY: Doubleday, 1966–70.
Danker, Frederick W., editor. *A Greek-English Lexicon of the New Testament and Other Early Christian Literature*. 3rd ed. Chicago: University of Chicago, 2000.
Davies, W. D., and Dale C. Allison. *The Gospel according to St. Matthew*. 3 vols. The International Critical Commentary, vol. 26.1–3. Edinburgh: T. & T. Clark, 1988–2000.
Delitzsch, Franz. *Commentary on the Epistle to the Hebrews*. 2 vols. Edinburgh: T. & T. Clark, 1868.
Denniston, J. M. *The Perishing Soul; or The Scriptural Doctrine of the Destruction of Sinners with a View of Ancient Jewish Opinion and Christian Belief during the First and Second Centuries*. 2nd ed. London: Longmans, Green, & Co., 1874.
Denzinger, Heinrich. *The Sources of Catholic Dogma*. Translated by Roy J. Deferrari. Fitzwilliam, NH: Loreto, 2010

Bibliography

Dieterich, Albrecht. *Nekyia: Beiträge zur Erklärung der neuentdeckten Petrusapokalypse.* Stuttgart: Teubner, 1969.

Dixon, Larry. *The Other Side of the Good News: Confronting the Contemporary Challenges to Jesus' Teaching on Hell.* 1992. Reprint. Tain, UK: Christian Focus, 2003.

Dudley-Smith, Timothy. *John Stott: A Global Ministry: The Later Years.* Downers Grove, IL: InterVarsity, 2001.

Dumbrell, William J. *The Search for Order: Biblical Eschatology in Focus.* Grand Rapids: Baker, 1994.

Edwards, David L., and John R. W. Stott. *Evangelical Essentials: A Liberal-Evangelical Dialogue.* Downers Grove, IL: InterVarsity, 1988.

Edwards, Jonathan. "Marks of a Work of the True Spirit." In *The Works of Jonathan Edwards.* Vol. 1, 525–62. 1808. Reprint. New York: Leavitt & Allen, 1858.

———. "Sinners in the Hands of an Angry God." In *The Works of Jonathan Edwards*, edited by Edward Hickman. Vol. 2, 7–12. London: William Ball, 1840.

Eichrodt, Walther. *Theology of the Old Testament.* 2 vols. 5th ed. London: SCM, 1967.

Ellis, E. Earle. "II Corinthians v. 1–10 in Pauline Eschatology." *NTS* 6 (1960) 211–24.

———. *The Gospel of Luke.* 7th ed. Grand Rapids: Eerdmans, 1996.

———. "Life." In *The New Bible Dictionary*, 2nd ed., edited by J. D. Douglas, 697–701. Leicester, UK: InterVarsity, 1982.

———. "New Testament Teaching on Hell." In *The Reader Must Understand: Eschatology in Bible and Theology*, edited by K. E. Brower and M. W. Elliott, 199–219. Leicester, UK: InterVarsity, 1997.

———. *The Old Testament in Early Christianity.* Wissenschaftliche Untersuchungen zum Neuen Testament 54. Tübingen: Mohr Siebeck, 1991.

———. "Sōma in 1 Corinthians." *Interpretations* 44 (1990) 132–44.

Emmet, Cyril W. "Retribution." *Dictionary of Christ and the Gospels*, edited by J. Hastings, 2:518–20. Edinburgh: T. & T. Clark, 1908.

Erickson, Millard J. *Christian Theology.* Grand Rapids: Baker, 1985.

Evangelical Alliance. "About Us." eauk.org. Online: http://eauk.org/connect/about-us/.

Farrar, Frederic W. *Mercy and Judgment: Last Words on Christian Eschatology with Reference to Dr. Pusey's "What is of Faith."* 2nd ed. London: Macmillan, 1882.

Flew, Anthony. *God and Philosophy.* London: Hutchinson, 1966.

Flusser, David. "The Dead Sea Sect and Pre-Pauline Christianity." In *Aspects of the Dead Sea Scrolls*, edited by Chaim Rabin and Yigael Yadin, 215–66. Scripta Hierosolymitana 4. Jerusalem: Magnes, 1958.

Foucault, M. *Discipline and Punish: The Birth of the Prison.* New York: Vintage, 1979.

Frend, W. H. C. "Arnobius." In *Oxford Classical Dictionary*, edited by N. G. L. Hammond and H. H. Scullard. 3rd ed. Oxford: Clarendon, 1970.

Froidevaux, Léon M., translator. *Irénée de Lyon, Démonstration de la Prédication apostolique.* Source Chrétienne 62. Paris: Cerf, 1971.

Froom, LeRoy E. *The Conditionalist Faith of our Fathers.* 2 vols. Washington, DC: Herald and Review, 1965–66.

Fudge, Edward W. "The Final End of the Wicked." *JETS* 27.3 (1985) 325–34.

———. *The Fire That Consumes: A Biblical and Historical Study of Final Punishment.* 1st ed. Houston: Providential, 1982.

———. *The Fire That Consumes: A Biblical and Historical Study of the Doctrine of Final Punishment.* 3rd ed. Eugene, OR: Cascade, 2011.

———. "A Loving Challenge to the Evangelical Church." *Resurrection* 93.4 (1990).

Fudge, Edward W., and Robert A. Peterson. *Two Views of Hell: A Biblical and Theological Dialogue*. Downers Grove, IL: InterVarsity, 2000.
Garrett, James L. Jr. *Systematic Theology*. 2 vols. Grand Rapids: Eerdmans, 1990–95.
Geffcken, J. *Komposition und Entstehungszeit der Oracula Sibyllina*. Leipzig: Hinrichs, 1902.
Gerstner, John. *Jonathan Edwards on Heaven and Hell*. Grand Rapids: Baker, 1980.
———. *Repent or Perish*. Ligonier, PA: Soli Deo Gloria, 1990.
Girdlestone, Robert B. *Dies Iræ: The Judgment of the Great Day, Viewed in the Light of Scripture and Conscience*. London: William Hunt, 1869.
Goff, Jacques Le. *The Birth of Purgatory*. Translated by A. Goldhammer. London: Scholar, 1984.
Gomes, Alan W. "Evangelicals and the Annihilation of Hell, Part One." *Christian Research Journal* (Spring 1991) 14–19.
Goulbum, Edward. M. *Everlasting Punishment: Lectures Delivered at St. James's Church, Piccadilly, on the Six First Sundays After Trinity, in the Year 1880*. London: Rivington, 1880.
Grant, R. M. *Theophilus of Antioch, Ad Autolycum*. Oxford: Clarendon, 1970.
Gray, Tony. "Destroyed for Ever: An Examination of the Debates concerning Annihilation and Conditional Immortality." *Themelios* 21.1 (1996) 14–18.
Green, Michael. *Evangelism through the Local Church*. London: Hodder & Stoughton, 1990.
Gregg, Steve. *All You Want to Know about Hell: Three Christian Views of God's Final Solution to the Problem of Sin*. Nashville: Thomas Nelson, 2013.
Guillebaud, Harold E. *The Righteous Judge*. Taunton, UK: Phoenix, 1964.
Gundry, Robert. H. *Matthew: A Commentary on his Literary and Theological Art*. Grand Rapids: Eerdmans, 1982.
———. *Soma in Biblical Theology*. 2nd ed. Grand Rapids: Zondervan, 1987.
Hammer, Reuven. *Sifre*. New Haven, CT: Yale University Press, 1986.
Harmon, Kendall. S. "The Case against Conditionalism." In *Universalism and the Doctrine of Hell*, edited by Nigel M. de S. Cameron, 193–224. Grand Rapids: Baker, 1992.
Harnack, C. G. Adolf von. *History of Dogma*. Vol. 2. Translated by Neil Buchanan. Boston: Little, Brown, and Co., 1907.
———. *Outlines of the History of Dogma*. Boston: Beacon, 1957.
Harris, Murray J. *Raised Immortal*. London: Marshall, 1983.
Helm, Paul. *The Last Things: Death, Judgment, Heaven and Hell*. Edinburgh: Banner of Truth, 1989.
Hendriksen, William. *The Bible on the Life Hereafter*. Grand Rapids: Baker, 1959.
———. *More Than Conquerors*. Grand Rapids: Baker, 1995.
Herford, T. R. "Pirqe Aboth." In *The Apocrypha and Pseudepigrapha of the Old Testament*, vol. 2, edited by R. H. Charles, 686–714. Oxford: Clarendon, 1978.
Hick, John. *Death and Eternal Life*. London: Collins, 1976.
Hilborn, David. *The Nature of Hell: A Report by the Evangelical Alliance Commission on Unity and Truth among Evangelicals (ACUTE)*. Carlisle, UK: Paternoster, 2000.
Hilborn, David, and Ian Randall. "The Evangelical Alliance: A Brief History." eauk.org. Online: http://eauk.org/connect/about-us/upload/The-Evangelical-Alliance_-A-brief-history.pdf
Himmelfarb, Martha. *Tours of Hell*. Philadelphia: Fortress, 1983.

Bibliography

Hodge, Charles. *Systematic Theology*. 3 vols. London: Nelson, 1871–74.
Hoekema, Anthony A. *The Bible and the Future*. Exeter, UK: Paternoster, 1979.
Hopper, Jeffery. *Understanding Modern Theology*. 2 vols. Philadelphia: Fortress, 1987–88.
Hughes, Gerard. *God of Surprises*. London: Darton, Longman and Todd, 1985.
Hughes, Philip E. *The True Image*. Leicester, UK: InterVarsity, 1989.
Jacoby, Douglas. *What's the Truth about Heaven and Hell? Sorting Out the Confusion about the Afterlife*. Eugene, OR: Harvest House, 2013.
Johnson, Aubrey R. *The Vitality of the Individual in the Thought of Ancient Israel*. Cardiff: University of Wales, 1949.
Jürgens, Williams A., translator. *The Faith of the Early Fathers*. 3 vols. Collegeville, MN: Liturgical, 1970.
Kannengiesser, C. *Athanase d'Alexandrie: Sur l'incarnation du Verbe*. Source Chrétienne 199. Paris: Cerf, 1973.
Käsemann, Ernst. *Romans*. 4th ed. Grand Rapids: Eerdmans, 1980.
Keck, Leander E. "Rethinking 'New Testament Ethics.'" *JBL* 115.1 (1996) 3–16.
Kelly, John N. D. *Early Christian Doctrines*. 5th ed. London: Black, 1977.
Kidner, D. *Psalms*. 2 vols. London: InterVarsity, 1973–75.
Kittel, Gerhard, and Gerhard Friedrich, editors. *Theological Dictionary of the New Testament*. Translated by G. W. Bromiley from *Theologisches Worterbuch zum Neuen Testament*. Grand Rapids: Eerdmans, 1964.
Klijn, John "2 Baruch". In *Old Testament Pseudepigrapha*, vol. 1, edited by James H. Charlesworth, 615–52. London: Danton, Longman and Todd, 1983.
Knibb, Michael A. "Ascension of Isaiah." In *Old Testament Pseudepigrapha*, vol. 2, edited by James H. Charlesworth, 143–76. London: Danton, Longman and Todd, 1985.
———. "The Date of the Parables of Enoch: A Critical Review." *New Testament Studies* 25 (1979) 345–59.
———. *The Ethiopic Book of Enoch*. 2 vols. Oxford: Clarendon, 1978.
Köberle, Adolf. "Das griechische und das biblische Verständnis von Seele." *Theologische Beiträge* 14 (1983) 133–42.
Kraus, Hans J. *Psalms*. 2 vols. Minneapolis: Fortress, 1988–89.
Krauss, C. Norman. *God Our Savior: Theology in a Christological Mode*. Scottdale, PA: Herald, 1991.
Küng, Huns. *Eternal Life? Life after Death as a Medical, Philosophical, and Theological Problem*. New York: Doubleday, 1984.
Kvanvig, Jonathan L. *The Problem of Hell*. Oxford: Oxford University Press, 1993.
Lane, William L. *Commentary on the Gospel of Mark*. Grand Rapids: Eerdmans, 1974.
Lawson, Penelope. *St. Athanasius, On the Incarnation*. 3rd ed. London: Mowbray, 1953.
Leiman, Shnayer Z. *The Canonization of the Hebrew Scriptures*. Hamden, CT: Archon, 1976.
Lewis, Clive. S. *The Great Divorce*. London: Bles, 1946.
———. *Out of the Silent Planet*. London: Lane, 1938.
———. *The Pilgrim's Regress*. 1933. Reprint, London: Collins Fount, 1977.
———. *The Problem of Pain*. London: Bles, 1940.
Lightfoot, Joseph B., and J. R. Harmer, editors. *The Apostolic Fathers*. London: Macmillan, 1891.
Lilla, Salvatore R. C. *Clement of Alexandria*. Oxford: Clarendon, 1971.
Lincoln, Andrew T. *Ephesians*. Word Biblical Commentary 42. Dallas: Word, 1990.

Lund, Nils W. *Chiasmus in the New Testament: A Study in the Form and Function of Chiastic Structure*. Peabody, MA: Hendriksen, 1992.
MacDonald, Gregory. *The Evangelical Universalist*. 2nd ed. Eugene, OR: Cascade, 2012.
Malherbe, Abraham J. *The Letters to the Thessalonians*. Anchor Bible Commentaries 32:2. New Haven, CT: Yale University Press, 2000.
Man, Ronald E. "The Value of Chiasm for New Testament Interpretation." *Bibliotheca Sacra* 141 (1984) 146–57.
Mansoor, Menahem. *The Thanksgiving Hymns*. Leiden: Brill, 1961.
Maritain, Jacques. *The Range of Reason*. London: Bles, 1953.
Markus, Robert A. "Augustine." In *The Cambridge History of Later Greek and Early Medieval Philosophy*, edited by A. H. Armstrong, 341–424. Cambridge: Cambridge University, 1970.
Marshall, I. Howard. *Endorsement of Rethinking Hell*. Online: http://www.rethinkinghell.com/about/endorsements.
———. *The Gospel of Luke*. New International Greek Testament Commentary. Exeter, UK: Paternoster, 1978.
———. "The Nature of Christian Salvation." *EuroJTh* 4.1 (1995) 29–43.
McGrath, Alister E. *Evangelicalism and the Future of Christianity*. London: Hodder & Stoughton, 1993.
———. *A Passion for Truth: The Intellectual Coherence of Evangelicalism*. Leicester, UK: Apollos, 1996.
———. *Roots that Refresh: A Celebration of Reformation Spirituality*. London: Hodder & Stoughton, 1992.
Mearns, C. L. "Dating the Similitudes of Enoch." *New Testament Studies* 25 (1978–79) 360–69.
———. "The Parables of Enoch: Origin and Date." *Expository Times* 89 (1978) 118–19.
Metzger, Bruce M. "4 Ezra." *Old Testament Pseudepigrapha*, vol. 1, edited by James H. Charlesworth, 517–60. London: Danton, Longman and Todd, 1983.
Meyer, R. "Σαδδουκαῖος." *TDNT* 7 (1971) 35–53.
———. "φαρισαῖος." *TDNT* 9 (1974) 21.
———. *Hellenistisches in der rabbinischen Anthropologie*. Stuttgart, 1973.
Milik, Józef T. *The Books of Enoch: Aramaic Fragments of Qumran Cave 4*. Oxford: Clarendon, 1976.
Miller, Perry. *Jonathan Edwards*. 1949. Reprint. Lincoln, NE: University of Nebraska Press, 2005.
Milne, Bruce. *Know the Truth: A Handbook of Christian Doctrine*. Leicester, UK: InterVarsity, 1982.
Moberly, Elizabeth R. *Suffering, Innocent and Guilty*. London: SPCK, 1978.
Moberly, Walter. *The Ethics of Punishment*. London: Faber & Faber, 1968.
Moltmann, Jürgen. *The Coming of God*. Translated by Margaret Kohl. 1996. Reprint. Minneapolis: Augsburg Fortress, 2004.
———. "The End of Everything is God. Has Belief in Hell had Its Day?" *ExpTim* 108.9 (1997) 263–64.
———. *Jesus Christ for Today's World*. London: SCM, 1994.
Montgomery, J. A. "The Holy City and Gehenna." *Journal of Biblical Literature* 27 (1908) 24–47.
Moody, Dale. *The Hope of Glory*. Grand Rapids: Eerdmans, 1964.
Morey, Robert A. *Death and the Afterlife*. Minneapolis: Bethany House, 1984.

Bibliography

Morgan, Christopher W. "Annihilationism: Will the Unsaved Be Punished Forever?" In *Hell under Fire: Modern Scholarship Reinvents Eternal Punishment*, edited by Christopher W. Morgan and Robert A. Peterson, 195–218. Grand Rapids: Zondervan, 2004.

Morris, Leon L. *The Apostolic Preaching of the Cross*. London: Tyndale, 1955.

Motyer, J. Alec. *The Prophecy of Isaiah*. Leicester, UK: InterVarsity, 1993.

Moule, Handley. C. G. "Arnobius." In *DCB* 1:167–70.

Mounce, Robert H. *The Book of Revelation*. New International Commentary. Grand Rapids: Eerdmans, 1974.

Neusner, Jacob. *Judaism: The Evidence of the Mishnah*. Chicago: University of Chicago Press, 1981.

Newman, Albert Henry. *A Manual of Church History*. 2 vols. Philadelphia: The American Baptist Publication Society, 1933.

Noll, Mark A. *The Scandal of the Evangelical Mind*. Grand Rapids: Eerdmans, 1994.

Packer, James I. "Evangelical Annihilationism in Review." *Reformation & Revival* 6.2 (1997) 37–51.

———. "Evangelicals and the Way of Salvation." In *Evangelical Affirmations*, edited by Kenneth G. Kantzer and Carl F. H. Henry, 107–37. Grand Rapids: Zondervan, 1990.

———. "The Problem of Eternal Punishment." *Crux* 26 (1990) 18–25.

Page, Sydney H. T. *Powers of Evil: A Biblical Study of Satan and Demons*. Grand Rapids: Baker, 1995.

Papaioannou, Kim. *The Geography of Hell in the Teaching of Jesus*. Eugene, OR: Pickwick, 2013.

Pedersen, Johannes. *Israel: Its Life and Culture*. 4 vols. London: Oxford University Press, 1959–63.

Pelikan, Jaroslav. *The Shape of Death*. Nashville: Abingdon, 1961.

Percy, Martyn. *Words, Wonders and Power: Understanding Contemporary Christian Fundamentalism and Revivalism*. London: SPCK, 1996.

Pétavel-Olliff, Emmanuel. *The Problem of Immortality*. London: Elliot Stock, 1892.

Peterson, Robert A. *Hell on Trial: The Case for Eternal Punishment*. Phillipsburg, NJ: Presbyterian and Reformed, 1995.

———. "A Traditionalist Response to John Stott's Arguments for Annihilationism." *JETS* 37.4 (1994) 553–68.

———. "Undying Worm, Unquenchable Fire." *Christianity Today* 44.12 (2000) 30–37.

Pink, Arthur W. *Eternal Punishment*. Swengel, PA: Reiner, n.d.

Pinnock, Clark H. "The Conditional View." In *Four Views on Hell*, edited by William Crocket, 135–66. Grand Rapids: Zondervan, 1996.

———. "The Destruction of the Finally Impenitent." *CTR* 4.2 (1990) 243–59.

Pinnock, Clark H., and Robert C. Brow. *Unbounded Love: A Good News Theology for the 21st Century*. Carlisle, UK: Paternoster, 1994.

Plumptre, E. H. "Eschatology." In *DCB* 2:189–97.

Powys, David J. *"Hell": A Hard Look at a Hard Question: The Fate of the Unrighteous in New Testament Thought*. 1997. Reprint. Eugene, OR: Wipf & Stock, 2006.

Pressensé, E. de. "Augustinius." In *DCB* 1:216–28.

Prestidge, Warren. *Life, Death, and Destiny*. Auckland, NZ: Resurrection, 1998.

Puech, E. "Messianism, Resurrection, and Eschatology at Qumran and in the New Testament." In *The Community of the Renewed Covenant*, edited by E. Ulrich and J. VanderKam, 235–56. Notre Dame, IN: Notre Dame University, 1996.

Bibliography

Quasten, Johannes. *Patrology*. 3 vols. Westminster, MD: Christian Classics, 1983.
Quinn, Jerome D. "The Scriptures on Merit." In *Justification by Faith*, edited by H. G. Anderson et al., 82–93. Minneapolis: Augsburg, 1985.
Rad, Gerhard von. *Old Testament Theology*. 2 vols. London: SCM, 1975.
Reimensnyder, Junius B. *Doom Eternal: The Bible and Church Doctrine of Everlasting Punishment*. Philadelphia: Nelson S. Quiney, 1880.
Reiser, Marius. *Jesus and Judgment: The Eschatological Proclamation in Its Jewish Context*. Minneapolis: Fortress, 1997.
Ringgren, Helmer. *The Faith of Qumran: Theology of the Dead Sea Scrolls*. 2nd ed. New York: Crossroad, 1995.
Roberts, Alexander, and James Donaldson, editors. *The Ante-Nicene Fathers. Translations of the Writings of the Fathers down to A.D. 325*. 10 vols. 1867–73. Reprint. Buffalo, NY: Christian Literature Company, 1885–96.
Robertson, Archibald. T. *A Grammar of the Greek New Testament in the Light of Historical Research*. London: Doran, 1914.
Robinson, H. Wheeler. *The Christian Doctrine of Man*. 3rd ed. Edinburgh: T. & T. Clark, 1947.
Robinson, Joseph A., translator. *St. Irenaeus: The Demonstration of the Apostolic Preaching*. London: Christian Knowledge Society, 1920.
Rogers, Adrian P. "Response" (to Clark Pinnock's "Parameters of Biblical Inerrancy"). In *The Proceedings of the Conference on Biblical Inerrancy: 1987*, 101–6. Nashville: Broadman, 1987.
Rubinkiewicz, R. "Apocalypse of Abraham." In *Old Testament Pseudepigrapha*, vol. 1, edited by James H. Charlesworth, 681–705. London: Danton, Longman and Todd, 1983.
Saville, Andy. "Hell without Sin—A Renewed View of a Disputed Doctrine." *Churchman* 119.3 (2005) 243–61.
Sayce, Archibald H. *The Religions of Ancient Egypt and Babylonia*. Edinburgh: T. & T. Clark, 1902.
Schaff, Philip. *History of the Christian Church*. 7 vols. New York: Scribner's, 1882–1910.
———, editor. *A Select Library of the Nicene and Post-Nicene Fathers of the Christian Church, First Series*. 14 vols. New York: Christian Literature Company, 1886–89.
Schaff, Philip, and Henry Wace, editors. *A Select Library of the Nicene and Post-Nicene Fathers of the Christian Church, Second Series*. 14 vols. New York: Christian Literature Company, Scribner's, 1890–1900.
Schürer, Emil. *The History of the Jewish People in the Age of Jesus Christ*. 3 vols. Edinburgh: T. & T. Clark, 1973–87.
Shedd, William G. T. *The Doctrine of Endless Punishment*. New York: Scribner, 1886.
———. *Dogmatic Theology*. Vol. 2. New York: Scribner's, 1888.
Silvester, Hugh. *Arguing with God: A Christian Examination of the Problem of Evil*. London: InterVarsity, 1971.
Smick, E. B. "The Bearing of New Philological Data on the Subjects of the Resurrection and Immortality in the Old Testament." *WTJ* 31 (1968) 12–21.
Smith, William, and Henry Wace, editors. *Dictionary of Christian Biography, Literature, Sects and Doctrines; during the First Eight Centuries. Being a Continuation of "The Dictionary of the Bible,"* edited by William Smith and Henry Wace, 2:189–97. 4 vols. London: 1877–87.

Bibliography

Son, Sang-Won (Aaron), editor. *History and Exegesis: New Testament Essays in Honor of Dr. E. Earle Ellis for His 80th Birthday*. London: T. & T. Clark, 2006.

Spanner, Douglas. "Is Hell Forever?" *Churchman* 110.2 (1966) 107–20.

Spurgeon, Charles H. *Sermons of the Rev. C. H. Spurgeon*. New York: Sheldon, Blakeman, 1857.

Stokes, George. G. *Evidence of Missionaries as to the Practical Effect of Presenting Christianity to the Heathen in the Form Associated with the Doctrine of "Life in Christ."* Cambridge: C. J. Clay at the University Press, 1882.

Stone, M. E. *Fourth Ezra*. Hermeneia. Minneapolis, MN: Fortress, 1990.

———. "Greek Apocalypse of Ezra." In *Old Testament Pseudepigrapha*, vol. 1, edited by James H. Charlesworth, 561–79. London: Danton, Longman and Todd, 1983.

Stott, John R. W. *The Cross of Christ*. Leicester, UK: InterVarsity, 1986.

Strack, Hermann. L. and Paul Billerbeck. *Kommentar zun Neuen Testament*. 4 vols. München: Beck, 1922–28.

Stuckenbruck, Loren T. "Revision of Aramaic-Greek and Greek-Aramaic Glossaries in 'The Books of Enoch: Aramaic Fragments of Qumran Cave 4,' by J. T. Milik." *Journal of Jewish Studies* 36 (1990) 12–48.

Swinburne, Richard G. *The Evolution of the Soul*. Oxford: Clarendon, 1986.

Talbott, Thomas. *The Inescapable Love of God*. 2nd ed. Eugene, OR: Cascade, 2014.

Theron, Daniel J. *Evidence of Tradition*. 1959. Reprint. Eugene, OR: Wipf and Stock, 2009.

Thielicke, Helmut. *Death and Life*. Philadelphia: Fortress, 1970.

Thompson, Fred P. *What the Bible Says about Heaven and Hell*. Joplin, MO: College, 1983.

Thompson, Mark. *Saving the Heart: What is an Evangelical?* London: St. Matthias, 1995.

Thomson, Robert. W. *Athanasius, Contra Gentes De Incarnatione*. Oxford: Clarendon, 1971.

Tidball, Derek J. *Who are the Evangelicals?* London: Marshall Pickering, 1994.

Tillich, Paul. *Systematic Theology*. Vol. 3. London: Nisbet, 1964.

Tixeront, Joseph. *History of Dogmas*. London: Herder, 1923.

Torrey, Reuben. A. *What the Bible Teaches*. London: Nisbet, n.d.

Travis, Stephen H. *Christ and the Judgment of God: Divine Retribution in the New Testament*. London: Marshall & Pickering, 1986.

———. *Christian Hope and the Future of Man*. Downers Grove, IL: InterVarsity, 1980.

Toon, Peter. *Heaven and Hell, A Biblical and Theological Overview*. Nashville: Nelson, 1986.

Tromp, Nicholas. J. *Primitive Conceptions of Death and the Nether World in the Old Testament*. Rome: Gregorian Biblical BookShop, 1969.

Tugwell, Simon. *Human Immortality and the Redemption of Death*. London: Darton, Longman and Todd, 1990.

Turner, Alice K. *The History of Hell*. New York: Harcourt, 1993.

Volf, Miroslav. *Exclusion and Embrace: A Theological Exploration of Identity, Otherness, and Reconciliation*. Nashville: Abingdon, 1996.

Walvoord, John. "The Literal View." In *Four Views on Hell*, edited by William Crockett, 11–29. Grand Rapids: Zondervan, 1996.

Webb, Barry. *The Message of Isaiah*. Leicester, UK: InterVarsity, 1995.

Weber, Ferdinand. *Jüdische Theologie auf Grund des Talmud und verwanter Schriften*. Hildesheim: Olms, 1975.

Wells, David F. *No Place For Truth, or Whatever Happened to Evangelical Theology?* Leicester, UK: InterVarsity, 1993.
Wenham, John W. "The Case for Conditional Immortality." In *Universalism and the Doctrine of Hell*, edited by Nigel M. de S. Cameron, 161–91. Grand Rapids: Baker, 1992.
———. *The Enigma of Evil*. Guildford, UK: Eagle, 1994.
———. *Facing Hell: An Autobiography*. Exeter, UK: Paternoster, 1998.
White, Edward. *Life in Christ: A Study of the Scripture Doctrine on the Nature of Man, the Object of the Divine Incarnation, and the Conditions of Human Immortality*. 3rd ed. London: Elliot Stock, 1878.
Wingren, Gustaf. *Man and the Incarnation: A Study in the Biblical Theology of Irenaeus*. 1959. Reprint. Eugene, OR: Wipf & Stock, 2004.
Wisbrock, George. *Death and the Soul After Life*. No loc.: Wisbrock, 1986.
Wright, N. T. *What Saint Paul Really Said*. Oxford: Lion, 1997.
———. "Towards a Biblical View of Universalism." *Themelios* 4.2 (1979) 54–58.
———. "Universalism and the World-Wide Community." *Churchman* 89.3 (1975) 197–212.
Woodcock, Eldon. *Hell: An Exhaustive Look at a Burning Issue*. Bloomington, IN: WestBow, 2012.

Ancient Document Index

Old Testament / Hebrew Bible

Genesis

2–3	12
2:7	15, 125
2:17	124
3:3	32
3:17ff.	124
3:19	15, 120, 125
3:22–24	15
3:22	8
6:1	251
6:7	32
7:4	32
7:22	125
18:23–25	199
19:23	38, 141–42
19:24–29	32
19:24–28	86, 190
19:24	37, 110
19:25	110
19:28	37, 38, 110, 141–42
25:8	125
37:35	125

Exodus

3:2	104
14	263
14:30	36
21:23–25	54
21:23–24	229
32:32	50

Leviticus

13:24	105
24:20	229

Numbers

21:28	104

Deuteronomy

4:24	105, 107
5:23	105
19:20	229
29:23	32, 38, 86, 141, 191
31:16	125
32:2	123
35:15	136

Joshua

2	263
15:8	247
18:16	247

Judges

16:17	246

1 Samuel

27:8	136

2 Samuel

14:14	125

Ancient Document Index

2 Kings

1	40
16:3	65
18:17—19:36	36
21:6	65
23:10	111, 129

1 Chronicles

15:2	136

2 Chronicles

28:3	111, 247
33:6	111, 247

Nehemiah

11:30	247

Job

3:13ff.	125
3:17	110
7:9	125
10:9	125
16:9	36
17:13–16	125
18:5–6	104
18:15–17	38, 141
19:26	127
21:17	104
21:20	38
31:12	105
34:11	209
34:14	125

Psalms

1:4	31
2:9	31
2:21–22	263
3:6	127
6:5	123, 125
9	31
9:83:5ff.	134
21	209
16:8–11	127
16:9ff.	127
16:10–11	129
17:15	127
21:4–10	31
21:9	105
24:7	136
30:3	126
30:5	216
30:9	125
31:5	186
33:19	126
35:16	36
36:9–12	31
37:2	64
37:9–10	64
37:9	209
37:12	36
37:20	31, 64
37:33	209
37:35–37	263
37:38	64
39:3	105
49:8–20	31
49:12	125, 127
49:14–15	127
52:5–9	31
57:4	106
58:8	31
58:10	36
58:12	209
59	31
59:13	104
60:3	38
62:10	209
62:13	209
68:2	31
69:28	300
71:20	212
72:17	125
73	31
73:20	31
73:23–28	126
73:23–27	127

320

Psalms (cont.)

73:24	127
75:8	38
79:13	104
88:3	126
89:48	126
91:8	36
92	31
97:3	106
103:6–14	222
103:14	89
107:26	212
112:10	36–37, 100
115:17	123
118:12	35, 104
139:18	127
144:4	125
146:4	125

Proverbs

2:21–22	32
10:16	209
10:25	32
12:7	32
12:28	16
22:28	136
24:12	209
24:15–20	32
25:21–22	107

Ecclesiastes

2:14	125, 209
3:19ff.	125
9:10	125
12:7	15, 125, 186

Isaiah

1:9	32
1:28	104
1:31	31, 35, 257–58, 268
2:3	19
3:10–11	209
5:24–25	257
6:5	232
9:5	120, 257
9:18–19	257
10:16–17	257
11:9	19
13:19–22	32
13:19	86
14	125
14:4–11	125
14:9ff.	129
25:7–8	40
25:8	127
26:19	127
30:27–33	38, 141
30:30	257
30:33	108, 246, 257
33:12	31
33:14–15	8
33:14	105
33:15	105
34:1–17	149
34:8–17	143
34:8–12	144
34:9–11	38, 141–42
34:9–10	110, 143–45
34:9	37, 144
34:10–11	35
34:10	37
34:11–15	149
36–37	36
37:36	36
43:17	104, 257–58
44:6	232
50:11	246
51:17	38
51:22	38
53:4–12	134
59:18	209
65:17–18	197
65:17	134
66:16–24	32
66:16	35
66:17	35, 104
66:22–23	118
66:22	35, 125, 134

Isaiah (cont.)

66:23	35
66:24	32–33, 35–36, 52–53, 69, 85, 112, 119, 127, 129, 135, 151, 167–68, 172, 213, 246, 253, 257–58

Jeremiah

4:4	35
7:20	35, 107
7:29–34	257–58
7:31–32	45, 111, 247
9:1	49
13:17	49
14:17	49
17:10	209
17:27	35, 107, 172–73, 257
19:1–13	257–58
19:2	111
19:6	111, 247
21:12	35
25:14	209
25:27–28	38
25:27	38
32:19	209
32:35	111
49:18	32
50:40	32, 86, 190

Lamentations

2:16	36
3:33	216
3:64	209
4:6	32, 86

Ezekiel

18:4	32, 124
18:29	199
20:47–48	35
27:36	171
28:11–19	171
28:13–16	171
28:19	113
31–32	125
37	127
38–39	40
38:22ff.	38, 141
39:9–22	32, 36

Daniel

7:2	113
7:9–12	39
7:11–12	148
12:2	16, 32, 36, 50, 118, 127, 168, 176, 246, 253

Hosea

4:9	209
13:14	129

Joel

3:1ff.	250
3:1–3	253

Amos

4:11	32, 86
5:5–6	35

Obadiah

15	103
16	32, 38

Jonah

2:1–10	127

Habbakuk

2:13	105

Zephaniah

1:2–3	104
1:14–18	32
1:14	100
2:9	32, 86

Malachi

4:1–3	36
4:1	64, 106
4:3	31–32, 106, 125

Apocrypha/ Deuterocanonical Books

2 Baruch

54:21–22	249
59:10	249, 253
85:13	249

4 Ezra

2:28–29	248
3:1	248
7:36	248, 253

Acts of Paul

3	126
8	126
24–27	126

Acts of Peter

17	126

Judith

16:17	33, 52–53, 70, 123

Pseudepigrapha

1 Enoch

1–36	251
27:1–2	252–53
37–71	251
48:9	246
52:1	252
52:2	252
54:1–6	251
54:1–2	246
54:1	252
54:4	252
54:5	252
56:1–4	252
56:5–7	251
62:12–13	246
69	251
86–88	251
90:20–27	253
90:25ff.	123
90:26	253
97:1	123
98:10	123

2 Enoch

18:7	251

3 Enoch

43:1–3	250
44	250
44:3	249
44:5	250
48D:8	249–50

4 Maccabees

9:9	123
12:12	123

Apocalypse of Abraham

15:6	250, 253

Apocalypse of Pseudo-Peter

7–10	126

Ascension of Isaiah

1:3	126, 249
4:14	249
4:17–18	249
10:8ff.	126

Ancient Document Index

Greek Apocalypse of Ezra

1:9	250
3:5ff.	250

Jubilees

5	251

Psalms of Solomon

2:31	176
2:34	176

Sibylline Oracles

1:104	250–51
2:292	250–51
2:307	251
4:171–78	251
4:181–82	251
4:186	250–51

∼

Rabbinic Writings

Mishnah

Eduyoth 2:10	125
Pirqe Aboth 1:4–5	255
Sanhedrin 10:1	123
Tosefta Sanhedrin 13:4	125

∼

New Testament

Matthew

2:13	22, 51
3:7	80, 130, 135, 208–9
3:10–12	257
3:10	65, 107, 157, 258
3:12	35, 52, 65, 80, 85, 107, 130, 136, 151, 157–58, 190, 213, 258
5:2	129
5:12	208
5:22	52, 80, 111, 130, 134–35, 209, 211, 222, 257–58
5:22–23	258
5:25–26	102, 169
5:26	137, 165, 208, 239
5:29–30	129, 209, 211
5:29	80, 111, 135, 257–58
5:30	65, 80, 111–12, 135
5:46	208
6:1–6	208
6:16–21	208
7:11	232
7:13–14	22, 134, 222
7:13	51, 80, 130, 135, 209, 224, 288
7:14	129, 208
7:15–23	222
7:19	80, 108, 130, 136, 157, 257
7:21–23	197, 222
7:21	81
7:23	50, 156
7:24–27	222
7:27	80, 130, 136
8:11–12	209, 211
8:11	81, 134
8:12	49, 99, 110, 130, 137, 156, 190, 233
8:18	191
8:23	81
9:36	89
10:6	80
10:15	208–9, 223
10:28	8, 22–23, 45, 51, 65, 80, 111, 129, 131, 134–35, 159, 163, 186, 194, 208–9, 211, 217, 231, 257–58, 288
10:32–33	222
10:32	81
10:33	208
10:39	80, 131, 134

Matthew (cont.)

10:41	208
11:20–24	208
11:21–24	209
11:22	204, 209
11:23	129, 211
11:24	209
12:14	22, 51
12:31–32	118, 208
12:32	85
12:36–37	208
12:36	82, 222
12:37	94
12:40	127, 209
12:41	82
13:30	65, 208
13:36ff.	190
13:38	222
13:40–43	134
13:40–42	22
13:40	80, 108, 130, 136, 158, 257
13:41–42	108, 208–9, 211
13:42	65, 80, 130, 156, 209, 213, 257, 296
13:47–50	158
13:48	130, 136
13:49–50	108, 134, 190
13:49	65
13:50	65, 80, 130, 156, 209, 211, 213, 257
15:13	80, 130, 136
16:18	129, 211–12
16:25–26	80
16:25	82, 131, 134
17:15	106
18:3–4	222
18:8–9	80, 209, 211
18:8	50, 52, 84, 108, 136, 156, 176, 190, 258
18:9	52, 80, 111, 129, 290
18:10	257
18:18	82
18:24	166
18:34–35	82, 137, 151, 155, 164, 168
18:34	220
18:35	208
19:16–19	222
19:17	121
19:25	121
19:28–29	208
19:29	129, 208
20:1–16	208, 223
21:41	22, 80, 130, 136
21:43–44	209
21:44	80, 130, 136, 159
22:1–16	223
22:7	80
22:13–14	134
22:13	49, 81–82, 99, 130, 137, 156, 190, 209, 211
22:23	123
22:32	127
23:5–12	222
23:15	111, 129, 135, 209, 211, 257–58
23:33	80, 111, 129, 135, 209, 211, 257–58
23:35–38	209
23:35–36	82
23:37–38	49
24	285
24:13	82
24:35	30
24:38–39	32
24:41	209
24:46–47	208
24:51	49, 82, 99, 100, 130, 134, 136, 156, 190, 209, 211, 220
25:1–13	222
25:10–12	50, 222
25:11–12	197
25:14–30	222
25:14	134
25:21	208

Matthew (cont.)

25:23	208
25:30	49, 81–82, 99, 130, 134, 137, 156, 190, 209, 211
25:31–46	133, 208, 222, 301
25:34	46
25:41–46	118, 288
25:41, 46	151, 161, 168
25:41	46, 50, 52, 80–81, 84, 108, 113, 130–31, 136, 156–57, 171, 176, 191, 208, 290
25:46	12, 30, 41–42, 46, 50, 53, 70, 81, 84, 100–101, 118–19, 129–33, 135–36, 155, 190–91, 208, 217, 223, 302
26:39	38
27:4	51

Mark

1:15	213
1:24	131, 134
3:6	22
3:25	131
3:28–29	208
3:29	41, 50, 82, 84–85, 136, 218
3:39	131
5:7–8	131, 134
8:34–38	222
8:35–36	80
8:38	81
9:22	22, 106
9:41	208
9:42–48	127, 129, 209, 211, 222
9:42–43	46, 119
9:42	208, 220
9:43–48	151, 155, 164, 166–69, 172, 257–58, 288
9:43, 48	35, 213
9:43–44	111
9:43	45, 80, 85, 112, 258
9:44–47	106
9:44	109, 112, 190–91
9:45–46	112
9:45	45, 80, 258
9:46	109, 112
9:47–48	112, 119, 130, 134–35, 209
9:47	45, 80, 190, 258
9:48–49	80
9:48	35, 52, 69, 82, 85, 109, 112, 172, 213
9:49	106
10:15	81
10:21	208, 222
10:28–30	208
10:29–30	209
10:30	133
12:9	80, 208
12:30–33	128
12:40	82, 223
13:32	285
16:16	82
14:4	161
14:21	50, 208

Luke

3:7	80, 208
3:9	82, 109, 257–58
3:17	52, 80, 85, 109, 157, 257
6:9	22
6:23	208
6:38	208
6:46–49	222
6:49	80
8:31	212
9:25	80
9:54	106
9:60	160
10:12–14	223
10:13–15	209
10:15	129, 211
10:25–37	222
10:25	129, 208

Ancient Document Index

Luke (*cont.*)

10:27–28	222
11:11	89
11:22–24	223
11:31	82
11:48	205
11:50	82
12:4–5	209, 211, 257–58
12:5	80
12:8–9	222
12:8	86
12:9	81
12:10	82
12:20	82
12:33–34	208
12:40	134
12:46ff.	134
12:46	82, 103, 220
12:47–48	103, 209, 220, 223
12:47	82, 208
12:48	204
12:49	106
12:51–53	106
12:57	199
12:58–59	102
13:2	130, 136
13:3	80, 131, 134, 159
13:4	130, 137
13:7	80, 130, 136
13:9	208
13:22–30	208
13:23–27	222
13:27–28	81
13:27	156
13:28–29	133, 208–9, 211
13:28	49, 82, 156, 213
13:34–35	222
14:12	208
14:14–15	208
14:21	81
14:34	81
15	81
15:11–32	223
15:17	51
16	301
16:8	222
16:19ff.	186
16:19–31	23, 45, 86, 125
16:22–23	53
16:23ff.	70
16:23–31	208
16:23–24	53, 82
16:23	129, 211, 220
16:24	213
16:26	50, 81, 220, 288
16:28	53, 82
17:7–10	223
17:27	130–31, 134, 137
17:28–33	32
17:28–32	86
17:29–30	130, 209
17:29	80, 106, 130–31, 134, 137
17:32	130, 137
17:33	80
17:34	81
18:7–8	130, 135, 208, 209
18:9–14	223
18:28–30	208
19:10	80
19:11–27	222
19:11	134
19:14	130, 137
19:22	224
19:27	80, 130, 134, 137, 159, 208
19:41–44	222
19:41–42	49
20:16	131, 134
20:18	80
20:27–40	127
20:35–36	8, 82
20:36	81, 131, 134
20:47	82, 223
21:19	82
23:33	134, 209
23:41	208
23:46	186

John

2:19	186
3:15–16	129, 208
3:16–17	303
3:16	51, 80–81, 159, 175
3:17	82
3:19	239
3:36	80, 82, 93, 135, 208–9, 222
5:6	134
5:16	288
5:21	214
5:24	175, 196
5:28–29	127, 133, 208
5:28	82
5:29	16, 129, 175, 190, 208
6:39	80
6:40	16, 133, 222
6:47	222
6:51	222
7:53—8:11	298
8:21	82
8:24	82, 93, 131, 134
8:51	81, 222
10:28	51, 175
11:26	81, 131, 134, 175
12:25	80, 131, 134
12:32	54, 226
12:48	30, 82
15:6	81, 109, 130, 136, 157
15:22	205
17:3	53
17:12	51, 130, 135, 209
19:30	186
20:31	222

Acts

2:21	222
2:24	82
2:25	80
2:26	127
2:27	129, 211
2:31	80, 129, 211
2:40	82
3:21	7, 118, 195, 226
3:23	131, 135
4:12	82
7:30	106–7
7:54	36
7:59	186
8:20	130, 135, 159, 209
8:22	82
10:42	82
11:18	129, 208
13:26	82
13:28f.	82
13:41	80, 159
13:46ff.	129
13:46–47	208
13:46	159, 224
13:47	82
15:1	82
15:11	82
16:17	82
16:30	82
17:25–29	214
18:6	159
20:19	50
20:26	159
20:31	50
23:8	123
24:15	127, 133, 190, 208
24:25	82
26:18	82
28:5	106

Romans

1:16	82
1:18–32	175
1:18	82, 130, 135
1:23	189
1:27	209
1:32	65, 81, 130, 135, 209, 224
2:1–16	209
2:1–11	209, 222
2:3	82

Romans (cont.)

2:5–8	93
2:5	82, 130, 135, 208
2:6–11	208
2:7–10	222
2:7	12, 16, 83, 129, 133, 208
2:8	130, 135
2:9	82, 103, 110, 156, 159–60, 209
2:12–16	222
2:12	41, 51, 80, 131, 134, 204, 217
2:16	82
3:5	130, 135, 209
3:6	82
3:23–24	223
3:23	22
3:25–26	134
4:7	82
4:15	209
4:17	81, 127
5:9	82, 130, 135, 209
5:12	81, 129
5:18–19	129
5:18	226
6:13	81
6:21ff.	130, 135
6:21–23	209
6:21–22	135, 209
6:21	41
6:23	41, 65, 129, 133, 159, 175, 182, 209
6:25	224
7:5	130, 135, 209
8:6	130, 135, 209
8:13	159
8:18–27	226
8:21	195
8:24	82
9:1–4	50
9:22ff.	130, 135
9:22–24	209
9:22–23	209
9:22	51, 80, 130, 135, 175, 217
9:27	82
9:29	80
10:1	50
10:7	212
10:9–10	82
10:10–13	222
11	296
11:15	81
11:26	82
11:32–36	226
11:32	82, 118
11:36	214
12:19–21	209, 226
12:19	209
12:20	106, 107
14:7–12	209
14:10	82, 208
14:15	80
16:25	136

1 Corinthians

1:18	51, 80, 82, 159, 175, 222
1:21	82
3:5–15	208
3:10–17	209
3:13	80, 82, 106–7
3:15	106–7
3:17	23, 41, 65, 131, 135, 209
3:19	121
4:1–5	209
4:4–5	208
5:1–5	209
5:5	176
6:9–11	209
9:22	82
9:24–27	209
10:9	51
10:10–11	131, 134
10:10	80
10:33	82
11:27–34	209
11:32	82

1 Corinthians (cont.)

15	16, 294
15:2	82
15:17	82
15:18	51, 80, 81, 127, 131, 134
15:21–22	130, 135, 209
15:22–28	226
15:22–23	129, 133, 222
15:22	81
15:23	12, 16
15:24–28	19
15:24–26	196
15:25	118
15:26	12, 40
15:27	214
15:28	46, 54, 69, 115, 170–71, 195, 214, 226, 230
15:41	209
15:43	187
15:50	121
15:51–57	194
15:51–55	66
15:52	129
15:53ff.	133–34
15:53–54	129
15:53	12, 83, 121, 231
15:54–57	129, 195
15:54	40, 81
15:55–56	189
15:55	129
15:56	130, 135, 209
16:22	82

2 Corinthians

2:15	51, 80, 81, 159
2:16	130, 135, 209
5	294
5:4	187
5:8	223
5:10	208
4:3	51, 80, 159
4:11	196
4:16	131, 134, 196
5:1–5	194
5:3	127
5:4	81, 129, 208
5:8	231
5:9–10	209
5:10	93, 127, 133, 208, 222
5:18	222
6:2	82
7:10	81, 130, 135, 209
11:15	135, 209
17:10	82

Galatians

5:17	187
5:19–21	209, 222
6:7–10	209
6:8	23, 40, 65, 130, 135, 209

Ephesians

1:6	169
1:9–10	18, 226
1:10	54
1:23	195
2:1	160, 288
2:3	130, 135, 209
2:5	81
2:7	169
2:8–10	223
4:32	205
5:5	81, 222
5:6	82, 130, 135, 209, 222
6:8–9	208
6:8	209

Philippians

1:23	223
1:28	23, 41, 51, 65, 80, 130, 135, 175, 176, 209, 217
2:5–11	296
2:10–11	54, 226
3:11	121, 127
3:12–16	208
3:18	50

Ancient Document Index

Philippians (cont.)

3:19	23, 41, 51, 65, 80, 130, 135, 159, 161, 175, 209, 217, 224
3:20	66
4:3	82

Colossians

1:17	214
1:19–20	226
1:20	54, 118, 195, 214
3:6	82, 130, 135, 209
3:24	208
3:25	82, 209

1 Thessalonians

1:9–10	209
1:10	82, 130, 135
2:14–16	209
2:16	82, 130, 135
4:6	82, 209
4:17	223
5:3	51, 80, 130, 135, 175, 209, 217
5:9	82, 130, 135, 209
5:10	223

2 Thessalonians

1:5–10	295
1:6–10	209
1:6–9	118
1:6	82, 159, 209
1:7ff.	134
1:7–9	157, 190
1:7–8	109
1:7	80
1:8–9	175, 302
1:8	82, 130, 135, 209, 222, 239
1:9	22–23, 30, 41–42, 46, 50–51, 65, 80–81, 84, 101, 108, 110, 130–31, 135–36, 159, 161, 175, 194, 209, 217–18, 223
2:3	80, 130, 209
2:8–10	170
2:8	80, 135
2:9–12	209
2:10–11	110
2:10	51, 80, 82, 131, 134, 159
2:23	135

1 Timothy

1:17	52
2:4	82, 218
4:10	82, 226
5:24–25	209
6:9	80–81, 130, 135, 159–60, 209
6:15–17	189
6:16	12, 52, 66, 83, 128, 189, 194, 214, 231

2 Timothy

1:9–10	16, 189
1:9	82, 136
1:10	8, 52, 66, 81, 83, 133, 135, 194–96
1:18	82
2:10–11	222
2:10	82
4:1	82
4:14	82, 209
4:16	82

Titus

1:2	136
2:11	82, 226
2:13	82
3:5	82

Hebrews

1:3	214
1:11	131, 134
2:3	222

Hebrews (cont.)

2:8	196
2:9	21, 226
2:10	82
2:14–15	189, 195
2:14	132, 135, 213
4:12–13	187
5:7	81
5:9	41, 82, 131–32, 208, 222
6:1	82
6:2	41, 46, 50, 84, 131–32, 136, 176, 218
6:8	80, 131
7:27	132
9:12	41, 85, 131–32, 208, 218
9:26	195
9:27f.	82
9:27	92, 133, 187, 208
9:28	132
10:9	130, 135
10:10	132
10:26–27	131, 134–35
10:27	80, 82, 109, 130, 157, 161, 163, 209, 213
10:28–30	209
10:28	101
10:29	82, 101, 222
10:30–31	130
10:31	196
10:39	51, 65, 80–81, 130, 135, 176, 209
11:28	131, 135
11:31	263
11:34	35
11:35	121–22, 127
12:27–29	191
12:29	80, 106–7, 213
13:1	293

James

1:12	222
1:15	130, 135, 160, 209
1:21	82
2:5	222
2:13	82, 226
3:1	94
3:5	106
3:6	113, 129, 135, 209, 211
4:12	80, 82, 131, 134, 217
5:3	109
5:12	82
5:20	81, 130

1 Peter

1:4	133
1:5	82
1:9	82
2:24	103, 134
3:7	129, 208
3:18	21
3:19	186
4:5f.	82
4:12	51
4:17	82, 135, 209

2 Peter

1:4	130, 135, 209
2:1–3	81
2:1, 3	23, 65
2:1	80, 130, 135, 209, 224
2:3	80
2:5	32
2:6	22, 32, 65, 86, 191
2:9	82, 101, 131, 135, 209
2:12	80, 130–31, 135, 209
2:17	82, 156
3:3–7	32
3:5ff.	134
3:6ff.	131
3:6–7	65
3:7–13	134
3:7	23, 51, 65, 80–81, 106–7, 130, 135, 160, 176, 191, 209, 217, 296
3:9	51, 80, 176, 217–18
3:10–12	81

2 Peter (cont.)

3:10	80
3:11–13	191
3:13	134
3:16	80, 135, 176, 209

1 John

2:2	104, 226
2:17	20, 80, 222
2:28	82
3:5	195
3:14	81, 175
4:17–18	175
4:17	82
5:16	81, 130, 135, 209

Jude

5–7	131, 134
5	80
6	45
7	32, 65, 80, 84–86, 106, 108–9, 119, 131–32, 136–37, 142, 156, 191, 209, 218
10–11	80
10	41
12	81
13	45, 82, 85, 156
15	82
21	82
23	32, 80, 109

Revelation

1:8	232
1:18	129, 211
2:7	81
2:10	81
2:11	130, 134–35, 176, 190, 209, 213
2:23	222
3:5	82, 300
4:8	169
4:9–10	171
5:8	158
6–19	285
6:8	129, 211
6:10	82
6:12–17	147, 148
6:15–17	196
6:16–17	148, 209
6:17	82, 130, 135
7:9	226
7:10	82
7:14–15	169
8:7	106
9:1	212
9:11	212
9:18	106
10:6	171
11:5	130, 209
11:15–18	147
11:15	171
11:18	82, 130–31, 134–35, 176, 191, 208–9
13:2–3	170
13:8	301
13:11–15	170
14	23
14:1–5	38
14:6–20	147
14:6–13	146
14:6–11	148
14:8	147
14:9–11	38, 109, 143–50, 176
14:10–11	143, 151, 155–56, 169, 190, 213
14:10	53, 114, 131, 134, 146, 209, 213
14:11	37, 46, 52, 70, 82, 85–86, 138–44, 146–48, 151, 153–54, 164, 171–73, 191
14:12–13	147
14:13	110
14:14–20	146–47
14:19	209
14:20	146

Revelation (cont.)

15:1	209
15:7	171, 209
16:1	209
16:6–7	144
16:8	110
16:17–21	147
16:19	130, 135, 209
17:1—19:5	147
17:8	51, 81, 301
17:11	51, 81
17:16	106
18:1—19:3	147
18–19	37, 147
18:2	37
18:7	53, 213
18:8	37, 106, 130–31, 209
18:9–10	134
18:9	37
18:10	53, 142, 213
18:15	53, 213
18:18	142, 147
19	23
19:3	37, 46, 52, 86, 110, 147, 169, 171
19:6—20:21	147
19:8	158
19:15	130, 135, 209
19:17—20:10	147
19:20	39, 113–14, 130, 158, 170, 190, 209
20	23, 290, 294
20:1–10	148
20:1	212
20:2	114, 170
20:3	114, 212
20:5–6	127
20:6	81, 130, 134–35, 190, 209, 213
20:7–10	40, 170
20:7	114
20:9–10	130, 209
20:9	106
20:10–15	134
20:10	39, 46, 53, 70–71, 86, 113, 131–32, 134, 148, 151, 156, 158, 164, 170–72, 176, 190, 211, 290
20:11—21:8	147
20:11–15	133, 148, 208
20:12	54, 222
20:13–15	196
20:13–14	129, 211
20:13	54
20:14–15	52, 65, 80, 130, 190, 209
20:14	40, 81, 87, 114, 130, 134–35, 158, 209, 211, 213, 288
20:15	39–40, 81, 114, 301
21–22	303
21:1–4	197
21:3–5	227
21:4	134, 195–96, 214, 288
21:5–8	133, 208
21:5	69
21:6	158
21:8	39–40, 80–81, 114, 130, 134–35, 158, 176, 190–91, 209, 213, 297
21:27	112, 191, 300
22:5	171, 195
22:12	82, 208, 222
22:15	81, 288, 297
22:18–21	208

~

Dead Sea Scrolls

1QH 3:19–22	124
1QH 3:24	123
1QH 4:21–22	124
1QH 6:29–30	124
1QH 10:3	123
1QH 11:12	124

Ancient Document Index

Dead Sea Scrolls (cont.)

1QH 12:25–31	123
1QH 18:25–29	124
1QH 34	124
1QS 11:20–22	123
4Q418 69:7–8	123, 124
4Q521 12	124

Greco-Roman Writings

Josephus

Antiquities

10.277–78	123
13.173	123
18.14	123
18.16	123

Wars of the Jews

2.154–66	123
2.162–65	123
5.12.2–3	254
6.8.5	254

Philo

opificio mundi

135	123

Early Christian Writings

Apostolic Fathers

Barnabas

7–10	266
11–12	267
20	267
21	14

1 Clement

4	262
9	262
12	263
14	263
17	261–62
22	263
35	119, 262
36	262
39	261, 263
41	263
48	262
51	263
53	263

2 Clement

6.7	119

Ignatius

Ign. Eph.

3	264
11	264
16	264
17	14, 264
18–19	264
20	119, 264

Ign. Magn.

1	265
5	265
10	14, 119, 265

Ign. Trall.

2	265
4	265
9	265

Mart. Pol.

2.3	119
11.2	119

Ancient Document Index

ANTE-NICENE FATHERS

Arnobius

Against the Heathen
1.54–58	121
2.6	121
2.14	15, 121, 272–73
2.34.2–3	120
2.53	121
2.64	121
4.39.1	120

Athenagoras

Ath. Res.
13.1	118

Clement of Alexandria

Fragments
"The Book on the Soul"	13

Irenaeus

Against Heresies
2.33.5	269
2.34.2	270
2.34.3	15, 270
2.34.4	270
5.27.2	16

Apostolic Preaching
15	120
56	120

Justin Martyr

Second Apology
7	119

Dialogue with Trypho
5	119
80	120

Marcus Minucius Felix

Octavius
35	13

Mathetes

Diogn.
6	118

Origen

Orig. Prin.
1.6	118

Against Celsus
7.32	118

Tatian

Address to the Greeks
13	120

Tertullian

Treatise on the Soul
4	118
22	118

Against Marcion
2.5	118

The Shows
30	118

Theophilus of Antioch

ad Autolycum
2	120, 121
27	120, 121

Ancient Document Index

NICENE AND POST-NICENE FATHERS

Athanasius

Against the Pagans

32–33	121
33	274
47.4	274

De Inc.

1	273
3–5	274
4	122
6	274
6.1	15
7–9	274
11	274
20–26	122
21.5ff.	122
56.3	122
57.3	122

Augustine

City of God

6.12	118, 188
8.5	119
21	58, 118
21.3.1	192, 193
21.3.2	14
21.5.2	192
21.9.2	193
21.23	84, 192

Enchiridion

111	192, 195
112–13	238
113	239

Basil

Reg. Brev. Tract.

267	239

Eusebius

Church History

1	126
6	126
14	126

Gregory of Nyssa

The Great Catechism

5	187

www.ingramcontent.com/pod-product-compliance
Lightning Source LLC
Chambersburg PA
CBHW032012300426
44117CB00008B/1003